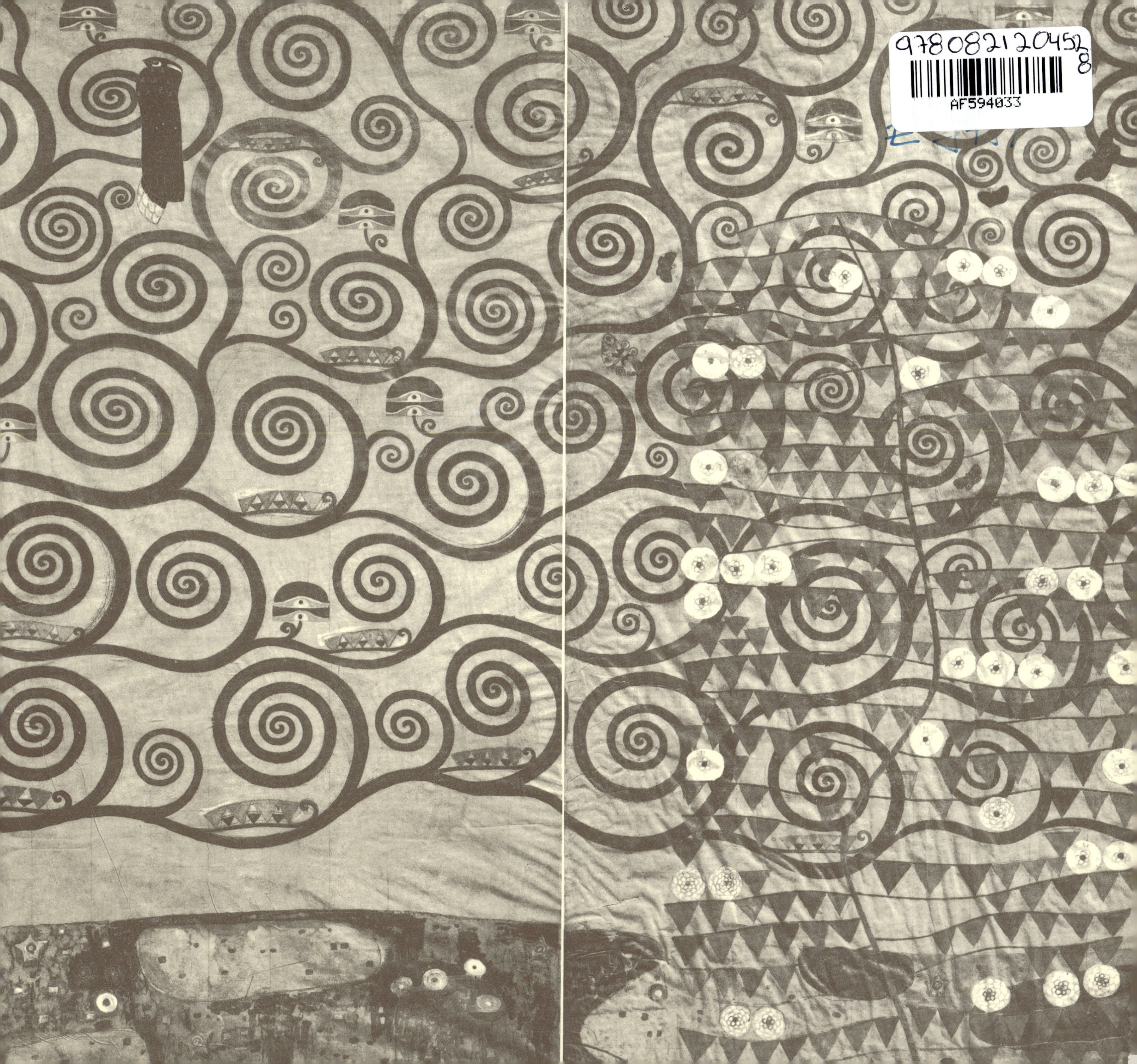

To my sensuous Elizabeth:
A reflection on every page
with love from her man.
Christmas. 1974. Richard.

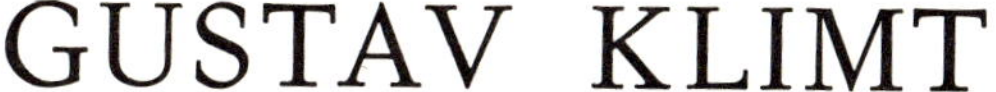
GUSTAV KLIMT

Translated by Inge Goodwin
Original edition in German published by
Verlag Galerie Welz Salzburg
Standard Book Number 8212-0452-1
Library of Congress Catalog Card Number 70-186455

Printed in Austria by R. Peichär, Saalfelden

Third printing 1974.

DEDICATED TO OSKAR KOKOSCHKA

WERNER HOFMANN

GUSTAV KLIMT

NEW YORK GRAPHIC SOCIETY LTD.
GREENWICH, CONNECTICUT

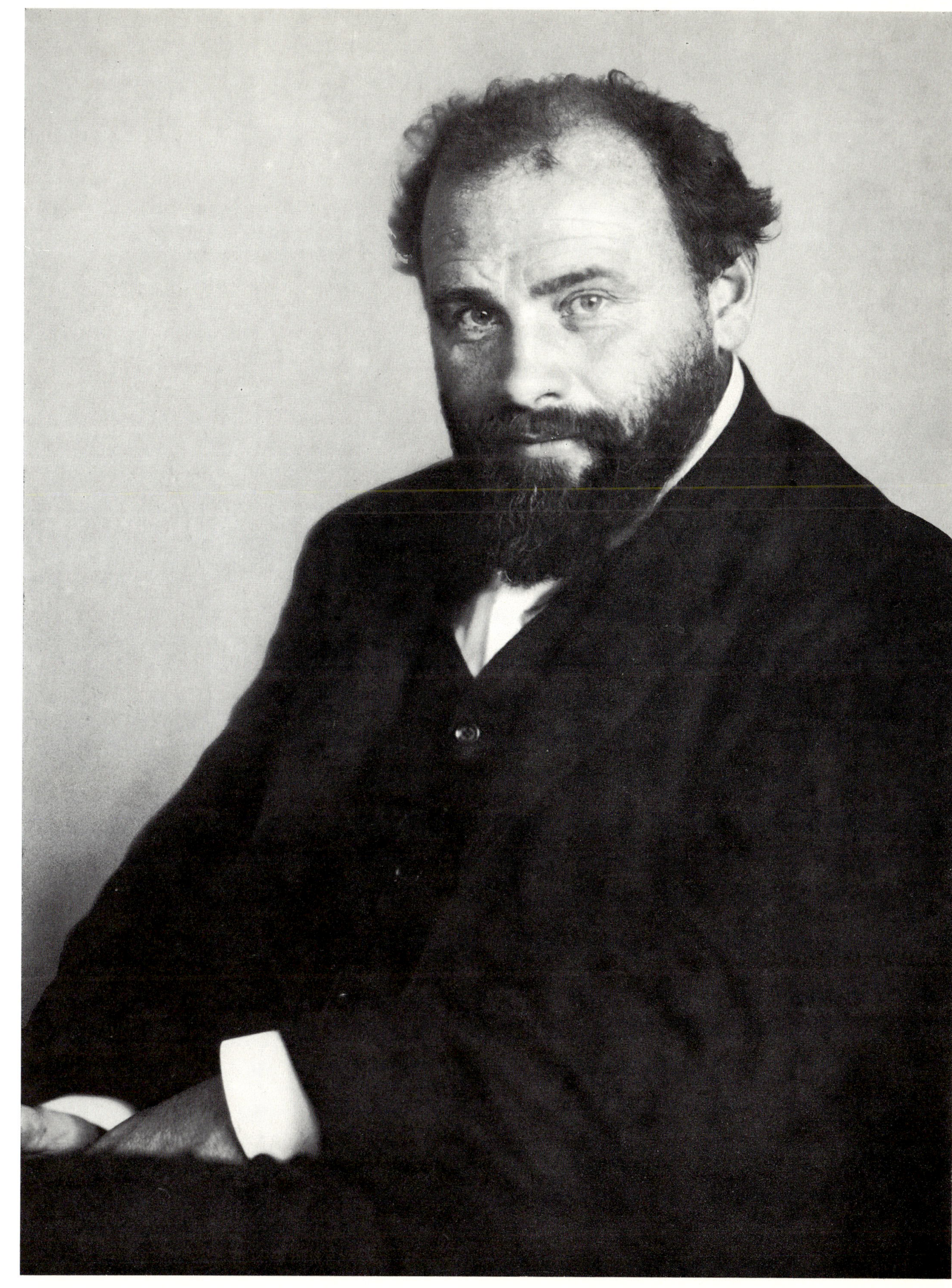

GUSTAV KLIMT, 1908
Photo: d'Oro Benda, Vienna
Photoarchive of the
Österreichische Nationalbibliothek

GUSTAV KLIMT AND VIENNA AT THE TURN OF CENTURY

I.

1.

In 1908 the Danube Monarchy of the Habsburg dynasty was celebrating the sixtieth anniversary of the accession of its now aged emperor, Francis Joseph I. The Austrian establishment, rocked by crises, saw in this survivor from the first half of the nineteenth century a guarantee of its own continuance. By means of constant festivities it fostered both a reassuring euphoria and the monarch's apotheosis as a folk hero. In a spectacular procession on the 12th of June, through the broad avenues of the Ringstrasse, which circles Vienna's proud inner city, his subjects paid homage to their ruler. The pretentious facades of Vienna's Ringstrasse, which the architect Adolf Loos had ridiculed in 1898, [1] formed the perfect setting for this patriotism-cum-folklore, just as the pageant lent to the flamboyant architecture a dramatic content missing in ordinary life.

Very close to this splendid street, on the site now occupied by the Konzerthaus, the First Vienna Art Exhibition was being held from May to October 1908. It was organized by the Klimt-Gruppe, founded in 1905, and represented their first (and indeed their only) stocktaking. Klimt in his opening speech claimed the show was "a review of the forces of Austrian artistic aspirations, an accurate report on the state of Culture in our Empire." [2] This cultural optimism echoed the optimism of the festive procession; but behind the stagy power and glory of the pageant, behind the exhibition's triumphant promise of a nobler aesthetic world, were layers of another reality. The fictitious window dressing of these two parades covered up a reality of social misery. Earthly paradise and hell on earth lay right next to each other, and the facades of prosperous society were brittle, resting as they did on the vaults where the underworld of Vienna had created its own city within a city. The kiosks beside the covered-over Wien Canal, not far from the Ringstrasse, enabled the homeless vagrants of the great capital and metropolis to go down into their labyrinthine hiding places. In 1908 that section of the public which refused to be lulled into complacency by pageants or exhibitions heard all about it in a lecture given by Emil Kläger at the Vienna Urania. This in turn led to a book, "Through Vienna's Areas of Poverty and Crime" (Vienna, 1908). The author of this penetrating social analysis proposes to "examine the substratum of our society," which, "furtive and solicitously covered up, seeps along beneath the marvels and showpieces of our civilization"; his aim is to unmask "the progress-mad, pretentious sophistication of the city." The canal system in Vienna, pride of the civic authorities, to him is merely a part of the topography of the homeless, and he lists the bridges, named after members of the Most Gracious Imperial family, not as impressive traffic routes but as nocturnal asylums.

Adolf Loos, too, wanted to unmask the deceit of contemporary culture in his subsequently famous "Ornament and Crime" [3] in 1908. The decorative stylization practiced by Klimt and his circle in the name of progress to him actually meant a retrogression, and he regarded the official fostering of this "plague of ornaments" as one of the "crimes against the political economy" perpetrated by a state which preened itself with surface culture while forcing its soldiers to walk about for three years with rags on their feet instead of properly made footwear. Loos believed that by clinging to archaic methods of production, the cult of ornamentation wastes and cripples the forces of productivity. It acts as a layer of whitewash over what should in fact be completely changed, and is thus essentially in collusion with a reactionary order of state, confirming it in the belief put forward by Loos that "a people with a low standard of living is easier to rule." Ornament stands exposed as the tool of aesthetic paternalism and political interdiction. Loos accuses the Secessionist architects and designers, who regard every vital function of the bourgeois consumer as an occasion for obtrusive decoration, of fraud against reality. Whoever, like Klimt, [4] considers "the most ordinary object, if perfectly executed" (i.e., bearing the signature of an artist) as promising the gradual "penetration of the whole of life by artistic purpose," is acting as a hypocritical propagandist of a false culture: in its name he violates elemental nature and domesticates art to a decorative accessory that serves for comfort and distraction from the facts of life.

Karl Kraus took a similar line. The philistine, lapping up ornaments like a dog guzzling sausages, expecting to be uplifted by art, represented for Kraus the whole bourgeois ideology of art as a doctrine in which aesthetic values play a subordinate role. [5] According to this doctrine, art is either just the more beautiful side of life, or a sheltering, soothing screen that keeps unpalatable reality at a distance. Kraus' criticism is directed mainly against the unwitting partner and beneficiary of this conception of art, the bourgeoisie's two-faced morality, which makes good business out of sexuality, the violation of instincts and desires, using the taboos to incite and to heighten the perverse excitement of their breaking. As Loos [6] prefers the plain craftsman to the arty-craftsman and the builder (regarding himself as one) to the architect, so his friend Kraus also pleads the cause of the natural against the factitious, the elemental against the slickly stylized. In culture he sees a mere crutch, in the newspaper industry, a new form of illiteracy. [7] To his mind the aesthete treats beauty as a pornographer does love, or the politician, life. [8] Aesthete, pornographer and politician alike aim to institutionalize, castrate and regulate, denying a man the right to uninhibited self-realization. Because Kraus senses that each institution which the rulers of society use to adorn or legally bolster their facade inevitably leads to coercion and paternalism, he does not stop as Loos does at despising the aesthetic "prostituters of art," but, deliberately breaking the taboos, he positively speaks out for the art of prostitution. His conviction — set down in the pamphlet 'The Veith Case' of 1908 [9] — "that the way of life of the humblest 'fallen woman' is cleaner and culturally more valuable than that of a public prosecutor" agrees with the tenet: "Art can come only out of protest: out of the cry, not the lulling." [10] Both statements tilt against the deforming institutions of the establishment, the first against the repressive hypocrisy of class-based justice, the second against the suppression of instincts by ornament and stylization, forbidding art to "cry out" and ordering "appeasement" instead.

2.

We chose the year 1908 because it brings the tensions surrounding Klimt into historical focus. Were this book primarily concerned with describing Klimt's niche in art history, evaluating him in a purely art critic's sense, the social context could be ignored. But our purpose is different: we are concerned with the problem of the artist in society. Klimt above all, whose art with its overtones of political partisanship contributed so greatly to the passionate controversies about the public duties and possibilities of artistic action, must not be exempted from this line of investigation. Of the many ways in which Klimt's work can be considered let us choose the one we can justifiably assume, in view of present-day awareness of the problems involved, will make the most relevant contribution to a critical evaluation of twentieth century art. Gustav Klimt will therefore be seen as the most notable exponent of a concept of art and culture which the bourgeoisie used in a last effort to arrange the way of life of a democratic society on an elite basis. It is not intended to give the reader a complete picture of the period, but rather to analyze the headings under which "Art" was practiced and discussed in Vienna around the turn of the century, to delineate the disputed territory. For our purposes, there were three main points of view. Firstly, there was the stylized art of Klimt and his circle, based on an optimistic and visionary ideology, which regarded art, culture and society as well-defined values interacting harmoniously with each other. The second attitude was completely opposed to this, based on Kraus' and Loos' declared view of art as refusing to fit in with or profit from established society. This point of view burdened art with the need for absolute truthfulness, meaning that its healthy, altruistic intransigeance should denounce a corrupt society trying to cover up its evils behind a facade of culture and ornament. The third attitude makes the work of art itself the problem — as in the case of Freud, Kubin, et al. In this way art, a dubious practice or institution in its own right, is consigned to a no-man's-land of ambiguity and uncertainty, forfeiting its former positive cultural function. Instead of an alibi for, it becomes a challenge to, every kind of established order.

The first attitude makes for wholly coherent relations between art, culture and society; the second postulates an irreconcilable rupture between truthful art and the cultural facade serving a defective society; the third destroys any confident definition of all three factors — art, culture and society. Roughly corresponding to these ideological distinctions would be Jugendstil, Expressionism and Dadaist Anti-Art. Our textbooks would claim that these three trends belong purely to the history of art and that they form a chronological succession. Both of these assumptions are wrong. The situation in Vienna shows clearly that these attitudes do not belong exclusively or even primarily to the history of art, also that they lie close together in time so that there is actually some overlapping. One cannot deny that the initial stimulus usually came from the stylists' exaggerated view of art. From the conflict of opposing attitudes provoked by the stylists one can deduce the social importance of Klimt's artistic achievements and art-political intentions.

3.

Gustav Klimt was born on the 14th of July, 1862, in Vienna. His father, Ernst Klimt, was a goldsmith and engraver of Bohemian origin. While Klimt was still a student at the State Technical College in Vienna (1876—83) he was already being asked to assist with important schemes of decoration. A contemporary critic ranked one of his more distinguished teachers, Ferdinand Laufberger, among the leading group of artists "who founded the style of modern Viennese decorative painting and art industry in the Sixties." Collaboration with Franz Matsch and Klimt's younger brother Ernst led to a communal studio in 1883, which in the following years was given several important commissions: a curtain for the theatre at Karlsbad in 1886, painted ceilings for the side staircases of the new Burgtheater during 1886–8, and in 1890 the plaques and intercolumnar pictures for the staircase at the Kunsthistorische Museum (immediately below the lunette paintings which Hans Makart had contributed to the decor in 1883). For his work at the Burgtheater Klimt received the Emperor's Prize. The studio group was broken up by the death of his brother in 1892. In 1894 Klimt and Matsch were commissioned to decorate the ceiling of the new University banqueting ball. Matsch did the centerpiece, "The Triumph of Light over Darkness," and "Theology"; Klimt produced "Medicine," "Philosophy" and "Jurisprudence." It took several years to complete the work. In 1893 Klimt joined the conservative-dominated "Wiener Künstlerhaus" society of artists. This association forced him to some critical rethinking of his work and eventually made him the spokesman of the discontented younger generation. Together with some like-minded friends he formed his own group inside the "Künstlerhaus" society in April 1897; however, this move met with hostility from the senior members, and he was asked to resign. And so the Secession, association of Austrian artists, was founded and elected Klimt its President. In March 1898 the Secession held its first exhibition, and in the same year moved into its own exhibition premises, the "Secession" built by Olbrich, where their second exhibition took place in December 1898.

Klimt saw his activities as serving the patriotic cultural mission which inspired all the Secessionists. It was this impetus which gave him both the desire and the force of personality to found the group. Their aim, based on historical examples, was the interaction of all the arts with life. This all-embracing "Creative Impulse" (the term "*Kunstwollen*" was coined by the Viennese art historian Alois Riegl) was meant for "everyone, without distinction of class or income." The Secessionists announced: "We recognize no distinction between 'High Art' and 'Minor Art,' or between art for the rich and art for the poor. Art is common property." [12]

After the first exhibition Hermann Bahr wrote an admonitory greeting which appeared in VER SACRUM (Sacred Spring), the movement's monthly magazine. He said: "Painting alone is not enough. We shall not have a truly Austrian art until it becomes a living force in our daily lives. Behold! As I write, I look over my desk and out of the window at the Liechtenstein Gardens: there the grey palace rests in all its severe elegance, behind it the Kahlenberg is turning green: here is a beauty you will not find anywhere else in the world. I feel really happy. But then I look at the desk at which I am writing, and that desk annoys me. It might just as well be standing in a house in Berlin. Now what I want is a desk that really belongs with my Liechtenstein Gardens and my Kahlenberg, a desk as specifically Viennese as that Viennese garden, that Viennese hill — my desk, my lamp, my chair should all be Viennese in that unmistakable way. Do you understand what I mean? I should like to live exclusively among the products of a Viennese style of art — whose forms and colors can evoke for me the happy hours of a Viennese spring. That is what you should be giving us: not to me alone, not to some connoisseur or other, but to our entire nation. Swathe our people in Austrian beauty!"

The glorious hours of a Viennese spring were stylized into the "sacred spring" of a new epoch in art. Art was to fit itself to reality, improving it with ornament. From one's desk and the smallest ornament to the Kahlenberg, everything was to be one total work of art, with harmony its dominant visual characteristic, and spreading joy and splendor where formely "barren desolation" reigned. Beauty, seen as a wrapping, has a protective, sheltering and concealing function. Thus "the weary and laden," thirsting "for a refreshing draught from the fountain of youth, of eternal beauty and truth," are to receive the New Gospel. [13] For all their rapturous rallying calls the Secessionists were not, however, unaware that, to achieve the desired transformation of reality, practical measures, meaning political action, must accompany the thrilling rhetoric. "Our Secession is therefore an organization for agitation," was Bahr's unambiguous conclusion. And he adds: "Whoever wants to achieve anything in Vienna by agitation, must be unafraid of ridicule." The ridicule came thick and fast. It was in the May-June issue of VER SACRUM that Bahr appealed: "Swathe our people in Austrian beauty!" The July issue contained Loos's essay "The Potemkinesque City," [13a] which accused the mock classicism of the nineteenth century of immorality and dishonesty. The same month the *Neue Freie Presse* published a no less militant article by Loos in which he wrote: "Instead of spending money to create Art, they should try to create a true culture. Build public baths next to the academies, and engage swimming pool attendants as well as professors. A higher culture will then give rise to a higher form of art, which can manifest itself, when it chooses, without the help of the State." [14] Loos at this stage was already dissociating himself from the "*Kunstwollen*" of the Secessionists. He thought it more important to clothe the Austrian people adequately and acquaint them with the habit of bathing, before immersing them in Art. To take the second step before the first, to erect pretentious cultural facades without regard for the basic necessities of civilization, he considered immoral as well as undemocratic. The respective demands of Bahr and Loos exemplify the diametrically opposed views which in the first decade of the century struggled to redefine concepts of art and culture.

4.

Ten years later, in 1908, when the dream of the "sacred spring" was well over and the Secession had broken up, Klimt still believed in Bahr's design for living and art. The break-up had taken the form of a second "Secession." In 1900 Klimt exhibited the first of his three paintings for the University, "Philosophy," at the Secession. The hostile response of the public gave the reactionary press an excuse for a campaign of persecution, which became positively hysterical when Klimt showed "Medicine" in 1901, and "Jurisprudence" and the Beethoven frieze in 1902. The wild abuse doubtless hastened the split within the movement, intensifying the differences between stylists and naturalists. The stylists — Klimt and his friends (Böhm, Hoelzel, Hoffmann, Kurzweil, Luksch, Metzner, Moll, Orlik, Roller and Wagner) — formed the radical wing, in opposition to the naturalistically orientated majority of the members. The test, within the movement and against the Ministry, came in 1904 when the Secession was invited to exhibit at the St. Louis World's Fair. The stylists wanted to restrict the contribution to four works by Klimt — two of the controversial University paintings and two landscapes — with Hoffmann to arrange the room and works by Metzner, Andri, Lenz and König to provide the background. The Ministry would not agree to this, whereupon the movement refused to contribute to the World's Fair. Not surprisingly the moderate wing felt injured by this decision, and group solidarity suffered. The tensions eventually led to separation. In the spring of 1905 Klimt's group left the Secession, and three years later appeared before the public for the first time as a definite group in the First Vienna Art Exhibition.

Klimt in opening this comprehensively planned progress report said: "As you know, we do not regard an exhibition as the ideal medium for making contact between artist and public — the carrying out of large-scale public art commissions, for example, would serve this purpose infinitely better." [15] The statement savors of disappointment. Not all the Secessionists' hopes had been fulfilled in the past decade. The only composite work of art surviving today to transmit the Secessionist artistic ideal undiminished is Hoffmann's Maison Stoclet in Brussels, and this is not a public work involving the whole population, but the mansion of an art-loving industrialist. For the dining room of this house Klimt created his last monumental decorative work, a mosaic mural in three parts. Completed in 1911, the Maison Stoclet remains the last communal work of Jugendstil. In the same year Gropius started the construction of the Fagus Works: a new era in architecture had begun. The First Vienna Art Exhibition proved that Klimt and his friends were backing a future that was already in the past. Their vision of a new culture of taste was based on the principles of the "*Wiener Werkstätte*" founded by Hoffmann and Moser in 1903: "The craftsman's work should be judged by the same standards as the painter's or sculptor's." [16] An artistic craftsmanship, rejecting mass-produced articles, which could realize Klimt's belief that "no sphere of human life is too insignificant or mean to offer scope for artistic endeavor" was possible only for an affluent elite. To the degree that it unconditionally surrenders to the magic charm of good taste and rejects the technological norm, so it becomes an exclusive preserve. The anachronisms of the 1908 exhibition are revealed even more clearly by their contrast with progressive ideas in the periodical *Deutsche Kunst und Dekoration.* The year 1908, beside a detailed report of the Klimt-Gruppe exhibition, contains the first publication of Peter Behrens' designs for AEG arc lamps and ventilators. Here function creates its own value, whereas in the other value is overlaid by a veneer of exquisite taste.

The patriotic tenor of Klimt's opening speech reveals that the exhibition was intended as homage to the Francis Joseph epoch: it is "a review of the forces of Austrian artistic aspirations, an accurate report on the state of Culture in our Empire." [17] It was a sort of pendant to the pageant, acting as a mass review of the state of patriotism in the Empire of the Danube. Exhibition and pageant alike proclaimed concord and harmony, and satisfaction with an ornament-loving mentality. The procession decoratively illuminated history and a folklore-trimmed contemporary scene; the art show made an ornamental display of the life of the upper classes. Eighteen tableaux vivants of "Moments in Habsburg History" passed along the Ringstrasse, ten thousand people in regional costume personified the nations within the Austrian Empire. [18] The picturesque procession of costumes both glorified paternalism and at the same time proved Loos right in saying "The stragglers slow down the pace of cultural advance." [19] It was also Loos who said that every State starts with the assumption "that a people with a low standard of living is easier to rule," in which case a nation of stragglers like the Austro-Hungarian Empire, two-fifths of whose population in 1900 was illiterate, [20] cultivated its folklore as a symbol of its supremacy and raison d'être.

There was no direct outward connection between exhibition and pageant, yet they both, in relation to each other, bolstered the official version of the artistic and intellectual history of the monarchy. Both built up an aesthetic facade; both served, in fact, to disguise. For one single day, according to Karl Kraus, the pageant promised to solve all social problems. The exhibition extended this shop-window euphoria to half a year. "That passion for beauty which has no ideas of its own to express yearns for the chance to dress up in gorgeous clothes." [21] Kraus was criticizing the pageant, but he might equally have meant the stylists, whom he despised, and some of whom, incidentally, had helped to mount the procession. Both criticism and admiration seized upon the metaphor of dress: Kraus criticizes the empty state robes of the procession, and Lux praised the exhibition as "a festive robe around Klimt." [22] Behind both spectacles one senses the influence of Hans Makart, the famous painter and designer of the late nineteenth century. Otto Stoessl in the *Fackel* (Torch) wrote off the exhibition's attitude to art as thoroughly domesticated by Good Taste, and he represented Klimt as its victim: "Klimt for all his marvellous gifts, for all the most elegant refinement of his powers, has been wholly defeated by this monster, Good Taste, and now shares the fate of all things so relative and communally acceptable — to be ephemeral. He seems, in a manner peculiarly typical of Vienna, to be repeating the character and career of Makart." [23] One may query whether Klimt's career ended in defeat. It was not by chance that the exhibition appeared as a homage to Klimt. The artist, far from being a victim, was a leading, active exponent of the aims which the exhibition had taken over from the Secessionist manifesto: in 1908 as in 1898, the artist was to dedicate himself to creating a reverent "House of Life," the arts were to experiment with mutual interpenetration and combination, the aesthetic was to reach out into the realm of the profane, achieving the total fusion of art and life.

The exhibition lent Klimt that same festive robe which his work aimed to throw over life — to revert to Bahr's metaphor of art as a beautiful wrapping. "The exhibition represents a House of Life," according to Lux, [24] "or rather a mirror of life as the artist would wish it to be. A universal building, or at any rate an allegory of the universe, encompassing the entire calendar, everyday life and domestic arts, the high days and holy days, the choice moments of great art which surpass religion, the working days bearing noble gifts in joyful hands, the early hours of art in the dawning consciousness of a child, guided by sure instincts. We can only gain by seizing on this art-transfigured image of life and using it to enrich our minds with a new dimension." As against this sentimentality, the voice of a skeptic, Loos, regarded the urge to beautify everything with ornamentation not merely as a covering up of reality but as a denial of the human right to free choice. Applied beauty — beauty applied to *everything* — was taking away the power of choice: "A time will come when the furnishing of a cell by Court Decorator Schulze or Professor Van de Velde will be used as an additional punitive measure." [25]

In the most representative room of the exhibition complex created by Hoffmann, Klimt was showing sixteen pictures. Peter Altenberg called this room "The Gustav Klimt Church of Modern Art." [26] The ironic ambiguity of this remark is evident when one realizes that the rooms to right and left of Klimt were reserved for ecclesiastical and cemetery art respectively. This disposition confirmed the words of Lux: great art shall be ranked above religion. The artist of genius, raised to godlike status by the Renaissance, was now driving out "the other God." Lux speaks of Klimt's works as having an almost mystical illumination, a certain ecstasy "bordering on the religious, although there is nothing of the church about it." Kolo Moser's arrangement of Klimt's pictures did not shrink from the comparison with the sacred art next door. The "altar wall," as it were, displayed "The Kiss," the mystic union of the human couple, opposite the painting of "The Ages of Man," while the longer walls were reserved for profane themes, portraits and landscapes.

The exhibition was an exclusive "house of life," glorifying the liberal bourgeoisie's leisure rites, consecrated to luxury consumption and creative leisure, encouraging emulation. Meanwhile the economic basis of this devoutly hedonistic leisure — the world of industrial workers — was shamefully excluded. What the exhibition meant by "life" was that part of life amenable to creative decoration. Reality was distilled into artistic reality, once again identified with "style" and "taste." By contrast Loos insisted that it was the working world which with its anonymous mass-produced goods created "the style of our time": bathtubs, American washbasins, tools and machines and all "that has not fallen into the hands of the artists." [27]

In the exhibition premises private and public building coalesced, the public sphere was reabsorbed into the private, personalized into a world of idyllic retreats. The "House of Life" comprised an inexpensive dwelling house with garden, designed by Josef Hoffmann, a public day nursery, a restaurant, a poster hall, i.e., a street closed to traffic, a garden theatre, a pseudo-church and a pseudo-graveyard. Children and the aged, comfort-seekers, pleasure-seekers, all aesthetically catered to — the visitor could take his pick out of the interaction and juxtaposition of all artistically processable requirements of life and culture. Blurring the boundaries between work and leisure, lucrative profession and dilettante hobby, this cultural idyll even found fringe space for laymen's efforts — works by women and girls from Adolf Böhm's art classes. The Ages of Man, which Klimt had used as a theme for his painting, turned into a series of occasions for applied art. Apropos of the cosmetic treatment of life, Loos in 1903 had already pleaded for those extremities of human experience in which good taste is useless: "Tell me how birth and death, the agonized screams of an injured son, the death rattle of a dying mother, the last thoughts of a daughter about to commit suicide, will go with a bedroom designed by Olbrich." [28] One could, of course, with equal justice make the same remark about a bedroom designed by Loos.

The exhibition, literally, aimed to be an encyclopaedic exposition of all the arts, sacred and profane, creative and interpretative. It showed children's art and art for children, amateur art and commercial posters, evening dresses and mosaics, flower arrangements and postage stamps, wall hangings and stage sets. Categories were done away with not only to free art from its isolation; the artist himself was to dissolve in "the community of all creators and consumers" (Klimt). All distinctions of class and talent were to disappear. According to Lux, everyone is born an artist. It was in homage to this inborn capacity that the stylist borrowed elements from "primitive folk art," or devoted time to teaching amateurs and uncovering the artistic urge in children, for "the childhood of nations and the beginnings of art are repeated atavistically in every human life." [29] The results of these efforts were, however, far from naive; they bore, as one might expect, the stamp of Jugendstil art. The latter believed it could command all ages of man and all levels of art by pulling out all the stops of naiveté and virtuosity, playing off the primitive against the artificed, the decadent against the archaic.

All the composite creations were not only meant to promote a mingling of the arts; ultimately, in the Garden Theatre, they led to a complete dissolution of boundaries: "Garden, stage, audience, music, magnificent decor, all melted into one unified work of art," said Lux. Exhibition and life, artistic and profane reality, united indeed, but not in risky public exposure, as the idea of street exhibitions had suggested ten years before, [30] but within the confines of a semi-public retreat from the world. Looked at critically, the result of this fusion was restricted to one precious aesthetic enclave, where the artistic revolution appeared universal though in fact it could only reach a few carefully filtered ornamental departments of life. The idea may have been to go beyond the conventional "exhibition" [31] — symptom of art cut off from life and turning inward upon itself — to a much wider definition of art, but the upshot was a super-exhibition. A life of glorious leisure and creative self-realization was sanctified, with the production and consumption of art coupled in one permanent ritual. Like the pageants of 1879 and 1908 this sample of the arts preserved the fiction of a tight little world where all is harmony.

Something had changed, however. The "palatial belt of the Ringstrasse" [32] — an urban ornament — and the Makart pageant had set each other off perfectly: together they turned the everyday into a festival. The procession — "a frieze of many hundreds of people in festive garments, dreaming for a few hours at least of that heightened existence which art can realize for us" [33] — like its backdrop, the Ringstrasse, induced "a voluptuous feeling of feudal splendor and power." [34] By 1908 the situation was different. No longer was the procession a parade of all the professions, starting with manual workers and culminating in allegories of science, progress and the arts — it was a mere folklore spectacle. Arts and crafts had emigrated to the snug retreat and aesthetic sublimation of the Klimt-Gruppe exhibition, leaving the field to patriotic entertainment. Comparisons between the neo-classicism of the Ringstrasse period and the Jugendstil of the turn of the century usually postulate a complete break. Certainly the Secessionist manifestos proclaimed one. A closer analysis shows nevertheless that quite a number of characteristics are common to both periods. The architect who insisted on designing everything himself down to the doorhandles was not a Secessionist innovation: the builders of the Ringstrasse, too, did not fail in attention to detail. [35] The composite works of the Ringstrasse period made the highest demands on the arts and the luxury industries; these standards of workmanship and versatility later profited the Secessionist reformers. Lux calls the rooms devoted to the *Wiener Werkstätte* at the exhibition "the peak of artistic taste and materials," he sees painting as ever more closely linked to the medium and considers "materials and technique the decisive style-forming forces." These criteria derived from Semper's theories of art were claimed twenty years earlier by Lützow for the neo-classical buildings: "The style is not stuck on deliberately from the outside, but developed with constructive logic out of the materials themselves."[36] Dressed up in historical allusions, the materials of the Ringstrasse mansions show a rich variety, and many of them turn up again in the work of Wagner, Hoffmann and Olbrich: costly stone, colored marble, unglazed brick, glazed terracotta, majolica and mosaic decorations. Ferstel's cottage villas which combine "solid simplicity with comfort and elegance"[37] are just as dependent on English models as the later family dwellings of Olbrich and Hoffmann. In their bizarre excrescences of form, too, the two epochs resemble each other. The uncertain taste of the Victorian art industry mixed up "form and function, the inkwell was shaped like a powder flask, the cigar box like a dog kennel . . . ."[38] In 1904 Loos makes fun of the Secessionists: "Did you want an inkwell? Here it is: naiads bathing around two rocky reefs, one containing ink, the other sand. You want an ashtray? Here it is: a serpentine dancer lies spread-eagled before you and you can knock the ash off your cigar on the tip of her nose." The Secessionist style rejected the antique trimmings but carried on the decorative urge of the Ringstrasse period: it is ornamental, tasteful art and bears out what Lützow, anticipating Bahr's clothing metaphor, said of Makart: "Everything he touched blossomed, surrounding itself with ornaments and glowing colors." An ecstatic review of the 1879 procession welcomed the painter-producer's giant enterprise for "boldly attempting, in the spirit of our fathers, to introduce the full power and brilliance of art into the light of our contemporary day."[40] The man who wrote that overlooked (just as Lux did when he called the exhibition a House of Life) the fact that art was not entering life, but reality was being theatrically dressed up; he forgot that Makart's rejection of the contemporary conjured up idyllic anachronisms. The railway was removed into the realm of allegory and the style of the sixteenth century. "The light of contemporary day" was hidden behind a mock-classical mask. Transposed into the "healthy" world of trade guilds, the Industrial Age lost its challenging and disturbing individual character. Art as an ideological wrapping: with somewhat more refined methods the exhibition of Klimt and his friends was pursuing the same goal. The "House of Life" bore the same decorative relation to reality as the 1908 pageant.

Every nicely-cleaned-up model world must be a substitute world, corresponding to the complex, contradictory features of cultural and social reality only as — according to Karl Kraus[41] — the newspaper report does to the event, which it does not reproduce so much as produce. It is a perfect production, down to the last detail — but a shop-window reproduction of reality.

The organizers of the exhibition were aware that they had withdrawn to a substitute position, but though they regretted being confined to an exhibition ghetto they refused to see the elitist and anachronistic nature of their artistic aims, let alone to overcome it by taking the step into industrial production and so to the actual democratization of their design for living. That step would have meant the abdication of the total art ideal — it was not worth discussing.

Taking Loos's and Kraus's criticisms of Jugendstil art, if one deducts the often embarrassing resentment and the personal polemics, they are obviously concerned to expose the cleft in bourgeois-mercantile society which the Secessionist slogan of the artistic penetration of the whole of life tries pathetically and conciliatingly to cover up. The theory of ubiquitous super-art, an aesthetic substitute-religion with the exhibition as one of its temples, requires an unlimited consumption of art and art tailored wholly to the consumer. This is using art like small talk,[42] yet no expense of form and price is spared to make the useful object into an artistic cult-object, to be judged by the standards of painting or sculpture. Art is sanctified and made a disposable object in the same breath. The task of beautifying life has in fact limited its total sphere of action.

It was not the first time an artist has thought his own corner the universe: but unfortunately the Klimt-Gruppe's claim to represent Austrian culture reduced them to the handymen-accomplices of the Potemkinesque facade world. Clearly the naive desire of Jugendstil art to adorn reality, while it may not have conformed with the artistic taste and judgment of the ruling class, did inevitably conform with their vested interests. Such artists have no cause to question or meddle with the powers that be — out of whom they make their living, by tirelessly designing forward-looking model worlds for them. On the contrary, by making their ultimate aim "the penetration of the whole of life with artistic intentions" they presuppose the lasting quality of the package to be enhanced by wrapping it in beauty, and must therefore try to integrate with society as it is. We do not know whether the 1908 exhibition was deliberately designed to coincide with the celebrations of the jubilee year. At any rate the Klimt-Gruppe demonstrated — even if they were not thinking primarily of dynastic glory — their acceptance of state and society in the shape of a firmly optimistic apotheosis of culture. That justified the 30,000 Kronen with which the government subsidized the exhibition and the powerful support given by the permanent committee and the City of Vienna. For their part, the artists showed their interest in official commissions. Two examples: In the show there was an unrealized design by Hoffmann for the Emperor's Pavilion in the pageant. The commission had gone to an artist outside the stylist camp, who had, however, adopted their principles to the extent of giving the pavilion the form of an Imperial crown — rather as Hoffmann in 1899 designed a sideboard reminiscent both of "an oversized hatbox and an altar niche." [44] The province of Bosnia-Herzegovina, under Austrian administration since 1878, received special notice both in the folklore display of the procession and, at the exhibition, in a set of postage stamps designed by Kolo Moser. If only the Ährenthal Cabinet's de jure annexation of this province (in October 1908) had been carried through sooner, it might even have made a glorious and colourful "Moment of Habsburg History". The consequences of that piece of masked colonialism are well known: six years later they exploded in the shots at Sarajevo which started the First World War.

5.

The craftman's work should be "judged by the same standards as the painter's or sculptor's," demanded Hoffmann and Moser's working program for the *Wiener Werkstätte*. Reversing this sentence proves the equivalence theory doubly false, both by its denying the painter's or sculptor's work any special dimension of its own, and by demanding of an article of common use what it cannot supply without failing in its purpose. The useful object loses its utility when it has been designed primarily by the criteria of fine art. Kraus expressed this in a famous aphorism: "Adolf Loos and I, he verbally and I linguistically, have simply shown that there is a difference between an urn and a chamber pot, and it is precisely this difference which enables culture to grow. The others, however, the Positivists, either use the urn as a chamber pot, or the chamber pot as an urn." [45] The egalitarian policy of the Secessionists in practice contradicted its professed aim, by proceeding in an aristocratic and not a democratic manner. The object made was elevated to its utmost significance, as a confession, for reverent contemplation. Olbrich, a designer for every occasion, equally at home with vignettes and mausoleums, coffee houses or tombstones, called forth a praise that treated his useful creations as profound revelations: "What he creates is not English, or Belgian, or Japanese — it is Olbrichesque. A confidential communication from the artist, a self-revelation." [46] With corresponding magnanimity the results of this revelation were accorded sacred rank, the exhibition became a place of reverence. Hevesi writes about the Beethoven Exhibition: "This is a Church of Art, which one enters to be edified and leaves as a believer."[47]

This ideology of the total work of art bears an uneasy relationship to utility, as its central vision of aristocratic equalization refuses to accept any distinctions between the profane and the spiritual needs of life. A totally aesthetic orientation must therefore lead to the pseudo-church, to museum-style obsequies, in short, to exhibition art. Only as an exhibit can the spoon be divorced from its function, or the chamber pot appreciated as a piece of craftsmanship.

Though it is certainly relevant to identify Klimt with the ideology and practice of the stylist design for living, it would be quite wrong to judge his works by the narrow, unrealistic standards which Hoffmann and Moser imposed on their fellow painters and sculptors. This does not mean there has to be a categorical division between the artistic purpose of the painter and the craftsman. What does matter is the quality of the difference. Two of Olbrich's "Lines of Flowers," which reminded Hevesi of an embrace, may derive from "the selfsame imagination" as the oak armchairs in the dining room of the Villa F., [48] but it makes a great difference whether this linear inspiration emerges as a drawing or solidifies into an object of use, thus finding itself in a completely different context. Indeed, the difference is vital. Our analysis must now most emphatically concern itself with Klimt's autonomous development, his individual qualities of form and content. Nevertheless we shall not lose sight of the various underlying threads which this first chapter has tried to bring out.

II.

1.

The visitor to the Klimt room at the 1908 exhibition found a collection of sixteen paintings, representing the three themes on which Klimt's work concentrated: there were scenes of human life, portrayals of women, and landscapes. The paintings of human life included "The Kiss" (Pl. 47) and "Three Ages of Woman" (Pl. 30). Three paintings showed women in the world of erotic mythology: Danae (Pl. 39) is an allegory of perpetual responsiveness; the Water Serpents (two versions, Pl. 33 + 34) portray alluring nature spirits akin to the naiads of antiquity. The Sisters (Pl. 38) led on to the four portraits in this exhibition: Fritza Riedler (Pl. 35), Adele Bloch-Bauer (Pl. 42), Margaret

Stonborough-Wittgenstein (Pl. 32), and Portrait of a Lady in Red and Black. Six pictures presented aspects of nature: the interior of a wood, gardens, fruit trees and flowers (Pls. 36, 40, 41). The traditional point of view would have no difficulty in tidying Klimt's oeuvre into the iconographic scale of values which classical art criticism relied upon well into the nineteenth century. The works which were most ambitious in form and thought, the human life pictures filled with longing and despair, fulfillment and renunciation, would be placed at the top of the scale. Next would come the various incarnations of the female, extending from the girlish mother to the old woman (Pl. 30), from the Viennese society ladies to the mythological characters, among which one can recognize the *femme fatale* and the *demi-vierge* of the turn of the century. The landscapes would come lowest on the scale.

Such a classification would be superficial and over-simplified, making firm divisions where they do not exist. Closer study reveals that the three thematic ranges are linked by transitions and interconnections. The unifying factor is not hard to find. In the human-life paintings the woman has more importance than the man, the key role is invariably hers: she seduces or threatens, she withholds herself or yields. The second category of subjects more overtly confirms her dominance. The portrayals of women, apart from the actual portraits, seem like episodes taken from the great complex context of the human-life pictures, but still augmented by and reminiscent of that background. What is the connection between these two categories and the landscapes? One must agree with the opinion of Fritz Novotny: "The full sensibility of Klimt's art is no less evident in the landscapes than in the figure paintings . . . ." [49] Confirmation of the painter's stature emerges from the poetic interrelation of the two kinds of paintings. Klimt's women and girls are filled with a knowing, refined sensuality, ranging from the fragile pose of a portrait to the open self-surrender of a Danae. Refinement is also an essential ingredient of the landscapes. Klimt is not a painter of the primeval, be it artless human sensuality or nature. The early landscapes are somber in mood (Pl. 21). Slender soaring trees become images of man's aristocratic isolation, dark swamps and ponds, allegories of impermanence, but also of the seductive spell exerted by the unfathomable (Pl. 17). Such scenes of melancholy and deliberate loneliness promote a feeling of solemn seclusion. After the turn of the century the extravagant desolation gradually disappears. Klimt has found his touch as a landscape painter. Paralleling the development in his human scenes, which pass from the shadow of death and uncertainty to the brighter regions of "Expectation" and "Fulfillment" (Pl. 45, 46), the mood of nature loses its gloomy cast. Yet Klimt does not render burgeoning nature as an elemental organic process (like Cézanne or Van Gogh), but as a world of artificial enchantment (like that of his women). The flourishing beauty of gardens, flowers and fruit (Pl. 55) is gorgeously wrapped in a mosaic of paint which, defying the laws of nature, seems to promise permanence, a complete state of being. The dense texture of the brushstrokes welds the layers of space into a floating curtain of colors whose impenetrability fascinates the observer as does the veiled picture at Sais. The distance is assimilated into the foreground, but that foreground offers no entry, it remains inaccessible (Pl. 78). As linear axes intrude only gingerly, if at all, into the thicket, all the groping vegetation seems weightless. Herein the "Apple Tree" (Pl. 55) resembles "Danae" (Pl. 39). The square shape of the picture supports an impression of powerless spreading in all directions. The delicately graduated color of these paintings seems equally unaffected by light and shade, times of the day or seasons of the year. This is not loneliness, "only a completely integrated fusion," as Weininger has remarked about women. [50] This enchanted, veiled scene both conceals and provides an ornamental setting for the female. A sunflower (Pl. 36) transmutes the female body back into a plant, like another Daphne. [51] These interpenetrations of meaning show that the artist's world cannot be simply equated with the classic hierarchy of themes. A brief but emphatic insistence on the high quality of these landscapes should prevent misinterpretation.

2.

It was in 1897—98, the year the Secession was founded, that the preliminary studies for the University pictures were painted (Pl. 8, 10, 13). Klimt at the age of 35 was no longer a beginner: together with his brother and with Matsch he had already produced a substantial body of work. These youthful works, starting around 1880, established him as a painter of decorative historical and allegorical pictures and also as a portrait painter. Klimt acquired his tremendous competence in carrying out monumental paintings for the Ringstrasse public buildings. But soon he turned away from the baroque style magnificence of the older generation (such as Rahl, Canon and Makart) in favor of a coolly exquisite naturalism which he cleverly augmented with historical associations. Grounded on an academic discipline of form which upheld the dignity of art, he succeeded in combining the descriptive illusion of the supposed eyewitness with an instructive fidelity to historical facts without producing

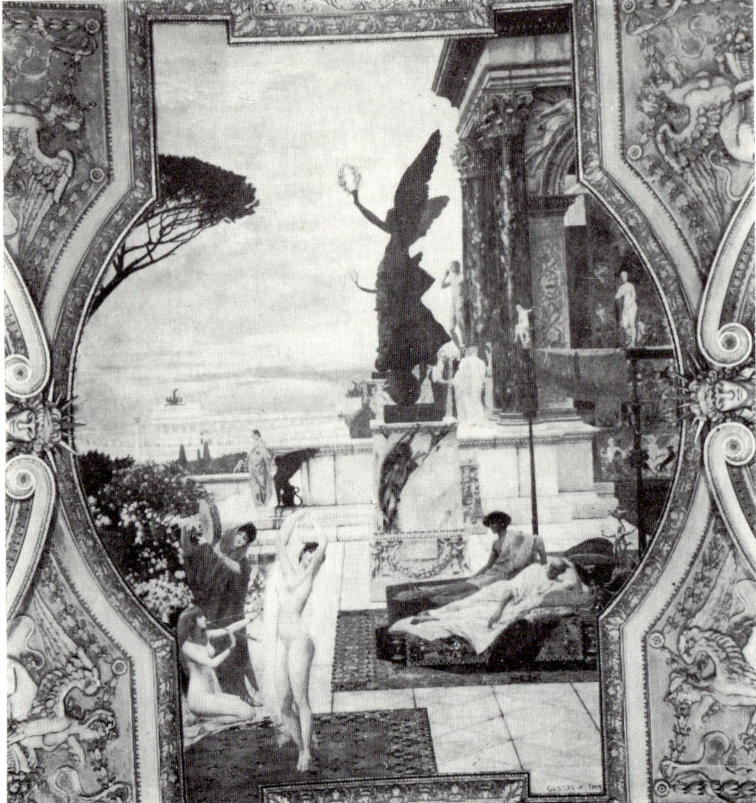

Ill. 1 *G. Klimt: Theatre at Taormina, Burgtheater*

a mere anecdote. Even the scenes from the history of the theatre (at the Burgtheater) and the embodiments of various art styles (in the Kunsthistorische Museum) already convey the moving quality of remoteness. The young painter's subtle talents are most happily employed with figures seen in ceremonial action or reclining. Stately passivity is his strong suit. The ideal figure already shows an elongated slimness of line. The animate is delicately juxaposed with the inanimate: carefully-thought-out carpet ornamentation or the veining of polished marble pedestals form glossy accessories for the human beings (Ill. 1). Particularly in the pediment and intercolumnar decorations at the Kunsthistorische Museum, there is a strong tendency to scatter the work of art, the painting itself, with painted works of art (Ill. 11). These works reveal archaeological diligence, an expert knowledge of costume and a delight in illusionist detail, all directed by a refined taste, but they give no hint of the turn Klimt's work took in the late nineties and how this led to the particular language of form that is linked with his name. Nevertheless one would not be justified in separating all the early "official" work from "the true Klimt." Such a foreshortening of Klimt's development would not only be a falsification, it would leave unanswered vital questions about the genesis of certain elements of form and content. A search for constants would find in the early work access to a view of the world which underlies his entire oeuvre. Gesture, women, histrionic exaggerations, and the enhancement of reality are already hallmarks of Klimt's early style. The artistic consequences of these interests will be found in the "true" Klimt.

3.

Every man is born an artist, wrote Lux in his essay on the 1908 exhibition. Klimt in his opening speech went even further: he would like to create an "ideal community" of creators and their audience which he calls "*Künstlerschaft.*" Admission to this community is open to everyone who feels a part of the communal work of art. Among the perfect architectural harmony of the exhibition, Lux thinks, "even man himself appears a work of art . . . if he does not botch his own bearing at the outset." [52] Whoever accepts the aesthetic rules of the game can fashion himself into a work of art. Dressed in his best and trained in choice poses, he forms a part of the festive garment the exhibition drapes over reality. He becomes a costume among costumes, a prop in the decor, a specialized work of art that successfully equates life with art. He does not represent Art as a separate category of objects, he is independent of saleability, he himself is the lasting work of art. [53]

The perfect example of an attitude that one cannot even imag-

Ill. 2 *Gérôme: Phryne before the Judges (detail), 1861*
Kunsthalle, Hamburg

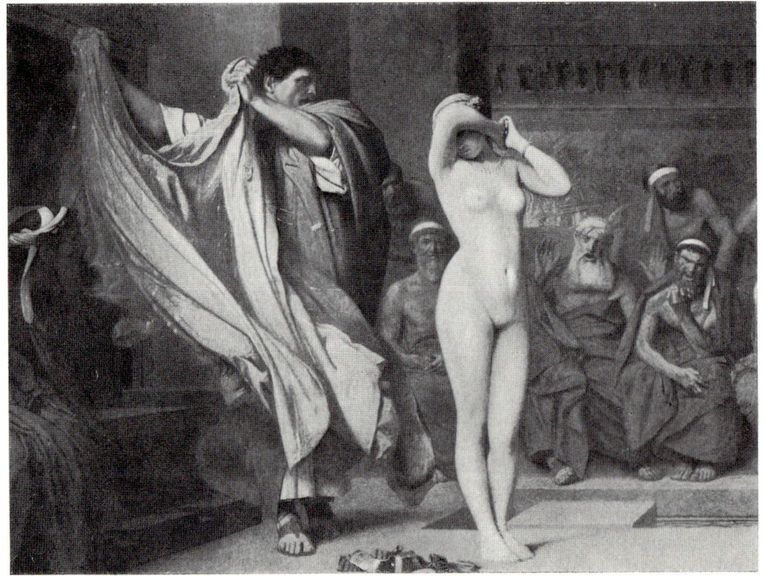

ine "botched" is the portrait of Fritza Riedler (Pl. 35). The figure seems as aloof as an icon. Insofar as there is a breathing body under that dress, it exists in a narrow space between the flattened armchair and the wall hanging. Hevesi noticed that the ornamental motif behind the head almost becomes a part of the figure. "One of these mosaic arcs rests right behind her head, like a half-halo — or perhaps like the bell-shaped gala hairstyle billowing out round the head of Velásquez' Infanta Maria Teresa in the Imperial Gallery." [54] The spheres of reality appear interchangeable, the exquisite lady floats suspended between the second and the third dimension. She is like an inlay upon the surface, and yet raised above it; in her ornamental aura she is offered up to us as a precious work of art, yet withdrawn from us as a human being. Klimt has painted a human being fitting in with her own decor in order to become a work of art. We are in fact confronted by three separate yet interacting forms of artistic reality. A work of art — the painting itself — portrays a work of art within a work of art: the human being as a work of art in surroundings realized by the painter as an artistic scene — the mosaic wall and the armchair. Painter and model both belong to the "*Künstlerschaft*" which unites creators and consumers.

Removing the distinction between these classes worked in the converse way when man as a work of art stepped out of the picture to enter reality. Such a liberation occurred at the Garden Theatre. In a performance of Wilde's "The Infanta's Birthday," the actresses seemed like figures out of Velásquez paintings. Assuming that the audience could fit into the decor and did not "botch" their attitudes, it must have seemed possible to create a communal work of art that justified Lux's statement: "Garden, stage, audience, music, magnificent decor all melted into one integrated work of art." This ideal performance took the communal work of art back to its theatrical origins: not to the opera, but to the classical situation, where there is no distinction between chorus and audience. As Nietzsche remarked in "The Birth of Tragedy," "It is all one great sublime chorus of dancing and singing satyrs, or those whom the satyrs represent." Obviously the ideology of the Secessionist comprehensive work of art was bound to agree with Nietzsche in demanding "an aesthetic audience" and condemning the arrangements of the modern theatre. He called them vulgar in comparison with those of classical antiquity. Lux saw the Garden Theatre as realizing, in a modest way, that dream "which we have taken over from the classical age, and for which our present commercial stage is about the most unsuitable setting."

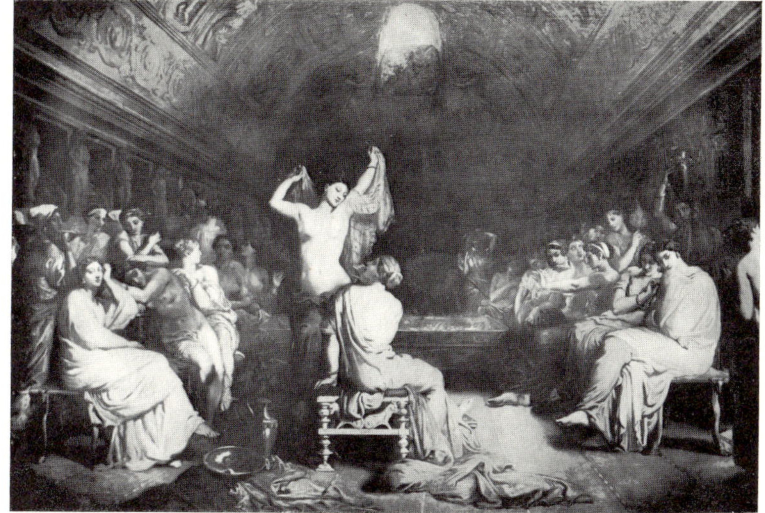

Ill. 3 *Chassériau: The Tepidarium, Louvre*

The moment the stage impinges on real life, everything becomes part of a play, the "festive garment" which art throws over life takes on the function of decoration and costume, and the wearer of the costume plays an unremitting role so that he can never afford to miss his cue or relax his posture. What the Secessionist art lover — the "aesthetic audience" — celebrated in the exclusive regions of the 1908 exhibition and the Garden Theatre, the pageants parades in streets and squares acted out. In such happenings the practice of amateur and improvised drama takes over the public spaces. They represent cult actions of the collective sense of theatre which permit everyman, within the framework of the conventions of style and costume, to appear in the role society has cast him for. Processions and pageants support the existing patterns of power precisely by not showing the social relations between consumers and creators, rulers and ruled, upper and lower classes, as they really are, but by veiling them in the promiscuity of a masquerade. The festive procession — this is what makes it so popular — has something of the saturnalia's reversal of roles: the populace rules the streets and directs the action, and the ruler whom it is honoring has to be content with the passive role of an applauding audience. The social distinction between creators and consumers briefly vanishes as for a few hours the creators become the enjoyers. Yet their performance lies under aesthetic interdiction: in the interests of style and folklore all performers are limited to the medium of the *tableau vivant,* they are elements of a composition on the same level as the tools and emblems which exemplify their class, their nationality or their trade. The festive sham world dominates the objects and their

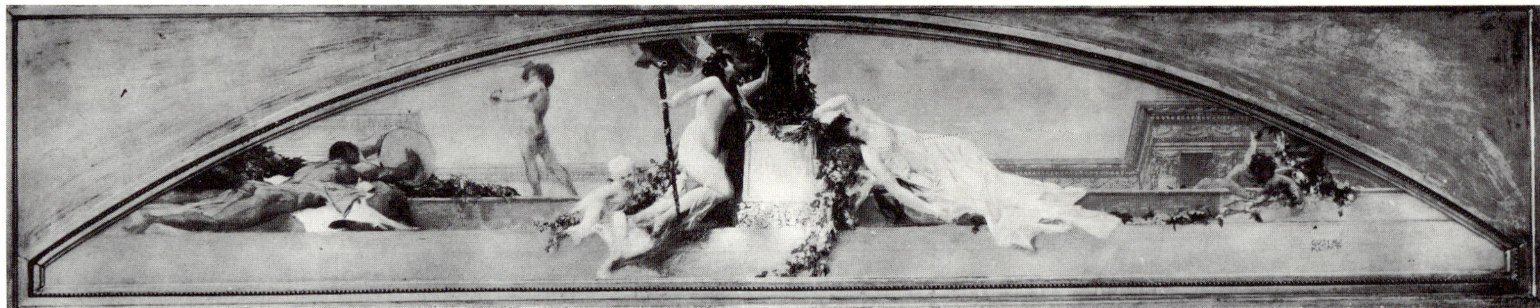

Ill. 4 *G. Klimt: The Altar of Dionysus*

makers, and reveals what it meant to conceal: that human beings too can be manipulated as objects.

4.

The theatre as the meeting place of reality and illusion interested Klimt when he was designing theatre curtains (1882—86) and the five paintings he contributed to the decorative plan worked out by Adolf von Wilbrandt for the new Burgtheater (Ills. 4, 5, 6.). His compositions are reminiscent of the *tableaux vivants* of a pageant. The program starts with the visions described by Nietzsche at the end of "The Birth of Tragedy": in the Altar of Apollo and the Altar of Dionysus the two elemental strains of art confront one another "in strictly alternating proportion" (Nietzsche). The origins of drama are followed by the Thespian chariot — prototype of the pageant float: there is still no division between creators and audience. In the Theatre at Taormina (Ill. 1) the scene shows a young girl dancing in the nude; she is not isolated in her own corner of space, but appears as part of an architectural setting with a distinctly staged effect. [55] The living nudes set off the nude statues: the dancer finds herself in a world which is half artificial, half natural. Where the whole world is a stage, the footlights vanish, every object becomes a prop, and the onlooker a costumed bit player. The fifth picture shows a performance of "Romeo and Juliet" at the Globe Theatre in London. Klimt takes the theme as though, Hamlet-like, this were a play within a play. The audience on the stage resembles that in the pit, but seems more immediately involved in the happenings onstage. This ambivalence obscures the distinction between creators and consumers. [56]

Long before Klimt demanded this partnership on principle, he set it down in two commissioned paintings, which flattered the self-consciousness of the onlookers and satisfied their desire to be actors as well as audience. In 1888 Klimt and Matsch were commissioned to paint two interior views of the old Burgtheater with portraits of the most prominent patrons of the Viennese theatre. Matsch painted a view of the stage from the entrance, Klimt the opposite view, the auditorium as seen from the stage (Ill. 8). In 1893 he chose the same perspective for the auditorium of the Schlosstheater in Totis. Stage and auditorium, actors and public, are equivalent — here as there, a common theatrical consciousness operates, roles are played, costumes displayed.

The representations of various art epochs on the staircase of the Kunsthistorische Museum show an ambivalence similar to the portrait of Fritza Riedler. The figures seem like paraphrases

Ill. 5 *G. Klimt: The Thespian Chariot*

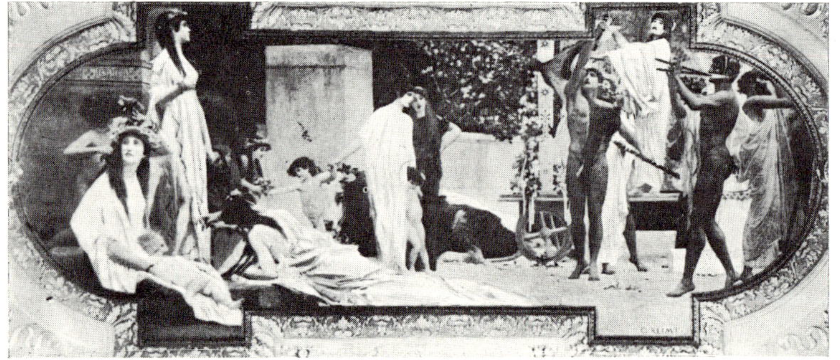

Ill. 6 *G. Klimt: Romeo and Juliet*

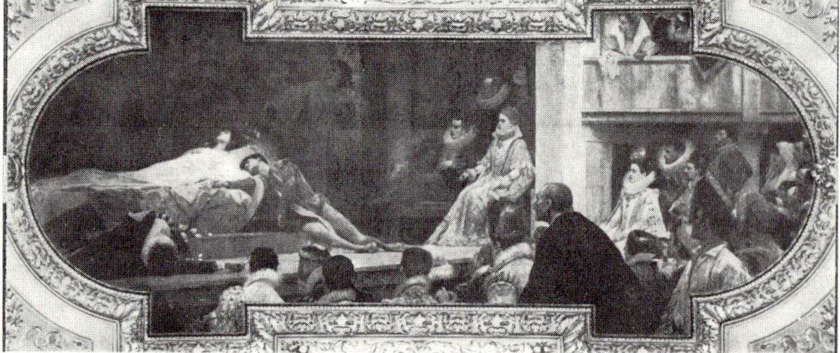

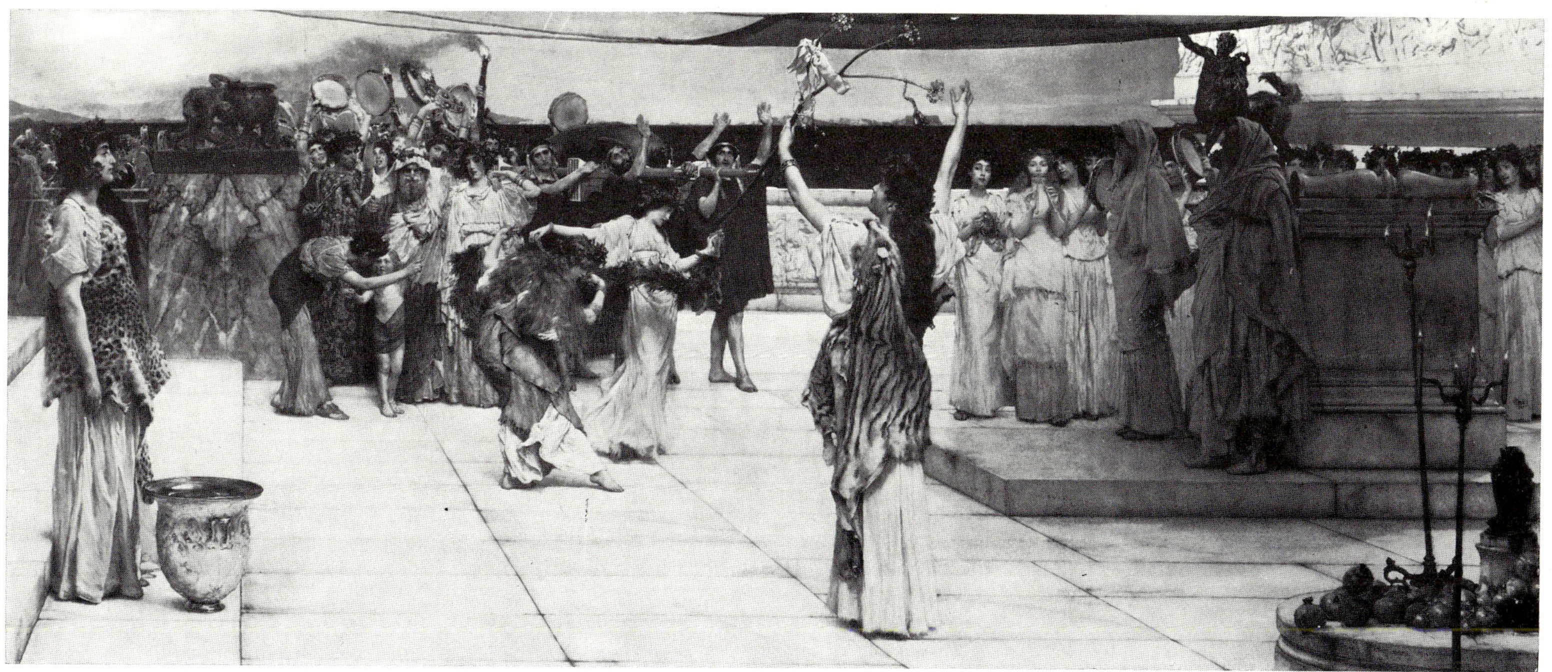

Ill. 7 *Sir Lawrence Alma-Tadema: The Festival of the Grape Harvest in Ancient Rome, 1871, Kunsthalle, Hamburg*

of existing historic works of art and yet also give a trompe l'oeil effect of having stepped out of pictures, or as though statues had come to life — or perhaps, conversely, as though these people had modeled for the artists or taken part in a fancy-dress parade (Ills. 9, 10, 11).

Ill. 8 *Gustav Klimt: Auditorium of the old Burgtheater, Vienna Historisches Museum der Stadt Wien*

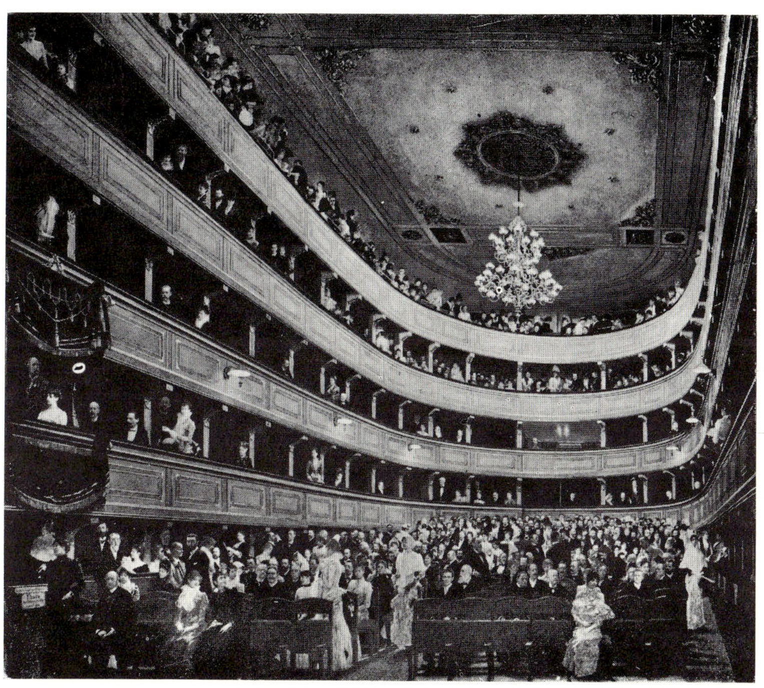

5.

Theatrical self-consciousness may manifest itself at various levels: in the confident, it can be satisfied with the superficial showiness of pageants; but it can also give rise to doubts which rob people and things of their identity. That was how it worked for the young Hofmannsthal. One of his early poems, the prologue to Schnitzler's "Anatol" (1892), describes with nostalgia and some affectation the transformation of reality into a stage, or the stage into real life. This seems to anticipate the Garden Theatre at the 1908 exhibition. Everyone is acting, playing not himself but some role in which he has been cast. Self-portrayal turns into a masquerade:

A garden house instead of stage,
Summer sun instead of footlights,
Thus we play at playacting,
Acting dramas of our own,
Precocious, delicate and sad,
A comedy about our souls,
Feelings today and yesterday,
Wicked things prettily expressed,
Polished words, high-coloured scenes,
Secret, half-felt sensations,
Agonies and episodes . . .

The actor who can play any and every role pays for it with a complete loss of identity, as described in Hofmannsthal's epitaph on the actor Mitterwurzer:

Who was he — who was he not?
He crept from one disguise into the next,
Leapt from the father's body to the son's
And changed his personalities like clothes.

Everything is only an outer garment, disposable wrapping, covering up. The compulsion to put on disguises and play parts is common to humanity, which can never achieve true self-knowledge. That is how the pessimist views human life. Whether alienation is in fact conditioned by society, or whether man is merely the prisoner of self-made lies, masks and conventions, he hardly considers. But this is the question which makes actors so important to the artistic ideologies of the nineteenth century, of which Nietzsche wrote that it was "The first age which has been studied as regards its 'costumes,' meaning morals, articles of faith, tastes in art and religions." [57] The actor personifies the alienation of man and art in the Capitalist Age. His availability for any role is the measure of his impotence. To the pessimist this involves the concept of certain ineluctable, inscrutable powers of fate, handling men like puppets on strings: we think we move of our own volition, but we are in fact being manipulated.

In 1900 Hofmannsthal wrote a curtain-raiser to the Antigone of Sophocles. The scene, Creon's palace, is shown up as a make-believe world. Deliberate destruction of the stage illusion causes the happenings of the prologue to carry all the conviction of real life. [58] The rehearsal is over, actors are leaving the stage, stagehands are extinguishing the lights. Two students are left behind. Suddenly a masked genie appears. One of the students seems at first embarrassed — then dismayed to discover there is no actor under the disguise. Reality and play, this world and beyond, life and dream coalesce:

What, am I here, is that Beyond?

asks the Student. Where is the borderline between him and his uncanny confronter?

How did you find the space
From your Beyond to drift in here?

The Student sees the vision he is shown "as though through mists." The genie denies him hope of a foothold or firm contours:

Grasp where you may, nothing you touch is solid.

He justifies his disguise:

But do not let the mask dismay you:
The most beloved of human beings
Show you a face that is a mask:
No human eye can bear reality.

Not only does man hide from man behind a mask, the powers that rule him also appear in disguise. Unable to bear reality,

Ill. 9 *G. Klimt: Pallas Athena*

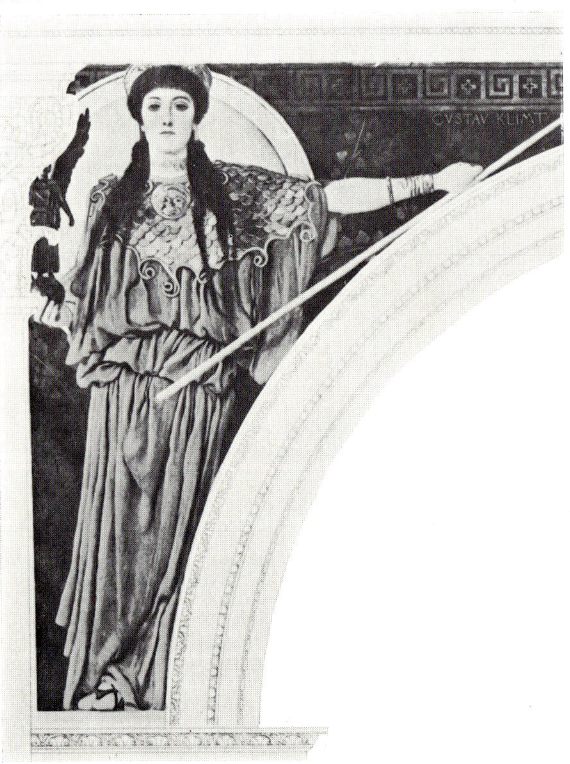

Ill. 10 *G. Klimt: Girl of Tanagra*

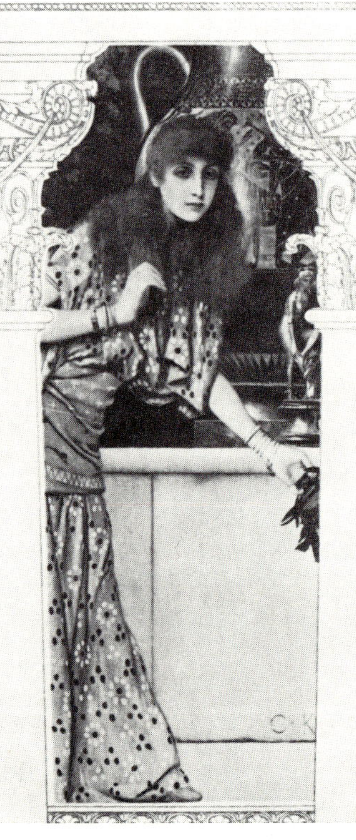

Ill. 11 *G. Klimt: Egyptian Girl*

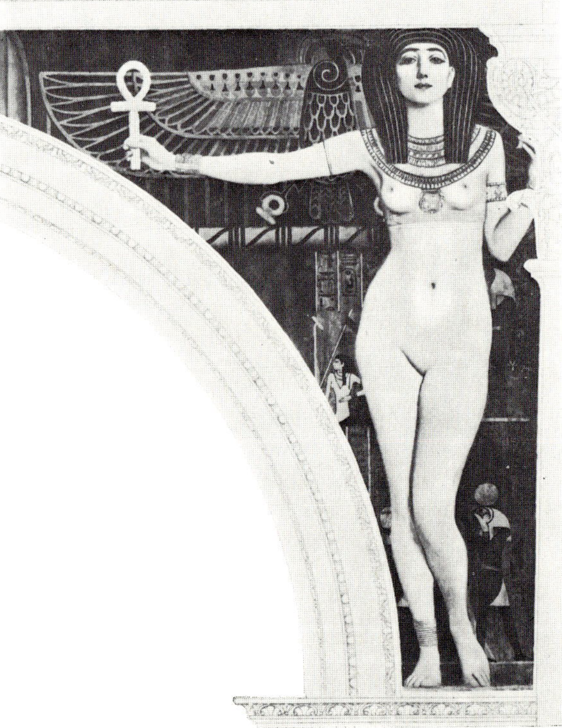

he seeks escape in the world of art. The work of art alone seems to overcome alienation, "strip the veils . . . from the abysses of life." But actually it merely transports one beyond the constraints of real life without attempting to overcome them, it denies what it claims to expose, rejecting any reference to the real world outside art. Only the work of art, the genie maintains, "is reality, all else is allegory, a game in a mirror." Here is the change of emphasis demanded by the ideology of the communal work of art: the desire to bring life and reality into complete aesthetic harmony depends on the work of art giving a meaning to life. This substitute religion finds support in Nietzsche's *"Artisten-Metaphysik,"* which holds that "the existence of the universe can only be *justified* as an aesthetic phenomenon." [59]

6.

In our view this creative metaphysics underlies the University pictures (Pl. 9, 11, 12), and that is why most of the professors, offended by the artist's sense of superiority, interpreted and rejected Klimt's pictures of human fate as blasphemous distortions of the role of science. The practical intelligence could not accept riddle-allegories of its impotence or its limitations. We would interpret Klimt's conception thus: it is not academic philosophy that brings enlightenment, it is not medical progress that relieves human agony, and it is not a jurisprudence which has hardened into a pompous, showy institution that can protect man against the devouring caprice of the "avenging fates." [60] Only the work of art, which truly shows the vulnerable helplessness of mortal creatures, can help the blind to see and to find their way. Looking at a work of art, man is granted insight by the mere fact of being the observer, an insight denied to men in action. The latter appear — to quote from a contemporary description of "Philosophy" — "just an apathetic mass, swept along in the service of endless procreation, for better for worse, in a sort of dream, from the first stirrings of life to the final exhausted descent into the grave. In between lies a brief illusion of loving union and a long, painful drifting apart. Love proves a disappointment, bringing neither true happiness nor illumination. Yet life goes on in the same way. Far removed from the cold certainties of science, as far from the veiled mystery of the universe, mankind labors and struggles for happiness and enlightenment, yet always remains a mere instrument in the hands of nature, which uses it for its own unvarying purpose, procreation." [61] ("Knowledge" is represented by the head at the lower edge of the picture, while the sphinx symbolizes the mysteries of the universe.)

In "Medicine" (Pl. 12) Klimt is also dealing with the human predicament. Bundled human bodies float — "as though through vapors" — into the picture. Their emergence is at the same time a sort of drowning, they are swept away. These figures are profoundly unfree, at the mercy of some higher power. Only one figure stands apart. Her body entices with bacchantic ecstasy. Has it escaped the collective entanglement, or is it the unattainable ideal of all the others who yearn out of the darkness of their suffering for the full light of health? Here is no final Last Judgment, pronouncing salvation or damnation, but "the eternal recurrence" which Nietzsche contemplates in "Zarathustra." The mass of humanity is involved in a cyclic, not an ascending or descending motion. In the center of "The Wheel of Life," of which the asymmetrical composition shows only a segment, Death waits. In the foreground of the picture stands Hygieia, who has somewhat the air of a priestess. But the cult she serves seems devoted to aesthetic worship rather than to comfort or healing. "Jurisprudence" (Pl. 11) shows an attenuated figure succumbing without resistance to the tentacles of an octopus-like monster. This "condemned criminal" (Hevesi) is one of the nameless crowd who, in both "Medicine" and "Philosophy," are tied to the Wheel of Life. Klimt reverses the situation of The Judgment of Paris: the man in command has become a feeble bowed creature whose lot is decided by the three Goddesses of Fate. Their dark domain is closed to "Justice," who has been relegated to the background.

Mockingly, yet tellingly, Kraus remarked about "Medicine" that Klimt had given his patrons at the Ministry a picture "in which the chaotic muddle of decrepit bodies symbolizes conditions at the General Hospital." [62] Hygieia and "Knowledge" are the hollow emblems of yet another civilized facade which covers up reality. Similarly, "Jurisprudence" can be seen as referring to the conflict between the facade of justice and the practice of law. The three unapproachable figures in the background — "Justice" flanked by "Truth" and "Law" — stand for the institutionalized judicial system, set in its self-perpetuating ceremonial and rejecting all change. The heads of the judges, not very convincing representatives of their profession, according to Hevesi show that "legal face" which the painter can find in all ranks of society. Actual legal practice is carried on by the three "goddesses of vengeance" and their assistant the sea monster. There is no path that leads from their world to the sublime regions of the background. Two interpretations are possible: either the three Fates may be taken to represent the destructive side of femininity, [63] *femmes fatales* in dark contrast to the three radiant figures of "the good mother," or else they reveal what is left of justice, law and truth when their deceptive finery is stripped off.

The visionary pathos of the three fate-of-humanity pictures extends to the social conventions, the institutions that enchain man. The painter set himself the task of painting the failings arising out of social taboos as they really are, opening up new dimensions to his work. In 1893 the young Hofmannsthal criticized the trivial oleograph tastes of the Viennese public, insisting that "art is connected with ideas, dreams and poetry . . . ," that it can "force open sunken, overgrown trap-doors of the soul." Klimt's University paintings afford proof of this. They reveal what Hofmannsthal, in advance of Freud, sensed behind the repressions of civilized man: "a half-conscious being that vegetates, dreams, lives on anxiety, drugs and longing, and never dares face daylight because of its own fancied inferiority, ashamed of being dependent on instincts and not on principles." [64] When Klimt tried to portray these instincts, there were reactions of disgust and outrage.

Each of the University pictures has two interacting fields of force: one is the ordinary varied human experience; the other is the rigid power of the forces that govern man. The latter do not have to act, their mere immobile presence proves their superiority. They control the game, whereas the others, given up to their instincts, are condemned to an unaware "*semper eadem.*" The observer can tell what is happening: the artist lets him see the forces which the human actors must blindly obey. These forces have several layers of significance. Knowledge, Truth, Justice, Law and Hygieia are not solely allegories of the facade of civilization, their role in the picture is one of theatrical proclamation, comparable to the Genie, the Heralds and Announcers of Hofmannsthal. They address themselves directly to the "aesthetic spectator," and, with the painter's connivance, reveal to him a layer of meaning beyond alienation and broken taboos. This is not to rouse him to criticism of society, but to reconcile him to his role.

Again the sense of drama achieves comparable results in painting and playwriting. In Hofmannsthal's "Death of Titian" (1892) it is said of the aged painter that he

bade us enjoy the flow and flooding of each day
As though it were a play
To understand the beauty of all shapes
And be spectators at our own lives.

This verse elucidates the theatrically evocative form of the University pictures. Klimt too extends beauty to all shapes, letting harmonious stylization take over what was ugly. That "universal mediator, style" [66] once more acts as a disguise.

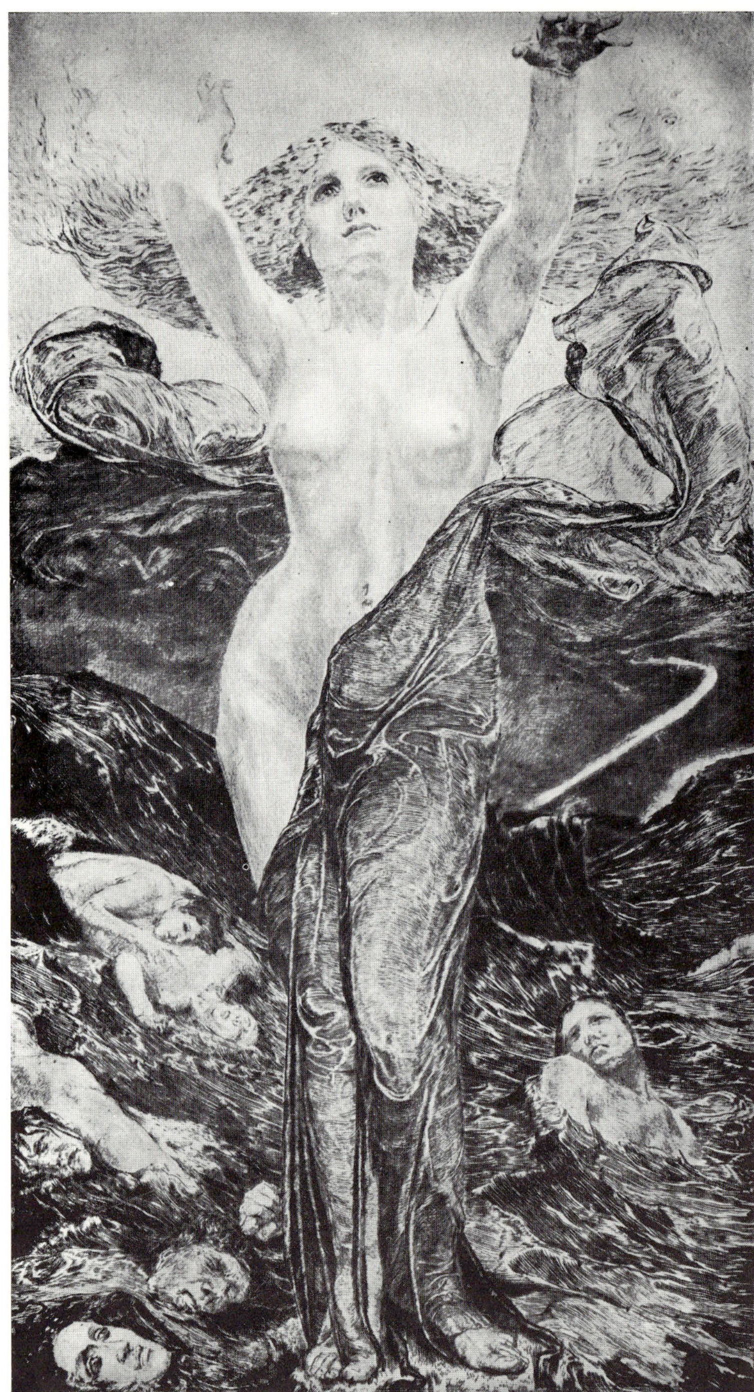

Ill. 12 *Klinger: Aphrodite, 1894*

Klimt's intention of showing the sufferings of unredeemed humanity loses its edge of truthfulness through the conventions of stylization. Liberation itself gives rise to fresh compulsions: not only must man suffer, he must suffer in stylized attitudes. All this is logical enough in view of an artistic outlook that wants to tie art wholly to aesthetic values, the true and only

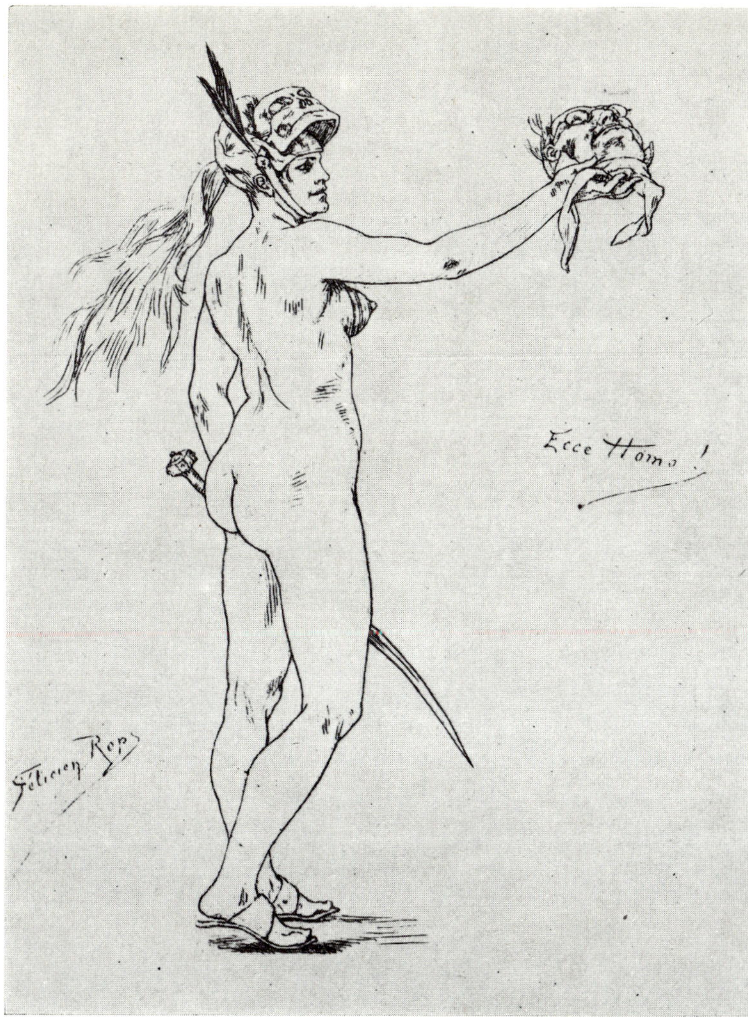

Ill. 13 *Rops: Ecce Homo*

justification for the universe; but it becomes the accomplice of cultural deceit the moment the critical consciousness of such skeptics as Kraus, Loos and Kokoschka dissolves the alliance of truth and beauty.

The full frontal stance, an important dramatic formula of symbolist art (not only in the late nineteenth century), is used by Klimt to stress the hieratic pose. It is chiefly found in his female figures, giving their outlines an untouchable, menacing force, drawing the observer under its spell with the power of a revelation. This frontal stance brooks no opposition. One could compare Hygieia with the Aphrodite in Klinger's "Brahmsphantasie" (Ill. 12), but while the latter, surrounded by drifting human wreckage, attempts a human, pleading, nearly Christian gesture, Hygieia remains in uncaring, sphinxlike immobility. Both the Athena (Ill. 9) and the Egyptian Girl (Ill. 11) among the staircase pictures at the Kunsthistorische Museum make use of this deliberate full-face confrontation. A subsequent line of development is close to traditional iconography — Athena, or Minerva, which incidentally constantly occurs amid Ringstrasse art[67] — leading to the Pallas Athena of 1898 (Pl. 5).[68] However, this particular painting opens up a further level of significance to the University pictures. The naked figure presented by the Goddess recurs at the left-hand edge of "Medicine" (Pl. 12), separated from the Human Wheel. The frontality of Pallas Athena is taken over by Hygieia, no longer holding just one human being but the whole of mankind in her power. Soon afterwards the revealing pose acquired a new dimension of meaning in "Judith" (Pl. 15): in place of humanity, it is now Man whom the woman dominates. Félicien Rops did similar interpretations of the battle of the sexes. His "Ecce Homo" (Ill. 13) shows a naked quasi-Minerva with a sword in her left hand and the severed head of a philistine in her right. Rops' frontispiece for F. Champsaur's *Masques modernes* in 1889 (Ill. 14) shows Folly, a woman, holding all men in her power — the Punch puppet, the famous writers of the day, the whole City of Paris, whose burning head she displays as Judith might Holofernes'. Had Klimt seen this frontispiece when he painted his Egyptian girl (Ill. 11), or was it in his mind when he was working on "Judith"? It is idle to speculate on this; even the early Dionysus Altar at the Burgtheater has a young priestess holding up a statuette of Athena (Ill. 15). More important than the question of influences is that two artists of the late nineteenth century, at their different levels, are expressing man's subjugation to woman. Between the statuette of the Dionysus Altar and the head of Holofernes a metamorphosis occurred, a change and increased profundity of meaning, with the marks of cruelty and aloofness invading the symbolic female figures. "Knowledge" and Hygieia anticipate Judith (Pl. 15) and the Judith-Salome (Pl. 43): both have mankind in their power. In the first version of Jurisprudence (Pl. 10) Justice appears as a Winged Victory, brandishing a sword but no scales. That sword is the weapon of the murderess of Holofernes.

Thus one of the great fin de siècle themes, the rule of woman over man, contributes to the multivalent symbolism of the University pictures. This might seem to contradict our previous suggested interpretations and force a choice between two alternatives: either the female protagonists of the three pictures symbolize the powerlessness of progress, or they proclaim a new matriarchy. This apparent contradiction can, however, be seen as a double meaning,[70] a union of opposites, if we consider the gradual evolution of ideas in successive versions of the

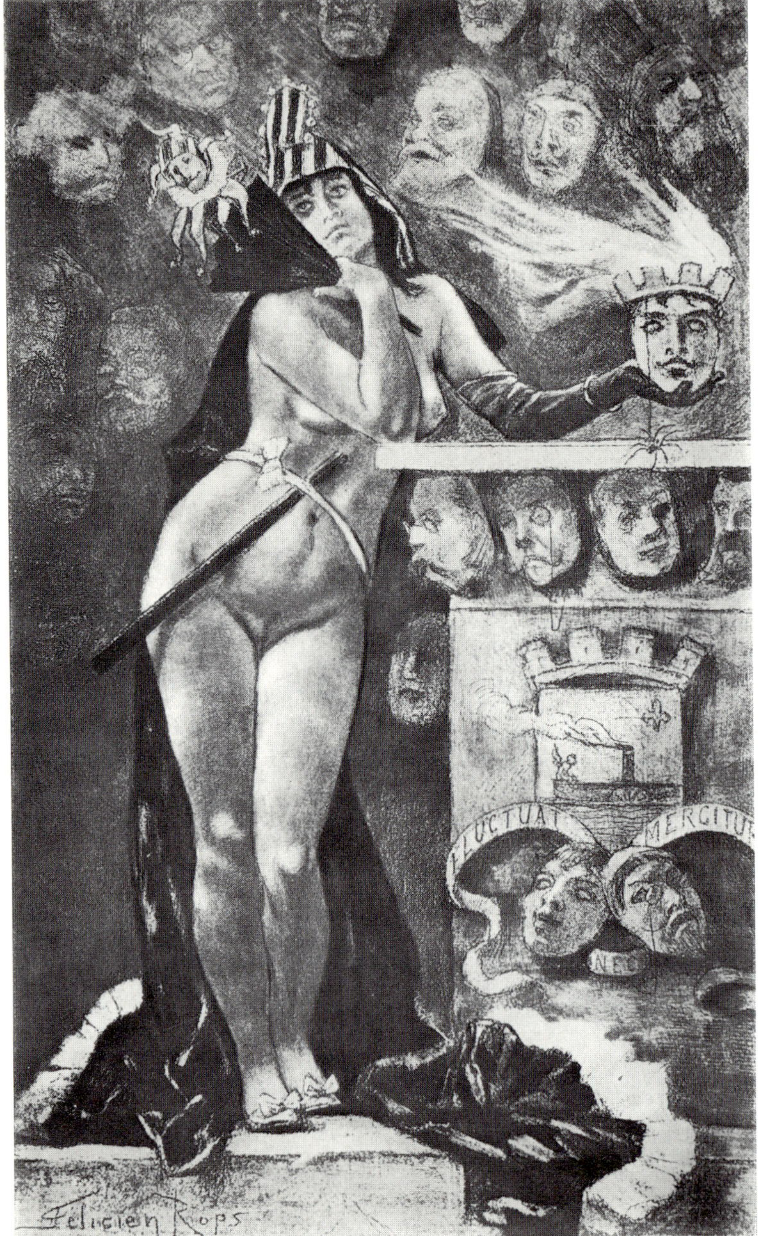

Ill. 14 *Rops: Masques Modernes*

pictures. The first Justitia overwhelms an octopus (Pl. 10), the final one lets him proceed. The first design for "Philosophy" (Pl. 8) shows Knowledge in the traditional pose of unworldly contemplation: from this grows the full-face head of the final version, which no longer reveals any concern for the fate of humanity. The figure of Hygieia also becomes transformed. Originally she is closer to the Wheel of Life; only in the final version has her frontal stance become majestic isolation.[71] Clearly this change of emphasis implies a neglect, an obscuring, of the commission's original purpose, to the same degree as the sphinx-like erotic character of the female protagonists is stressed. This may be seen most explicitly in the last picture, "Jurisprudence," which shows the two basic female characters, the "good" and the "wicked" mother, in polar opposition and alternate emergence.

The professors' protest against the University pictures touched upon the vital intellectual controversies of the nineteenth century. The academics' resistance to Klimt's "muddled ideas" reflects the conflict between the research worker and the visionary, between "Science" and "Wisdom," rationalism and irrationality. That conflict in which Nietzsche thought he could see the beginning of a new, tragic culture "whose most important characteristic is that wisdom replaces science as the ultimate goal — wisdom which, undeceived by the seductive distractions of science, turns an unwavering glance on the total world picture and seeks to apprehend eternal suffering with affectionate sympathy as its own."[72] This conflict places the artist, always in sympathy with eternal suffering, on the side of "Wisdom." It is not progress which matters to him, but the understanding of eternal constants. This is what inspired Klimt's attempt to add further depth to his subjects by turning from the theatre scene to mythological evocation. Again, Nietzsche is a witness to this rejection of a historical received style: "And now the man without a myth stands, eternally hungry, among all the past ages, and searches, digging and scrabbling for roots, though he may have to dig among the most remote antiquities." In the paintings for the Burgtheater and the Kunsthistorische Museum Klimt labors towards this historical self-realization. In the University paintings he turns from the history of civilization to the mythological painting of human destiny. "To what does it all point, that huge historical

Ill. 15 *G. Klimt: Altar of Dionysus, detail*

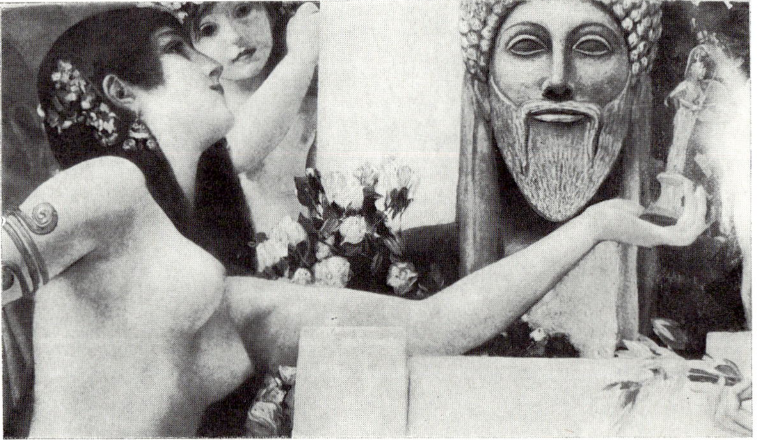

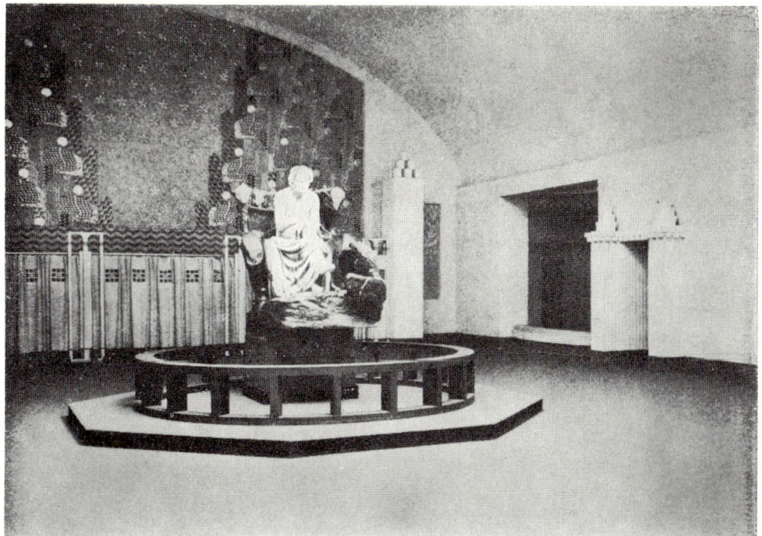

Ill. 16 *Klinger: Beethoven*

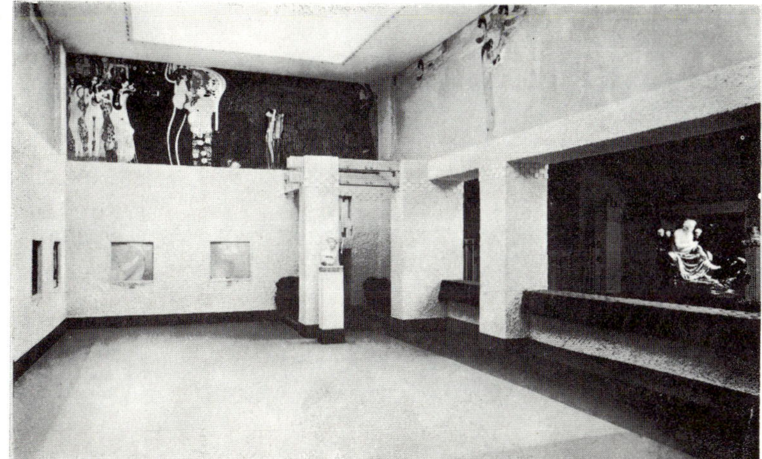

Ill. 17 *G. Klimt: Beethoven frieze*

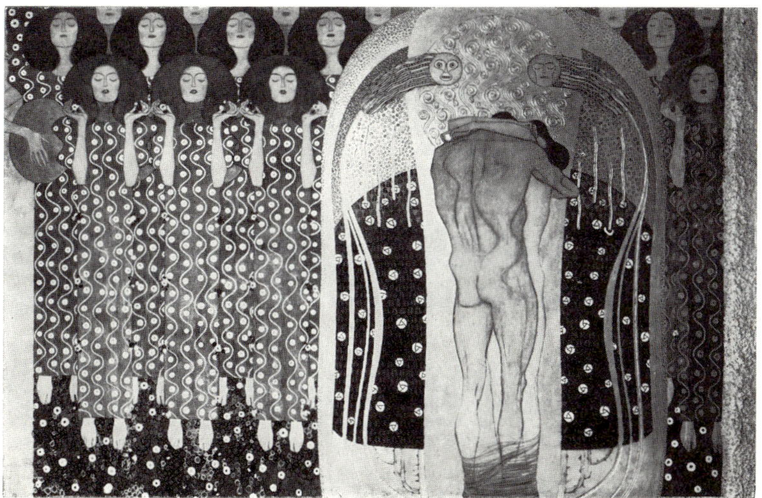

Ill. 18 *G. Klimt: Detail from the Beethoven frieze*

need of unsatisfied modern culture, the gathering to oneself of numerous other civilizations, the consuming desire for enlightenment?" asks Nietzsche, "if not to the loss of the myth, loss of the mythical homeland, the mythical womb?" [73]

7.

The aesthetic cult of the turn of the century usurped the place of religion, and the exhibition of Klinger's Beethoven at the Secession in 1902 was an example of this (Ill. 16, 17). The Secession pays homage to Klinger, Klinger pays homage to Beethoven; the latter, the Artist-Messiah himself, with all his apostles, serves the Deity, Art. Josef Hoffmann designed three rooms for the sacred rites. In the central hall Klinger's colorful sculpture sat enthroned. The most illustrious members of the Association had contributed to the decoration of the rooms. For the left-hand room Klimt painted a frieze approximately 24 meters long (Pl. 28, 29). The exhibition catalogue explains the design in terms of Beethoven's Ninth Symphony. But once again in this picture of the human condition Klimt is chiefly concerned with his own imaginative world, above all the relations between man and woman. The catalogue reads: "Longing for happiness. The sufferings of feeble humanity: their pleas to the well-armed strong man as the outer, compassion and ambition as the inner moving forces, persuading him to take up the struggle for happiness." "The hostile powers. The Giant Typhoeus, whom even the gods could not overcome, his daughters, the three Gorgons. Sickness, madness, death. Lust and wantonness, intemperance, nagging sorrow" (Pl. 28). "The longings of men rise above it all." "Longing for happiness finds satisfaction in poetry. The arts take us into the realms of the ideal where alone we can find pure joy, pure happiness, pure love." "Chorus of the angels of paradise: 'Joy, beautiful divine spirit.' 'This kiss for the whole world!' " (Pl. 29, Ill. 18). The ideas behind the painting give the pessimism of the University pictures a turn towards optimism. In "Jurisprudence" mankind was represented by one individual, the condemned criminal. His subjection to the dark powers of fate bitterly summed up the total concept of the three pictures. This time a single individual has been chosen to break the cycle of eternal recurrence, overcome the powers of darkness and direct the human quest to a sublime goal. Representing all men, a well-armed strong man takes up the search for happiness. The figure of a knight occurs frequently in allegorical art around 1900: it embodies the heroic liberator and conqueror, but also the messenger from a purer, more beautiful world. [74] Klimt's knight

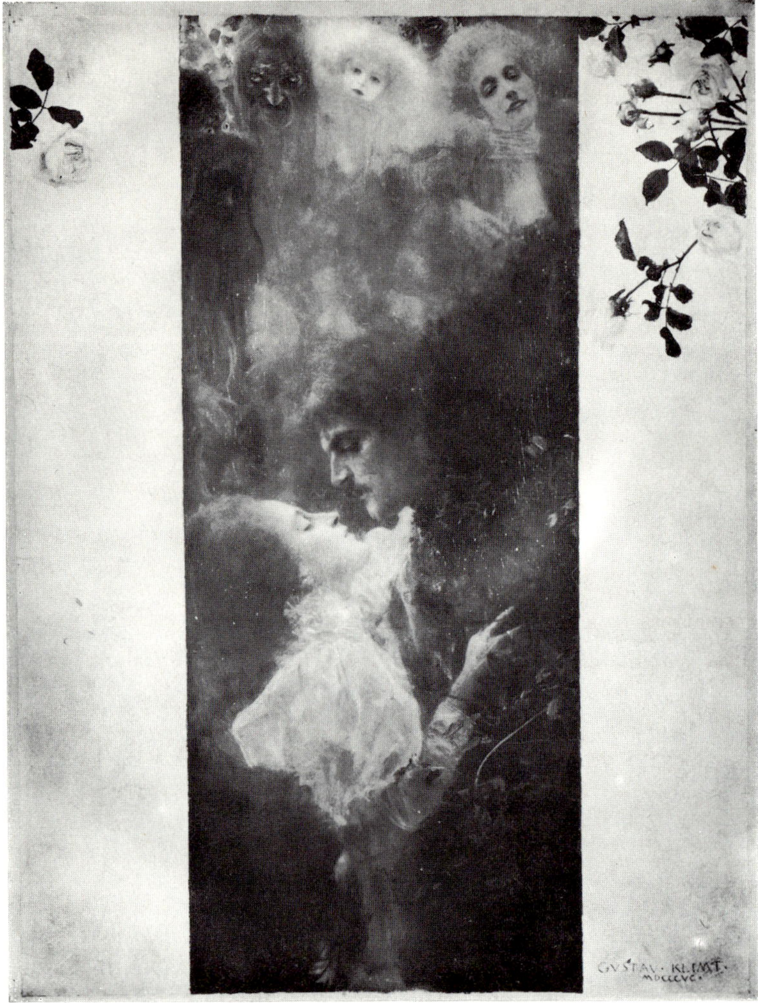

Ill. 19 *G. Klimt: Love, Historisches Museum der Stadt Wien*

is no liberator — he himself seeks deliverance. After he has doffed his armor, the attribute of manly resolution, he finds release and fulfillment at the end of the road in embracing a woman. This embrace cannot be uncompromisingly classed as male subjection, but it does seem final, indissoluble, and therefore becomes — like any irrevocable settlement — enslaving for the man who sought it. Sun and moon, cosmic symbols for man and woman, hint at the ascendancy of the woman. Questing man stares with hungry, demanding eyes into the unknown; the woman's secretive expression is one of passive expectation, which might well turn into rejection.

Before the embrace the "well-armed strong man" has overcome — we are not shown how — Death and the hostile powers that bar the way to the ideal regions beyond. We recognize these characters from "Jurisprudence." But this time the embodiments of the dark aspect of femininity do not have the last word. Triumphing over the fatal Eros is an Eros we might call life-giving, could one but remove him from the shelter of stylization and ornamentation. The spellbound immobility of the pose may be due to Klimt's trying to accommodate yet another idea in this embrace: Man finds joy and happiness in purified, unadulterated art, which unites its liberating message with that of "pure love." It can succeed where science fails; through the power of music it leads man into the arms of that cult-figure, Ideal Love, and at the same time into the "realms of the ideal" of which Creative Metaphysics, like every salvationist religion, holds that it is the only justification for our "vale of tears." [75] The feeling of apotheosis refers not only to the concluding chorus of the Ninth Symphony. It reinforces the optimism of the stylist who strives to change the world through art. "This kiss for the whole world!" — a promise that echoes the tenet "Art is communal property." The Secession did not live up to its motto, and like the embraces in Klimt's paintings, their communal work of art turned away from the world and sought precious seclusion.

Thematically the Beethoven frieze harks back to the early work "Love" (1895, Ill. 19). Death and the hostile powers are already foreshadowed here, representing the dangers and temptations of a man's life. Has love freed the man for complete self-fulfillment? Will the encounter with the unspoilt girl remain an episode or mark the beginning of a lifelong union? Consequently, are the background types past or future temptations and attackers? All these questions were left open: in the Beethoven frieze they were answered by the gospel of pure art and pure love.

8.

In the Beethoven frieze man's desire for happiness travels a long and dangerous path, beginning with the resolute departure and ending in fulfillment. In the mosaic mural for the dining room in Hoffmann's Maison Stoclet (1905—1909, Ill. 20, 21) Klimt drops both the provocative act of will that sets off the aesthetic-erotic self-fulfillment, and also the hostile powers which the seeker has to overcome. Here, surrounded by a "House of Life" where the dream of an ideal realm has materialized, man is no longer involved in a sequence of events, he is in a pure state of being. This sanctuary has no room for "hostile powers." More prominent than man is the vegetable ornament which, in the shape of a wide-spreading Tree of Life occupies the total length of the two longest walls. The spiral branches centering in themselves, pointing back to their own

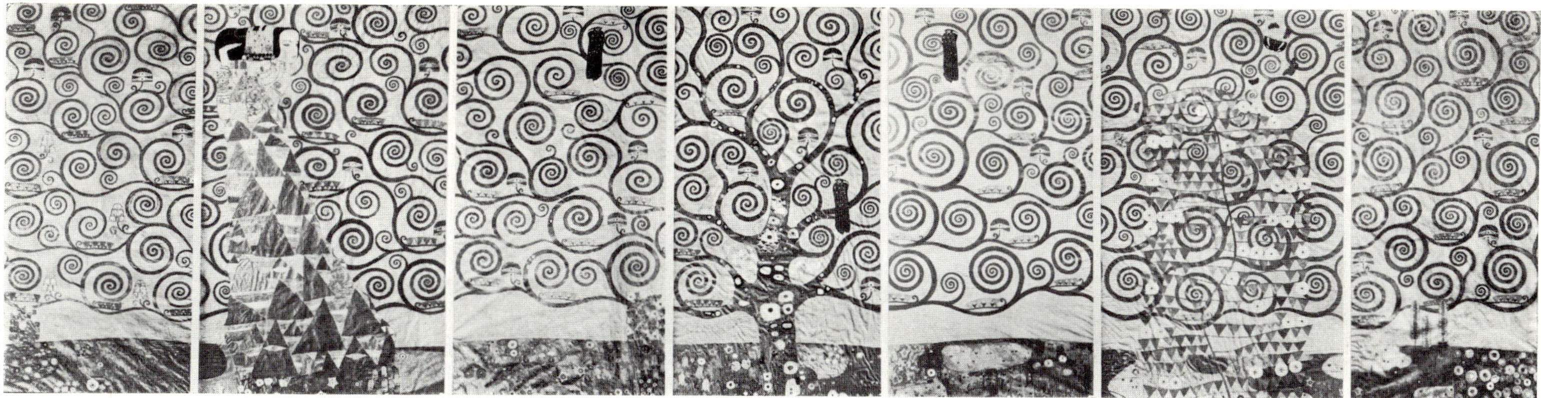

Ill. 20 *G. Klimt: Working drawings for the left-hand wall of Stoclet frieze. Museum für angewandte Kunst, Vienna*

origin, also emphasize a resting state rather than a natural growth process. In front of this decoration yet invaded by it stand the girl and the couple: excessively rich ornamental creatures, works of art within a work of art (Pl. 45, 46).

Ornament not only takes over the human figure, but displaces it to the periphery: "Expectation" and "Fulfillment" occupy lateral, subordinate positions to the Tree of Life. They share this inferior, flanking position with their symmetrical counterpart, a delicate plant with triangular leaves and round blossoms, motifs which also figure in the ornamental dress of the humans. The common motifs and the compositional balance hint at a possible metamorphosis of human beings into natural growths. A relatively small change of formal emphasis would suffice to change "Expectation" and "Fulfillment" into stylized plants, just as the shrubs might reveal themselves as human figures. This interchangeability is based on a common ornamental denominator. Surrender to a pervasive ornament is the price both man and nature pay for their precious symbiosis.

In this chief work of his "golden" style Klimt so closely approached the formal and material means of craftwork that Hoffmann and Moser's criteria can apply. The frieze, which incorporates the white marble of the wall, displays an abundance of costly materials: copper plates, silvered tin, coral, semiprecious stones and gold mosaic. Klimt, in delegating the execution of it to the *Wiener Werkstätte,* subjected both painting and craftwork, which in the final result unite to form one whole, to the same set of standards. The fact that he does not bring out the end wall of the room with an anthropomorphic theme, but decorates it with an abstract composition, could mark the painter's retreat to the decorative and ornamental limitations of the craftsman, and thus imply the equality of the two realms of creative activity. (Ill. 22) However, this equality only holds true for the encroaching complex of the communal work of art. In Klimt's easel pictures abstract ornament loses its autonomy and becomes a subsidiary factor. An instance of this can be seen in the narrow rectangle filling the upper right-hand corner of the portrait of Margaret Stonborough-Wittgenstein (Ill. 23): its structure roughly coincides with the abstract end wall of the Brussels dining room — but there the composition is autonomous, in the portrait a mere accessory.

9.

During the years of working on the Stoclet frieze Klimt also painted several pictures dealing with the life stages of women. These include "Three Ages of Woman" (Pl. 30), "Hope" (Pl. 26), "Danae" (Pl. 39) and the "Water Serpents" (Pl. 33, 34). The "Ages of Woman" takes up the basic theme of the human

Ill. 21 *Dining room of Palais Stoclet, Brussels*

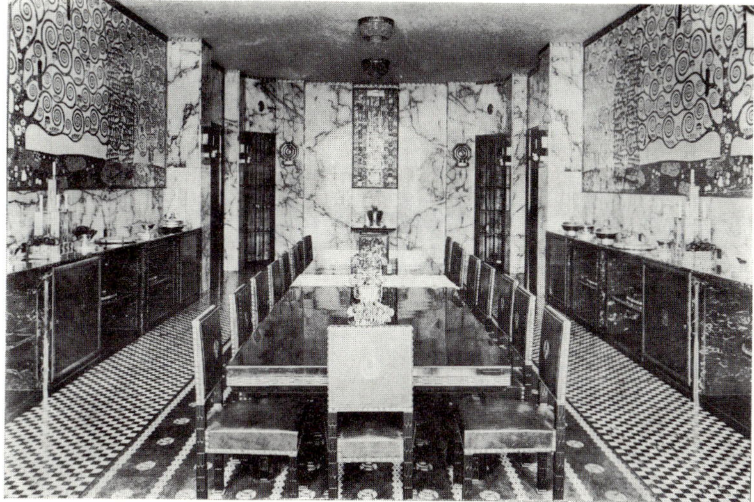

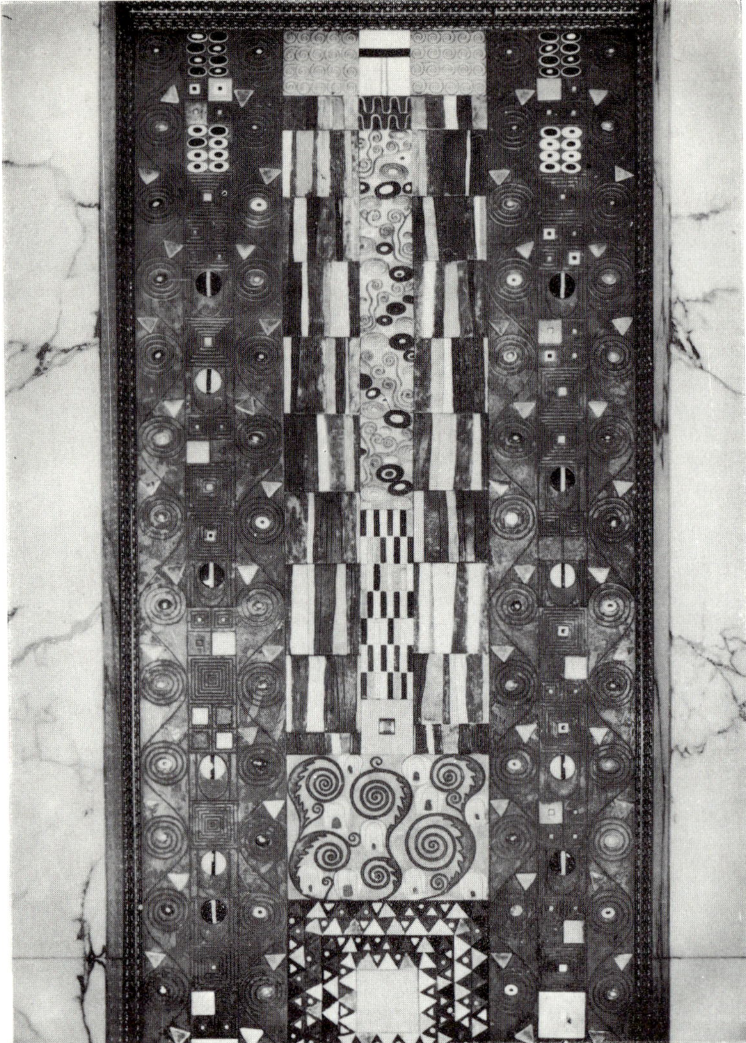

Ill. 22 *G. Klimt: Abstract mosaic, Palais Stoclet*

predicament pictures, the interaction and coexistence of growth and decay. Lux spoke of three phases of female beauty. From that point of view Klimt comes very close to a pictorial theme of Edvard Munch. In a more general way one can say that the pictures gives an insight into the evolution of Klimt's formal ideas. The three figures are set in a plane vertical strip. While the old woman stands out dry and sharp-edged from the carpet of blossoms, the body of the mother seems translucent to the encroaching ornament. Her hair is strewn with flowers, echoing the stylized flower decoration; at hip level a blue tongue-shape rests on her body, paralleling the transparent veil draping her legs. In front of this veil hover three squares, vertically divided. At the center of the body all this interpenetration and superimposition creates a highly ambiguous effect. Confronting this polyvalent disposition of forms is the body of the old woman. Here there is no mysterious intertwining of lines, there is no more creation of life or form. The rigidity of the final state is echoed by the painfully accurate formal record. The young mother, on the other hand, suggests the many ambiguities inherent in the genesis of form. The beginning of life and form alike is obscure and undefined, while the final stage is characterized by rigidity.

Organic growth has its counterpart in the act of artistic creation. As ornament can render childbirth in terms of artificed form, so it can also become a symbol of procreation, as in the "Danae" (Pl. 39). The shower of gold is made up of innumerable shimmering ornamental particles. These signify that every germ-cell, be it biological or artistic, draws its vitality from pre-representational abstract forms. The "Water Serpents" (Pl. 34) can do without man, for two reasons. They should not be seen only as votive pictures of lesbian love: these creatures are hybrids, still tied to the generative swamp from which they seem to have emerged. [76] The human anatomy of these hermaphrodites is intermingled with clinging water weeds and fish shapes, with waves and scales. Such promiscuity ensures them erotic satisfaction.

Klimt's creative procedure is rooted in linear forces not yet defined as objects. In other words, he works with a relatively limited repertoire of curves bearing the germ of many different representations. That is the cause of the poetic mystification and the mythical hybrids. The American architect Louis Sullivan expressed this characteristic of the Jugendstil line very well: "Forms emerge from forms, and others arise or descend from these. All are related, interwoven, intermeshed, interconnected, interblended." [77] Thus a certain curve can delimit a horizontal tongue of color with no representational significance (Ill. 24), or it can link two human limbs (Ill. 25). A swelling line can indicate pregnancy (Pl. 26), or form a bay around a figure — as in the portrait of Adele Bloch-Bauer (Pl. 42) — or become part of an intricate complex of curves (Ill. 26) posing problems of interpretation: is it "the tail of a comet" [78] or "billowing smoke drifts"? [79] We shall return to these problems when we consider the basic forms of Klimt's art.

10.

A variant of the mother in "Three Ages of Woman" recurs in "Death and Life" (1911—16, Pl. 58). In the "Ages of Woman" the delicate origin of life is juxtaposed with the living creature's proximity to death. The intimate confrontation of beginning and end in "Death and Life" is separated by an

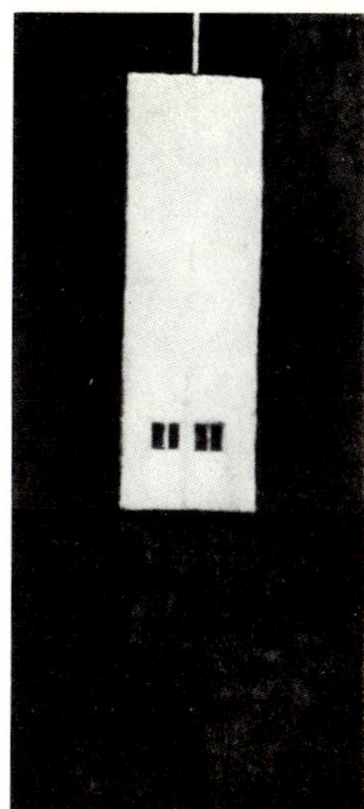

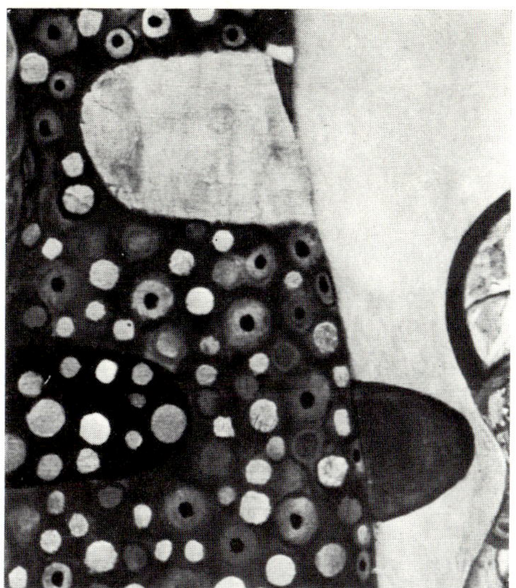

Ill. 23 Gustav Klimt: Motif from the portrait of Margaret Stonborough-Wittgenstein, cf. Pl. 32

Ill. 24 (right) Detail of Pl. 30

unbridgeable spatial tension. In this painting Klimt recapitulates the most important layers of meaning from his human predicament pictures. The spatial tension between a figure standing apart and a tightly packed bundle of bodies is anticipated in "Medicine," and there too we find the mother and child, figures expressing ecstatic longing, the decayed bodies of the aged, and the man reminiscent of Rodin's "Thinker," pressing his head against the shoulder of another. There have been some significant changes of emphasis. In "Medicine" both sexes played an equally important part in personifying humanity; now we have just one man surrounded by all the life stages of woman — as in "Love," but omitting the demoniacal dark side of feminity. Death is no longer the center around which human beings revolve. Banished from their midst, he assumes the definite shape of a threat from another world. In "Medicine," awareness of death was integrated into life, now it is rejected, suppressed.

And as the shapes all sank in darkness,
So ended everything on earth,
And like sleep in the soft rhythm of the waves
The approach of death would be welcome now.

Thus ends Hofmannsthal's poem "Life" (1892). In "Medicine," too, sleep seems to merge into death. Not so in "Death and Life": for this Death to get people in his power he would have to intrude violently and destructively into their sheltered world. The symbolism of the coloring confirms this interpretation. In "Medicine," a twilit morbid coloring prevails throughout, the bodies appear diaphanous, marked by sickness and death. In "Death and Life," Klimt separates the color zones: Death wraps himself in the colors of night, while the human bodies are sturdily modeled and display a thoroughly healthy complexion, whose rich diversity is interspersed with colorful, gay ornaments. Hermetically sealed off, the human tower soars into a somber surround, which belongs to the domain of Death. To drive out death reacts back on life: it only appears to be solidly established; in fact it is cut off, more isolated and more imperiled than before.

11.

This polarization is especially illuminating in view of the highly colored vitality of the late works, among the most important of which are two that belong basically with the human condition: "The Maiden" (1913, Pl. 54) and "The Bride" (1917/18, Pl. 82). Together with the "Baby" (1917/18, Pl. 81) and "Adam and Eve" (1917/18, Pl. 80) — two lesser paintings — they describe a life cycle, but completely ignoring the unpleasant side. The dark colors of death are not represented in the palette. Hand in hand with the loosening, increased movement and lightening of the pictorial structure, Klimt goes in for more youthful subject matter. He turns away from the demonic Eros, and increasingly relegates man to the background. His main theme is no longer "fulfillment," as in the "golden" style — Adam and Eve show that forgoing the hackneyed formula of the embrace does not necessarily produce a new and convincing pictorial image. [80] Klimt's imagination is now increasingly preoccupied with the "expectation" that precedes physical union.

Ill. 25 Detail of Pl. 12

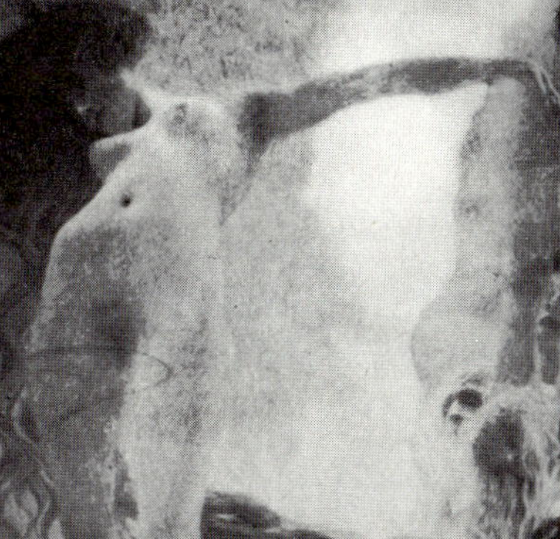

Ill. 26 Detail of Pl. 11

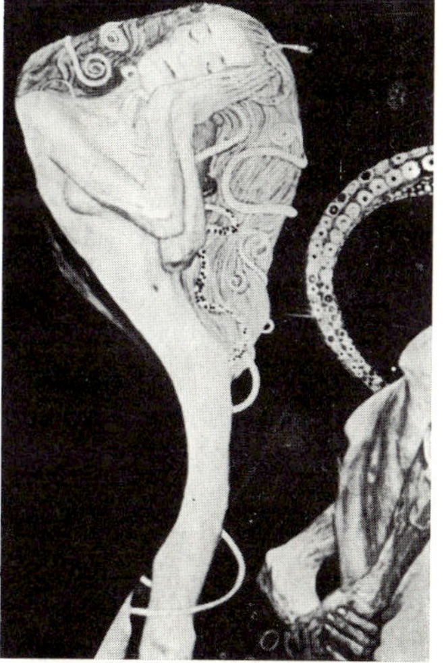

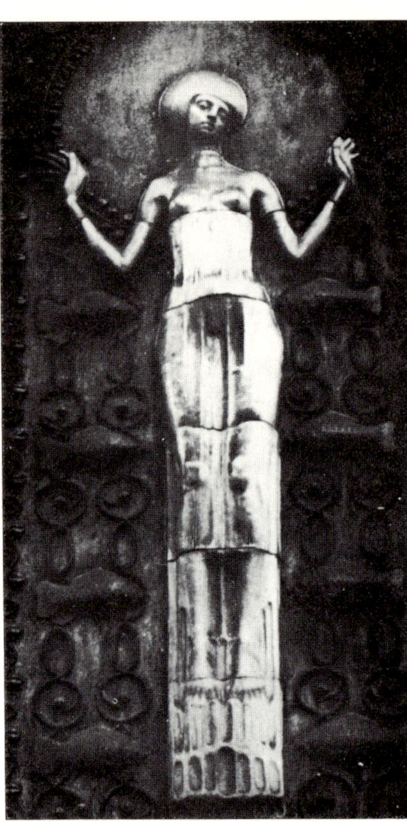

Ill. 27
Luksch: Relief 1907/08

The theme of expectation had a long, though not continuous, evolution. The first hint of it, lyrically restrained, comes in the young girl of Tanagra (Ill. 10) in the Kunsthistorische Museum, then one finds it in connection with portraits of young women and girls. These creatures seem to be hoping less for union with the male than for a more beautiful world in which woman is an object of adoration rather than lust. [81]
Why do women love to be painted by Klimt? Lux asked at the 1908 exhibition, and immediately answered his own question: "They have a great yearning to be raised above the humdrum . . . like princesses or madonnas . . . beauty that can nevermore be torn and devastated by the greedy hands of life." [82] In the Stoclet frieze, "Expectation" and "Fulfillment" confront each other, equal in importance. The pregnant women vary the theme to the expectation of new life (Pl. 26), which Klimt finds an eminently feminine state, combining psychological and physical elements, premonitions and dreams, desire for man and the longing to conceive.

Weininger says about woman: " . . . her desire for a man is simply a desire for the moment when she can be completely passive." [83] If expectation is that part of consciousness which processes precognitive imaginative material, Weininger deduces that men would progress more rapidly than women from these phases to active expression. It is precisely the differential behavior of the sexes regarding imaginative precognition that fascinates Klimt as a painter of women. Man, whose consciousness tends to clear, definite ideas, is not a rewarding subject for an artist who prefers ambiguity to singlemindedness. From the early works like "Love," (Ill. 19) down to "The Maiden" and "The Bride," Klimt continually re-enters the charmed circle of ambiguity with which woman, according to Weininger, has closer and more lasting converse than man. He mentions "preconceptions," meaning a stage "where flowing geometric forms, visual phantasmagoria, misty visions emerge and dissolve, 'wavering figures,' veiled pictures, mysteriously alluring masks appear." [84]

The "Maiden" (Pl. 54) represents such a preconception. In this picture Klimt attains to an astonishing freedom. It is as though we were viewing a multi-significant, multi-articulated prototype, a collective embryo as it were, articulated and suffused by forces of color, which is both bound and liberated. The comparison with the human tower in "Death and Life" (Pl. 58) is instructive. The bundling of bodies is resolved, and the tension has gone from the rhythm. The interaction of the partners in form occurs more loosely, on a larger scale — it teems with possibilities. The ornament is not a binding, fixing element, but carries the movement of the bodies, opens up both the girl and her clothing, encircles the event without encapsulating it. The overlapping of opening and closing is due to the spiral construction, which is at once a centripetal and centrifugal movement. [85] Exactly in the middle of the young woman's body there is a violet wreath of opposed spirals — we discover an echo of it when we look at the girl's arms in relation to the arms and heads of her companions. [86] Klimt's freedom in the use of this motif is shown by comparison with the Tree of Life in the Stoclet frieze (Ill. 20). The rotating pictorial form reminds one of a painted ceiling. And indeed its distant precursor is a painted ceiling done in 1884, "Poet and Muse" (Ill. 28). This relationship is not surprising, because the opening up and dynamism of the later Klimt allows baroque inspirations dating from the time before the static and hermetic stylization, to resurface.

"The Bride" is a puzzling picture (Pl. 82). Unfinished, as it has come down to us, it can hardly be interpreted. "To the left fragments of female bodies symbolize aspects of life, among which the monklike bridegroom in red clothing can be seen. To the right is the bride's dream image of her own body on the wedding night, portrayed with visionary intensity," is the not wholly convincing interpretation of Dobai. [87] Perhaps the incomplete state itself points to the idea behind the picture. It is strange that Klimt seems to anchor the composition in the two lateral centers and the execution is furthest advanced there. The body of the bride, only sketchily indicated, seems to be interstitial, but it could also mark the beginning of a formal rethinking, in the course of which the two flanking configurations might well have been brought closer together. As Klimt has left it, the composition reminds one of "Medicine": in both cases there is an ecstatic figure segregated from a human tower. However, it is possible that Klimt wanted to contrast the bride's slim unadorned figure with the splash of colors and that later stages would not have changed very much. The untouched girl between two bacchantic incarnations of femininity: perhaps that would have been Klimt's contribution to a theme which Toorop introduced with his Three Brides twenty-five years before.[88]

12.

When Klimt died on February 6, 1918, at the age of 56, he left several pictures uncompleted. He left no final message. For some time his work had not been in the spotlight of contemporary interest. In 1913 Hamann had already referred to Kandinsky's recent work as "the new monumental style" and placed Klimt, who was only three years older, among the traditionalists.[89] Eight years after Klimt's death Wilhelm Pinder's *Problem der Generation* did not draw this distinction: Pinder takes all those born around 1860 as one generation, which for him is the true "expressionist" generation, its fundamental concern mimesis. In this generation he includes (among others) Corinth and Segantini (1858), Toorop and Seurat (1860), Ludwig von Hofmann and Maillol (1861), Klimt (1862), Munch, Obrist and van de Velde (1863), Eckmann, Toulouse-Lautrec and Vallotton (1865), Minne and Kandinsky (1866), Nolde and Jawlensky (1867) and Slevogt (1868). Missing from the list are Ensor (1860), Stuck (1863), Bonnard (1867), Vuillard (1868) and Matisse (1869). "All of them," Pinder concludes, "are artists of attitude: in all of them, with the exception of Kandinsky, mimesis effects the rehabilitation of the poetic." It is arguable whether this statement truly characterizes the artistic behavior of this generation, or whether Pinder's *Kunstgeschichte nach Generationen* (History of art by generations), persuaded by the implied or overt need for conformity, has settled for a common denominator that cannot stand close analysis, asserting both too much and too little. Be that as it may, Pinder's characterization of the generation "around 1860" fits no single artist better than Klimt. From his beginnings to his last works

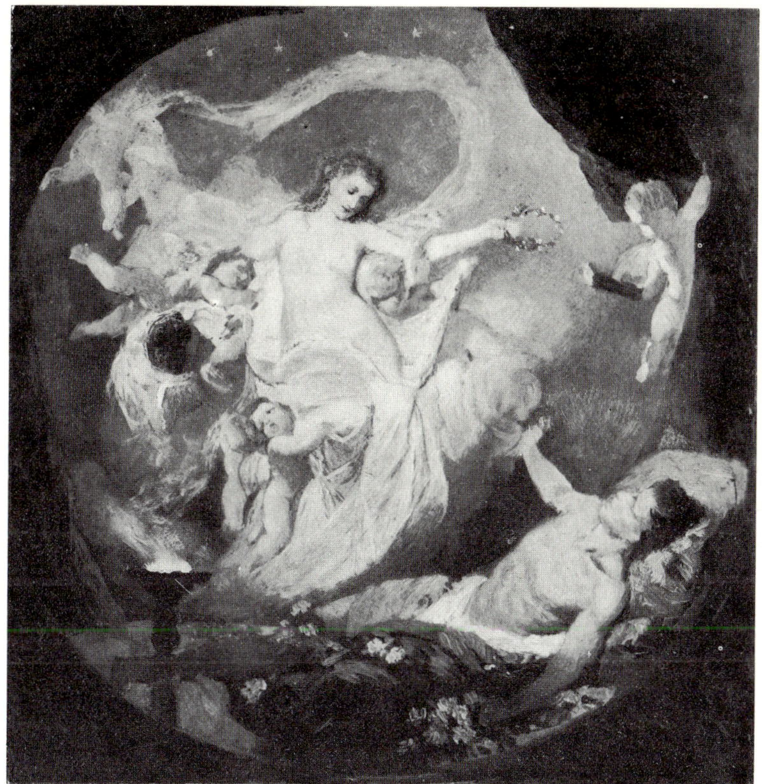

Ill. 28 *G. Klimt: Poet and Muse*

Klimt was a painter of attitudes, arranging the actors in his pictorial world in evocative poses and performances. The showy exhibitionist element starts with his early paintings for the Burgtheater and the Kunsthistorische Museum, rooted in the histrionic self-consciousness of the historical style; acquires depth in the dark enchantment of the cult of Death at the turn of the century, above all in the University pictures, and works through the aristocratic fulfillment visions of the "golden" style to the optimistic expansiveness of the late pictures which pay homage to the cult of Life.

What was Klimt's place in the art of his time? That depends on what we mean by an artist's time. If we measure him by his contemporaries, there is no doubt that of the paths open to those born in the sixties — one need only think of Munch, Matisse and Kandinsky — Klimt by no means took the most out of the way, but neither did he choose the well-trodden. Why this was so the generation theory can only answer in terms of the specific historical situation in which the painter found himself. Of the art of his time, from the eighties to the end of the First World War, only a small part impinged on Klimt's consciousness, and that which did could not persuade him to take a radical turn. It was not ignorance of the situation in

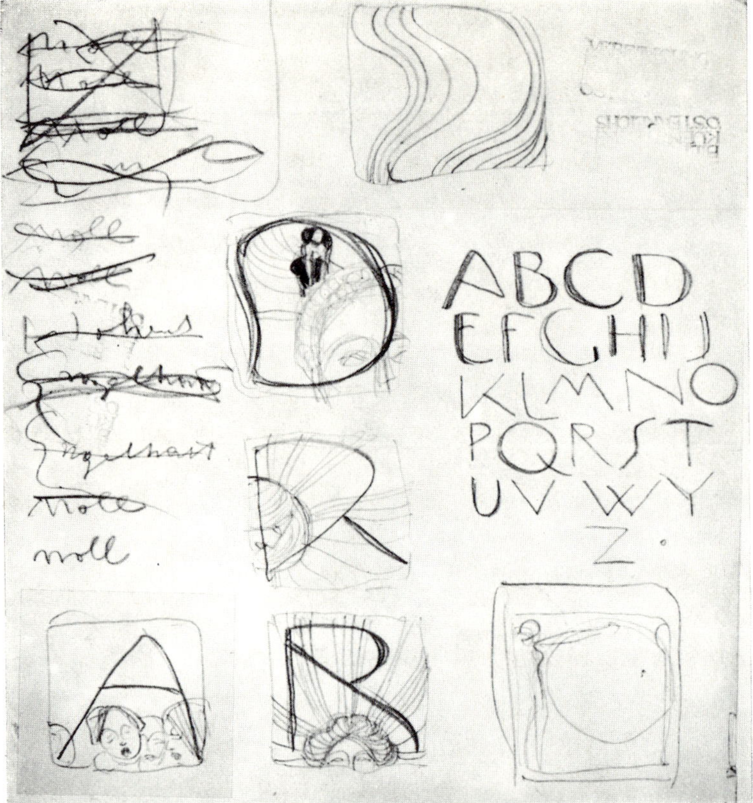

Ill. 29 *G. Klimt: Page of Sketches*

Europe that kept Klimt from the boldness of the Expressionists and the unexplored territory of the abstract; it was rather that his personality was involved in the interplay of tradition and innovation, and he would seem to have judged his own possibilities and limitations correctly. His artistic personality harmonized with a certain aspect of Viennese culture at the turn of the century. The two ensuing chapters will deal with the interaction of Klimt and this particular historical moment. This does not mean, however, that Klimt should be reduced to the size of local events. We shall re-examine Klimt's contribution to the Secessionist plan for art and life and try to estimate its value in the context of the intellectual and artistic horizon of contemporary Vienna. It will be seen that the controversies of the time gave rise to some of the most decisive ideas of twentieth century art.

III.

1.

So far we have spoken mainly of the content of Klimt's work. Questions of form offer themselves to analysis from the points of view of development and recurrence. Traditional stylistic criticism regards changes in chronological sequence as processes of development and tries to discover their causes. The analysis of formal constants seeks to elucidate the persisting framework without considering the dynamics of stylistic phases, occasional breaks of style, inventions or retrospection. The two points of view should of course interrelate. For the moment, however, as Klimt's work has so far been examined by the criteria of style analysis, it seems opportune to introduce some observations of structure analysis into the discussion and thus prepare a basis for a future analytical synthesis. The advantage of this will be twofold. We shall discover that Klimt's use of form is structurally related to that of other creative personalities in Vienna around 1900. It also will emerge that Klimt's world view, which the previous section discussed in connection with his paintings of the human predicament, is not a literary or symbolical accessory, but the logical consequence of that use of form. In the words of Delacroix: "There is a consecrated mold into which one puts good and bad ideas." [90] Information about Klimt's basic forms is supplied by sixty colophons which the artist drew for a luxury edition of his works. Invented as a species of reduced formulae to elucidate and paraphrase his complex pictorial structure, these abbreviations are at the same time ornamental manifestations of the germ-cells from which the macro-forms of the compositions emerged. Insight into the shadowy beginnings of stylization is afforded by a page of sketches (Ill. 29) featuring a linear D-shape, which unites at least two levels of meaning; it could harden into an actual letter, or liquefy into an assembly of curves not necessarily, though potentially, representational. The protuberance to the

Ill. 30 *Venet. 16th cent. Copy of Michelangelo's Leda, Museo Correr, Venice*

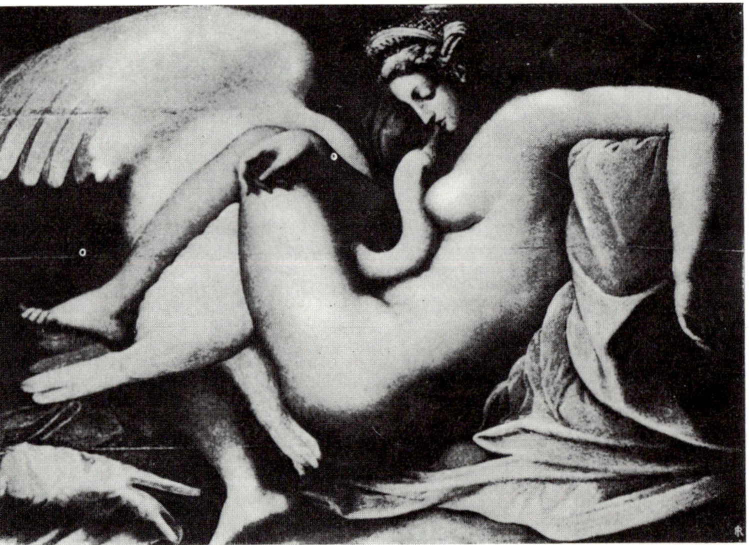

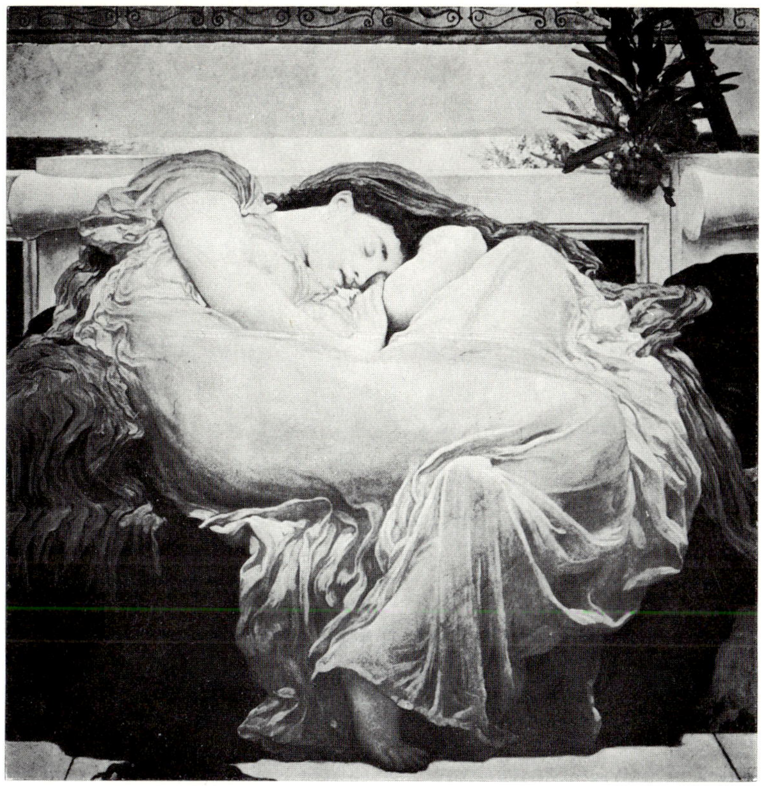

Ill. 31 *F. Leighton: Flaming June, Mus. Ponce, Puerto Rico*

right occurs in the belly of the pregnant woman and the left-hand edge of "Jurisprudence" (Pl. 11), while the kidney-shaped curve is the germ of "Danae" (Pl. 39).

"Danae" confirms Delacroix's dictum. A possible precursor is Michelangelo's Leda, of which copies survive (Ill. 30). Klimt achieves a greater intensity of passive surrender than the classical model. Using the picture surface to the full, he encloses the body in an embryonic oval which nevertheless is not cut off, but is seized and irradiated by the flooding shower of gold and the veil which mingles with the hair. The figure is both resting and suffused, simultaneously open and closed. The concentration of form conveys erotic suggestion in the same sense as Weininger's assertion that "Woman's entire body is an accessory to her sexual parts." [91] An aphorism of Kraus summarizes the total homogeneity Klimt was striving for: "The sexual instinct of woman, surely at the moment of use, becomes her sole significance." [92] Elsewhere we read: "The stream of female satisfaction from its source to its estuary has no tributaries." This metaphor also suits Danae.

The quality of Klimt's achievement is underlined by comparison with a contemporary painting, Frederick Leighton's "Flaming June" (Ill. 31). Danae is all of a piece, while in Leighton's picture, though the figure is no less pliant, the form seems diffuse and redundant. Whoever sees both pictures side by side will find the Danae more instantly memorable. This impressiveness is due to Klimt's use of a basic formula, a "mold" in Delacroix's sense, which suggests utter immediacy and inevitability. We recognize this lapidary outline from Klimt's signature (Ill. 32):

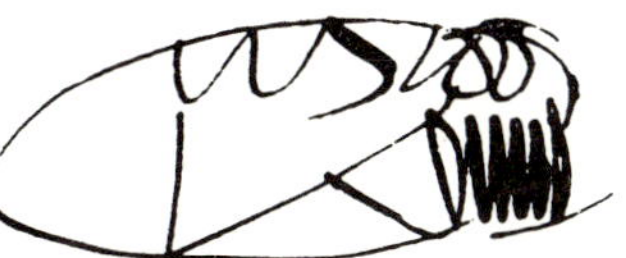

Ill. 32

here is the germ of the Danae. Precursors of this oval shape may be seen in two drawings of 1897. The allegory of Knowledge (Pl. II) already seems to hint at a similar disposition of limbs within a square as Danae. This shows more clearly in the study of a seated nude, where the passivity of Danae is already marked (Ill. 33). The second drawing (Ill. 34) also shows ideas for "Medicine," among them certain outlines reminiscent of the soundbox of a stringed instrument. Anyone aware of Klimt's stylized anatomy will recognize them for female bodies. The

Ill. 33 *G. Klimt: Study for Danae*

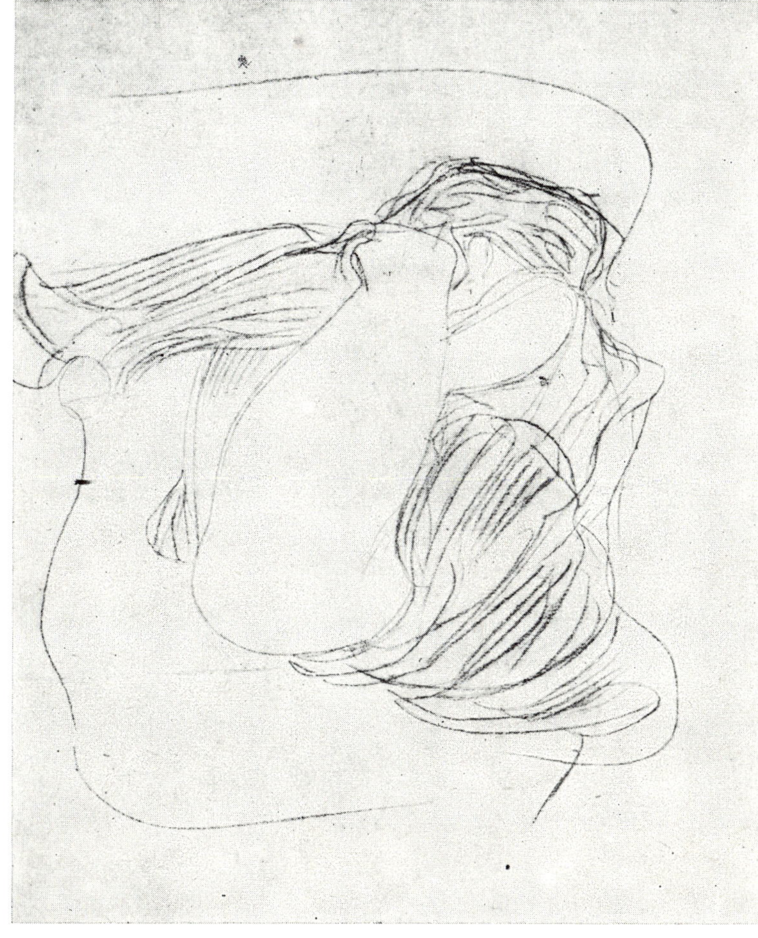

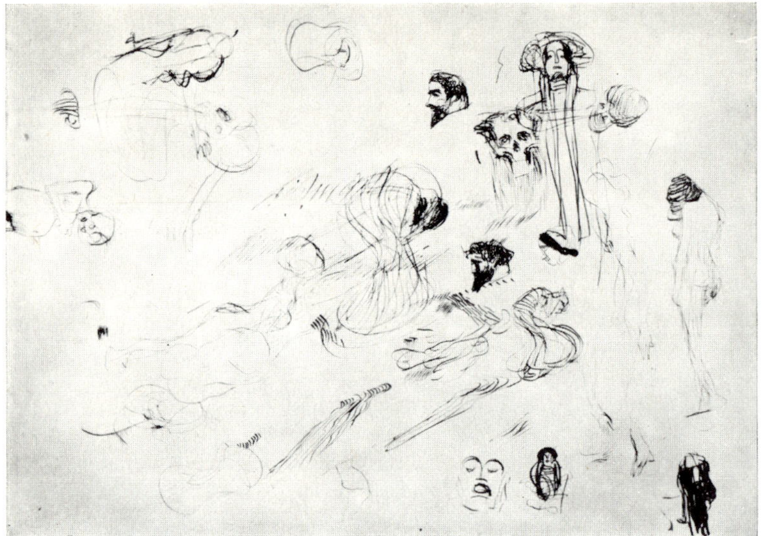

Ill. 34 *G. Klimt: Studies for "Medicine"*

curves of buttocks or of a head with billowing hair are interchangeable. [94] Tightened up and deprived of its waist indentations, the soundbox-contour becomes the oval of the signature device and of Danae.

The soundbox line may be modified: ornamentally emancipated, it reappears as a larger shape in the "bell" that surrounds the lovers in the Beethoven cycle (Ill. 18); diminished into a "tongue" shape it defines the wavy line of a dress (Pl. 15). This line is related to the lyre and all its variants. [95] Morphogenetic variability is characteristic of these recurring constants. Earlier we pointed out the arc of bodies in "Medicine," which we meet again in the "Ages of Woman" (Pl. 30). One of Klimt's colophons (Ill. 35), probably a stylized G. K. monogram, is given the simplified formula of "Medicine": the human tower and the solitary figure to the left, which yet remains linked to the right side of the picture. [96]

The linear formulae for arrangements of figures and setting are interchangeable. The body outline of Amalie Zuckerkandl (Pl. 76) corresponds to the stylized arch of the avenue at Schloss Kammer (Pl. 56). This relationship determines figure and ground, "positive" shape and "negative" interstitial space, as an analysis of "The Bride" (Pl. 82) also revealed. The narrow middle zone of the picture is an interval between the two flanking islands of bodies, but positively filled by the main figure central to the conception. A similar example of the potential tangibility of interstitial space is seen in the "Goldfish." The dark intervening space is at the same time a hollow mold of the monster which threatens the pregnant woman in "Hope" (Ill. 36). Similarly the line of blossom between the "Water Serpents" could turn into a reclining figure (Pl. 33). The contours are ambivalent, orientated in two opposite directions; the spaces between can become positive shapes. Klimt uses the same principle even when he renounces line. The arrangement of planes in the Sunflower (Pl. 36) is to the Garden Path with Chickens (Pl. 79) as positive is to negative: in one case the central band is pattern, in the other interstitial, but with the tangibility of an object. The mechanism of this reversal is explained by a device of six oval shapes (Ill. 37). The stressed, black-rimmed shapes of the upper row are unstressed in the lower. The observer can reverse this relationship and put the accent on the white shapes. The more diagrammatic and abstract the shapes, the more interpretations seem possible. We may compare two vertically subdivided squares (Ill. 38 a and b) and see they are alike. What are they meant to be — an abstraction or a symbol? It is not only how it is seen, but how the interrelationship is understood. In one case, it is the letter I, in the other, the Roman numeral II. The context therefore decides whether the two verticals delimit a "figure" (the letter I) or merely divide the square into three strips of varying breadth.

The problem of figure and ground is part of the central concern of Gestalt psychology. This school of perception psychology was more or less founded by the Graz scientist Christian von Ehrenfels, who in 1890 published an essay "On 'Gestalt Qualities' " in the Quarterly Review of Scientific Philosophy. The premises from which the process of perception selects distinctive Gestalt qualities were dealt with by Ernst Mach in 1886: "If we start two scales from two different notes and let them progress according to the same numerical proportion of oscillation, we shall perceive the same tune in both cases as immediately as we recognize the same figure in two geometrically similar constructions orientated in the same way." [98] A similar relationship links Klimt's signature with Danae, the microforms of the colophons with the organized rhythm of the compositions.

Ill. 35 *G. Klimt: Colophon*

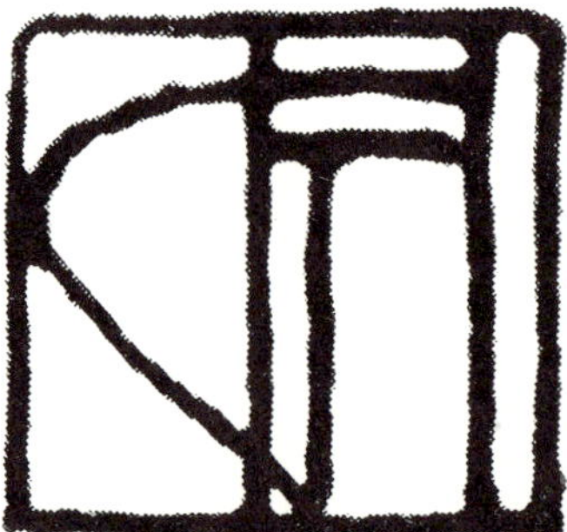

Ill. 36 *Detail of Pl. 24*

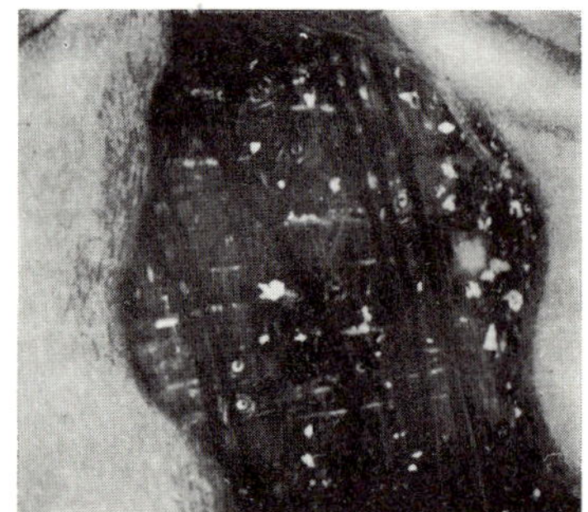

Klimt thereby proves that Gestalt qualities are transposable, and that they can form the basis, the "molds," for new realizations of a higher order. "Because we can compare Gestalt qualities like anything else, and the relative scale so produced can itself be regarded as a higher order of Gestalt quality." [99]

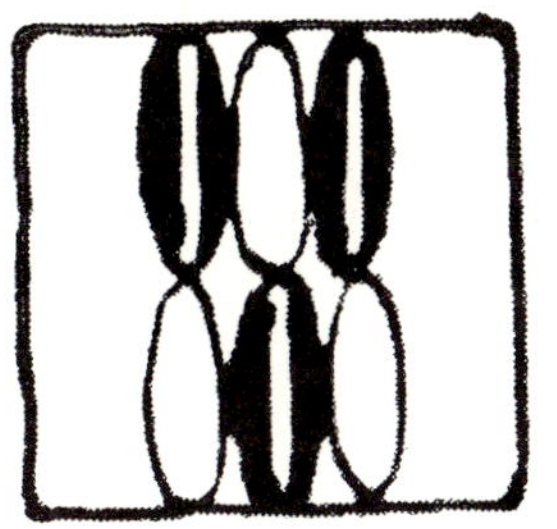

Ill. 37 Klimt: Colophon

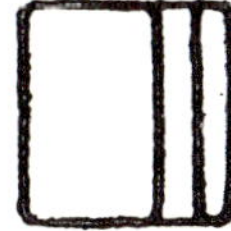

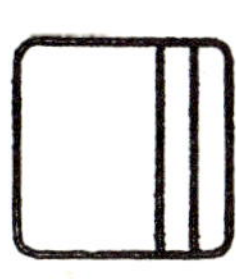

Ill. 38 a *b*

a Klimt, from Ver Sacrum, No. 8, 1900
b Klimt, from Ver Sacrum, 1901

2.

Their transposability makes the Gestalt qualities ambiguous, hence the previously mentioned comparison involving a Hoffmann sideboard, a hatbox and an altar niche. For a vision that strips perceived objects of their "banal meaning," a goblet might as well be "a hollow pineapple open at the top, or a fat gleaming snake's head." [100] The vision which ignores the connections of things makes an important artistic discovery: the artist stands "once more in his true native element, a myth-maker in the midst of . . . chaotic . . . reality." [101] The riddle of the meaning leaves the observer looking for interpretations with nothing but the phenomenal certitude of autonomous forms, committed to no object and no description. Of a woman outlined against the evening sky there is "nothing that means knee, breast or forehead: nothing but a curved line against the evening sky, pure form," stated Hofmannsthal. [102] In the spirit of this naive vision, (based on Ruskins "innocent eye") in 1903 Bahr demanded paintings that have no meaning, "so far removed from objects that people will give up trying to find any relation to reality in them or asking what it is 'actually' meant to be: because 'actually' color can be nothing but color." [103]

Ambiguity in Klimt's work occurs in varying degrees. There are also parallels with contemporary literature. In the pictures for the Kunsthistorische Museum, ambiguity results from the trompe l'oeil effect, in the Burgtheater pictures from the interaction of stage and auditorium, heightened and prosaic reality. Compare the stage on the stage in Schnitzler's "*Der grüne Kakadu*" (The Green Cockatoo, 1899). [104] The Viennese society ladies who have frozen into works of art are products of an alienating vision, which could be expressed equally in prose. Altenberg removes a hand from its realistic context and stylizes it into an "artificial exhibit." [105] In "*Der Tod Georgs*" (1900) Beer-Hofmann merges the figure of a woman with statuettes of saints; in another connection he places a figure in surroundings which in the course of a few sentences turn from "a grassy slope" into wallpaper strewn with narcissi." [106] It is not only Klimt's landscapes and the backgrounds of his portraits that show this tendency to turn into ornamentation: the people themselves have often lost a part of their corporeality to the two-dimensional wallpaper decor (Pl. 42). In Beer-Hofmann the woman, "a white picture of herself," stands disembodied in front of the flowered wallpaper, like a negative in front of the colored positive, sharply accentuated. This situation has been compared with a remark of Musil's about J. P. Jacobsen: "This no longer portrays a human being, only his pictorial aspect." [107] That is exactly what one feels about the ambiguity of Klimt's portraits. In the light of Goethe's universal philosophy of wholeness, Bahr tries to strip ambiguity of its disturbing aspects and place it on a sounder basis. His *Neue Studien zur Kritik der Moderne* (Berlin, 1897) contains an appreciation of Leopold von Andrian's *Der Garten der Erkenntnis* (The Garden of Enlightenment, 1895), in which he says about the hero of that tale: "He will have to learn that he is no different from the rest of the world, that what happens outside is no different from what goes on inside him. Only then will he be complete, and then he will have to die: because life is a singling out from the general to the particular. Whoever has achieved enlightenment and returned to the whole, has fulfilled his destiny."

In this connection one should mention Klimt's transmutation of color. Another quotation from Leopold von Andrian's *Garten der Erkenntnis* aptly characterizes it: "It seemed to him the Viennese manner had the attractive alluring quality of a light of which one is not sure whether it has two colors that continually intermingle, or one color iridescing in all its shades." This intermingling also extends to the inner experiences, the continuous stream of consciousness. *Der Garten der Erkenntnis* hints at the range of feelings Klimt touches in his scenes of human life: "Pain and exultation, grandeur and vulgarity and the whole abundance of all that is in heaven and hell, but combined in such a way, intermingling in such a movement, that the whole thing was experienced as a mysteriously trembling halo . . ." [108] Fifteen years later Schnitzler similarly described the shifting variety of experience: "So many feelings in us at any one time —! Love and deceit . . . Faith and faithlessness . . .

Adoration for one and desire for another — or for several. We do try to create some sort of order in our feelings, as best we can, but this order is just something artificial . . .. The natural state is chaos" *(Das weite Land*, 1910).

Klimt's basic "molds" and the symbolism of his pictures of the human predicament, with their formal versatility, match the many layers of significance and ambiguity which are the natural consequences embodying "so many feelings . . . at any one time."

3.

The transmuting dynamic of Gestalt perception and production is not confined to painting and literature. We encounter its characteristics — under varying insignia — in the sexual psychology of Otto Weininger, in Freud's psychoanalysis and in Karl Kraus's critique of language.

All that is transmutative and ambiguous negates the nature of conceptualism, which Weininger attributes to the male attitude and regards as absolutely constant and unequivocal. He condemns synaesthesia, effeminate Jugendstil art, the brilliant stylists and shapeless "mood art," [109] because they all glorify the feminine traits opposed to the active experience of the Self. Nonconceptual, formless, ambiguous, always blending in, woman is the symbol of this aesthetic mutability: she can turn into anything. [110] A few years later Kraus turned this dictum of the misogynist philosopher into positive admiration: "Woman has the characteristics of the Non-Self: she is everything, in *not* being herself." [111] The negative becomes a positive, the delimited but formless "ground" in front of which Weininger placed the strong contoured figure of man itself becomes a "figure."

Weininger differentiates between A and Non-A. What he formulates for the abstract thought schemata of logic does not hold for concrete Gestalt perception and reproduction: neither the perceptual world nor any of the artificial systems of signs which men have invented for their own orientation is unequivocal. A study of the ambivalent nature of Klimt's technique shows that the spectator has a choice among ambiguous patterns of significance. Every A is conditioned by its context, and our interpretation of A also depends on the corresponding Non-A. In a different context, with new expectations or changed habits of perception, A can become Non-A, and vice versa. Everything is potentially multivalent. Lux said of the variable towers of Roller's Mozart stage set that they could be "the balcony of a house or a box in a hall, as required." Musil's Young Törless confesses that he sees things "in two different guises." [112] Alois Riegl's analysis of the reliefs on the Arch of Constantine suggests two complementary points of view. From nearby, the observer notes "extreme formalistic beauty," a distant view on the other hand gives an impression of extraordinary liveliness. Conclusion: even works of art defy an objective, unequivocal, *correct* description.

The same goes for the potential meaning of words. The abuse of language by journalists and phrasemongers which Kraus castigated has its origins in precisely that availability and potential ambiguity of the units of language which the editor of the *Fackel* himself exploits for his deflating aphorisms. [113] On this transmuting ambiguity the psychoanalyst whom Kraus despised built his interpretation of dreams. Freud's diagnosis of dream experiences coincides with the non-conceptual nature which Weininger considers characteristic of woman and feminine art forms. [114] Dreams neglect the either-or alternatives and all the laws of opposites and contradiction, they produce strange word-combinations and puzzle pictures, choosing out of several possible associations. The same dream content can change its meaning completely for different people or in a different context; again, various symbols can be used to render a certain meaning. Dream symbols "are often ambiguous and multivalent, so that, as in Chinese script, only the context can supply the correct interpretation in any given case. Combined with this versatility of symbols is the characteristic of dreams to admit dual interpretations, to represent in one dream content several, often extremely divergent, thought formulations and wish motivations." Just as context-dependence marks our conventional script symbols, so dream symbols are also valid for the experiences of the waking consciousness — and not only of the artist. Again we are faced with a universal mutability. Freud later expressed the situation thus: "Our ego seems to us independent, unified, well marked off from everything else. It took psychoanalytical research to teach us that this appearance is a fraud, that the ego continues inwards without a sharp demarcation into an unconscious natural being which we refer to as the id, for which it acts as a kind of facade . . ." [115] One of the mutative "hinges" is studied in Freud's work on jokes, which appeared in 1905. [116] The characteristics of verbal and pictorial jokes — smooth transitions, hidden similarities, mixed metaphors, double meanings, etc. — resemble the formal behavior of dreams. In a traditional sense the unconscious supplies the archetypal, elemental "molds" which are the springs of consciousness.

4.

The units in a communal work of art are related to their context in the sense of Ehrenfels' definition of "feeling for style" as the ability to grasp and compare the Gestalt qualities of a certain category.[117] The stylist brings to such comparison an overall harmony, his creative sense of style inventing certain forms, Delacroix's "molds," which he then — mutatis mutandis — impresses upon all the articles in his communal work of art, resulting in the resemblance of a sideboard to a hatbox and an altar niche. Every component of the total complex enters into several different relationships at once, and thereby combines several layers of significance. A vase becomes a work of art and an article of use, the piece of furniture is architecture

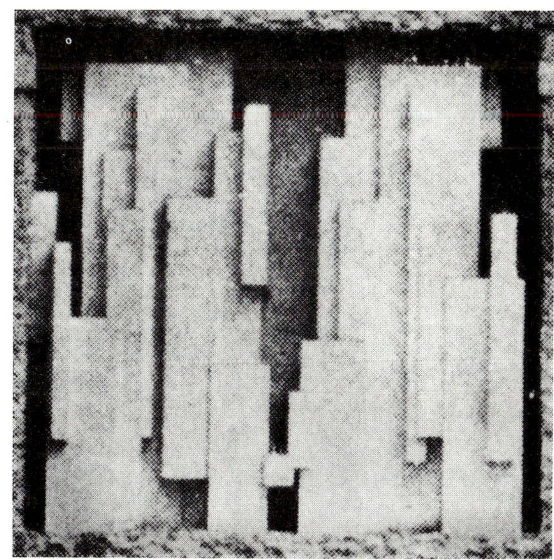

Ill. 39 *J. Hoffmann: Overdoor at the Beethoven Exhibition, Vienna, 1902*

in miniature, Hoffmann's relief above a doorway (Ill. 39) an abstract picture, a garden gate a magnified brooch, and the exhibition hall a sacred precinct, a cemetery, a theatre and a street of posters. In the sweeping mutations of stylist art, one can always point to the dynamics of creative vision involving several different ways of perception if:

1. the formal composition of one or several works of art displays hybrid mixtures or an interconnected continuum;
2. the norms of ideal beauty are dissolved and integrated (i.e., yield up their evaluating, limiting authority within this horizontal continuum);
3. the categories of art within the total work of art inter-communicate, and
4. the hitherto closed sphere of art encroaches upon non-art.

The symbiosis of work of art and useful object, so contrary to the postulates of logic, was probably one of the reasons why the Secession made free use of abstract elements but could not go on to proclaim abstract art a valid form of communication. Where everything is ambivalent, there can be no incompatibilities, no conceptual segregation between A and Non-A. Art and useful object, theatre and reality, dream and consciousness, art and non-art, representational and abstract, are all in a constant state of change, polyvalent, not committed to any one category.

The naively proselytizing mutationalism of stylist art may be viewed side by side with the linguistic reflections Schnitzler allows his characters. One word insensibly slides into another, thus exotic becomes erotic.[118] Kraus wants word-play limited strictly to the elect — among whom he includes "natural" women and children.[119] Schnitzler does not care whether the comparison of the soul with a far country comes from a poet or a hotel manager. It is equally immaterial to the Secessionist definition of art whether it is an artist, an artisan or a "lay artist" who designs a chair or paints a picture. All the arts have equal rank, and "consumers" and "creators" together form that ideal community, the "*Künstlerschaft.*"

5.

Comprehensive re-assessment along stylist lines occurs also in a theory of art history which was formulated in Vienna about this time. Indeed, several years before the Secession was founded, the art historian Alois Riegl planned his evolutionary history of the arts which would abolish the boundaries between categories. His conviction that scholarship ultimately takes its direction from "the leading intellectual tendencies of the time" is confirmed if we set his view of history beside the wishful thinking of the Secessionists. From 1887 to 1897 — the year he was made Professor of Art History at the University of Vienna — Riegl was in charge of the Austrian Museum für Kunst und Industrie.[120] It was doubtless in this capacity that he encountered and evaluated the aims of Jugendstil. This assumption is based on various passages in his recently published *Historical Grammar of the Plastic Arts,* which was written in 1897—98. Here he criticizes "art for art's sake" which is reserved for "connoisseurs," and notes that "Henceforth if things designed for decoration or use are to conform to the view of art as an end in itself, they must pass . . . from the hand of the philistine to the hand of the artist." Admittedly this demand differs in one important respect from the Secessionist ideology of stylist art and the *Wiener Werkstätte* — it is linked with the demand for a radical change in the economic means of production. Riegl foresees that "if developments continue logically in the planned direction, gradually even the most highly qualified work of artistic craftsmanship must submit to factory methods." [121]

Already in *Stilfragen* (Problems of Style, 1893) Riegl used the concept of "*Kunstwollen.*" In contrast to Semper's theory of art, which holds useful purpose, raw material and technique responsible for the creation of a work of art, Riegl postulates that the work of art is "the result of a definite and directed *creative drive*. . . that survives the struggle with useful purpose, raw material and technique." He deplores that the history of ornament has hitherto been excluded from histories of art dealing with the development of style. About this time the stylized ornamentation of Jugendstil was infiltrating all the arts. Indeed, a history of Jugendstil cannot be written without including ornament.

In his great work *Die spätrömische Kunstindustrie nach den Funden in Österreich-Ungarn* (Late Roman Art Manufacture Based on the Finds in Austria-Hungary, 1901) [122] Riegl makes the extent of his revaluing even plainer. He attacks the widespread prejudice which "considers figurative art not merely a higher form, but following special laws of its own . . . ." Riegl not only maintains one law of development, common to all art forms, which obeys an "inner necessity," he finds it "in positively mathematical purity" in architecture and craftwork, whereas in painting and sculpture it can seldom emerge with complete clarity and originality, as the subject matter inevitably distracts from what Riegl considers the actual pictorial art: "the appearance of things as form and color in plane and space." [123] The representational subject matter is thereby dismissed as expendable. Hoffmann's relief above a doorway of 1902 achieves the dignity of an abstract picture if one shares Riegl's conviction that different categories do not obey separate laws or a different scale of value. [124]

The same creative drive can be manifested in various techniques. This idea is reminiscent of the transposability of "Gestalt qualities." Riegl first expressed it in *Stilfragen,* revealing an unbroken development from geometric ornament to the most complex portrayals of human beings and animals. The historical process, according to this, is a metamorphosis of Gestalt qualities whose phases are all interconnected — as in the case of Klimt the colophon with Danae, the ideograph with the finished pictorial composition. Riegl's evolutionary theory contains a revolutionary thesis: there is no such thing as decadence in the history of art. Starting from this premise Riegl undertakes the favorable revaluation of the "non-classical" tendencies of late Roman art. He tries to prove that evolution is not directed towards one end, but is always Janus-faced and part of an endless chain. The destruction of formal arrangements is equally as important as their construction, there is neither retrogression nor stagnation. We should note, by the way, that this equalizing mutative drive cutting across the millennia differs radically from the purpose-directed conceptualism for which Weininger was the spokesman; on the other hand it can be brought into agreement with the theories of psychoanalysis. Weininger favors the process of articulation as against retrogression that loses itself in the darkness of the pre-conscious mind. He values the clear, distinct "male" conception above the diffuse "female" preconception. Freud, however, attempted to raise the standing of pre-conscious experiences. To this end he exposed, and devalued, the facade of conventionalized complexes of the conscious mind.

According to Riegl the art historian cannot far transcend the "artistic demand" of his contemporaries, he too is tied to his context; consequently his judgment of the past also suffers from this limitation and he cannot take up a point of view outside history. However this limitation harbors the possibility of uncovering the origins of the present in the past, explaining the former in terms of the latter. Consciously or unconsciously, that is what Riegl did. The concepts "ugliness" and "lifelessness" are dropped from his vocabulary. He attributes to the formal characteristics of late antiquity — massiveness, lack of detail in the outline, rigid crystallized immobility — a positive purpose, "a different kind of beauty"; he looks for harmony "in forms which would have struck earlier generations of antiquity as disharmony." Riegl's analysis of the Constantine reliefs argues that formal value is in the eye of the beholder. Applying his theory to the past, negative qualities become positive.

The "transitional forms" of late antiquity are the necessary presupposition for the development of newer forms of art and "modern conditions." The developments of late antiquity, studded with anachronisms, progressed in leaps; archaic persistence is countered by a radical anticipation of "positively modern attitudes." This characterization of late Roman art agrees in tenor with contemporary opinions of Klimt's art. What Richard Hamann wrote in 1913 remains one of the best interpretations: "The symbolism is of impenetrable obscurity, and in true Viennese fashion it is always slender and angular female figures who emerge as symbols. All this combines to raise these pictures above their decorative purpose. They fascinate, they flirt with us, they continually interest and

surprise us anew. And how all conceptions here are mixed up and reversed, the lean and haggard becomes attractive, the primitive, the ultimate in calculation, the purely decorative, stimulating, and impressionism wholly artificial: one could call it complete artistic, ethical and intellectual perversity." [125]
For Klimt ugliness was, as Riegl would put it, "a different kind of beauty." [126]

Riegl's theory of evolution corresponds significantly with the basic tenets of the "artistic demand" among Secessionist stylists. Their precious "art of the material" sets out to prove that the creative drive transcends the "negative factors" of function, raw materials and technology. Practice and theory of stylist art try to demonstrate the same evolutionary process in all categories. The creative drive offers itself persuasively, to all, "without distinction of class or income," raising all art forms to their highest possible level. "We make no distinction between 'high art' and 'minor art,' art for the rich and art for the poor. Art is common property." This tendency towards universal harmony coincides with the concept of "harmonism" by which Riegl wanted to replace the traditional term, "idealism."

Amid the actively reforming harmonism of stylist art, another aspect of Riegl's theory was shown to be valid: that every phase of development — since history does not stand still, ends in its own dissolution. The rise of stylist universal harmony went hand in hand with its decline, and that decline, too, was motivated by a zeal for reform. That is what our final chapter will show.

IV.

1.

At its periphery the sane, snug world of the 1908 exhibition was already growing uneasy. One critic noted the cynical coarseness of competitively shouting posters, which he compared to "a fevered vision." [127] Most disturbing of all was the debut of the young Kokoschka. His "Designs for Gobelins" reminded one writer of Peru, [128] another of Rimbaud. [129] When the first performance of Kokoschka's "Murderer Hope of Women" took place at the Garden Theatre, there was a scene that provoked the fusion of stage and audience in a totally unexpected sense, and not at all according to the ideology of the 1908 exhibition. Kokoschka describes the pre-Dadaist tumult in his memoirs: "In my first play I transgressed against the thoughtlessness of our male civilization with the revolutionary idea that man is mortal and woman immortal" — this revolutionary idea was lifted from Klimt — "and that only the murderer tries to reverse this basic fact in the modern world. That is how I became 'the bourgeois bogeyman.' Deeply disturbed, I discussed the events of the evening on the Stephansplatz with the friend who had played the chief male part. Gate-crashers, soldiers from the Bosnian barracks across the road, had joined in the fighting together with the ticket holders, and a literary altercation might well have turned into a bloody war, had not Adolf Loos with a handful of faithful followers rescued me from being battered to death." [130]

Ill. 40
O. Kokoschka: Murderer Hope of Women, 1908

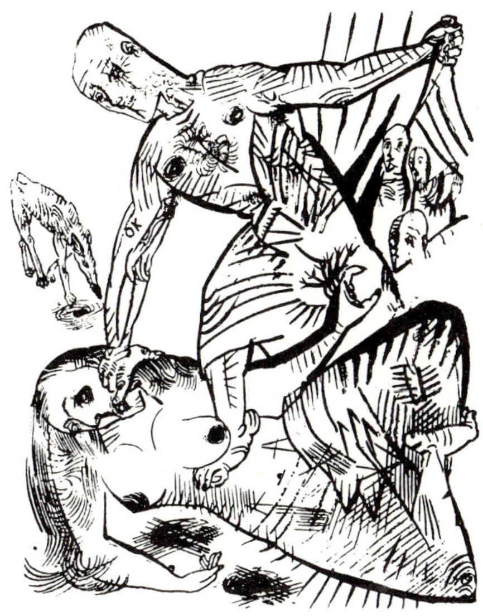

"Murderer Hope of Women" (Ill. 40) exposed the world of flawless harmony for which Klimt painted an icon in "The Kiss": it heralded a change, and Klimt seemed to sense this. Uneasily he wondered whether the coming generation would still find him valid. [131] Kokoschka, who dedicated "The Dreaming Boys" to him, and Schiele both benefited from his encouragement. He would have risked the existence of the 1908 exhibition for Kokoschka, whom he regarded as "the major talent of the young generation." The uncertainty Kokoschka, aged twenty-two, introduced into the pan-aesthetic conception of the exhibition was not merely the expected contribution of a romantic young rebel: it pointed in the direction Loos's and Kraus's polemics had indicated ten years earlier.

The stylist regarded form as all-powerful, laying its "festive" impress over the whole of life to produce one homogeneous whole. However, the mutative power of Jugendstil art was only apparently widespread and unlimited. In fact its attitude to reality was a defensive one. It maintained a closed system of aesthetic regimentation, an island of beauty shutting itself off from "The Other Side" about which Kubin wrote his novel of that name. Beyond this retreat blew the winds of disorder and decay, and creative action was challenged and stripped of the status of a near-sacred organizing power. Art no longer stabilized the structure of society, but became an index of society's dissolution.

The elevating mutative drive of the stylists was opposed by another that deliberately sought to profane. It distrusted the solemn gesture that forced an aesthetic aura on everything. Musil demanded: "Let us change everything as much as we can." [132] The profaning tendency did not believe in universal harmony. It wanted to show how things looked behind the scenes of civilization's festivals, the nature of suppressed forces and instincts, the undertones and double meanings of our conventions of speech, the traps concealed behind brightly lit street facades. Everywhere it postulated the "secret processes of a double life," [133] which betrayed any hopeful vision of a perfect world.

While Klimt was removing the relations between men and women to a sanctified or demoniac level, Schnitzler in *Reigen* (La Ronde, 1896—97) took up a cynically revealing point of view. If one substituted the word "love" for art throughout the Secession's manifesto, one would have the key to the profaning tendency in *Reigen:* Love is communal property, it does not distinguish between high and low, rich and poor. Everyone is at everyone's disposal. [134] The actress is successively the lover of the poet and the count, the count sleeps with her and then with the prostitute. There are no permanent relationships or class distinctions, only an unending state of change. The obvious formula for this linkage is ornamental. Take a colophon designed by Klimt and superimpose various formal readings (a, b, c) and you have a visual symbol of the availability of partners which is the subject of *Reigen.* The six cells stand for actors, three male, three female. Each cell has two partners and functions alternatively as figure or ground (Ill. 41).

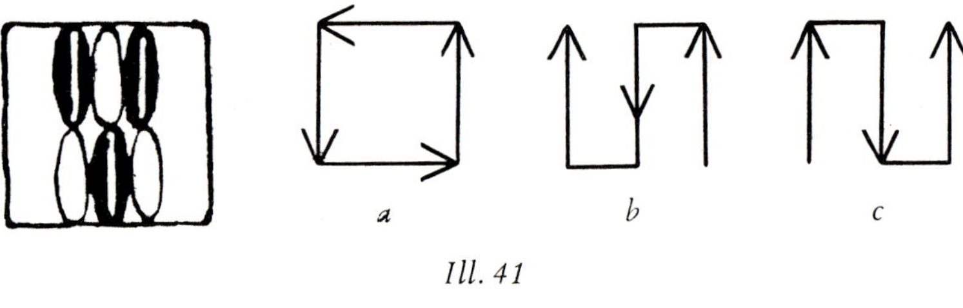

Ill. 41

There is a parallel in what Kraus realized to be the promiscuity of words. Their varying context is the equivalent of copulation:

An Orphic rhyme — but what's the betting
It turns up next in an operetta setting. [135]

Kraus, considering language at all its levels, is like a man who in the obligatory mutations of *la ronde* is continually entering new partnerships, thus exploring femininity in all its incarnations. This is shown by the metaphors Kraus uses to describe his relationship with language, playing on the feminine gender of the word in German. He does not want to use it as "a maid of all work" like those dashing feuilletonists who flirt with it, he prefers to entertain — negation of the negation — a "steady illicit relationship" [136] with it. Thus he tries to make up to it for the abuses it has suffered from others: he has turned the bold prostitute back into a virgin. [137] Others want to clothe their ideas in language — such as the stylists for whom art is decorative wrapping —but he wants the idea, the male element, to fit itself into the language. [138] The erotic overtones of this metaphor are unmistakable.

Loos called Vienna the potemkinesque city; and Schnitzler in *Reigen* penetrates behind that facade of moral-aesthetic values. He ignores the taboos and unmasks the sexual hypocrisy of bourgeois society. Instead of making that dim creature Man into a myth as Klimt does, he uncovers Man's total banality. Kraus is even more uncompromising in rejecting the stylists' mythopoeic attitude. It infuriates him to read in an advertisement that a "Jupiter seeks Leda with independent means," [139] and he sneers at Richard Strauss's female audience: "Women to whom one would give Jokhanaan's head on the sole condition that they *refrain* from dancing . . ." [140] He wants to destroy the sublime mythical facade behind which bourgeois society lets itself go. But Klimt was one of those who actually decorated that facade. He painted erotic idols (Pl. 15, 39, 43), and fulfilled — without ever exposing, like Kraus or Freud [141] — the desire of his aristocratic models "to be raised," as Lux remarked, "above the humdrum . . . like princesses or madonnas . . . beauty that can nevermore be torn or devastated by the greedy hands of life."

The devastation from which Klimt wanted to preserve woman, Kraus recognized as woman's destiny. The princess who sleeps with the coachman frees man to do the same, to become a prostitute. [142] Believing that perversion can, as far as society is concerned, be a sickness as well as a healthy sign, [143] he claims on behalf of the free man the right to all varieties of erotic experience — for he stands outside the convention of sexual bondage [144] with its perversions, and culture in general with its "deliberate neglect of natural capacities." [145]

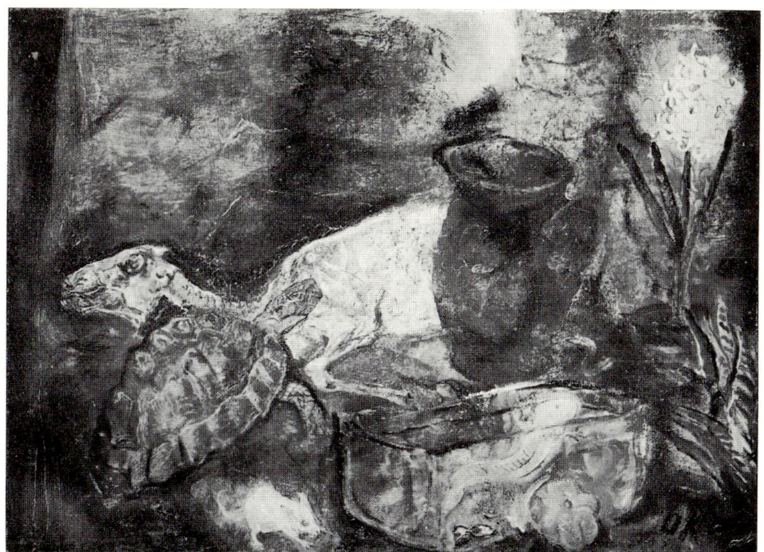

Ill. 42 *Kokoschka: Still Life with Ram and Hyacinth*
Österreichische Galerie, Vienna

The natural man whom Kraus champions, unlike the aesthete and the latter's half-brother, the politician, had no need for stylized eroticism. It is only the aesthete who is forbidden to interchange chamber pot and urn; to the natural man lust for woman or man is permitted, he has the right to "erotic versatility" and may even "adore . . . the features of his ideal woman in a cat's head." Kraus, like Freud, accuses morality of having "crippled sexual life." [146] That is his contribution to the realistic reappraisal of sexual relationships: the reponse may be seen in the drawings in which the young Kokoschka, having severed his connection with the stylists, re-interpreted relations between men and women (Ill. 40).

2.

The "dull fraternal round of submerged forces" (Hofmannsthal) is allowed its pathetically banal say in Schnitzler's "Leutnant Gustl" (1902). The inner monologue records a ceaseless round of free associations: Schnitzler seems to be restricting himself to reproducing the raw materials of language. The loosening of speech patterns borders on complete shapelessness. The hypocritically trivial "double life" of the young officer exposes established society as one that depends on servants such as this. The decadence of the world shown on stage proves the impotence of the aesthetic attitude.

What happens to Leutnant Gustl is paralleled by Hofmannsthal in his *Lord Chandos' Letter* of 1902, on the rather different level of a master of language whose medium suddenly becomes refractory: "I have suddenly completely lost the faculty of thinking or speaking coherently about anything." Hofmannsthal was writing out of his own experience, but his reflections about loss of eloquence had no sequel: he did not in fact stop writing. On the contrary, he goes on to describe at length the replacement of one kind of universal perception by another. Now he grasps the previously unnoticed: "At such moments a negligible creature, a dog, a rat, a beetle, a stunted apple tree, a cart track twisting over a hill, a moss-covered stone, means more to me than the happiest night with the most beautiful, most voluptuous mistress ever did." The new revelation includes the banal, the unlimited and the cruel. It is based on the "inexplicable selection" of apparently insignificant creatures and objects. The death agonies of poisoned rats give rise to "a godlike feeling."

Klimt knew neither the crisis of doubting one's means of expression nor the ensuing discoveries of new realities. His work shows only flourishing apple trees; it was left for Schiele to discover the stunted ones. An animal does not manifest savage, naked aggression, but reposes ornamentally in exquisite concealment (Pl. 11). The animal detritus which Hofmannsthal perceived was not considered worth painting until Kokoschka's "Still life with Ram and Hyacinth" of 1909 (Ill. 42). This apotheosis of silent decay and corruption shows the other side of the healthy world of the stylists. However, there is an early picture by Klimt — "Fable" of 1883 (Ill. 43) — that sets the stage for this uncanny experience.

Hofmannsthal's "inexplicable selection" is poetic shorthand for the isolation of a phenomenon from its accepted surroundings. In the "Letters of One Who Returned" (1907) Hofmanns-

Ill. 43 *G. Klimt: Fable*

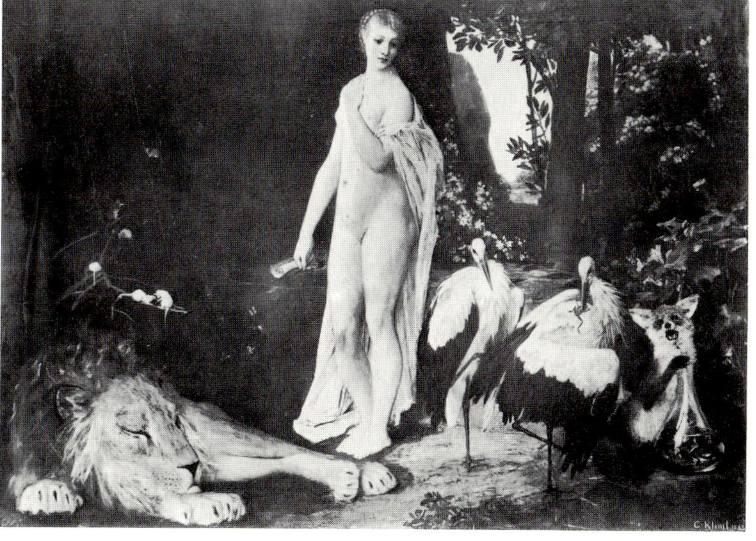

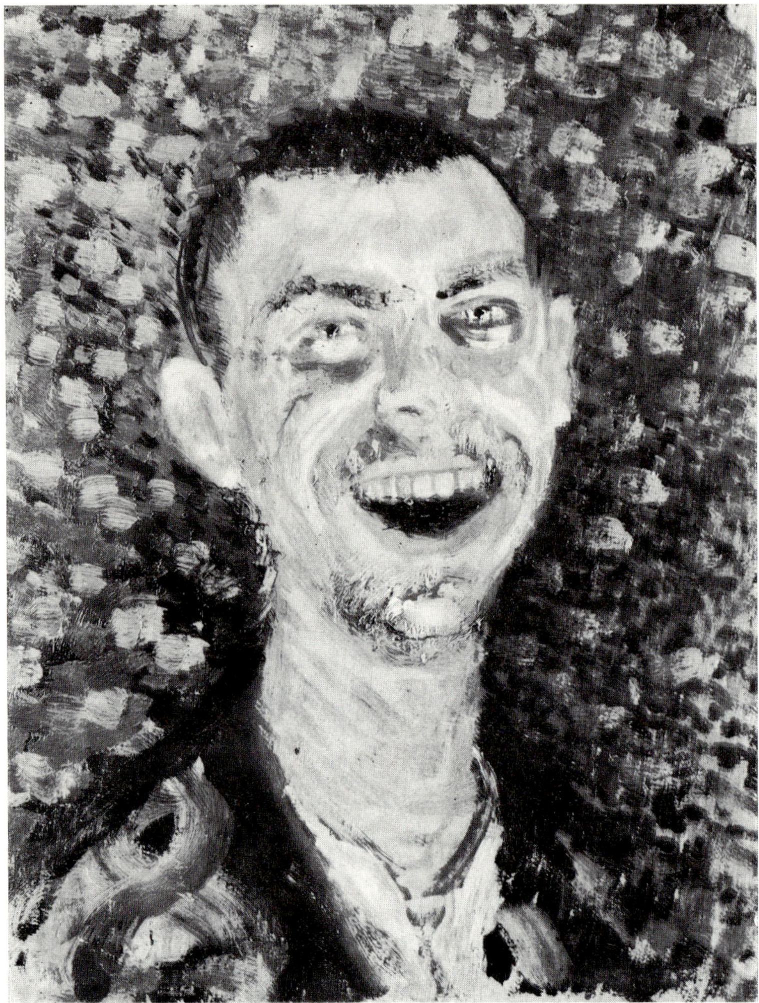

Ill. 44 *Gerstl: Laughing Self-Portrait, 1908*
Österreichische Galerie, Vienna

thal described the revelation of new, unexplored realities as a result of pathological alienation of perception: "Sometimes it happened in the morning in these German hotel rooms that the jug and washbasin — or perhaps a corner of the room with the table and the clothes-stand, seemed unreal to me, completely unreal, ghostly in a way, and at the same time provisional, waiting, so to speak keeping the place of the real jug, the real washbowl filled with water." Observing some cabs in the street caused nausea: "It was like a momentary floating above the bottomless, eternal void." Similar experiences are set off by the most ordinary house fronts, in which Musil several years earlier had already seen hints of "complexity, furtiveness, mystery." [147]

Experiences of formally unexplored emptiness, the fringe situations of total alienation, are almost completely missing from Klimt's work. Even the "condemned criminal" (Pl. 11) dies beautifully, wrapped in the splendor of the death-dealing octopus. Loneliness, according to Weininger a male privilege, [148] lies beyond the horizon of experience of Klimt's women and girls. They remain works of art within works of art, inmates of a secure, unendangered ideal world. In the Portrait of Elisabeth Bachofen-Echt (Pl. 61) the subject may appear to stand in our empirical reality, but at the same time two converging bands of ornament carry her off into the world of painted fairy tales, where she accepts the homage of various exotic figures. When one compares this aesthetically sheltered frontal figure with the anguished grimaces of the young Schiele (Ill.45), with the uninhibited colorfulness of Gerstl (Ill. 44) or with the flayed heads of Kokoschka, of whom Kraus said that he reduced flesh to jelly,[149] then one can measure the distance that lies between Klimt and the new generation. The comparison applies equally to the landscapes. Klimt paints a discreetly adorned natural scene wrapped in perpetual beauty. Domesticated to gardens and parks, it forms the well-cared-for ambiance of city dwellers who collect Klimt pictures. This unthreatened abundance contrasts with Schiele's landscapes, in which abide elemental dangers and mortal fears.

3.

Doubts about the identity of things can also affect the works of man, contesting the unmistakable character of the work of art. More insistently than Hofmannsthal, who soon got over the crisis expressed in the Chandos letter, Alfred Kubin consistently portrayed these doubts. On January 16, 1902, in the same year as the Chandos letter, he wrote to his friend Hans von Müller: "As life seemed to be running through my fingers, almost palpably, I began to doubt the reality of things." [150] Five years later he completed "The Other Side," and in that work the profaning tendency materializes as a definite anti-world. Scenes and events of the novel bear the same relation to the artistic intentions of the stylists as negative to positive, or dissonance to consonance. Though here too everything connects with everything else, it is chaos that rules the interacting forces. The distant City of Pearl is a parody of the communal work of art. Disinterested pleasure has no commercial value here, beauty no inherent value. "We have no special museums or picture galleries or anything like that. Everything is shared, being used, so to speak." That is exactly what the organizers of the 1908 exhibition wanted. In Pearl too there is no distinction between high and low art: "Treasures and obvious old junk are equally in demand." Where everything, however insignificant, is important, one can boast of "the penetration of the whole of life by artistic purpose" — in reverse. Consequently art, robbed of its autonomy, yields to reality its privilege of conferring significance. "Why should we need a theatre in Pearl? We have all the drama we want," say the citizens of the town. The exhibition of 1908 wanted state and audience to fuse into one unified work of art — in the City of Pearl the institution of the theatre is overwhelmed by the absence of art.

Kubin's reassessment of all values is based on the observation that one only has to take things out of their conventional context to discover new dimensions in them: "I became capable of an astonishing sort of amazement. Torn out of the connection with other things, every object acquired a fresh significance." Prerequisite for this amazement is that the observer should regard all designations and terms of reference as transitory and revocable. Thus the "ungrasped connection that suddenly, depending on our point of view, gives events and objects values that are not comparable or related," [151] as Musil had observed several years before, rests on a multivalent experience of reality. As everything touches on everything else, neither man-made nor received reality can ever be grasped categorically, unambiguously, but only as an active state of transition, always potentially part of several different composite realities. We dwell among revocable, uncertain relationships. A decade later the philosopher Wittgenstein expressed it thus: "Everything that we see could be different. All that we can even describe could be different. There is no a priori order of things." [152] That such statements are directed against the consensus ideology of the communal work of art is obvious and explains why the champions of this ideology could never grasp the process of alienation. In a smoothly harmonious combination of forms sheltered against disturbing factors, to take an object out of its assigned context amounts to a breach of the rules of universal harmony. [153]

Whoever denies the order of things a priori must also deny the validity of any dogmatic concept of art — of the pan-aesthetic attitude of the stylists no less than the narrow views of Kraus and Loos, who considered themselves able to differentiate unerringly between "art" and "non-art." The reasoning behind alienation leads logically to the paradox of "artlessness" — a step which Marcel Duchamp risked in 1913—14 with his "ready-mades." [154] Though Kubin described anti-art in his novel, he himself never practiced it.

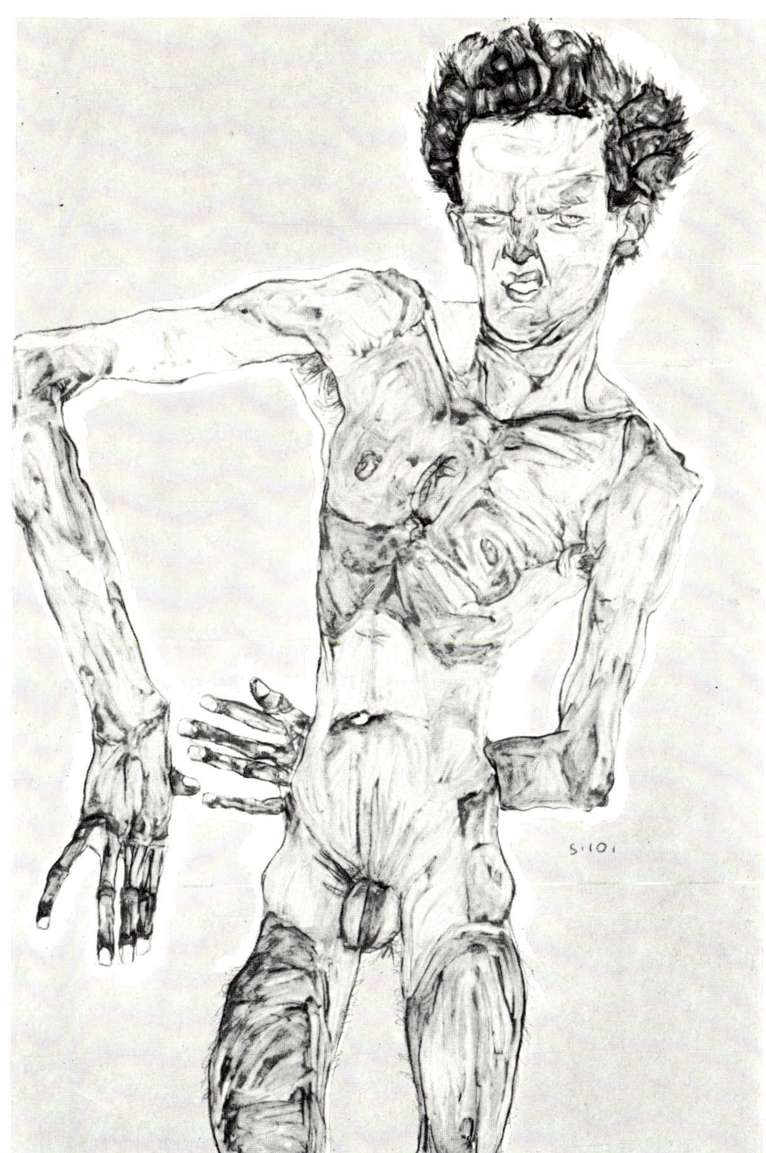

Ill. 45 *Egon Schiele: Self-Portrait, 1910*

4.

The formal stance of the stylists, smoothed and dogmatically buttressed in the cause of universal "harmonism," offered an eminently vulnerable area to attacks by skeptics, whose attempts to see through this self-righteous facade were motivated by a variety of factors, especially a tendency to the profane that sometimes extended into the realms of anti-art.

At every turn Kraus saw the prostitution of art. By day it was at the service of the businessman, in the evening it was supposed to open "the venetian blinds of the soul" for the philistine. [155] To mercantile drudgework the demand for war propaganda added patriotic misuse: "And gold for iron fell from the altar into the operetta, dropping a bomb made a subject for a song, and 15,000 prisoners got themselves into a special supplement, to be read out by a musical-comedy star and give a librettist a curtain call." [156] Worse, on April 28, 1916, at the Burgtheater there was a benefit performance for the widows and orphans of soldiers who fell at Uszieszko. Soldiers were played by actual soldiers: the survivors of the battle, just returned from the front, re-enacted the battle on the stage, supported by actors in uniform — "the spheres intermingled." Long before this crowning piece of bad taste occurred, Kraus saw only one way out of the baying for art of impresarios and temple guardians: "One longs for an end to all art and a prohibition of all freedom, just to clear the ground." [157]

Kraus carried out this thought to the extent of using Dadaist anti-art as a weapon of exposure: he made a feature of documents and reprinted quotations. This procedure, like the "ready-mades," meant both a rejection of art and the gain of a new artistic technique: collage. So Kraus contributed doubly to the destruction and discrediting of an art exploited by the consumer industries: first, by ferreting out the formal characteristics of humbug, be it in a poem or an advertising slogan, in the craftsman's talent or the hack novel, in a pageant or a legal report, and thus denouncing the "penetration of the whole of life by artistic purpose" as a plot on the part of the prostituters of art; second, by giving the quotations from reality, the crude fact of the document itself, a higher truthfulness than the formal rendering of reality in a work of art. [158]

When Kraus says that he has learnt more about people from those antitheses of beauty, the poster and the sentimental pop song, than from libraries or museums, [159] he is attacking the facades of civilization in the same way as Freud. To the psychoanalytical technique of getting at the truth, dream material is no less rewarding than a work of art, the production of the poet just as relevant as the bungled action, verbal wit, a child at play or a daydreamer. [160] The latter, a potential artist, has helped to bring the concept of art out of academic isolation and give it flexibility. Freud knew that his interpretation of the creative impulse offended two prejudices which the cultured bourgeois had made the pedestal of sacrosanct Art: the intellectual prejudice that would not admit the existence of "unconscious thought and unacknowledged desires," and a moral-aesthetic prejudice that obstinately denied sexual feelings any share in "the highest cultural, artistic and social creations of the human intellect." Meanwhile the work of art, removed from the hallowed precincts of the temple, became a source of hitherto concealed experiences. However, the man who committed this 'sacrilege,' which resulted in an increasingly complex concept of art, to the end of his life retained the artistic tastes of the average cultured bourgeois of the nineteenth century.

When we add to these rejections of the cultural facade the artists' dissatisfaction with traditional clichés of observation and execution, we should remember that the stimuli of painters and writers can never be entirely the same as those of the psychoanalysts and social critics. This is not to deny that in both cases there was a breakthrough towards a new truthfulness. Impatient with aesthetically flawless stylized art, Kraus cast about for material that had not yet received Jugendstil approval. The trivial, and kitsch in general, developed a fascination similar to *"le sublime d'en bas"* of Flaubert. Max Brod, [161] as well, wrote chattily and "from an unusual point of view" about music, drama, furniture and art, while constantly inveighing against Jugendstil's dictatorship of taste. He enthuses about the inadvertent grace of bad pictures, praises the "romance of bad taste," and admires posters for being "the popular accessory of everyday life." Beyond the reality which has been falsified by stylization into art, another reality emerges, which may be a disaster aesthetically but makes up for this by being genuine.

This links up with the validity of artistic interpretations — a question which did not exist, as far as the stylists were concerned. True, Hofmannsthal occasionally senses — though without acting upon it — that aesthetic expansionism may be unjustified: "No net can trap reality . . ." [162] Musil's Young Törless records the failure of words, their inability to convey feelings except by evasions. The motto quoted at the beginning of the novel is taken from Maeterlinck: "As soon as we express anything, we strangely devalue it . . . ." If art distorts reality, then to be really creative it should abdicate and leave the stage to life itself. Brod actually suggests this to dramatists: "Do not enact events, but simply scenes from the life of things." [163] These should not be interpreted, i. e., shaped, but just shown — a row of desks, perhaps. "The curtain rises, one sees what one sees." At another point, Brod recommends snippets of dialogue from a foreign phrase-book, and prophesies — correctly — that "in future it will be left to such shadow plays to stimulate the imagination." [164]

5.

The "discontents of civilization" which Freud diagnosed were already fermenting in the crisis-conscious Vienna of the early 1900's. The Secessionists' "content in civilization" was their target. An attitude to art based on aesthetic harmony was felt to be too easy, its unqualified affirmation asked to be contradicted. Everyone was left discontented who felt, like Kraus, that the task of art should be to query the easy solution, not to prostitute itself as "a maid of all work" that supplies a beautiful mask for every object, a satisfaction for every need, an answer to every question. For the young Musil the "horrid jumble of stylistic blasphemies" in the uncultured outside world opened up a greater breadth of experience than the distillate of the "stylized century,"[165] whose homogeneous snugness suppressed the darker aspects of existence. Kubin, seeking a "refuge for all who are dissatisfied with modern civilization" invented the "Other World of the City of Pearl" — a world of total anarchy. Weininger condemned the "arty-crafty armchair enthusiasms" and the falsity of "stylized" man. The purely aesthetic had, to his mind, no cultural value.[166] He saw its epitome in "secessionist taste," licensed by the effeminacy of the age.[167] Brod carried on Loos's polemics against Hoffmann and Olbrich: "We have escaped from the conventions of imitation Renaissance, but immediately got caught up in another, which is much more unpleasant, because it insists on being and staying in the best of taste . . . ." A few lines further on he exclaims, sounding almost like the Dadaists: "Oh God, this precious culture is enough to make one sick!"

Their discontent provoked by complacency, the opponents of "the penetration of life by artistic purpose" felt that the artist must free himself from all conventions that would tie him to an affirmative attitude, to the optimistic culture fiction. It was better to renounce art altogether, or to express rejection by the artlessness which would merge art with life, or alternatively — the course chosen by Kraus and Loos — to rescue art from the oppression of its hundred and one applications and confirm it in proud independence: "Art can come only out of protest. Out of the cry, not the lulling. Art, called upon for comfort, leaves the deathbed of humanity with a curse. Through hopelessness it attains fulfillment."[169] Only when it no longer has to sing hymns to progress and the transfiguration of life can its voice be heard uncompromisingly.

For the situation in Vienna, such ideas were more relevant than speculations about artlessness. They finally caused the defeat of the stylists by the "espressivo attitude." Krenek[170] coined this term for the composers Schönberg, Webern and Berg, but it could be applied equally well to the painters Gerstl, Kokoschka and Schiele. In the decisive years between 1908 and 1910, for both groups, the trend towards the "anarchist transformation of material" prevailed in Europe. However, the comparison between the painters and the composers — who incidentally maintained mutual contact[171] — must not obscure the fact that the innovations practiced and preached by Schönberg and his circle were infinitely more radical and hence historically influential, in the European context, than the contribution of the three artists.

The retreat from pure aestheticism, urged by various, often mutually opposed, factions, was not primarily due to formal inadequacy; it was a rejection of wishful thinking, of the all-embracing art and culture ideology, representing its own narrow-minded dogmatism as an expansion. The attempt to bring art and life into a total harmonious coherence requires stability, the secure basis of a static-affirmative establishment committing art and society to a common interest. This establishment put its trust in the refining power of art. The stylists, by refusing to test, limit or question the affirmative range of their creative means, robbed themselves of any chance to understand their own activities beyond the mission of giving pleasure, let alone to show up the faulty structure of society: blind to the surrounding social conflicts, they never found cause to query the omnipotence of their ideal of universal harmony.

6.

Klimt frequently painted pregnant women and mothers (Pl. 26). His interpretations stress the religious sublimity and the "common humanity" of the subject, whether they transfigure it into legend or dress it up in a timeless present (Pl. 30, 48). Karl Kraus had rather different intentions when in 1910 under the title of "Mothers" he published a montage of two articles.[172] One was a newspaper report of the trial of a servant girl who had killed her eleven-year-old child and been condemned to death for it. The other text, obviously also taken from a newspaper, described in detail a new method "of christening a child inside the mother's womb."

The comparison between Klimt and Kraus is illuminating. Klimt removes motherhood to the distance of an icon. Even though his previously noted fondness for swelling curves encourages him to portray pregnancy without inhibitions, to the point of being considered offensive,[173] he does not discard the allegorical accessories which exert the spell of the mysterious and pseudo-sacral (Pl. 26). Kraus aims to expose the pharisee lie, the hypocritical statement. He shows up instances of miscarriages of justice and the hypocrisy of the ruling classes. Without comment he invented a new technique to expose these outrages: a montage of newspaper reports without intervention of artistic means, i. e., without throwing an aesthetic gloss over the facts. He uses the technique of alienation — "the document is the feature"[174] — to add a further dimension of moral honesty. It is precisely this dimension which the stylist avoids, even though he may realize resignedly with Hofmannsthal that no artificial web can catch reality (hence the apparent entry into real reality in the prologue to Antigone), or like Klimt practice a technique related to montage.[175] In a distant way, Klimt's "Ages of Woman" (Pl. 30) recalls what Kraus presents to his readers. Here, too, there is a juxtaposition — the radiantly beautiful figure of the young mother contrasts with the used-up, worn-out body of the old woman. But even here Klimt's masterly command of varying styles succumbs to the spell of formal harmony. The polemical confrontations of text-montage consciously negate artistic means of expression, whereas Klimt uses all the formal means at his disposal to prove that the "penetration of life by artistic purpose" can extend to the body of an aged woman. His excursion into anatomical detail produces neither propagandist distortion nor true realism — but a stylized form of his early naturalism, a sort of naturalistic stylization.[177]

Obviously the question of "art and society" must come to grips with the problem of formal commitment. An artist who wants to expose the disharmonies of social structure must open up his technique to dissonance. The naive confidence in the ornamental possibilities of every shape, of ugliness itself, allows no dissonance, no truth without the decorum of beauty. The stylists would tolerate neither ugliness nor "that cursed everyday beauty, regular universal prettiness."[178] The two poles are brought close together, however, as style, that universal mediator, commands the whole range of mutable form. A small and therefore memorable repertoire of linear formulae effects the intercommunication of the most diverse worlds.

The formal discipline of stylization differs completely in principle from the reversal of all values which Kraus advocates in the *Chinesische Mauer* (The Great Wall of China, 1909): "Beautiful is ugly, ugly beautiful, and what is repulsive to the waking senses lures them into the trance of lust. The princes of life could not understand it. But the princesses lay with the coachmen, because they were coachmen, and because the princes could not understand it. Love conquered the horrors that resisted it, sought them out in order to conquer them. Chastity was in pawn to lewdness, grandeur the guarantee of a fall. A warning rouses desire; separation unites. The appetite whose tastes were supposed to be sublimated has become not more selective, but more aggressive. It chooses what it has been deprived of." Nothing is further from Kraus's intention than to advocate the aestheticization of the ugly. It is the values of truth and beauty supporting and covering up for each other that have caused the enslavement of man. The long withheld horizon of freedom lies beyond the conventions and taboos of class society, but also beyond good and evil, beauty and ugliness. The stylist regards liberation as a breach of the rules, a kind of "*libertinage de l'imagination.*"[179] Ornament "is wanton, where it is not positively perverse"[180] — this sentence referring to Klimt's decorative sensuality was Hevesi's. Used in a pejorative sense, it could be by the author of the *Chinesische Mauer*, to whom perversion seems "the culture of sexual unfreedom." There is a form of perversion which is the culture of artistic "unfreedom" — stylization, enslaved by ornament. The formal liberties and excesses which the stylist indulges in are conditioned by the discipline and restraint which dominate him from the start.

Stylization denies the artist the full run of the creative element: it means closed, never open-ended form; consonance, never dissonance. That is why creative activities ruled by it are restricted to self-consolidation and affirmation, and critical analysis of its own language is just as totally excluded as criticism of the establishment. The unifying festive garment woven by art fetters both itself and society. Gustav Klimt as an artist bears the burden of this one-sidedness: it makes for both the limitations and the greatness of his work.

NOTES

1. Adolf Loos, **Sämtliche Schriften,** (Collected Works) I, Vienna Munich 1962, 153 ff.
2. Christian M. Nebehay, **Gustav Klimt Dokumentation,** Vienna 1969, 394.
3. **Loc. cit.,** 276 ff.
4. **Keramika** (1904), **loc. cit.,** 258.
5. **Die Malerischen** (The Picturesque Ones), (1908), in **Die chinesische Mauer** (The Great Wall of China), Fischer-Bücherei, Frankfurt am Main 1967, 85.
6. **Architektur** (1910), **loc. cit.,** 302 f.
7. **Nachts** (At Night) (1918), Munich 1968, Deutscher Taschenbuch Verlag, 50.
8. **loc. cit.,** 32
9. **Die chinesische Mauer,** 7 ff.
10. **Nachts,** 34.
11. Carl von Lützow, **Die bildenden Künste in Wien** (The Plastic Arts in Vienna), **1848—1888,** memorandum of 2 December 1888, ed. by the Municipal Council of the City of Vienna, Vienna 1888, II, 227.
12. **Ver sacrum,** I, 1 (Jan. 1898), 6.
13. **Ver sacrum, loc. cit.,** 7.

13a. Refers to Grigori Potemkin, Russian statesman who in 1791 erected make-believe villages to line the prospective route of Catherine the Great during one of her travels through the Russian countryside.

14. **Loc. cit.,** 74. Cf. Kraus, **Von den Sehenswürdigkeiten** (Sightseeing) (1908) in **Unsterblicher Witz** (Immortal Wit), Munich 1961, 68.
15. Nebehay, 394.
16. Working program of the Wiener Werkstätte (1905), Catalogue of the exhibition "Die Wiener Werkstätte," Vienna 1967, 21.
17. Nebehay, 394.
18. Ludwig Hevesi, **Der Festzug, Kunst und Kunsthandwerk,** (The Pageant, Arts and Crafts), XI, 1908, 393.
19. **Ornament und Verbrechen** (Ornament and Crime) (1908), **loc. cit.,** 279 f.
20. **Meyers Konversationslexikon** (Meyer's Encyclopaedia), 1909.
21. **Der Festzug,** in **Die chinesische Mauer,** Collected Works, XII, 162 f.
22. Josef A. Lux, **Deutsche Kunst und Dekoration,** XXIII, 1908/9, 44.
23. **Die Fackel** (The Torch), 13 July 1908, 24 f.
24. **Loc. cit.,** 37.
25. **Loc. cit.,** 288. Hevesi **(Acht Jahre Secession,** 450), too, though an admirer of the Secession, calls ornament "wicked" and "perverted."
26. Nebehay, 423.
27. **Kulturentartung** (The Decadence of Culture) (1908), **loc. cit.,** 273.
28. **Loc. cit.,** 240.
29. **Loc. cit.,** 53.
30. **Ver sacrum,** I, 1, 23.
31. Cf. E. W. Bredt, **Die Ausstellung als künstlerisches Ganzes** (The Exhibition as an Artistic Unity), **Die Kunst,** 1908, 428.
32. Lützow, **loc. cit.,** 200.
33. Lützow, **loc. cit.,** 228.
34. Loos, **Die potemkinsche Stadt** (1898), **loc. cit.,** 154.
35. Rupert Feuchtmüller and Wilhelm Mrazek, **Kunst in Österreich 1860—1918,** Vienna 1964, 84.
36. **Loc. cit.,** 205. Cf. Theophil von Hansen: "Above all the artist must keep in mind the purpose of the exercise he has been set. . . ." (Feuchtmüller - Mrazek, **loc. cit.,** 15)
37. Lützow, **loc. cit.,** 214.
38. Jacob von Falke, **Das Kunstgewerbe,** Memorandum . . . (cf. Note 11), II, 248.
39. **Loc. cit.,** 257.
40. **Zeitschrift für Bild. Kunst,** XIV, 1879, 197.
41. **In dieser großen Zeit** (In this great period) (1914), in **Weltgericht** (World Opinion), Fischer-Bücherei, Frankfurt am Main 1968, 7 ff.
42. Kraus, **Nachts,** 32: "The Culture Lie has alienated the public even more from literature than from the other arts, because while they don't pretend to be able to daub like an artist or whistle a composition, they do claim to be able to speak the language as it is written. Yet for that very reason they would do better trying to daub or whistle. One lives far removed from the language, and because one can speak, one imagines one can speak it. People would respect language more if there were colloquial art and colloquial music, so that people could use daubs and whistles to tell each other what they had for dinner."
43. Ludwig Hevesi, **Zeitschrift f. Bild. Kunst,** N. F., IX, 1908, 245.
44. Richard Hamann & Jost Hermand, **Stilkunst um 1900, Deutsche Kunst und Kultur von der Gründerzeit bis zum Expressionismus,** (Style Art around 1900, German Art and Culture from the late nineteenth century to the rise of Expressionism), IV, Berlin 1967, 331.
45. **Nachts,** 37.
46. Hevesi, **Acht Jahre Secession,** (Eight Years of Secession), 209.
47. Hevesi, **loc. cit.,** 384.
48. **Loc. cit.,** 209.
49. Fritz Novotny & Johannes Dobai, **Gustav Klimt,** Salzburg 1967, 88.

50. Otto Weininger, **Geschlecht und Charakter** (Sex and Character), 2nd ed., Vienna Leipzig 1904, 389.

51. Cf. Hevesi, **Altkunst Neukunst** (Old and New Art), Vienna 1909, 319. In July 1917 Klimt wrote a short poem (Novotny - Dobai, 392) which contains the lines: **"Die Wasserrose wächst am See / Sie steht in Blüte / Um einen schönen Mann / Ist weh ihr im Gemüte."** (The water lily by the lake is in flower, she feels melancholy for a handsome man.)

52. **Loc. cit.,** 33.

53. Cf. Nietzsche, **Die Geburt der Tragödie** (The Birth of Tragedy), ed. v. Schlechta, Munich 1954, I, 25.

54. Hevesi, **Altkunst Neukunst,** Vienna 1908, 318.

55. Possible influences are: Chassériau's **Tepidarium,** 1853 (Ill. 3) and Gérôme's **Phryne before the Judges,** 1861 (Ill. 2). Alma-Tadema's **Wine Harvest Festival,** 1871, engraved by Blanchard in 1873 (Ill. 7), may have influenced Klimt's **Thespian Chariot** (Ill. 5). Possibly also two drawings — **Sculpture** (Nebehay, Ill. 162) and **"Duo quum faciunt idem non est idem"** (Nebehay, Ill. 234) — may be traced back to motifs used in Alma-Tadema's **"Ave Caesar in Saturnalia"** (1880).

56. Obliteration of boundaries is also characteristic of the work of F. Matsch **(Theatre scene in Classical Antiquity, Medieval Mystery Play)** and Ernst Klimt **(Harlequin, Le Malade Imaginaire).** (Nebehay, Ills. 116, 128, 131.)

57. **Jenseits von Gut und Böse** (Beyond Good and Evil), **loc. cit.,** II, 686. Bahr speaks of "the colorful carnival of eternal forces, incessantly changing masks" in his essay **"Ein Sonderling"** (An Eccentric) **(Renaissance, Studien zur Kritik der Moderne,** Berlin 1897, 27).

58. Cf. Rilke's poem **Todes-Erfahrung** (Experience of Death) **(Neue Gedichte,** 1907):

Noch ist die Welt voll Rollen, die wir spielen.
. . .
Doch als du gingst, da brach in diese Bühne
ein Streifen Wirklichkeit durch jenen Spalt
durch den du hingingst: Grün wirklicher Grüne,
wirklicher Sonnenschein, wirklicher Wald.

Wir spielen weiter. Bang und schwer Erlerntes
hersagend und Gebärden dann und wann
aufhebend; aber dein von uns entferntes,
aus unserm Stück entrücktes Dasein kann

uns manchmal überkommen, wie ein Wissen
von jener Wirklichkeit sich niedersenkend,
so dass wir eine Weile hingerissen
das Leben spielen, nicht an Beifall denkend.

. . . As yet,
the world is full of parts for us to act.
. . .
But, as you went, a segment of reality
flashed in upon our stage by that same crevice
through which you passed: the green of real verdure,
the real sunshine, and the real wood.

We go on acting, and reciting lines
learnt with anxiety and painful effort,
and now and then we raise our hands in gesture;
but your existence, far from us, removed
out of our play, can sometimes come upon us,
descending like experience of reality,
and for a brief while we act life itself,
carried away, not thinking of applause.
(Tr. by Ruth Speirs)

Even he who renounces the public does not escape the play situation: he plays — "Mir zur Feier" (for his own celebration) — being his own audience.

59. Nietzsche, **Die Geburt der Tragödie,** 14.

60. Hevesi, **Acht Jahre Secession,** 443.

61. **Die Kunst für Alle** (Art for Everyone), Munich 1900, 500 (quoted by Alice Strobl, **Zu den Fakultätsbildern von Gustav Klimt, Albertina Studien,** I, 1963, 152).

62. Quoted by Nebehay, 254.

63. **Zur Terminologie:** Erich Neumann, **Die große Mutter,** Zürich 1956.

64. **Die Malerei in Wien** (Painting in Vienna), Prosa I, Frankfurt am Main 1950, 193 f.

65. Hofmannsthal, **Das Kleine Welttheater,** 1897.

66. Hevesi, **Acht Jahre Secession,** 450.

67. Klimt's teacher Ferdinand Laufberger in 1877 designed the Minerva fountain between the Museum of Applied Art and the Kunstgewerbeschule; Carl Kundmann the Athena fountain in front of Parliament (1898/1902); and J. Benk placed Pallas Athena on top of the cupola of the Kunsthistorische Museum.

68. **Über die negative Reaktion des Wiener Publikums** (Concerning the negative reaction of the Viennese public): Hevesi, **Acht Jahre Secession,** 81.

69. At their third exhibition (1899) the Secession devoted one room to Rops, who had died in 1898. The Vienna Society for Art Reproductions had shown a selection of his work in 1895.

70. Regarding the various kinds of polyvalence in Klimt's work cf. Ch. III. According to Freud the same dream can mean different things in different people, as dreams resist definitive interpretation. **Die Traumdeutung** (The Interpretation of Dreams), 1900, Coll. Works, II/III, 109, 323. This Janus-head situation also applies to the joke (Jokes and their relation to the unconscious, 1905, Coll. Works, VI, 173, 144). Cf. William Empson, Seven Types of Ambiguity (1930), London 1965; Erwin Panofsky, **Der greise Philosoph am Scheidewege** (The Aged Philosopher at the Crossroads). An example of the 'ambivalence' of iconographic identity marks. **Münchner Jahrbuch der bildenden Kunst,** 1932, 285 f. Panofsky stresses "that the same attributes may signify opposing moral values . . ." i. e., attributes are also carriers of opposed psychological forces, leading to paradoxical inversions of meaning.

71. Cf. the composition study (Pl. 8) with the later conditions (Nebehay, Ills. 348—350).

72. Nietzsche, **loc. cit.,** 101.

73. Nietzsche, **loc. cit.,** 125.

74. W. H., **Von der Nachahmung zur Erfindung der Wirklichkeit** (From Copying to the Invention of Reality), Cologne 1970, 45.

75. Hevesi (**Acht Jahre Secession,** 384) writes of the Beethoven Exhibition: "A modern church or temple building has been incorporated in the Secession."

76. J. J. Bachofen, **Mutterrecht und Urreligion** (Maternalism and Primitive Religion), Leipzig 1926, 75 f.

77. Kindergarten Chats (1901), New York 1947, 45.

78. Hevesi, **Acht Jahre Secession,** 444.

79. Otto Benesch, **Hodler, Klimt und Munch als Monumentalmaler,** Wallraf-Richartz-Jahrbuch, XXIV, 1962, 343.

80. The picture is reminiscent of "Das Märchen" (The Fairy Tale) from the cycle **"Allegorien und Embleme"** (Nebehay, Ill. 101).

81. An "Adoration" was arranged for the International Art Exhibition at Mannheim in 1907: the Bloch-Bauer portrait I was flanked by two kneeling youths, by Minne (Nebehay, Ill. 636).

82. **Loc. cit.,** 46.

83. **Loc. cit.,** 356.

84. **Loc. cit.,** 122, cf. the drawing **"Träume"** (Dreams) from Klinger's **"Ein Leben"** (1884), which might have inspired Klimt in several ways.

85. Regarding double spiral movement, cf. Alois Riegl, **Stilfragen,** 1893, 77.

86. This attitude, whose precursors go back to Egyptian representations of Isis, is also anticipated in one of two ceramic reliefs which Richard Luksch, a member of the Klimt group, did in 1907 for a house in the Karpfengasse, Prague (Ill. 27).

87. Johannes Dobai, **Zu Gustav Klimts Gemälde "Der Kuß", Mitt. d. Österr. Galerie,** XII, 1968, 126.

88. About Toorop's picture: Hevesi, **Acht Jahre Secession,** 241.

89. **Die deutsche Malerei im 19. Jahrhundert,** Leipzig Berlin 1914, 345, 357 (where you find the comparison with Strathmann, later developed by Dobai).

90. Diary, 26 March 1854.

91. **Loc. cit.,** 353.

92. **Der Fall Riehl** (The Riehl Case) (1906) in: **Sittlichkeit und Kriminalität** (Morality and Delinquency), Fischer-Bücherei, Frankfurt am Main 1966, 193.

93. **Perversität** (1907) in: **Sittlichkeit und Kriminalität, loc. cit.,** 238.

94. Arthur Roessler reports a remark Klimt made about one of his models: "That girl has a body, even her bottom is more beautiful and intelligent than most people's faces." (Nebehay, p. 428.) Cf. Freud, **Die Traumdeutung, loc. cit.,** 152.

95. The lyre is a popular requisite of idealistic painting in the 19th century; the stylists removed it from realistic representation and made it a component of generalized curved form.

96. The suggestive power of the ɑ is made clear by comparison with a similar scene in Klinger's **"Abend"** (Evening) (Hessisches Landesmuseum, Darmstadt). The interplay of pulling away and returning is expressed much more concisely and suggestively by Klimt, without losing its ambivalence.

97. How much Klimt stylized the avenue, made it fit into his "mold," is shown by two photographs of the actual trees (Nebehay, Ills. 568, 569).

98. **Beiträge zur Analyse der Empfindungen** (Contributions to the Analysis of Sensations), Jena 1886 (quoted by Ehrenfels, **loc. cit.,** 251). Lorenz Dittmann (**Stil Symbol Struktur,** Munich 1967, 157) has proved that for the radically formalistic aesthetics of the Gestalt Theory "Art is merely a quantitative heightening of Gestalt qualities," "which are also found everywhere else," which gives rise to the boundary-obliterating postulates of Viennese Jugendstil — Man as a work of art. More recently there has been a polemically sharpened attempt to hold the Gestalt criterion of harmony responsible for the theory of the totalitarian State. (Martin Jürgens, **Bemerkungen zur 'Ästhetisierung der Politik'** in: **Ästhetik und Gewalt,** Gütersloh 1970, 20).

99. Ehrenfels, **loc. cit.,** 278.

100. Hofmannsthal, quoted by Wolfgang Iskra, **Die Darstellung des Sichtbaren in der dichterischen Prosa um 1900** (The Representation of the Visible in Poetic Prose c. 1900), Münster 1967.

101. Hofmannsthal, **Franz Stuck** (1894), Prosa I, 1950, 198.

102. Hofmannsthal, **loc. cit.,** 198.

103. **Impressionismus** (1903) in: Essays, ed. by H. Kindermann, Vienna 1962, 186. In the essay **"Malerei 1894" (Renaissance. Neue Studien zur Kritik der Moderne,** Berlin 1897, 179), Bahr singles out the "brave urge in painting to be nothing but painting." To him that meant: "Joy and sorrow, intoxication and magic, orgy and festival of light, ecstasy, babbling in colors." The prerequisite for this was naturalism, which made all objects paintworthy and therefore equivalent. Bahr stresses the role of Whistler, regarded by many as a "hero and liberator."
The neglect of subject matter in favor of "mood" was supported by the Viennese art historian Franz Wickhoff, an admirer of Klimt (cf. Note 126), in a lecture cycle **"Über moderne Malerei,"** which took place in 1897 in the Österreichische Museum für Kunst und Industrie. For Wickhoff Whistler was the most considerable of living artists. Doubtless the remark "what used to be confined to music and poetry, the ability to render a mood . . . has now become the true task of modern painting" was meant particularly for him. Bahr may have influenced Wickhoff's judgment of modern art. On the one hand Wickhoff praises modern artists for revealing "an aesthetic connection everywhere, between all events"; on the other hand he seems to regard the factual content of the wider experience as expendable: "Painting seems at its most picturesque, its most artistic, if we keep it free from all associations with poetic things, historical things, with all things of importance." This is amplified by the non-representational nature of a 'modern' subject: "When evening lights fall on an iron bridge, the light iron rods, seen from a

certain distance, all merge into one tone, like a web — the whole unites in one harmonious picture of maximum pictorial effect." What Loos wrote in 1908 about the "style of our time" (cf. Note 27), Wickhoff anticipated by almost ten years: "The new style for which architecture is always searching has already been found, and it would be better if one let the engineers and not the architects build everything." Wickhoff is more "progressive" than Loos, who wanted to replace the architect not by the engineer but by the traditional master builder. (The Works of Franz Wickhoff, ed. by Max Dvoràk, Berlin 1913, II, 21 ff.) It is conceivable that Wickhoff and Bahr were both basing their views on Ruskin. In "The Stones of Venice" (II, The Nature of Gothic) we read that "good colouring" is not a question of copying, but of creating "abstract qualities and relations" of colors.

104. The scene of the play is Paris on the eve of the 14th of July 1789. The blasé crowd at the low tavern, entertained by former actors miming criminals, is both partner and representative of the audience in the theatre below: it draws them, so to speak, onto the stage. The paying spectator identifies conspiratorially with the actor pretending to be a spectator, while the 'professional' actor, by slipping out of his criminal role, brings actual reality into it. The actor Henri boasts of having surprised the Duke of Castignan with his wife, and killed him. The audience does not believe him, because it knows the rules of the game. The Duc de Castignan enters the tavern: Henri hurls himself at him and stabs him. The boundary-obliterating play has become a two-dimensional backdrop, from which the gory grim reality beyond the bewildering quid pro quo stands out with cruel sharpness.

105. Iskra, 21.

106. Iskra, 9, 15.

107. Iskra, 9.

108. Cf. Musil's story **"Das verzauberte Haus"** (The Enchanted House) (1908) (Iskra, 16).

109. **Loc. cit.,** 90, 91, 244.

110. "Woman is nothing, and for that reason, **only** for that reason she can **become everything,** whereas Man can always only become what he **is." (Loc. cit.,** 399).

111. **Literatur und Lüge** (Literature and Lie), Munich 1962, 210.

112. Iskra, 46.

113. "A professor of Literature thought that my aphorisms are just mechanical reversals of platitudes. That is perfectly true. However, he has not grasped the idea that drives the mechanism: that a mechanical reversal of platitudes reveals more than mechanical repetition." Kraus was honest enough to admit that his judgment was also tied to context: "A poem is great, until one finds out who wrote it." **(Nachts,** 29) Conversely, this means that a transgression against the rules of language may be justified, if it testifies to a genuine feeling for language. **(Die Sprache,** Munich 1954, 27.)

114. **Loc. cit.,** 31, 57, 59, 109, 224, 253, 302, 321, 323, 357.

115. **Das Unbehagen in der Kultur** (Civilization and Its Discontents) (1930), Fischer-Bücherei, Frankfurt am Main, 66.

116. Coll. Works, VI, 7, 11, 19, 27, 42, 43, 173, 244, 246.

117. **Loc. cit.,** 279.

118. **Das weite Land** (The Far Country).

119. **Nachts,** 26.

120. This museum, the result of Semper's demand for new collections of examples and training colleges for applied art, is one of the achievements of the Neo-Classicists which offered a basis for the reforms of the Secessionists. Together with the adjacent technical college and its studios it not only caused the interaction of teaching, production and gallery exhibition — which the present day is again striving to achieve — it also seemed designed to guide commercial art along certain model lines. The exact nature of these models depended on the taste of the director. When in 1897 the anglophile Arthur von Scala took over the headship and in 1899 Felician von Myrbach, a Secessionist, became head of the technical college (with Hoffmann, Moser and Roller on his staff), it was not hard for the Stylists to make full use of the two educational and research centers of applied art.

121. **Historische Grammatik der bildenden Künste,** ed. Karl Maria Swoboda and Otto Pächt, Graz Cologne 1966, 126 f.

122. The following quotations are taken from the introduction (1—13).

123. This shows an error of thought or presentation, for if the appearance of things is the essence of (pictorial) art, it cannot be compromised by painting or sculpture unless one applies to these art forms the standards of architecture and craftwork. Riegl's tenet that the figurative arts follow no particular law of development seems to demand this. But this cannot be reconciled with the postulate that the appearance of things is the essence of art, because this criterion, true perhaps of sculpture and painting, does not cover architecture and crafts.

124. The picture which is a section of reality seems expendable to Riegl: "An excerpt of actual nature bounded by two trees, or a ring made by thumb and forefinger, gives an effect as good, if not better, than a copy of it in a rectangular frame. The painting arouses the required emotional reaction because there are no distracting side effects." **(Historische Grammatik,** 128). According to this thought artifact and natural formation share the same Gestalt qualities (cf. Note 98).

125. **Loc. cit.,** p. 346.

126. Cf. the chapter on "Negative Beauty" in my book **Von der Nachahmung zur Erfindung der Wirklichkeit,** Cologne 1970, 48 ff. The varying concept of beauty was discussed by Riegl's colleague Franz Wickhoff in his defense of Klimt's "Philosophy." The picture was exhibited at the Secession in Spring 1900. There was a positive storm of indignation. Prof. Jodl spoke for a whole group of professors in rejecting Klimt's painting out of hand: "We are fighting not against nudity in art, nor against liberality in art, but against ugliness in art." Wickhoff thereupon protested from Rome against the anti-Klimt agitation, holding the Rector personally responsible. Returning to Vienna he gave a lecture on 9 May to the Philosophical Society at the University, entitled "What is ugly?" Wickhoff argues evasively. He attributes to his oppo-

nents an ideal of beauty based on the pure style of classical antiquity and its imitators. Under its tutelage, they regarded every transgression against the pure style as ugly. In his **"Wiener Genesis,"** which he published in 1895 jointly with Wilhelm Ritter von Hartel, subsequently Minister of Information and patron of the Secession, Wickhoff already recognized in the "mixed style" opposed to classical taste the roots of medieval art. (Works of Franz Wickhoff, III, Berlin 1912, 204) Instead of using this to interpret Klimt's picture, as would have been appropriate to its mixture of naturalistic and stylized techniques, Wickhoff in his lecture went on to discuss lay opinion, which equates the incomprehensible with the ugly. Great works of art have never been completely open to explanation — but Klimt's "Philosophy" needed no indulgence in this direction. "The globe floats in space, the Sphinx hints at its riddle, limited and hard-pressed humanity passes in review. Amidst all this confusion the illuminated head of Wisdom emerges, radiant and consoling, like a star in the evening sky. The whole carried out with the finest means of modern art — mood and the magic of color." (Quoted from the report in "Fremdenblatt," reprinted in Hermann Bahr's **Anthologie Gegen Klimt,** Vienna 1903, 23, 27, 31 f.)

127. Kuzmany, **Dekorative Kunst,** XVI, 1908, 525.
128. **Loc. cit.,** 521.
129. Lux, **loc. cit.,** 50.
130. Oskar Kokoschka, **Schriften 1907—1955,** Munich 1956, 51.
131. Nebehay, 397, 400.
132. **Tagebücher, Aphorismen, Essays und Reden,** Hamburg 1955, 23. Cf. Bahr, **Renaissance, loc. cit.,** 27.
133. Musil, **loc. cit.,** 25, 28, 29.
134. Kraus notes the arbitrary and interchangeable nature of sexual contacts with reference to a court case: "As it happens, small-time corset-maker and shop assistant. Next time a tenor, a horse-trainer, or a lieutenant, with countess, lady's maid or housewife. Christian and Jewess, Jew and Christian girl." (Notes in **Sittlichkeit und Kriminalität, loc. cit.,** 240.)
135. **Der Reim** (Verse), in: **Auswahl aus dem Werk** (Selections) Munich 1957, 345. In the essay **"Der Reim"** (1927) Kraus brings out the connection between the erotic and the creative act and the degradation of both by the philistine: "As the philistine debases the ultimate values of eroticism, so he has made a pastime of creative activity in verse." **(Die Sprache,** Munich 1954, 393.)
136. **Hier wird deutsch gespuckt** (We spit in German) (1915) in **Die Sprache,** 13.
137. **Auswahl,** 340.
138. **Nachts,** 24.
139. **Sittlichkeit und Kriminalität,** 20.
140. **Literatur und Lüge,** 23.
141. Cf. the dream of a "highly respectable and cultured" widow of an officer, offering her "favors" **(Die Traumdeutung,** 148).
142. **Die chinesische Mauer,** 139.
143. **Sittlichkeit und Kriminalität,** 237.
144. **Die chinesische Mauer,** 147.
145. **Nachts,** 36.
146. **Die chinesische Mauer,** 144.
147. **Tagebücher . . .** (Diaries), 28.
148. Weininger, 255.
149. **Nachts,** 31.
150. Quoted by Anneliese Hewig, **Phantastische Wirklichkeit** (Fantastic Reality). Interpretative study of Alfred Kubin's novel **Die andere Seite** (The Other Side), Munich 1967, 55. Hewig among other things discussed the problem of "Actors and spectators" (p. 60) and the comparison of the world with a puppet theatre (p. 129).
151. **Die Verwirrungen des Zöglings Törless** (Young Törless), (1903, first published 1906). **Prosa, Dramen, späte Briefe** (Prose, Dramatic Works, Late Letters), Hamburg 1957, 145.
152. **Tractatus logico-philosophicus,** 5.634, **Schriften,** Frankfurt am Main 1960, p. 66.
153. Loos ridicules this in his story **"Von einem armen reichen Mann"** (About a Poor Rich Man) (1900), **loc. cit.,** 201 ff.
154 Cf. W. H., **Grundlagen der modernen Kunst** (Foundations of Modern Art), Stuttgart 1966, 329 f. (Duchamp), 343 ff. (Artlessness).
155. **Nachts,** 52.
156. **Weltgericht,** 7.
157. **Literatur und Lüge,** 23.
158. In his opinions about art Kraus is against extreme Modernism and avant-garde experiments. ("The Future of the Futurists is an exact Imperfect," **Nachts,** 31.) Probably he would have rejected any comparison of his montage method with Duchamp's "ready mades."
159. **Die Welt der Plakate** (The World of Posters) (1909), in: **Die chinesische Mauer,** 121 ff.
160. **Der Dichter und das Phantasieren** (The Poet and the Daydream) (1907), Frankfurt am Main 1969, X, 169 f.
161. Max Brod, **Über die Schönheit hässlicher Bilder** (The beauty of Hideous Pictures) (1913), Vienna Hamburg 1967, 10, 13, 18, 23, 39.
162. **Das kleine Welttheater.**
163. Brod, **loc. cit.,** 112.
164. Brod, **loc. cit.,** 110.
165. Diaries, 23, 24.
166. Weininger, **Über die letzten Dinge** (Concerning the Last Things), ed. Moriz Rappaport, Vienna Leipzig 1904, 25, 156.
167. **Geschlecht und Charakter,** 91.
168. **Loc. cit.,** 17.
169. **Nachts,** 34.
170. Cf. W. H., **Beziehungen zwischen Malerei und Musik** (Links between Painting and Music), Catalogue of the Exhibition of Schönberg, Webern, Berg. Vienna 1969 (Museum des

20. Jahrhunderts), 104 ff. Klimt shows a certain contact with the Expressionist attitude around 1910 (Pl. IX, 48 and 51.)

171. Gerstl did a portrait of Schönberg, to whom he probably also gave painting lessons; Schiele and Kokoschka portrayed Schönberg and Webern. (Ills. in the Catalogue of the Schönberg, Webern, Berg Exhibition, 11, 13, 31, 33, 49).

172. **Die chinesische Mauer,** 134 ff.

173. Nebehay, 428.

174. Preface to **"Die letzten Tage der Menschheit"** (The Last Days of Humanity). In this tragedy, begun in 1915, Kraus wrote the apocalyptic last word to the theatrical consciousness of Vienna at the turn of the century. The carnival of festive processions becomes a dance of death, peopled by masks and puppets, specters and evil spirits.

175. Klimt's use of montage was discussed by Dobai. This is how it appears to me: "In the mixture of different layers of reality there is an explosive element of disturbance and confusion, which the artist can conceal, but also accentuate. In a Cubist collage the deliberately fragmented newspaper cuttings have the shock effect of foreign bodies, however, when Klimt uses the technique of 'montage' it is for a different purpose. There is no violent juxtaposition of realistic and unrealistic pictorial zones, the various zones, i.e. the various layers of reality, have a common denominator: everything is choice and precious." **(Von der Nachahmung zur Erfindung der Wirklichkeit,** Cologne 1970, 100.)

176. Cf. W. H., **Grundlagen ...** (139 ff.). The concept of "a mixture of styles" first appears, to my knowledge, in Wickhoff (cf. Note 126). This is in connection with the problem of manner, which – apart from important assessments of Aby Warburg's – literary historians found more accessible than art historians. (Ernst Robert Curtius, **Europäische Literatur und lateinisches Mittelalter,** (European Literature and Latinate Middle Ages), Berne 1948; Erich Auerbach, **Mimesis. Dargestellte Wirklichkeit in der abendländischen Literatur** (Representations of Reality in Occidental Literature), Berne 1946. Cf. Jan Bialostocki, **Das Modusproblem in den bildenden Künsten** (The Problem of Manner in the Plastic Arts), **Stil und Ikonographie,** Dresden 1966, 9 ff.

177. What Hevesi wrote on the occasion of the Secession's Rodin Exhibition, regarding the model for La Belle Heaulmière, seems apt here: "... a sort of classical ruin, whose very decay was still decorative: every wrinkle an ornament." **(Acht Jahre Secession,** 395.)

178. Hevesi, **loc. cit.,** 450.

179. This is how the Encyclopédie (1751) defines caricature. Hofmannsthal in his essay on Stuck hints at the connection between caricature and style. For Stuck the drawing of caricatures was an important preliminary training, that was how he learnt to see life ornamentally, and ornament as living. **(loc. cit.,** 197).

180. Hevesi, **loc. cit.,** 450.

BIOGRAPHICAL NOTES

1862 Born 14 July at Baumgarten near Vienna, the son of an engraver of Bohemian origin.

1876 Entered Kunstgewerbeschule attached to the Österreichische Museum für Kunst und Industrie, Vienna. Attended the art classes of Prof. Ferdinand Laufberger, and after the latter's death (1881) studied with Prof. Julius Viktor Berger.

1879 Gustav and Ernst Klimt, together with their fellow student Franz Matsch, carried out Laufberger's decorative scheme for the courts of the Kunsthistorische Museum in Vienna.
All three assisted in preparing Hans Makart's pageant in honor of the Imperial Silver Wedding.

1880 The Klimt brothers and Franz Matsch collaborated on four ceiling pictures for the Sturany Palace in Vienna and a painted ceiling for the Kurhaus in Karlsbad.

1881 Work for the publication "Allegorien und Embleme."

1883 Finished studies at the Vienna Kunstgewerbeschule.

1885 Designs by the studio of the Klimt brothers and Matsch for the Hermes villa at Lainz near Vienna. Decorations for the Stadttheater in Fiume.

1886 Painted two ceilings in the Stadttheater at Karlsbad. Began work on the ceiling and lunette paintings on the staircases of the Burgtheater, Vienna.

1888 Completed work on the Burgtheater. Awarded the Golden Cross of Merit. Influenced by G. Moreau. "The Auditorium of the Old Burgtheater, Vienna." Journeys to Cracow, Trieste, Venice, Munich.

1890 Began work on the inset and intercolumnar pictures in the stairwell of the Kunsthistorische Museum, Vienna (completed 1892).

1891 Joined Association of Artists, Vienna.

1892 His brother Ernst died 9 December.

1894 Commissioned by Ministry of Education to produce designs for a painted ceiling at the University Hall, Vienna.

1896 Klimt and Matsch presented their proposed designs for the arrangement of ceiling and lunette paintings for the University Hall. Klimt to do "Philosophy," "Medicine" and "Jurisprudence."

1897 Secession from the Vienna Artists' Association. Founder member and first President of the Vienna Secession. That summer painted the first of his Attersee landscapes. Worked on oil composition studies for "Philosophy" and "Medicine."

1898 First exhibition of the Vienna Secession, to which Klimt contributed. The periodical Ver Sacrum founded.
In July, after lengthy discussions, definitely commissioned to do the university pictures.

1899 Completed decoration of the music room at the Palais Dumba ("Schubert at the Piano" and "Music").

1900 "Philosophy" (as yet unfinished) exhibited at the Vienna Secession, also various landscapes. "Philosophy" arouses violent controversy. The academics of Vienna took sides for and against Klimt's university paintings. At the Paris World's Fair Klimt received the Gold Medal for "Philosophy."

1901 "Medicine" exhibited at the Secession. Violently hostile reviews in the daily press, great public interest.

1902 "Beethoven Frieze" for the spring exhibition at the Secession.

1903 Continuing intensive work on the university pictures, which in some parts undergo considerable alteration. Hoffmann and Moser founded the Wiener Werkstätte, strongly influenced by Klimt. Friendship with Hodler. In autumn major exhibition of 80 works by Klimt at the Secession.

1904 Contributed to exhibitions in Dresden and Munich. Commissioned to design the mosaic frieze for the Palais Stoclet in Brussels.

1905 Abandoned the university pictures and returned the honorarium to the Ministry. "I want to escape from all

the unedifying absurdities and feel free again."
In May exhibited 15 paintings in Berlin. Klimt and his friends left the Secession.

1906 Travelled to Brussels and London in connection with Stoclet frieze.

1907 Completed the university pictures and exhibited them in Vienna and Berlin.
Peak of the "Golden Period." J. Zeitler, Leipzig, published Lucian's "Dialogues with Hetaerae" illustrated with Klimt's erotic nudes. Klimt met Egon Schiele.

1908 Exhibition of 16 paintings at the Vienna Art Show. "The Kiss," most important work exhibited, acquired by Österreichische Staatsgalerie.

1909 Took part in the International Art Exhibition, Vienna. Paintings show increasingly somber content, end of the "Golden Period." Stoclet frieze begun under Klimt's supervision at the Wiener Werkstätte. Journeys to Paris and Madrid. Contributed to International Art Show in Munich and to the exhibition of the Berlin Secession.

1910 Successful contribution to Venice Biennale. Took part in exhibition of the Association of German Artists, Prague.

1911 Participation in International Art Exhibition in Rome. Awarded First Prize for "Death and Life." Travelled to Rome and Florence.

1912 Contributed to Great Exhibition in Dresden.

1913 Summer by Lake Garda, where he painted "Malcesine" and "Church in Cassone."

1914 Journey to Brussels. Took part in exhibition of Association of Austrian Artists in Rome.

1917 Honorary member of the Academy of Arts in Vienna and Munich.

1918 Klimt had a stroke 11 January. Died 6 February in Vienna. Many unfinished paintings left in his studio.

BIBLIOGRAPHY

(Extract from the complete survey by Johannes Dobai, published by Verlag Galerie Welz Salzburg, 1967, with supplement to 1970)

PUBLICATIONS ILLUSTRATED BY KLIMT
(in chronological order)

Allegorien und Embleme. Edited by Martin Gerlach, with contributions by Gustav Klimt. Verlag Gerlach und Schenk, Vienna, 1822 ff. (in serial form).

Allegorien. Neue Folge. (From page 1896, in serial form.)

Ver Sacrum. Periodical of the Association of Creative Artists of Austria. Containing contributions by Gustav Klimt.

Die Hetärengespräche des Lukian. German translation by Franz Blei. With fifteen drawings by Gustav Klimt.
Published by Julius Zeitler, Leipzig, 1907.

Paul Verlaine, **Femmes.** With six drawings by Gustav Klimt. The Dandy Books, undated.

WORKS CONTAINING REPRODUCTIONS OF THE PAINTINGS
(in chronological order)

Das Werk Gustav Klimts. 60 art prints published by the Imperial (k. u. k.) Hof- und Staatsdruckerei, under the artist's supervision, in heliogravure facsimile prints, including 10 in color and gold. Verlag H. O. Miethke, Vienna 1914. (Appeared in installments, from 1908 onwards.)

Das Werk Gustav Klimts. Edition as above, with introductory text by Hermann Bahr and Peter Altenberg. Hugo Heller, Leipzig and Vienna, five installments, 1914—1918.

Gustav Klimt. Eine Nachlese. 30 color prints. Introduction by Max Eisler. Österreichische Staatsdruckerei, Vienna 1931. (Edition of 500 copies, 200 with German text, 150 each with English and French text.)

Gustav Klimt. Eine Nachlese (Second Edition). 30 color prints. Introductory text by Benno Fleischmann. Franz Deuticke Verlag, Vienna 1946. (The same color prints as in the 1931 edition.)

Gustav Klimt. Fratelli Fabbri Editori, Milan 1967, Maestri del Colore No. 162. (Selected and introduced by Werner Hofmann. Color reproductions.)

WORKS CONTAINING REPRODUCTIONS OF THE DRAWINGS
(in chronological order)

Gustav Klimt. 25 Handzeichnungen. (25 Drawings). Gilhofer and Ranschburg, Vienna 1919. (Folio, 500 copies, some color photographs of drawings from the Erich Lederer Collection, Geneva.)

Gustav Klimt. 10 Handzeichnungen, with accompanying text by Gustav Glück. Rikola Verlag, Vienna 1922. (Photogravure reproductions mainly of late drawings.)

Gustav Klimt. 50 Handzeichnungen, with an introduction by Hermann Bahr. Thyrsos Verlag, Leipzig and Vienna, undated (1922). (Drawings of the mature and late periods.)

Gustav Klimt. 25 Zeichnungen, selected and arranged by Alice Strobl. Edited by Walter Koschatzky in the series "Publications of the Albertina," I. Akademische Druck- und Verlagsanstalt, Graz 1964. (Two- to four-color facsimiles in folio, drawings from various phases.)

Gustav Klimt (und Henri Matisse), with a preface by Otto Breicha and Rudolf Leopold. Special exhibit at the Third International Exhibition of Drawings, Darmstadt 1970.

MONOGRAPHS AND ESSAYS
(in alphabetical order by author)

Dobai, Johannes: Das Frühwerk Gustav Klimts. (The early work of Gustav Klimt) Dissertation at the Philosophy Faculty of the University of Vienna, 1958. (Manuscript. With first version of oeuvre catalogue of Klimt's paintings.)

Dobai, Johannes: Zu Gustav Klimts Gemälde "Der Kuß". (About Klimt's painting "The Kiss") Mitteilungen der Österreichischen Galerie, Jahrgang 12, No. 56, Vienna 1968.

Eisler, Max: Gustav Klimt. Vienna, 1920. (1921, English edition with same title. The first — useful — monograph on Gustav Klimt, with illustrations.)

Hatle, Ingomar: Gustav Klimt, ein Wiener Maler des Jugendstils. Dissertation at the Philosophy Faculty of the University of Graz, 1955. (Manuscript.)

Nebehay, Christian: Gustav Klimt. Documentation. Verlag der Galerie Christian M. Nebehay, Vienna 1969. (Divided into three parts: Gustav Klimt, Youth and Apprenticeship. The Seven Years of Vienna's Artistic Spring, 1898-1905. The Last Years. A fundamental documentation of Gustav Klimt's life and work, with numerous illustrations.)

Novotny, Fritz and Dobai, Johannes: Gustav Klimt. Edited by Friedrich Welz. Verlag Galerie Welz, Salzburg, 1967. (The first comprehensive monograph, with an introduction by Fritz Novotny, a comprehensive section of plates in monochrome and polychrome reproduction, an illustrated list of the paintings with detailed commentaries and scholary appendix by Johannes Dobai.)

Pirchan, Emil: Gustav Klimt. Ein Künstler aus Wien. (A Viennese Artist.) Wallishauser Verlag, Vienna — Leipzig, 1942.

Pirchan, Emil: Gustav Klimt. With a preface by A. Grünberg. Bergland Verlag, Vienna 1956. (Text identical with Emil Pirchan's book published in 1942.)

Salten, Felix: Gustav Klimt. Occasional notes. Vienna — Leipzig 1903. (Personal details of Gustav Klimt.)

Strobl, Alice: Gustav Klimt. Drawings and Paintings. Verlag Galerie Welz Salzburg, first edition 1962 (59 reproductions of paintings and drawings, some in color); second, expanded edition 1965 (67 reproductions); third edition, containing a further 8 color plates, 1968, in German and English editions.

LIST OF DRAWINGS AND PAINTINGS

D. with following number: the number in the catalogue of paintings by Johannes Dobai (See bibliography, Novotny/Dobai: Gustav Klimt). In the dimensions given, height precedes width.

DRAWINGS

I **Studies for Medicine,** 1898/1900, pencil, 43 x 29 cm. Albertina, Vienna, Inv. No. 23657.

II **Study for Philosophy,** c. 1896, black crayon, 45,3 x 33,5 cm. Albertina, Vienna, Inv. No. 34556.

III **Working drawing for Philosophy,** 1898/99, black crayon, pencil, 89,6 x 63,2 cm. Historisches Museum, Vienna, Inv. No. 71506.

IV **Working drawing for Medicine,** 1899/1900, black crayon and pencil, 86 x 62 cm. Albertina, Vienna, Inv. No. 29545.

V **Study for Medicine,** c. 1898, blue crayon, 40 x 26 cm. Albertina, Vienna, Inv. No. 23651.

VI **Study for Goldfish,** 1900, pencil, dimensions unknown, signed lower center. Collection Erich Lederer, Geneva.

VII **Study for Expectation,** c. 1906, pencil, 55,8 x 36,9 cm. Dr. Hermann Goja.

VIII **Seated Girl,** c. 1903, pencil, 56,4 x 37,3 cm, estate stamp lower right. Private collection.

IX **Crouching girl,** c. 1909, pencil, crayon, gray and brown wash, 54,9 x 34,8 cm. Historisches Museum, Vienna, Inv. No. 101.692.

X **Study for a standing woman,** 1905/7, pencil, 56 x 37 cm, estate stamp lower right. Albertina, Vienna, Inv. No. 31514.

XI **Study for The Maiden,** 1913, pencil, 56,6 x 37 cm, estate stamp lower right. Drawing collection of the Federal College of Technology, Zürich, Inv. No. 1960/55.

XII **Studies for the portrait of Adele Bloch-Bauer, II,** 1912, pencil, 56,7 x 37,2 cm. Albertina, Vienna, Inv. No. 30696.

XIII **Kneeling woman,** c. 1916, pencil, 56,5 x 37,1 cm, estate stamp lower left. Viktor Fogarassy, Graz.

XIV **Supine nude,** 1914/17, pencil, 36 x 56 cm, estate stamp lower left. Galerie Gurlitt, Munich.

XV **Study for the portrait of Fräulein Lieser,** c. 1917, black crayon, 56 x 36 cm. Private collection.

PAINTINGS

1 **Music II,** 1898 (D. 89), overdoor in the Palais Dumba. Oil on canvas, 150 x 200 cm, signed lower right, Gustav Klimt. Destroyed in 1945 at Schloss Immendorf.

2 **Music I,** 1895 (D. 69), rough draft of Music II. Oil on canvas, 37 x 44,5 cm, signed lower left: Gustav Klimt 95. Bayerische Staatsgemäldesammlungen (Neue Pinakothek), Munich, Inv. No. 8195.

3 **Portrait of Sonja Knips,** 1898 (D. 91). Oil on canvas, 145 x 145 cm, signed lower right: Gustav Klimt. Österreichische Galerie, Vienna, Inv. No. 4403.

4 **Nuda Veritas,** 1899 (D. 102). Oil on canvas, 252 x 56,2 cm, signed lower right: Gustav Klimt. Theatre collection of the Vienna National Library (estate of Anna Bahr-Mildenburg), now on loan to the Museum des 20. Jahrhunderts, Vienna.

5 **Pallas Athene,** 1898 (D. 93). Oil on canvas, 75 x 75 cm, signed upper left: Gustav Klimt 1898. Historisches Museum, Vienna, Inv. No. 100680.

6 **Schubert at the piano,** 1899 (D. 101), overdoor in the Palais Dumba. Oil on canvas, 150 x 200 cm, signed right center: Gustav Klimt. Destroyed in 1945 at Schloss Immendorf.

7 **Schubert at the piano, preliminary study,** 1898/99 (D. 100). Oil on canvas, 30 x 39 cm, signed lower right: Gustav Klimt. Private collection.

8 **Philosophy, rough draft,** 1897/98 (D. 87). Oil on canvas, dimensions unknown, signed lower right: Gustav Klimt. Destroyed in 1945 at Schloss Immendorf.

9 **Philosophy,** 1899/1907 (D. 105), decorative panel for the Festival Hall of the University of Vienna. Oil on canvas, 430 x 300 cm, signed lower right: Gustav Klimt. Destroyed in 1945 at Schloss Immendorf.

10 **Jurisprudence, rough draft,** c. 1897/98 (D. 86). Oil on canvas, dimensions unknown, signed lower right: Gustav Klimt. Destroyed in 1945 at Schloss Immendorf.

11 **Jurisprudence,** 1903/1907 (D. 128), decorative panel for the Festival Hall of the University of Vienna. Oil on canvas, 430 x 300 cm, signed lower right: Gustav Klimt. Destroyed in 1945 at Schloss Immendorf.

12 **Medicine,** 1900/1907 (D. 112), decorative panel for the Festival Hall of the University of Vienna. Oil on canvas, 430 x 300 cm, signed lower left: Gustav Klimt. Destroyed in 1945 at Schloss Immendorf.

13 **Medicine, rough draft,** 1897/98 (D. 88). Oil on canvas, 72 x 55 cm. Private collection, Vienna.

14 **Hygieia,** detail from Medicine (plate 12).

15 **Judith I,** 1901 (D. 113). Oil on canvas, 84 x 42 cm, signed lower left: Gustav Klimt. Österreichische Galerie, Vienna, Inv. No. 4737.

16 **Farmhouse with birch trees,** 1900 (D. 110). Oil on canvas, 80 x 80 cm, signed lower right: Gustav Klimt. Österreichische Galerie, Vienna, Inv. No. 5448.

17 **The swamp,** 1900 (D. 109). Oil on canvas, 80 x 80 cm, signed lower right: Gustav Klimt. Present location unknown.

18 **Forest of fir trees I,** 1901 (D. 120). Oil on canvas, 90 x 90 cm, Galerie Würthle, Vienna.

19 **Forest of beech trees I,** c. 1902 (D. 122). Oil on canvas, 100 x 100 cm. Moderne Galerie, Dresden, Inv. No. 2479 A.

20 **On the Attersee I,** c. 1900 (D. 116). Oil on canvas, dimensions unknown, signed lower left: Gustav Klimt. Present location unknown.

21 **The tall poplar I,** 1900 (D. 111). Oil on canvas, 80 x 80 cm. Private collection.

22 **Portrait of Gertha Felsövanyi,** 1902 (D. 125). Oil on canvas, 150 x 45,5 cm, signed upper left: Gustav Klimt 1902. Private collection.

23 **Portrait of Gertha Felsövanyi,** detail.

24 **Goldfish,** 1901/1902 (D. 124). Oil on canvas, 181 x 66,5 cm, signed lower right: Gustav Klimt. Private collection Solothurn.

25 **Passage of the Dead,** 1903 (D. 131). Oil on canvas, 48 x 63 cm. Destroyed in 1945 at Schloss Immendorf.

26 **Hope I,** 1903 (D. 129). Oil on canvas, 181 x 67 cm. Galleria Galatea, Milan and Turin.

27 **Portrait of Emilie Flöge,** 1902 (D. 126). Oil on canvas, 181 x 84 cm, signed lower right: Gustav Klimt 1902. Historisches Museum, Vienna, Inv. No. 45677.

28-29 **The Beethoven Frieze,** 1902 (D. 127), frieze for the left hall of the Vienna Secession on the occasion of the exhibition of the statue of Beethoven by Max Klinger. Casein paint on stucco, inlaid with semi-precious stones. In seven sections over three walls. Height 220 cm, total length 2400 cm. Collection Erich Lederer, Geneva (stored in the Lower Belvedere, Vienna).
Hostile power, detail.
Joy, beautiful divine spark, detail.

30 **The three ages of life,** 1905 (D. 141). Oil on canvas, 180 x 180 cm. National Gallery of Modern Art, Rome, Inv. No. 951.

31 **Golden-Apple Tree,** 1903 (D. 133). Oil on canvas, 100 x 100 cm. Destroyed in 1945 at Schloss Immendorf.

32 **Portrait of Margaret Stonborough-Wittgenstein,** 1905 (D. 142). Oil on canvas, 180 x 90 cm, signed lower left: Gustav Klimt 1905. Bayerische Staatsgemäldesammlungen (Neue Pinakothek), Munich, Inv. No. 13074.

33 **Sea serpents II,** 1904/1907 (D. 140). Oil on canvas, 80 x 145 cm, signed lower right: Gustav Klimt. Private collection.

34 **Sea serpents I,** c. 1904/1907 (D. 139). Mixed media on parchment, 50 x 20 cm, signed lower right: Gustav Klimt. Österreichische Galerie, Vienna, Inv. No. 5077.

35 **Portrait of Fritza Riedler,** 1906 (D. 143), Oil on canvas, 153 x 133 cm, signed lower left: Gustav Klimt 1906. Österreichische Galerie, Vienna, Inv. No. 3379.

36 **The sunflower,** c. 1906/1907 (D. 146). Oil on canvas, 110 x 110 cm, signed lower right: Gustav Klimt. Private collection.

37 **Farmhouse garden with sunflowers,** c. 1905/1906 (D. 145). Oil on canvas, 110 x 110 cm, signed lower left: Gustav Klimt. Österreichische Galerie, Vienna, Inv. No. 3685.

38 **The sisters,** 1907/1908 (D. 157). Oil on canvas, 125 x 42 cm, signed lower left: Gustav Klimt. Private collection, Vienna.

39 **Danae,** c. 1907/1908 (D. 151). Oil on canvas, 77 x 83 cm, signed lower right: Gustav Klimt. Private collection, Graz.

40 **Poppy field,** 1907 (D. 149). Oil on canvas, 110 x 110 cm, signed lower right: Gustav Klimt. Österreichische Galerie, Vienna, Inv. No. 5166.

41 **Farmhouse garden,** c. 1905/1906 (D. 144). Oil on canvas, 110 x 110 cm, signed lower right: Gustav Klimt. Národni Gallery, Prague, Inv. No. 04107.

42 **Portrait of Adele Bloch-Bauer I,** 1907 (D. 150). Oil on canvas, 138 x 138 cm, signed lower right: Gustav Klimt 1907. Österreichische Galerie, Vienna, Inv. No. 3830.

43 **Judith II (Salome),** 1909 (D. 160). Oil on canvas, 178 x 46 cm, signed lower left: Gustav Klimt 1909. Gallery of Modern Art, Venice.

44 **Woman with hat and feather boa,** 1909 (D. 161). Oil on canvas, 69 x 55 cm, signed left center: Gustav Klimt. Österreichische Galerie, Vienna, Inv. No. 4046.

45-46 **Preparatory sketches for the mosaic in the Palais Stoclet,** details, c. 1905/1909 (D. 152). Tempera, gold and silver on paper, with handwritten instructions for execution. Österreichisches Museum für angewandte Kunst, Vienna, Inv. No. 37197.
Expectation, 193 x 115 cm.
Fulfillment, 194 x 121 cm.

47 **The kiss,** 1907/1908 (D. 154). Oil on canvas, 180 x 180 cm, signed lower right: Gustav Klimt. Österreichische Galerie, Vienna, Inv. No. 912.

48 **Mother with children,** 1909/10 (D. 163). Oil on canvas, 90 x 90 cm, signed lower right: Gustav Klimt. Private collection.

49 **Park,** before 1910 (D. 165). Oil on canvas, 110 x 110 cm, signed lower left: Gustav Klimt. The Museum of Modern Art, New York (Gertrude A. Mellon Foundation).

50 **Portrait of Adele Bloch-Bauer II,** 1912 (D. 177). Oil on canvas, 190 x 120 cm, signed lower right: Gustav Klimt. Österreichische Galerie, Vienna, Inv. No. 4210, now on loan to the Museum des 20. Jahrhunderts, Vienna.

51 **The black hat,** 1910 (D. 168). Oil on canvas, 79 x 63 cm, signed lower right: Gustav Klimt 1910. Viktor Fogarassy, Graz.

52 **Schloß Kammer on the Attersee III,** 1910 (D. 171). Oil on canvas, 110 x 110 cm, signed right center: Gustav Klimt. Österreichische Galerie, Vienna, Inv. No. 4318.

53 **Portrait of Mäda Primavesi,** c. 1912 (D. 179). Oil on canvas, 150 x 110 cm, signed lower right: Gustav Klimt. Mr. and Mrs. André Mertens, Westport, Connecticut.

54 **The maiden,** 1913 (D. 184). Oil on canvas, 190 x 200 cm, signed lower right: Gustav Klimt. Národni Gallery, Prague, Inv. No. 04152.

55 **Appletree I,** c. 1912 (D. 180). Oil on canvas, 110 x 110 cm, signed lower right: Gustav Klimt. Österreichische Galerie, Vienna, Inv. No. 3342, now on loan to the Museum des 20. Jahrhunderts.

56 **Avenue in the park of Schloss Kammer,** 1912 (D. 181). Oil on canvas, 110 x 110 cm, signed lower left: Gustav Klimt. Österreichische Galerie, Vienna, Inv. No. 2892.

57 **Forest ranger's house in Weissenbach on the Attersee,** 1912 (D. 182). Oil on canvas, 110 x 110 cm, signed lower left: Gustav Klimt. Private collection, U.S.A.

58 **Death and life,** before 1911, reworked 1916 (D. 183). Oil on canvas, 178 x 198 cm, signed lower right: Gustav Klimt. Private collection, Vienna.

59 **Church in Cassone,** 1913 (D. 185). Oil on canvas, 110 x 110 cm, signed lower left: Gustav Klimt. Private collection, Graz.

60 **Malcesine on Lake Garda,** 1913 (D. 186). Oil on canvas, 110 x 110 cm, signed lower right: Gustav Klimt. Destroyed in 1945 at Schloss Immendorf.

61 **Portrait of Baroness Elisabeth Bachofen-Echt,** c. 1914 (D. 188). Oil on canvas, 180 x 128 cm, signed lower right: Gustav Klimt. Collection Erich Lederer, Geneva.

62 **Portrait of Friederike Maria Beer,** 1916 (D. 196). Oil on canvas, 168 x 130 cm, signed lower left: Gustav Klimt 1916. Collection Friederike Beer-Monti, New York.

63 **Appletree II,** c. 1916 (D. 195). Oil on canvas, 80 x 80 cm. Österreichische Galerie, Vienna, Inv. No. 5447.

64 **Litzlbergerkeller on the Attersee,** 1915/16 (D. 193). Oil on canvas, 110 x 110 cm, signed lower left: Gustav Klimt. Private collection.

65 **Schönbrunn Park,** 1916 (D. 194). Oil on canvas, 110 x 110 cm, signed lower left: Gustav Klimt. Private collection, Graz.

66 **Landhaus on the Attersee,** c. 1914 (D. 189). Oil on canvas, 110 x 110 cm, signed lower left: Gustav Klimt. Private collection, Vienna.

67 **Church in Unterach on the Attersee,** 1916 (D. 198). Oil on canvas, 110 x 110 cm, signed lower right: Gustav Klimt. Private collection, Graz.

68 **The friends,** 1916/17 (D. 201). Oil on canvas, 99 x 99 (?) cm, signed lower left: Gustav Klimt. Destroyed in 1945 at Schloss Immendorf.

69 **Leda,** 1917 (D. 202). Oil on canvas, 99 x 99 cm. Destroyed in 1945 at Schloss Immendorf.

70 **Wally,** 1916 (D. 200). Oil on canvas, 110 x 110 cm, signed lower left: Gustav Klimt. Destroyed in 1945 at Schloss Immendorf.

71 **The fur coat,** 1916/18, unfinished (D. 206), oil on canvas, 100 x 57 cm, signed lower right: Gustav Klimt. Selected Artists Galleries, New York.

72 **Woman with a fan,** 1917/18 (D. 203). Oil on canvas, 100 x 100 cm. Private collection.

73 **The dancer,** c. 1916/18 (D. 208). Oil on canvas, 180 x 90 cm. Private collection, Paris.

74 **Portrait of a woman,** 1917/18, unfinished (D. 209). Oil on canvas, 180 x 90 cm. Neue Galerie, Linz, Wolfgang Gurlitt Museum.

75 **Portrait of a woman from the front,** 1917/18, unfinished (D. 212). Oil on canvas, 67 x 56 cm. Neue Galerie, Linz, Wolfgang Gurlitt Museum.

76 **Portrait of Frau Amalie Zuckerkandl,** 1917/18, unfinished (D. 213). Oil on canvas, 128 x 128 cm. Private collection, Vienna.

77 **Presshaus on the Attersee,** 1917 (D. 217). Oil on canvas, 110 x 110 cm, signed lower left: Gustav Klimt. Private collection, Holland.

78 **Garden with top of hill,** 1917 (D. 216). Oil on canvas, 110 x 110 cm, signed lower right: Gustav Klimt. Private collection.

79 **Garden path with chickens,** 1916 (D. 215). Oil on canvas, 110 x 110 cm, signed lower left: Gustav Klimt. Destroyed in 1945 at Schloss Immendorf.

80 **Adam and Eve,** 1917/18, unfinished (D. 220). Oil on canvas, 173 x 60 cm. Österreichische Galerie, Vienna, Inv. No. 4402.

81 **Baby,** 1917/18, unfinished (D. 221). Oil on canvas, 110 x 110 cm. Galerie St. Etienne, New York.

82 **The bride,** 1917/18, unfinished (D. 222). Oil on canvas, 166 x 190 cm. Private collection.

DRAWINGS

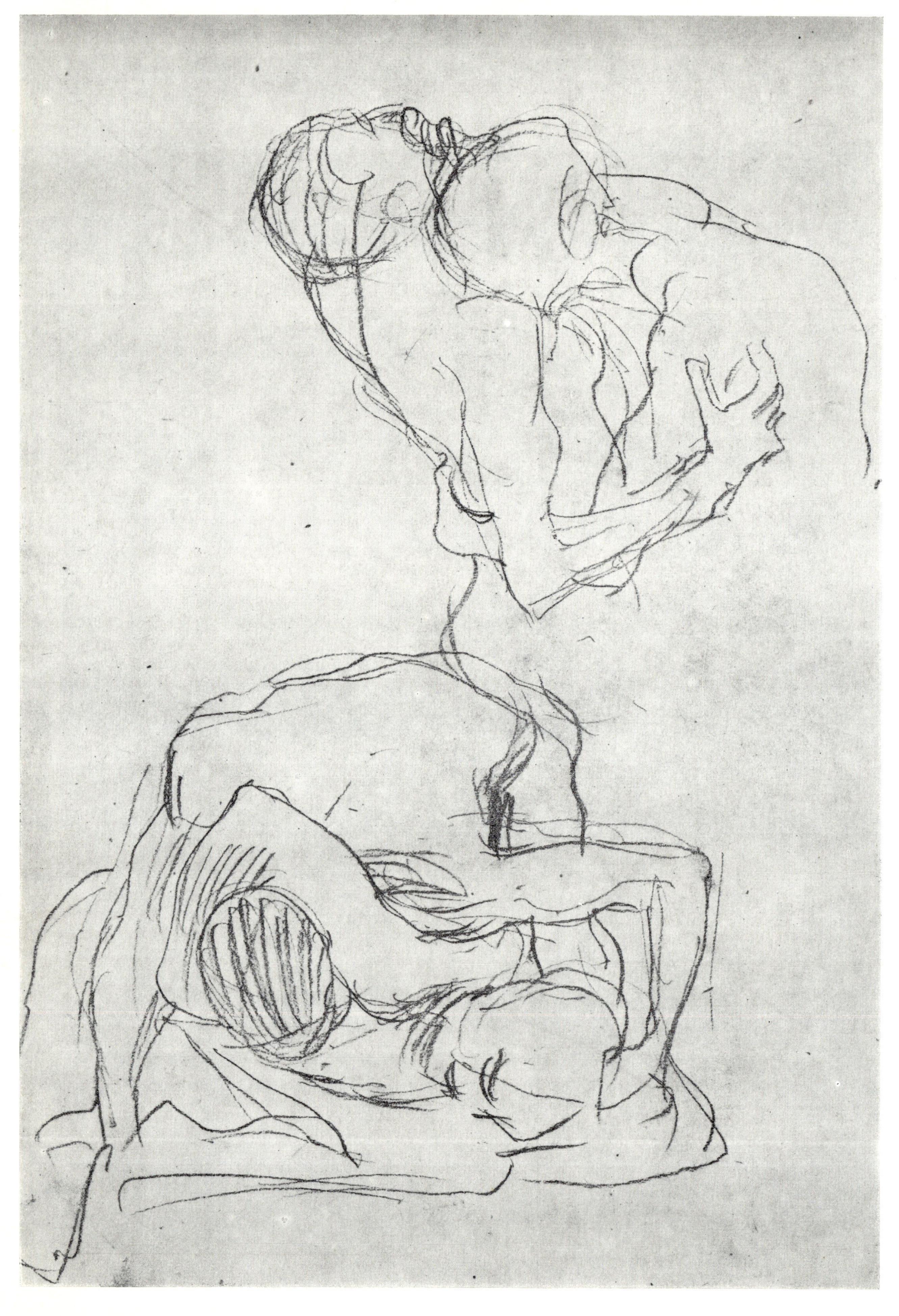

1 STUDY FOR MEDICINE, 1898/1900

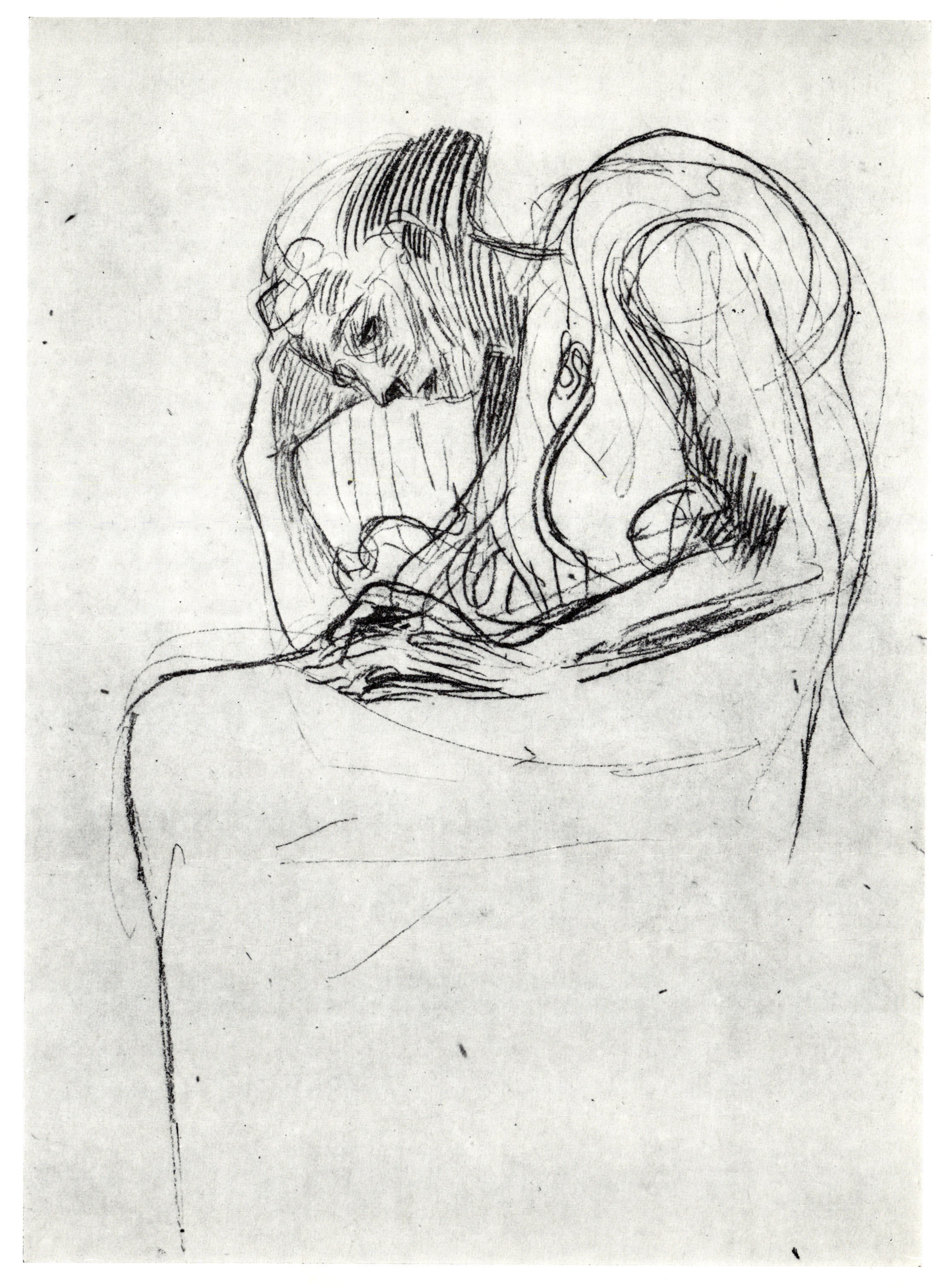

II STUDY FOR PHILOSOPHY, c. 1896
(Allegory of Knowledge)

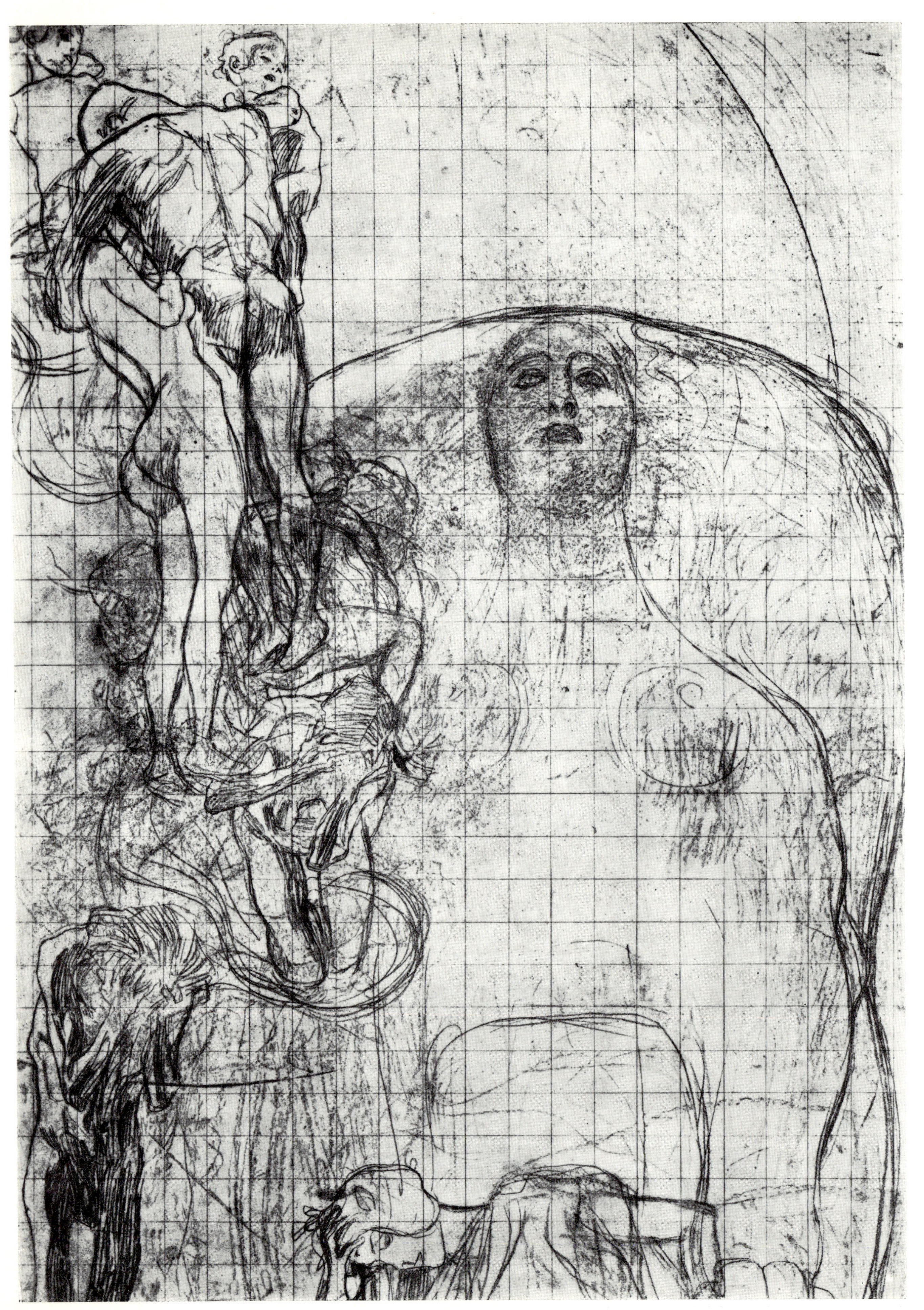

III PREPARATORY DRAWING FOR PHILOSOPHY, 1898/1899

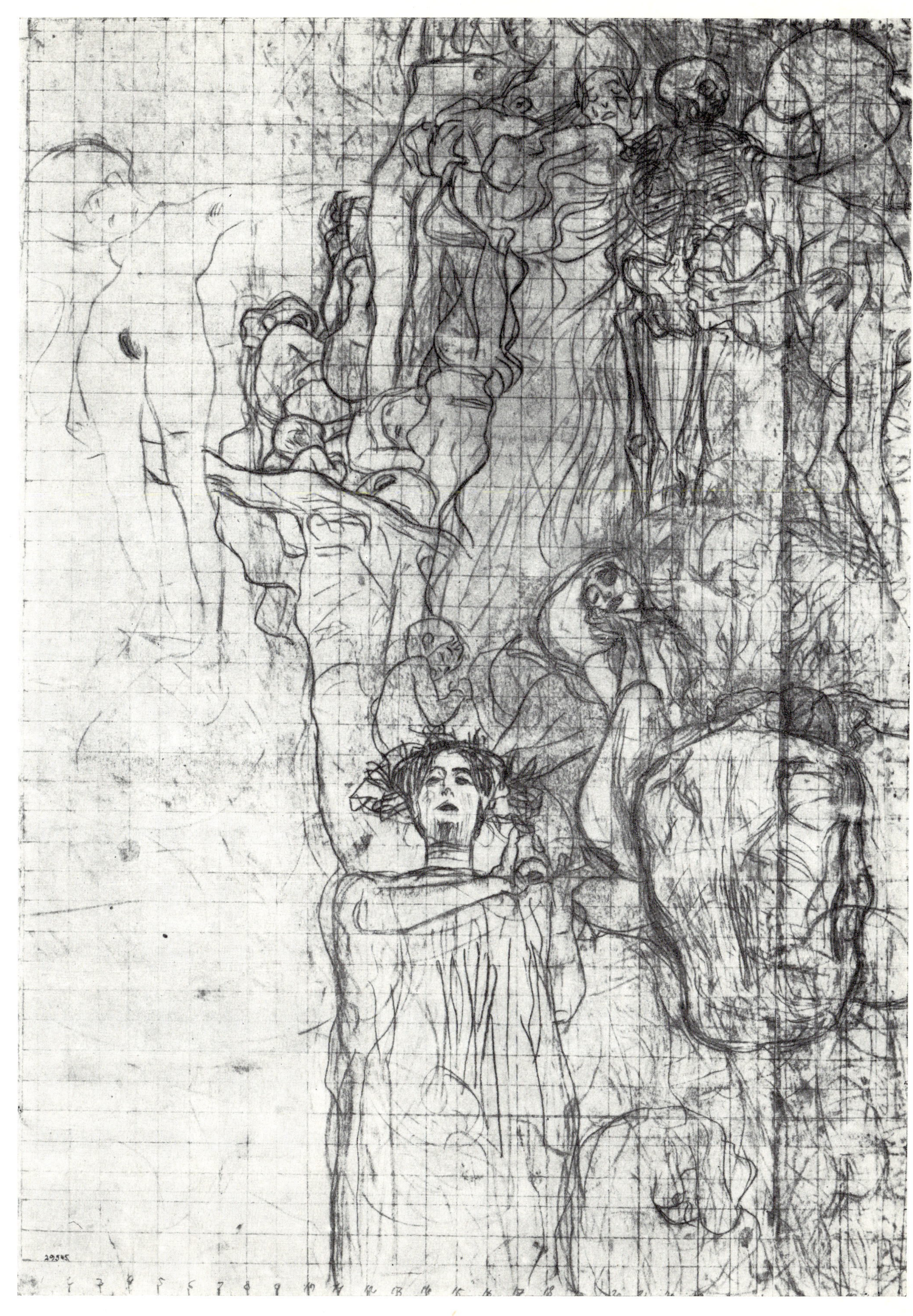

IV PREPARATORY DRAWING FOR MEDICINE, 1899/1900

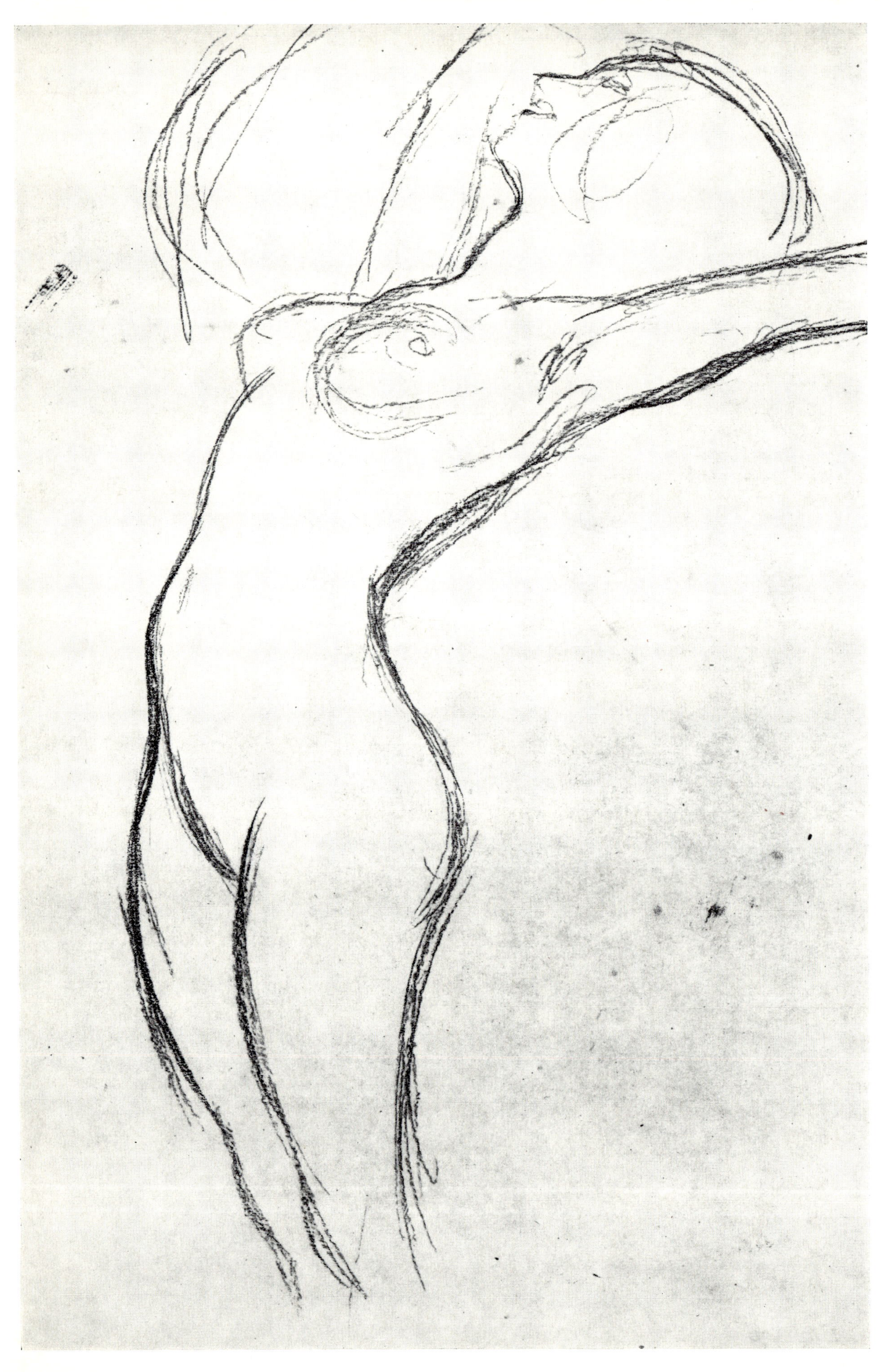

V STUDY FOR MEDICINE, c. 1898

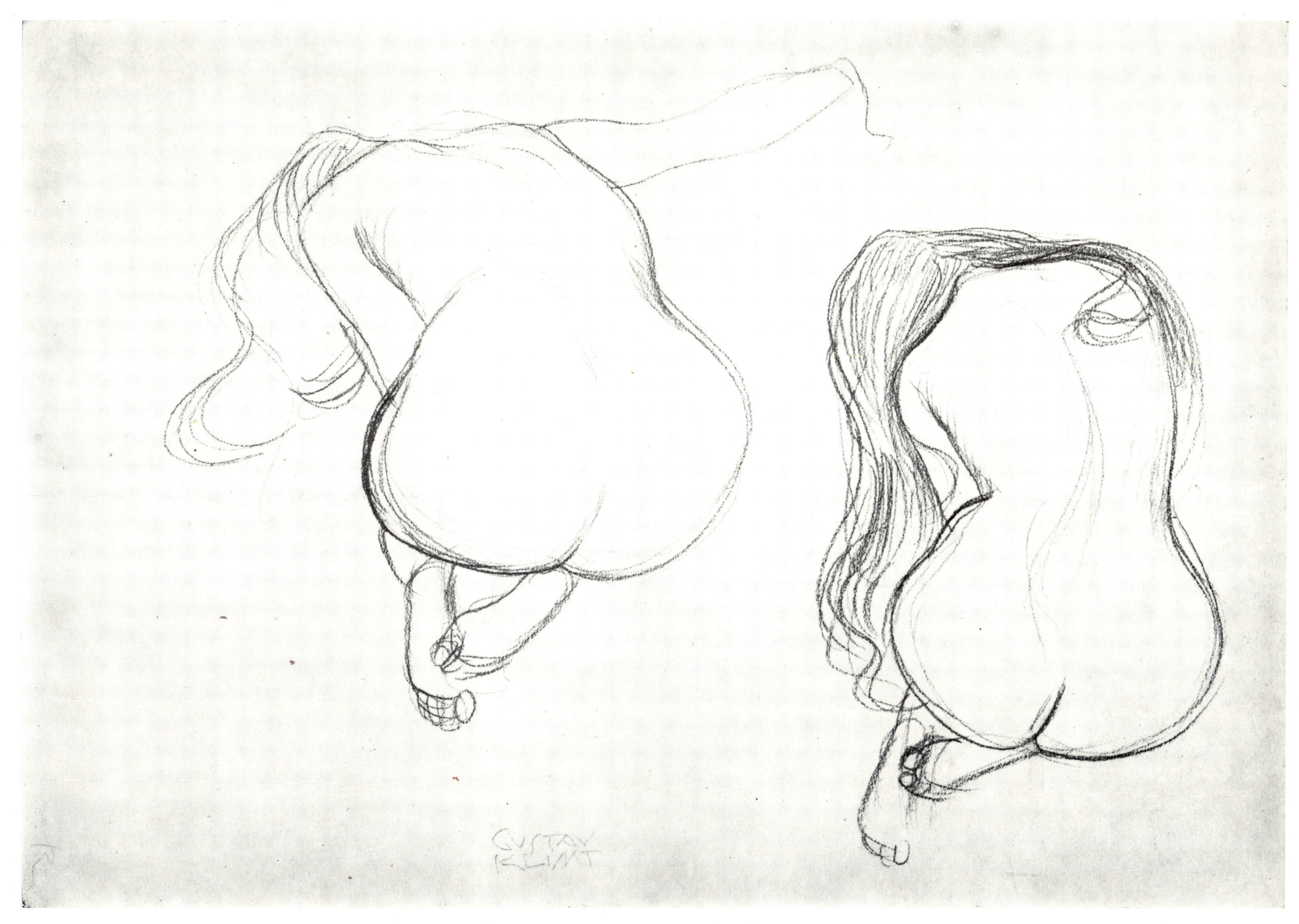

VI STUDY FOR GOLDFISH, 1900

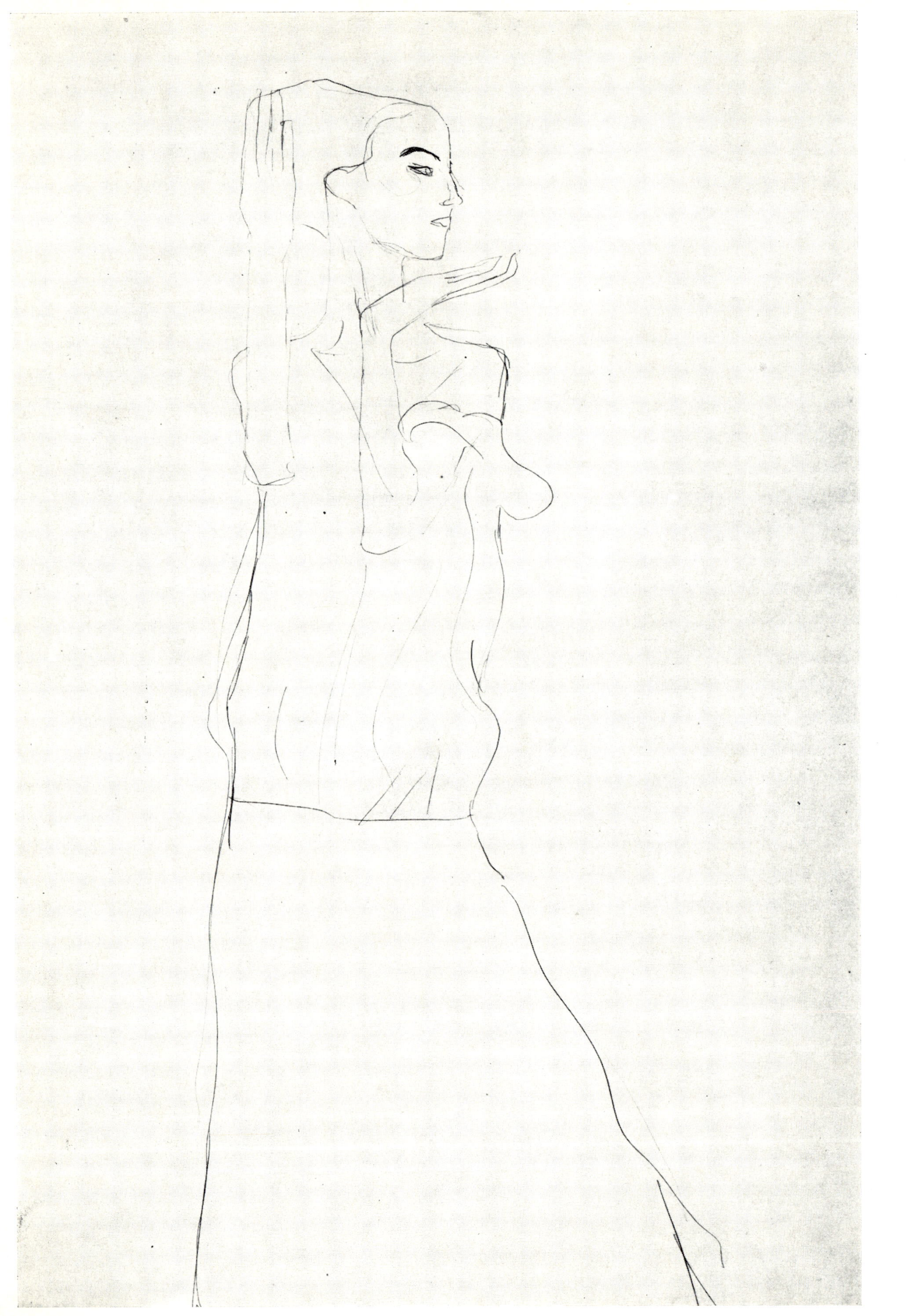

VII STUDY FOR EXPECTATION, c. 1906

VIII SEATED GIRL, c. 1903

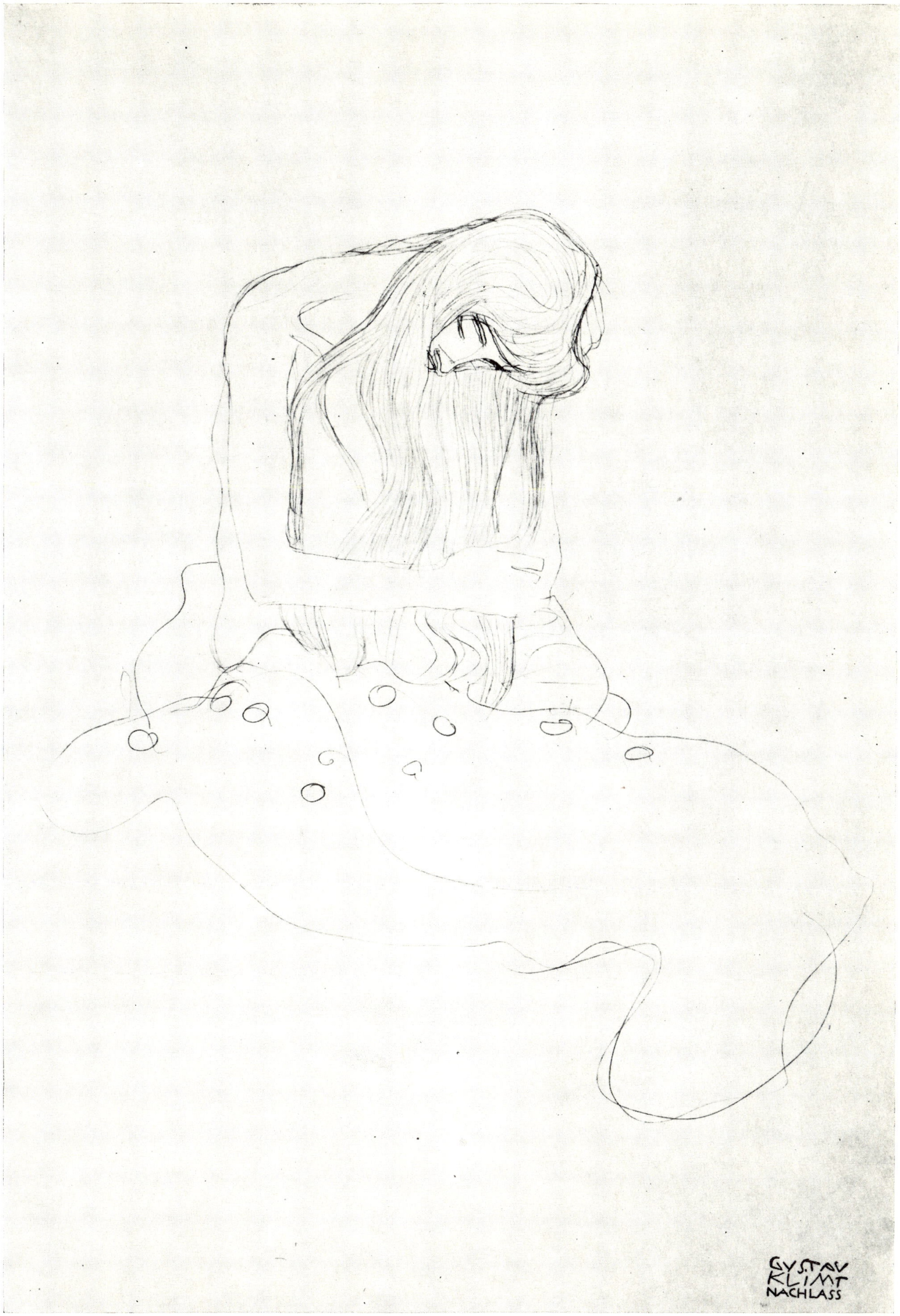

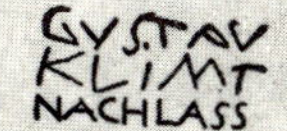

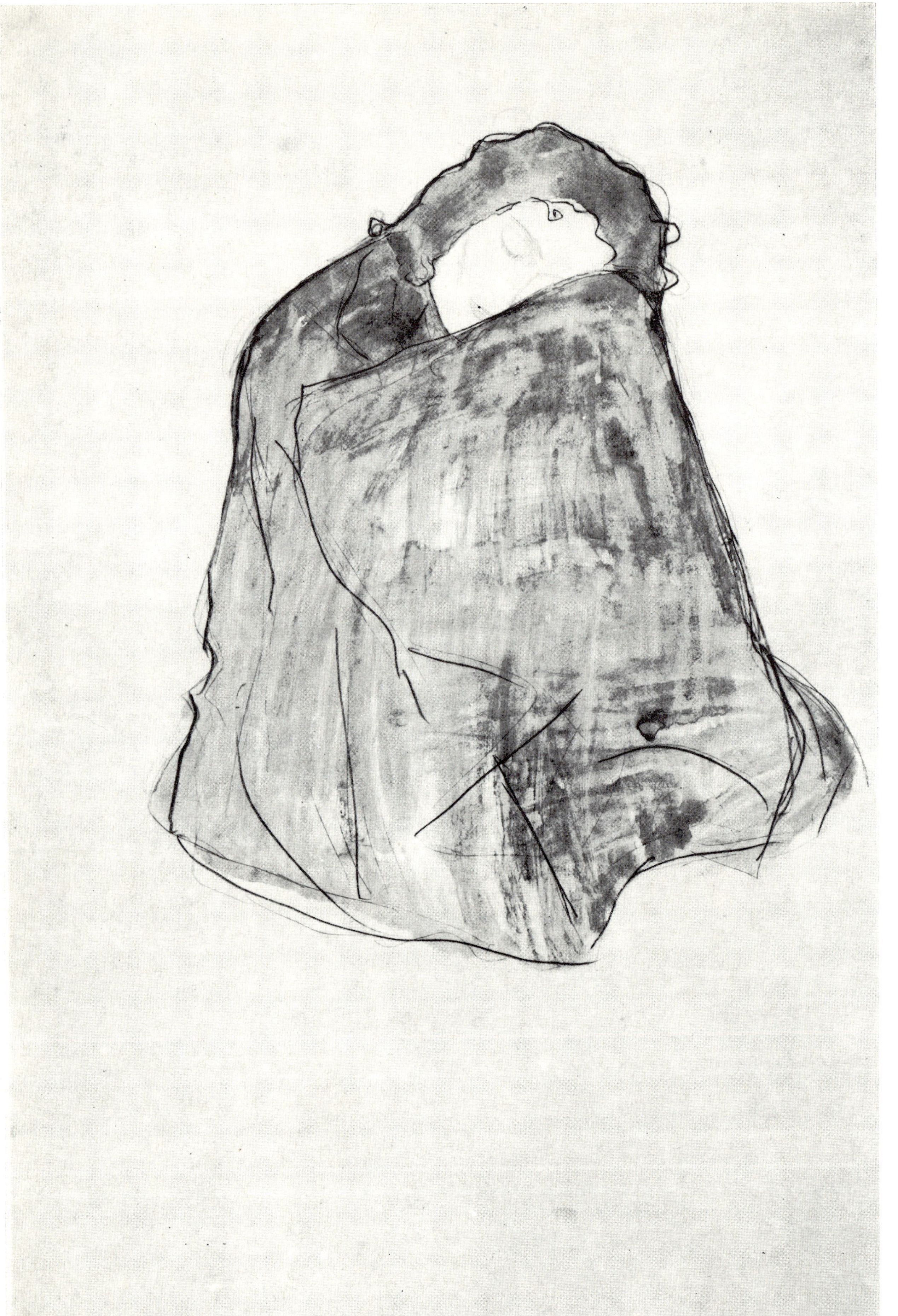

IX CROUCHING GIRL, c. 1909

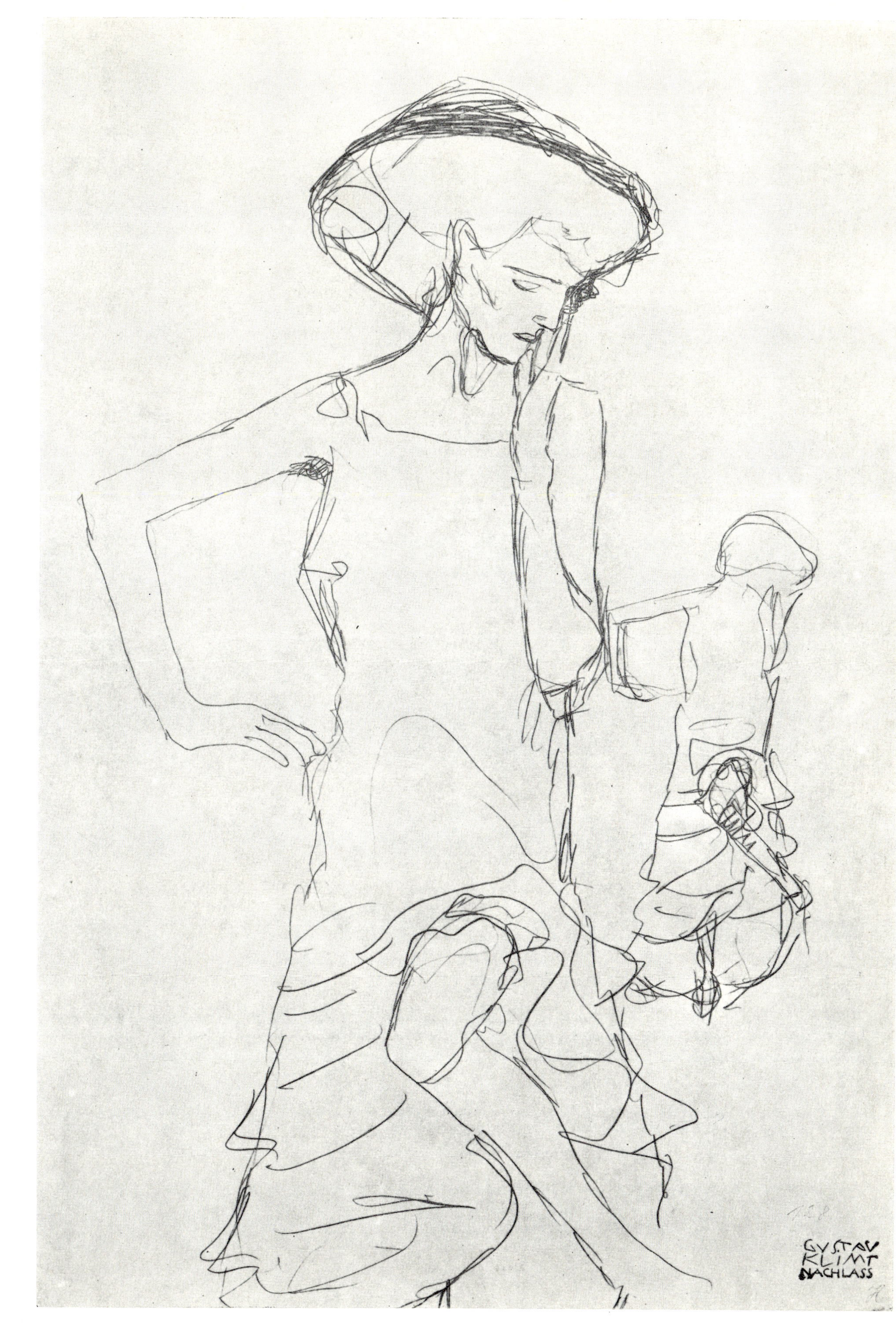

X STUDY OF A STANDING WOMAN, 1905/1907

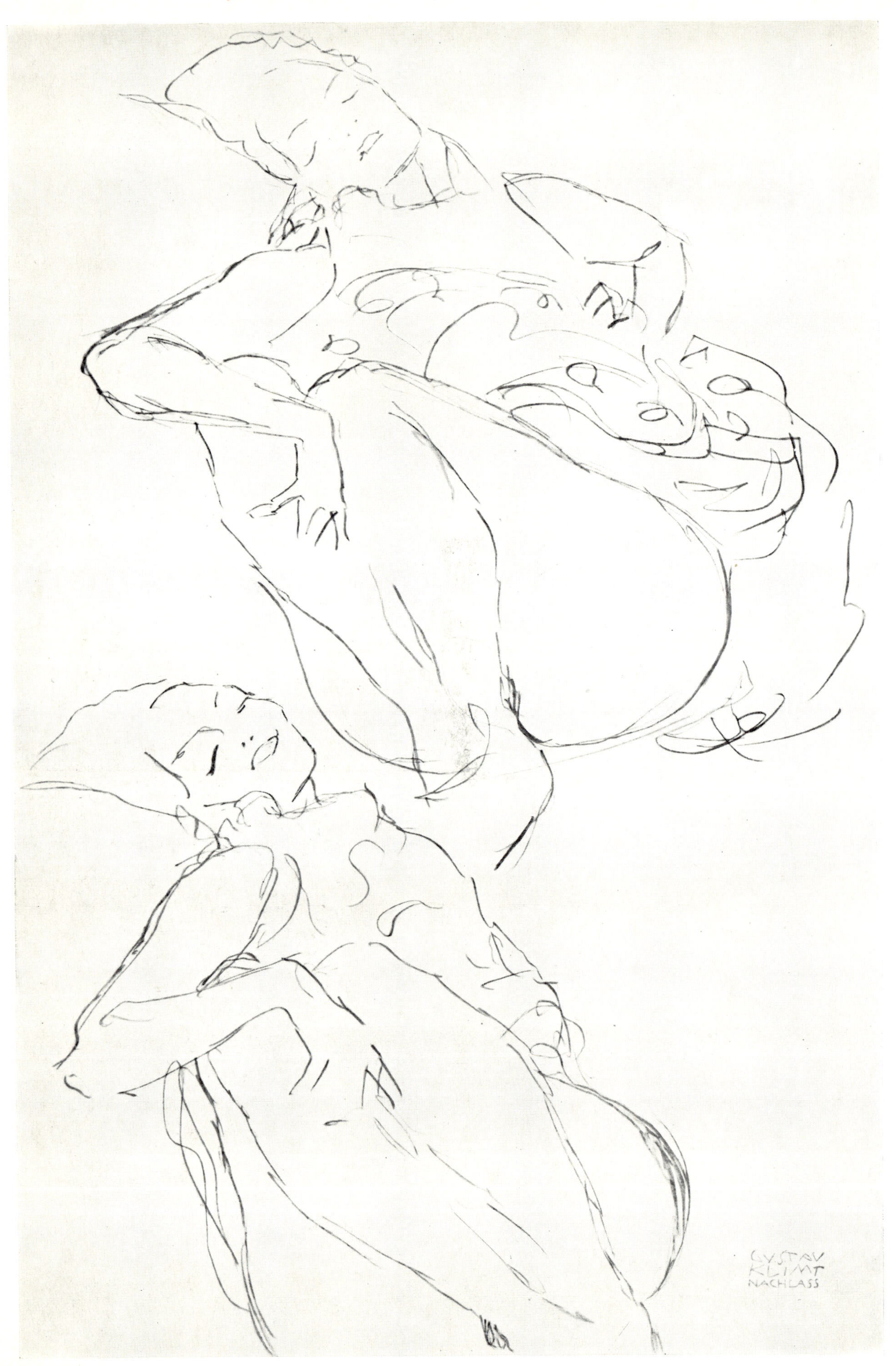

XI STUDY FOR THE MAIDEN, 1913

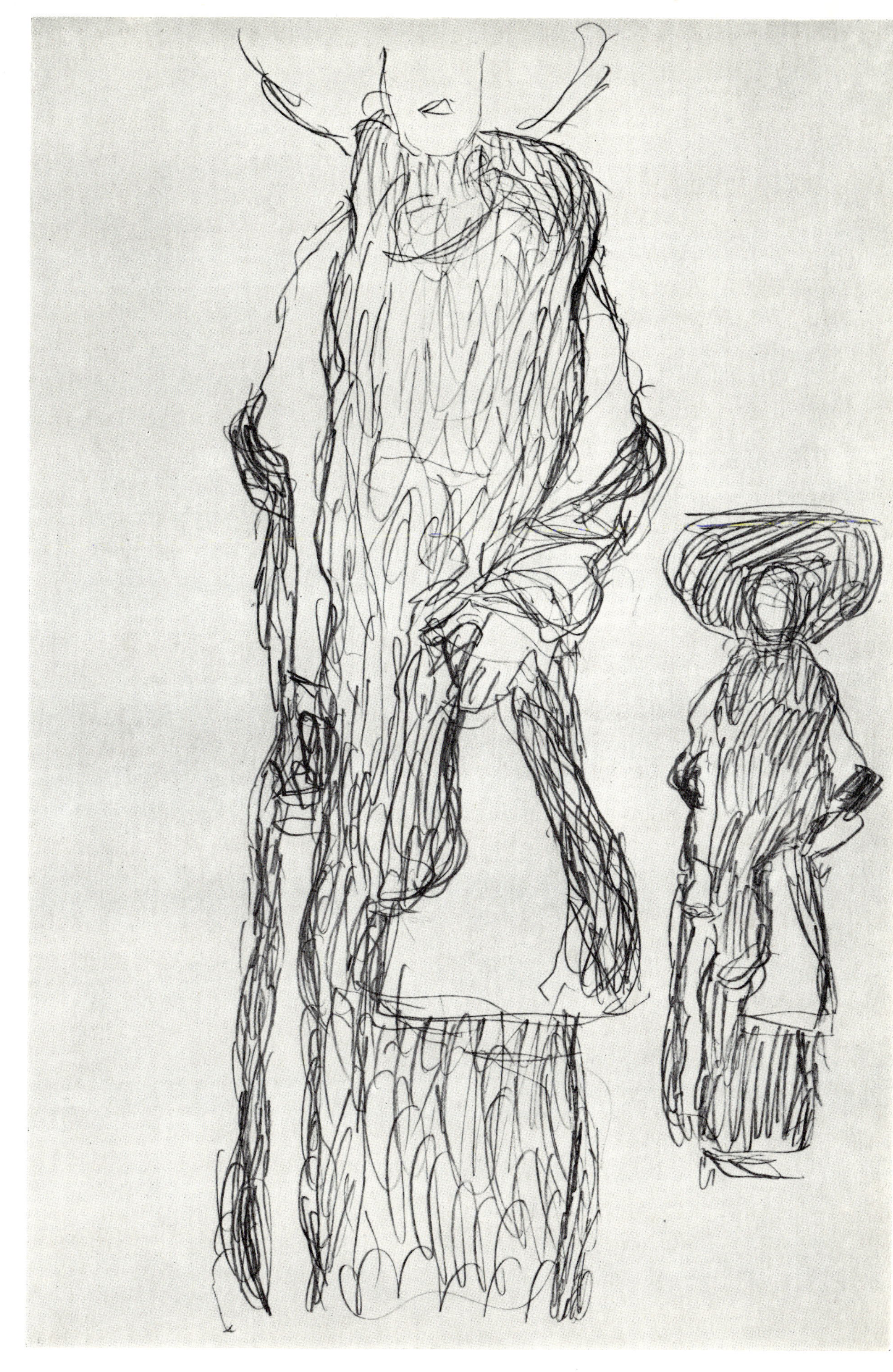

XII STUDY FOR THE PORTRAIT OF ADELE BLOCH-BAUER, II, 1912

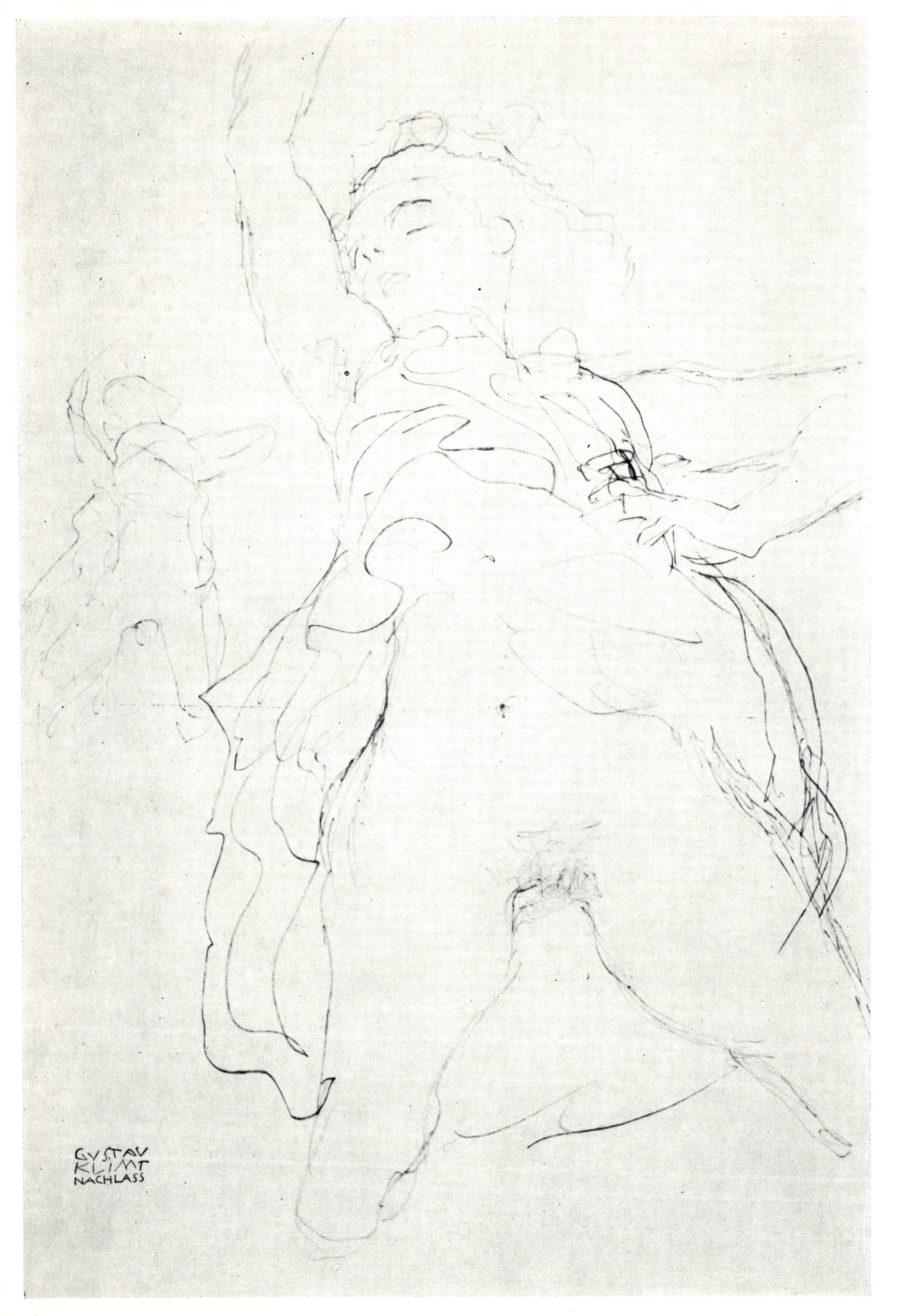

XIII KNEELING WOMAN, c. 1916

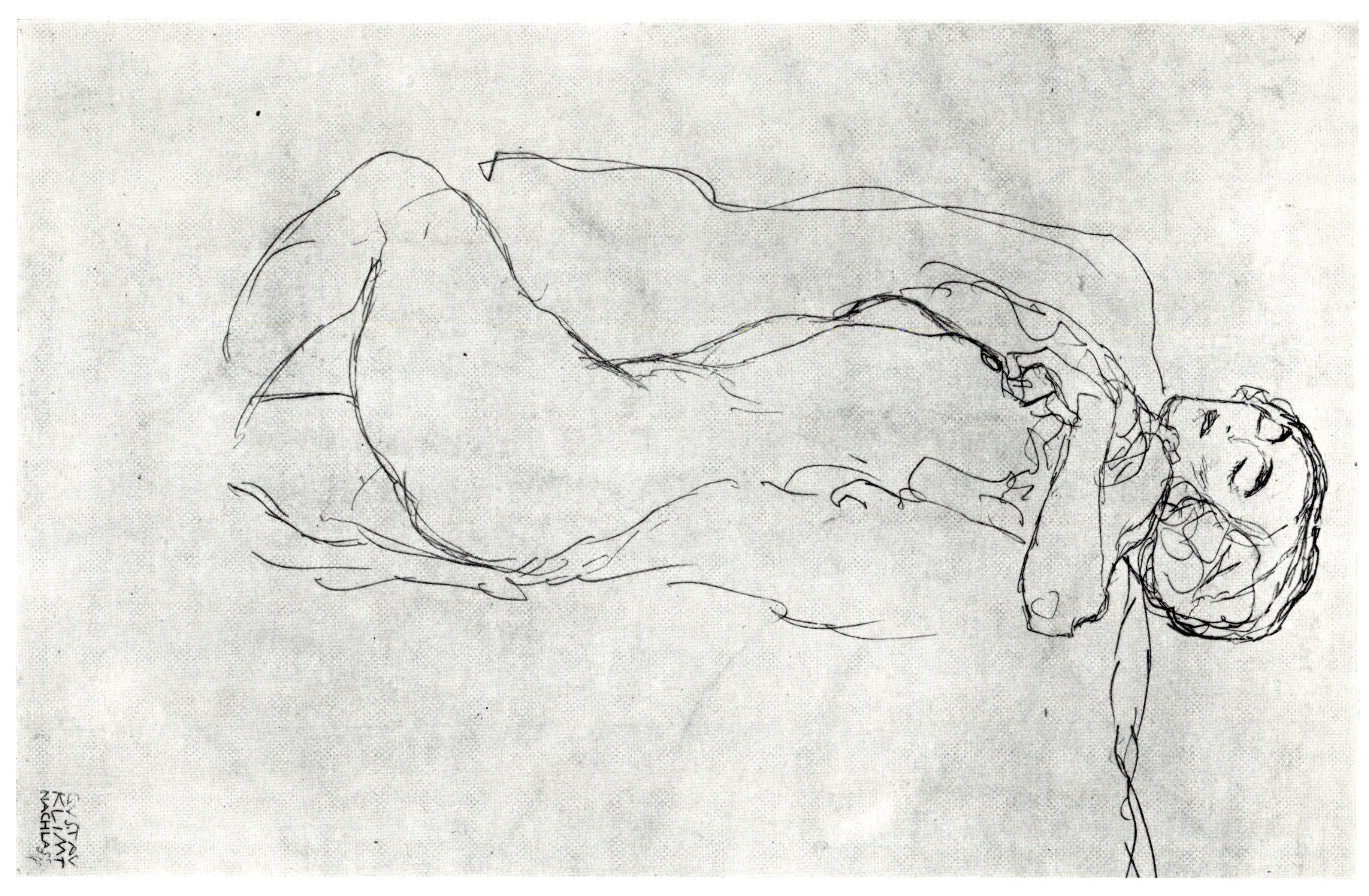

XIV SUPINE NUDE, 1914/1917

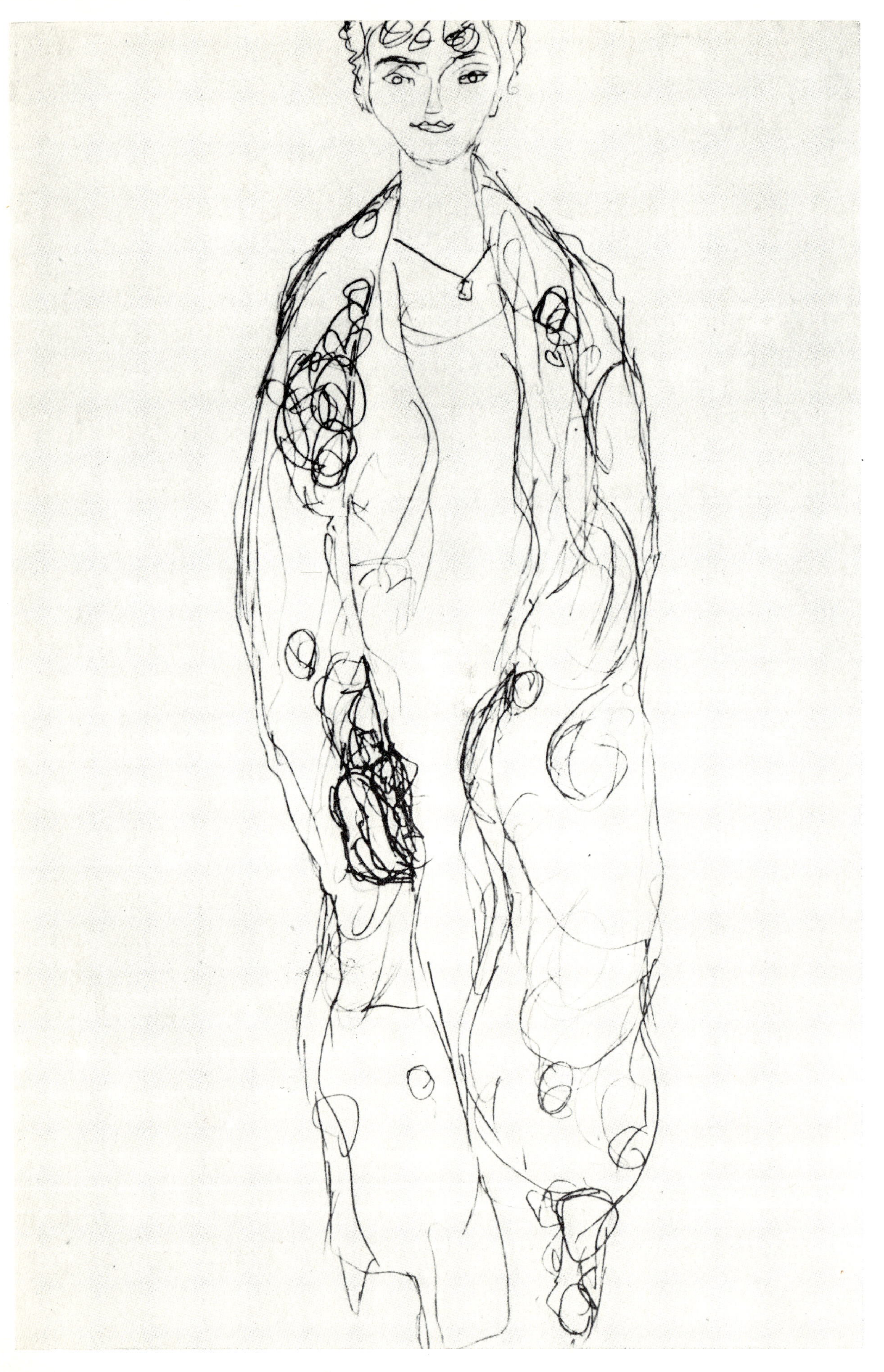

XV STUDY FOR THE PORTRAIT OF FRÄULEIN LIESER, c. 1917

THE PAINTINGS

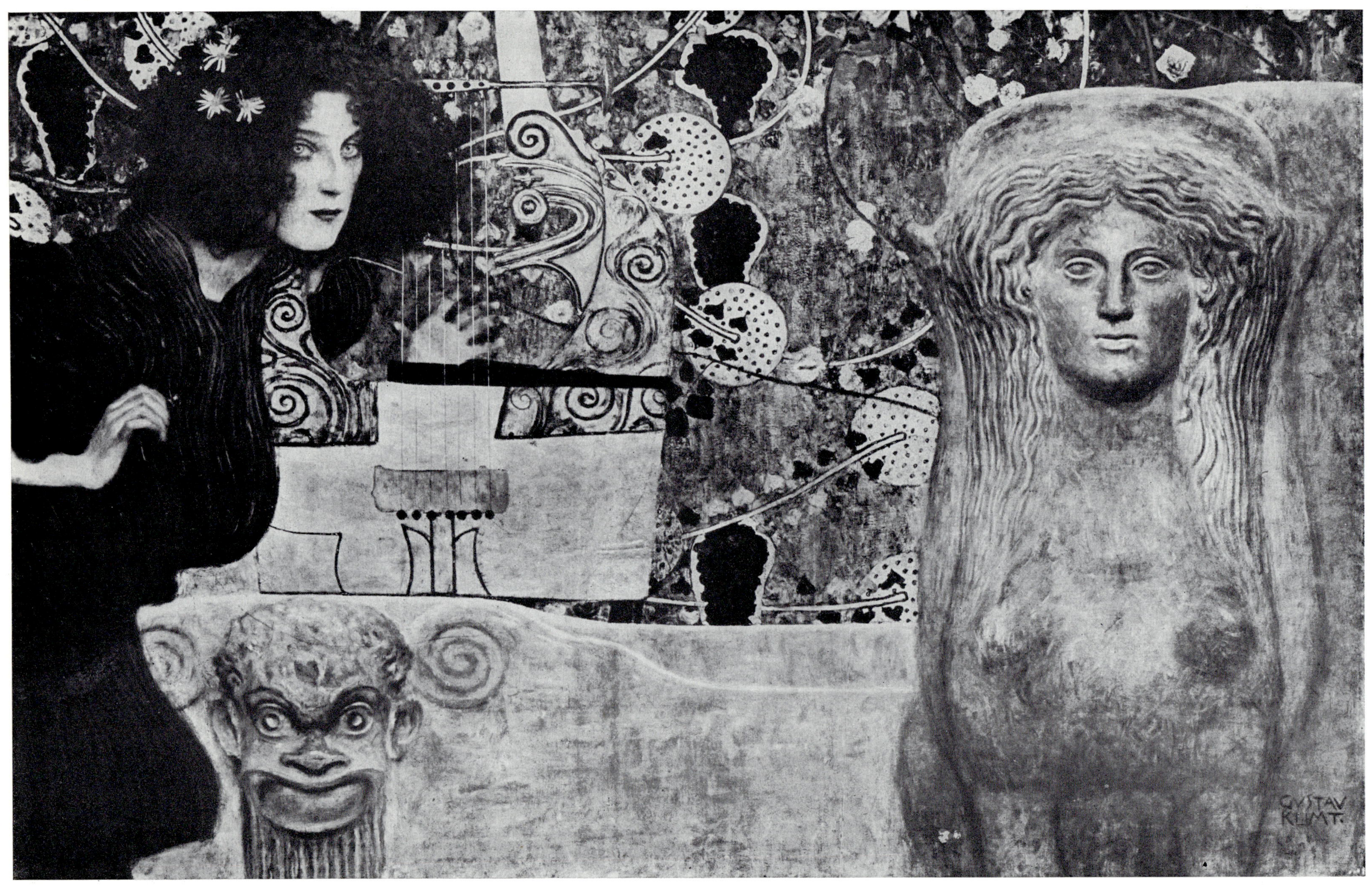

1 MUSIC II, 1898 (D. 89)

2 MUSIC I, 1895 (D. 69) ▸

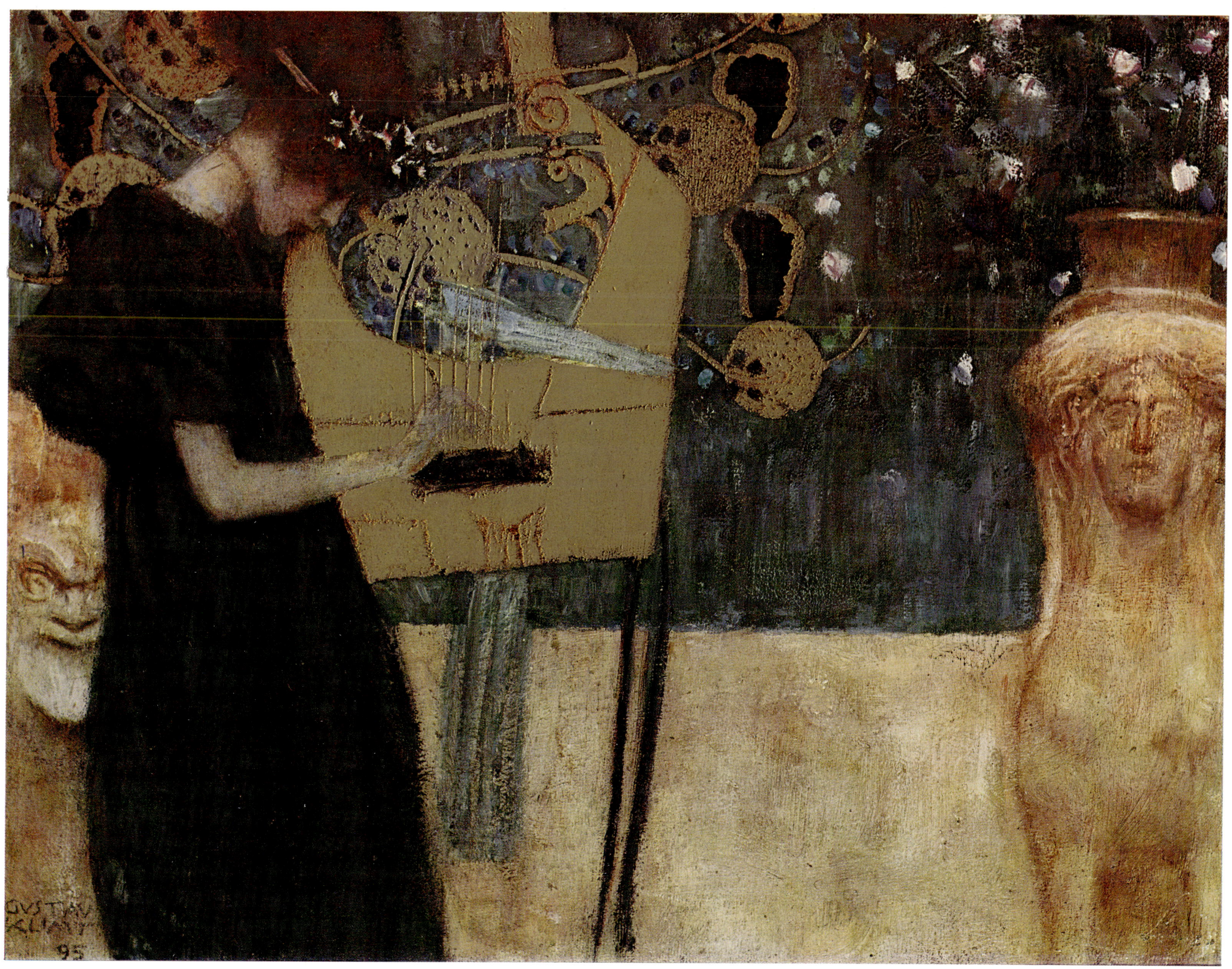

3 PORTRAIT OF SONJA KNIPS, 1898 (D. 91)

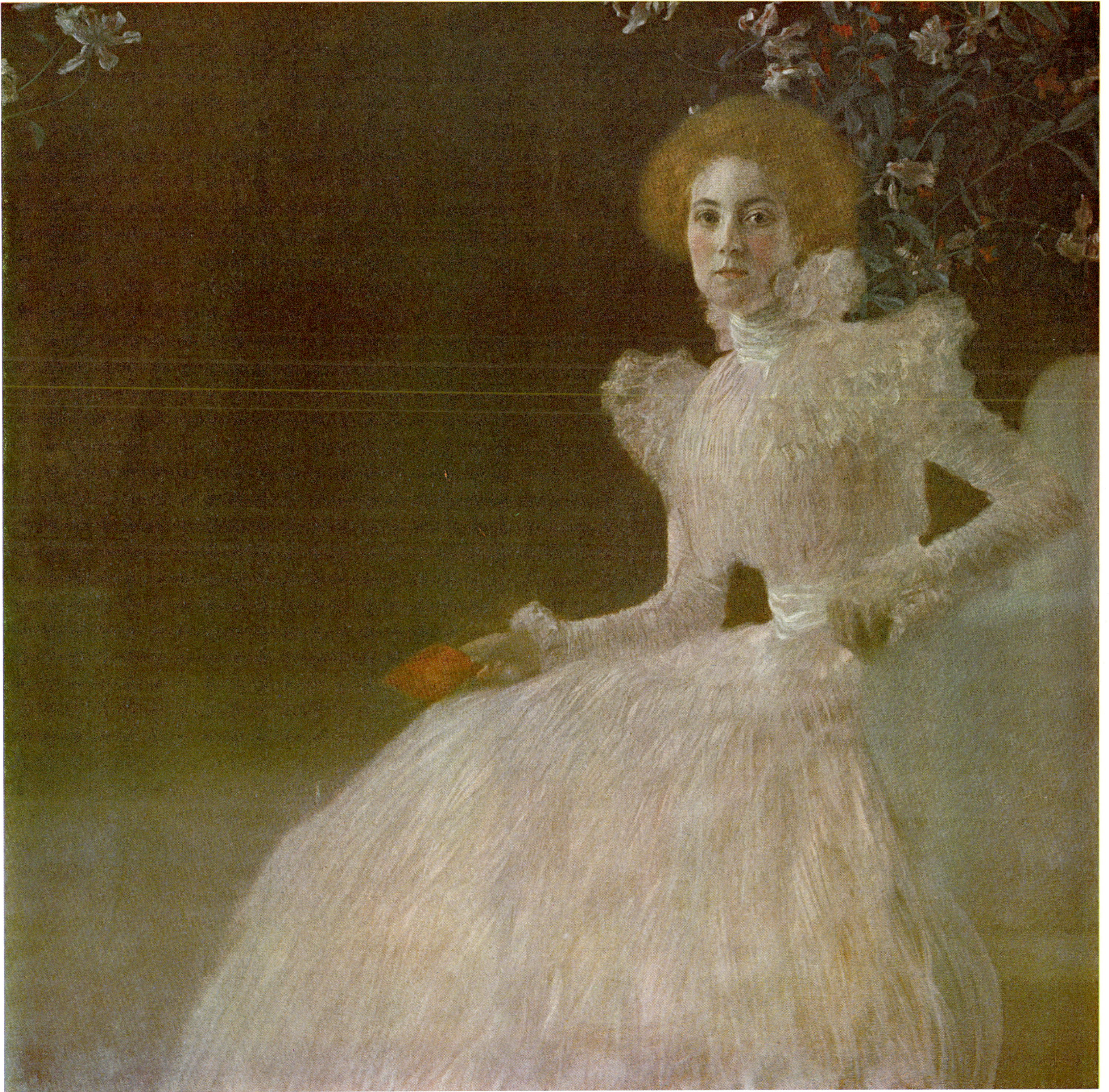

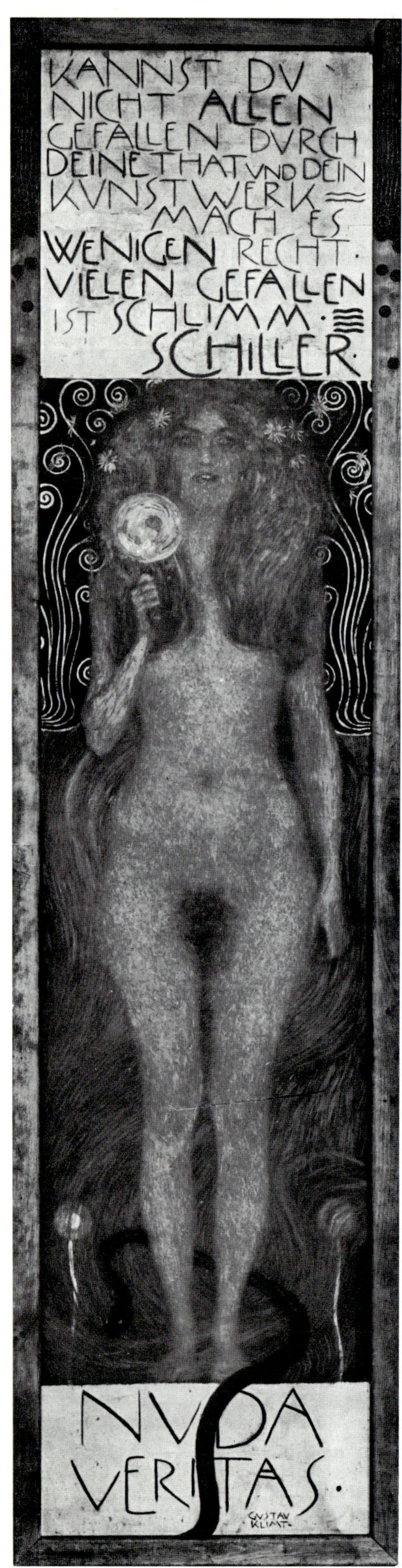

4 NUDA VERITAS, 1899 (D. 102)

5 PALLAS ATHENE, 1898 (D. 93) ▸

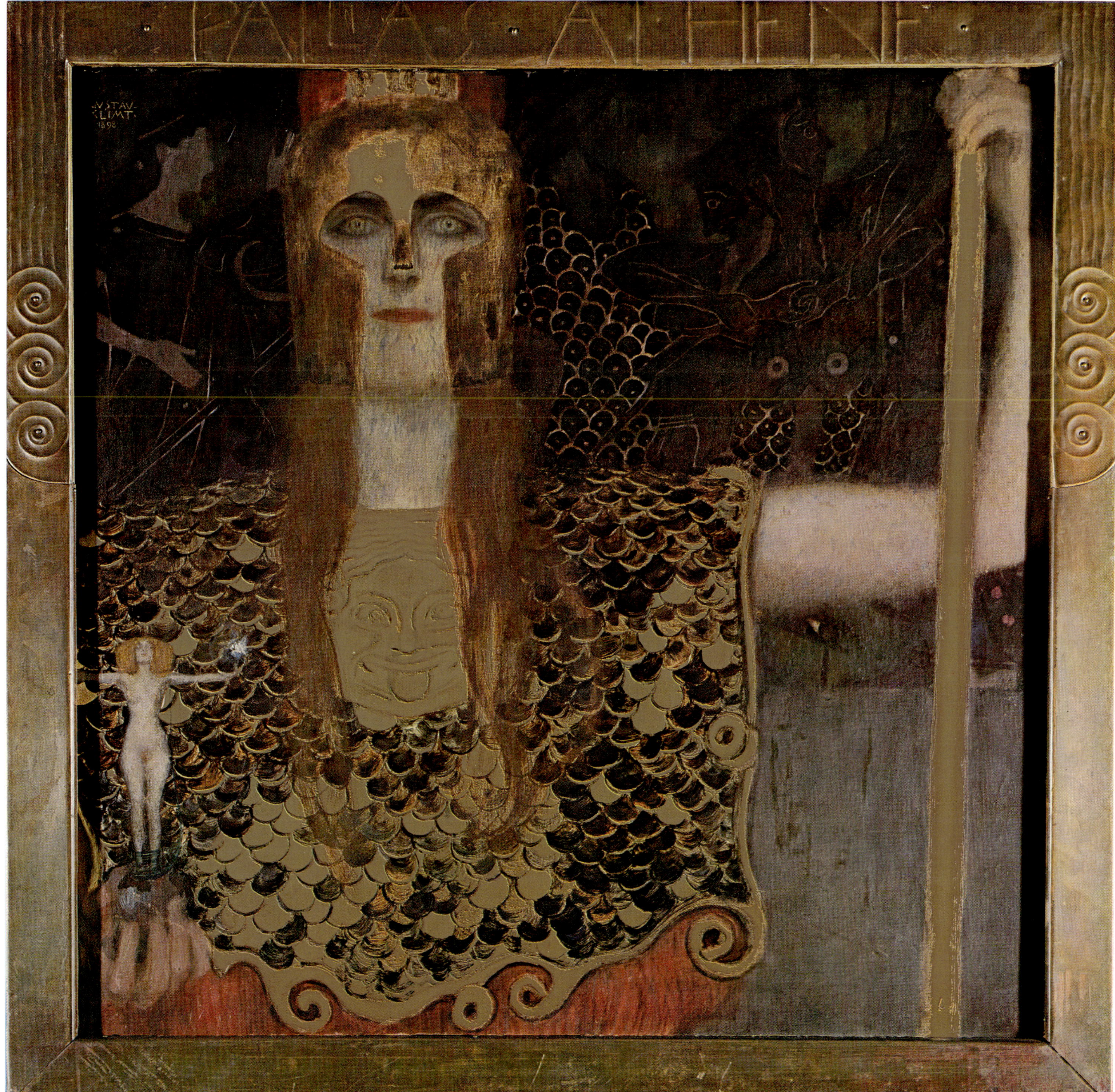
PALLAS ATHENE

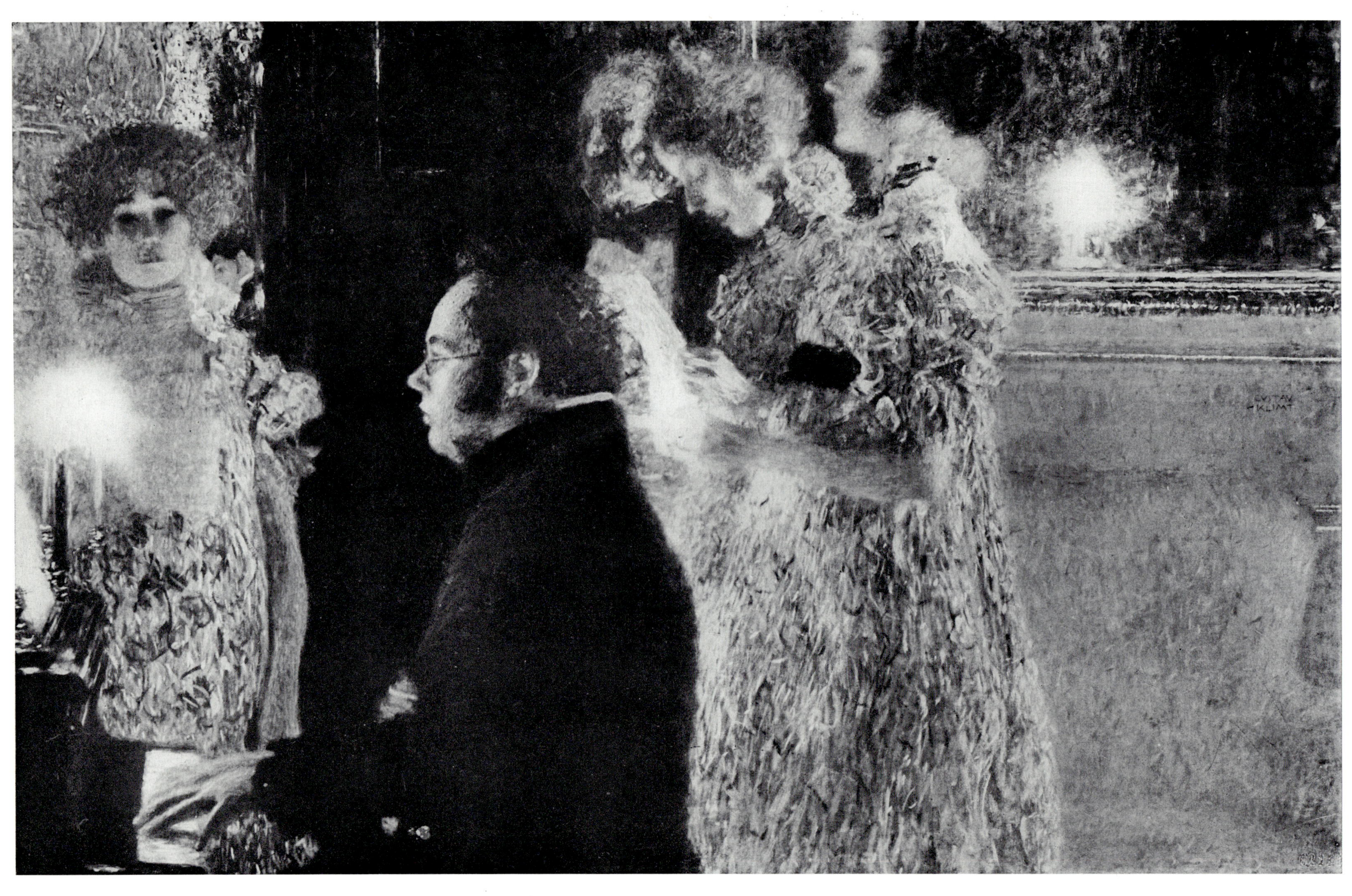

6 SCHUBERT AT THE PIANO, 1899 (D. 101)

7 SCHUBERT AT THE PIANO, study, 1898 — 99 (D. 100) ▸

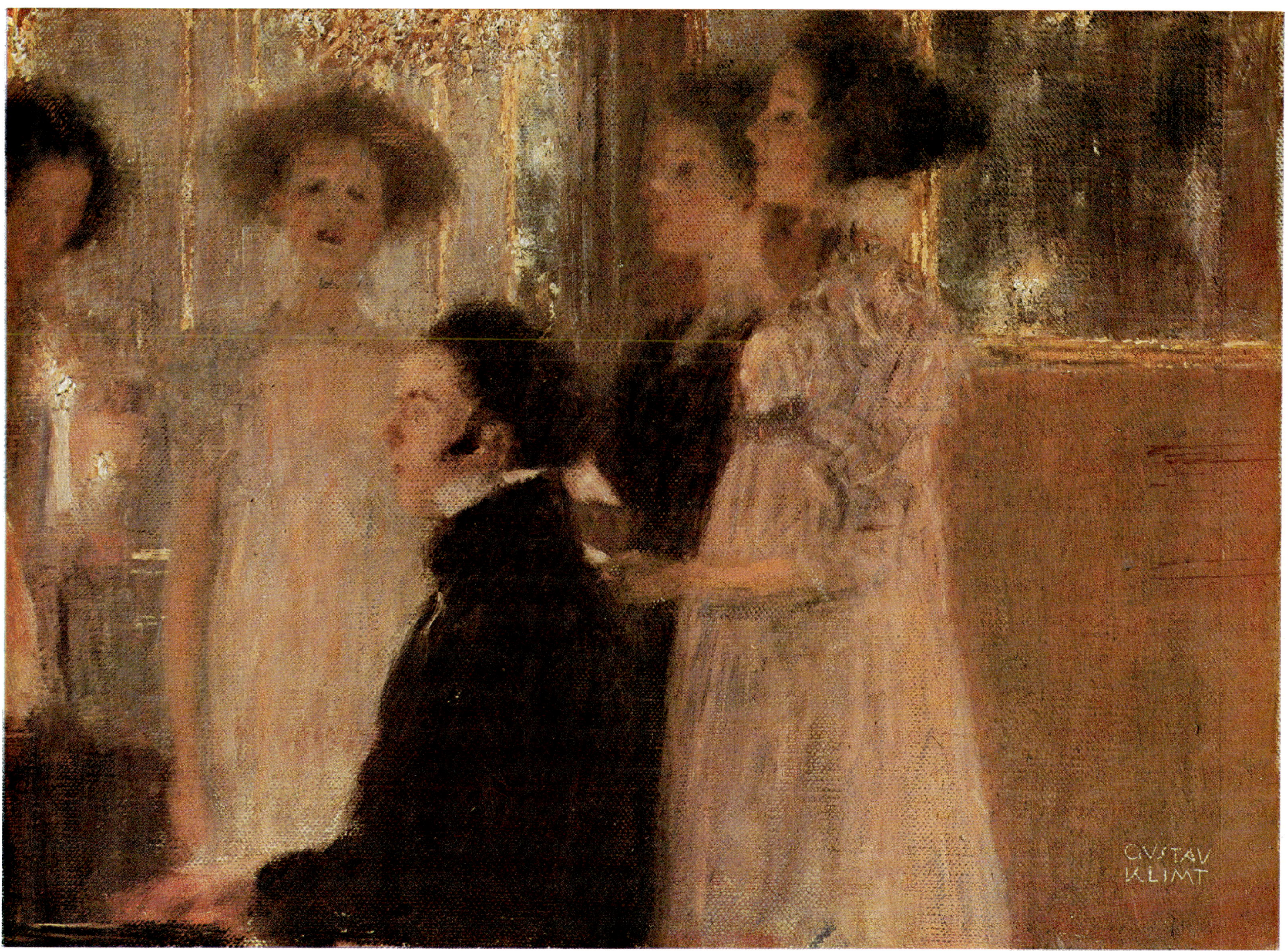
GUSTAV
KLIMT

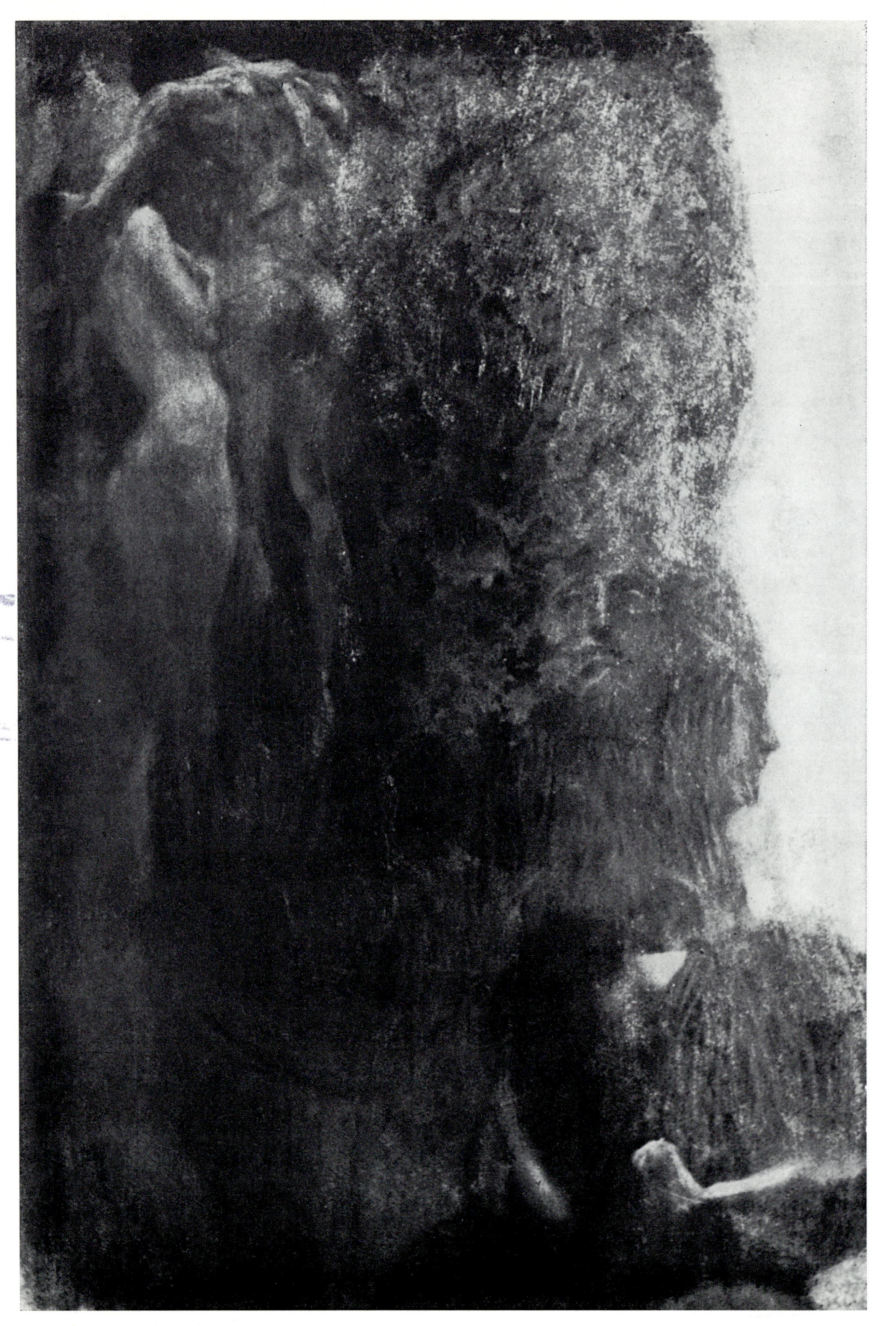

8 PHILOSOPHY, composition study, 1897 – 98 (D. 87)

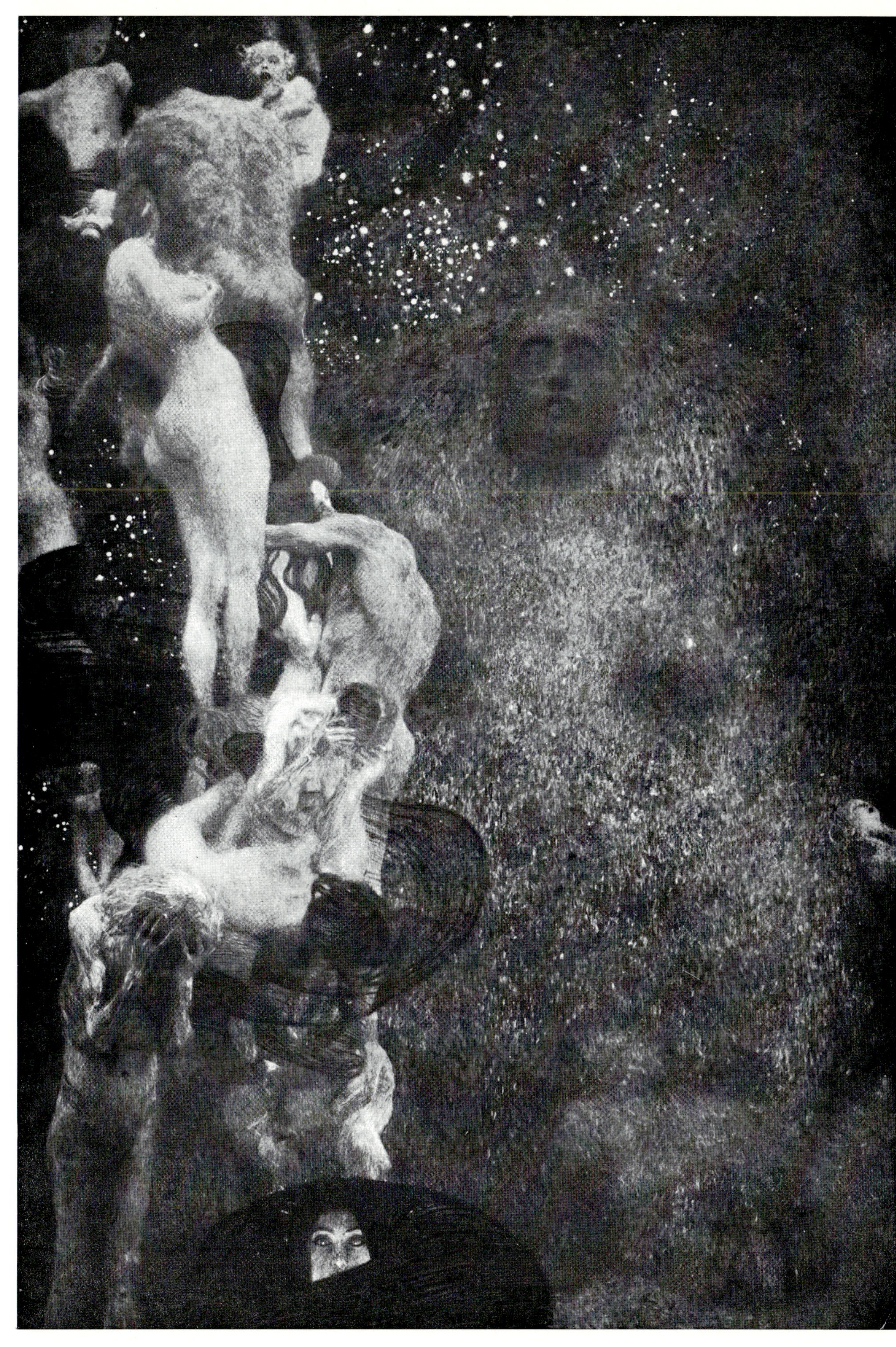

9 PHILOSOPHY, 1899 — 1907 (D. 105)

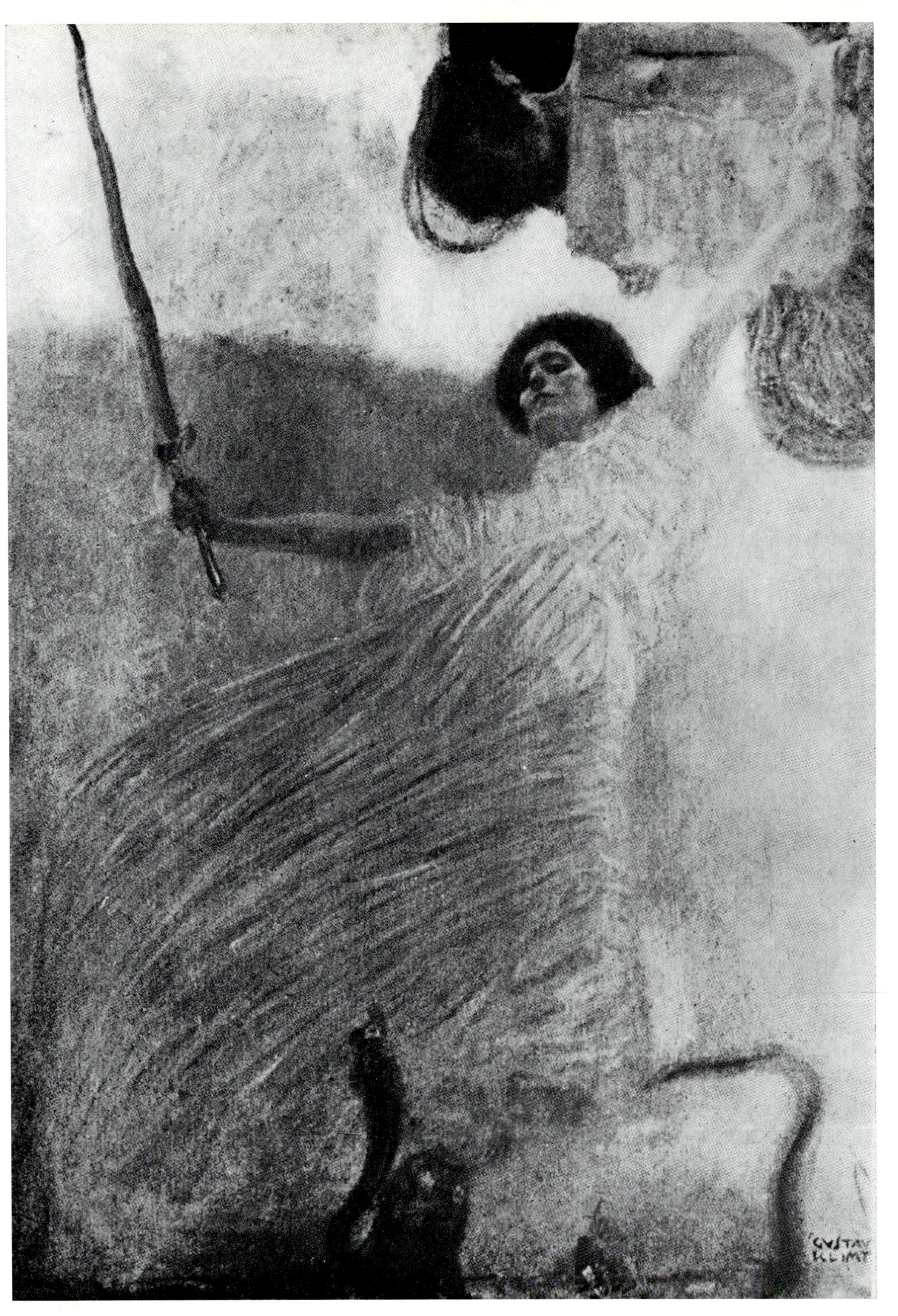

10 JURISPRUDENCE, composition study, c. 1897 — 98 (D. 86)

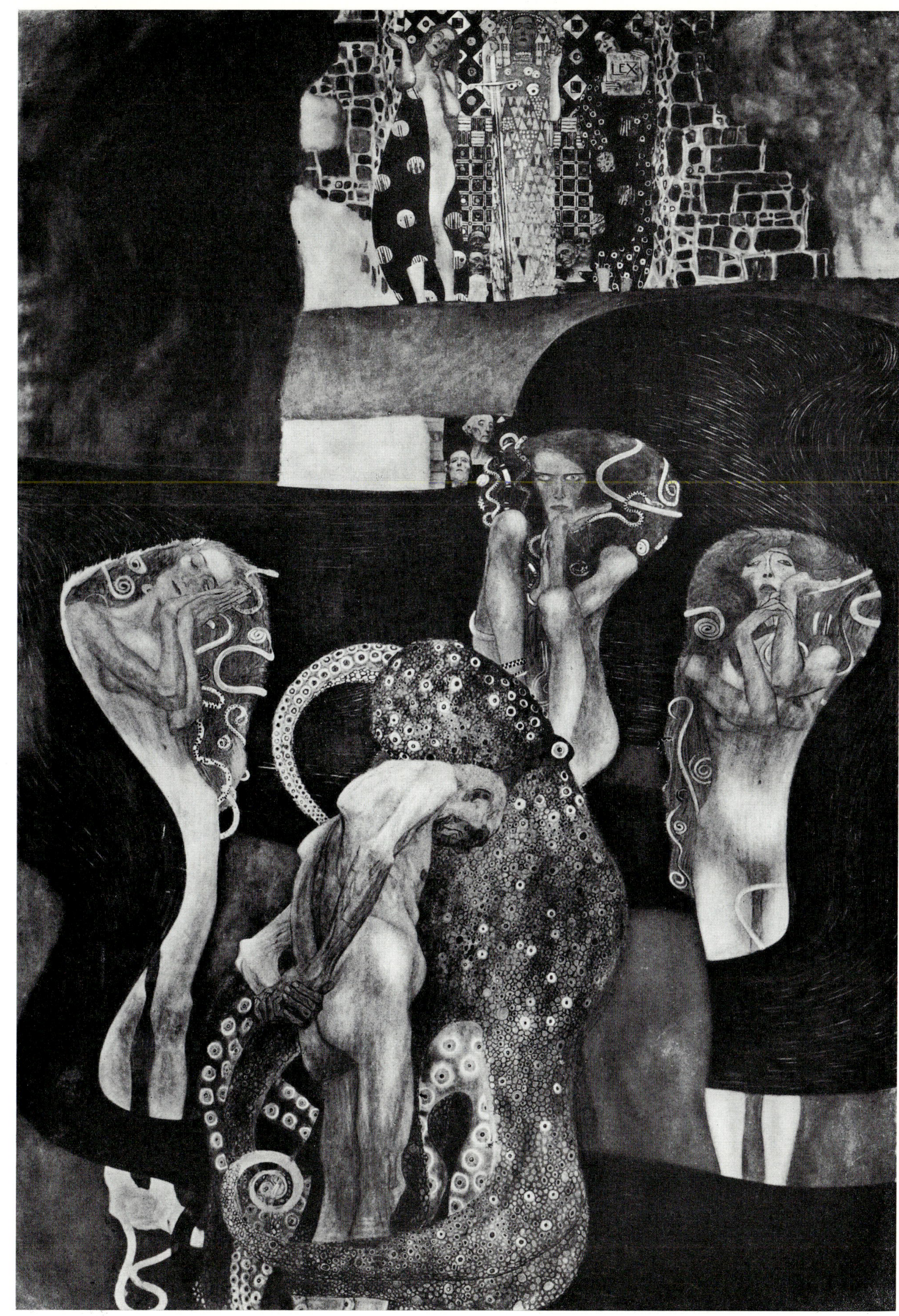

11 JURISPRUDENCE,
1903 — 07 (D. 128)

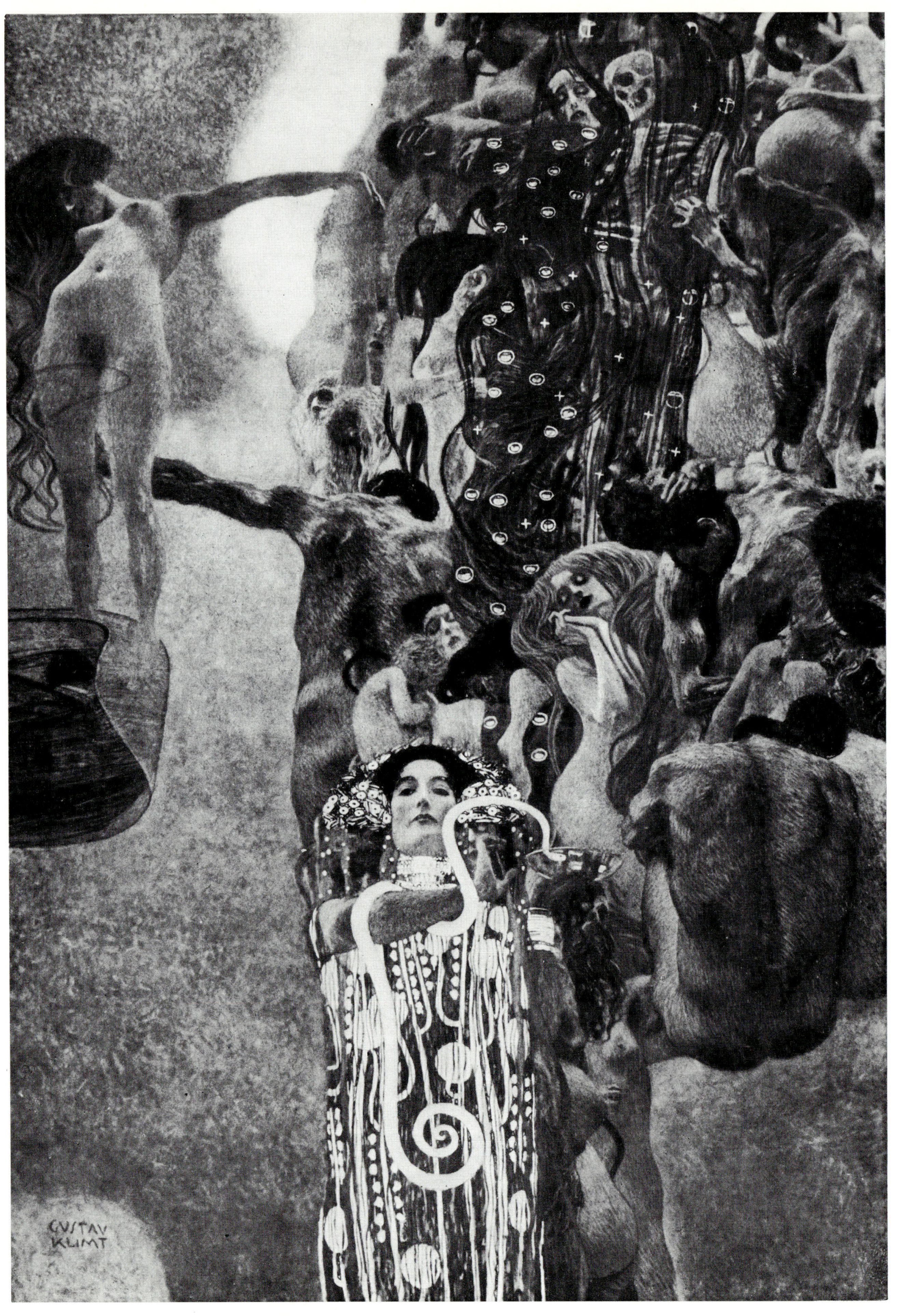

12 MEDICINE, 1900 — 07 (D. 112)

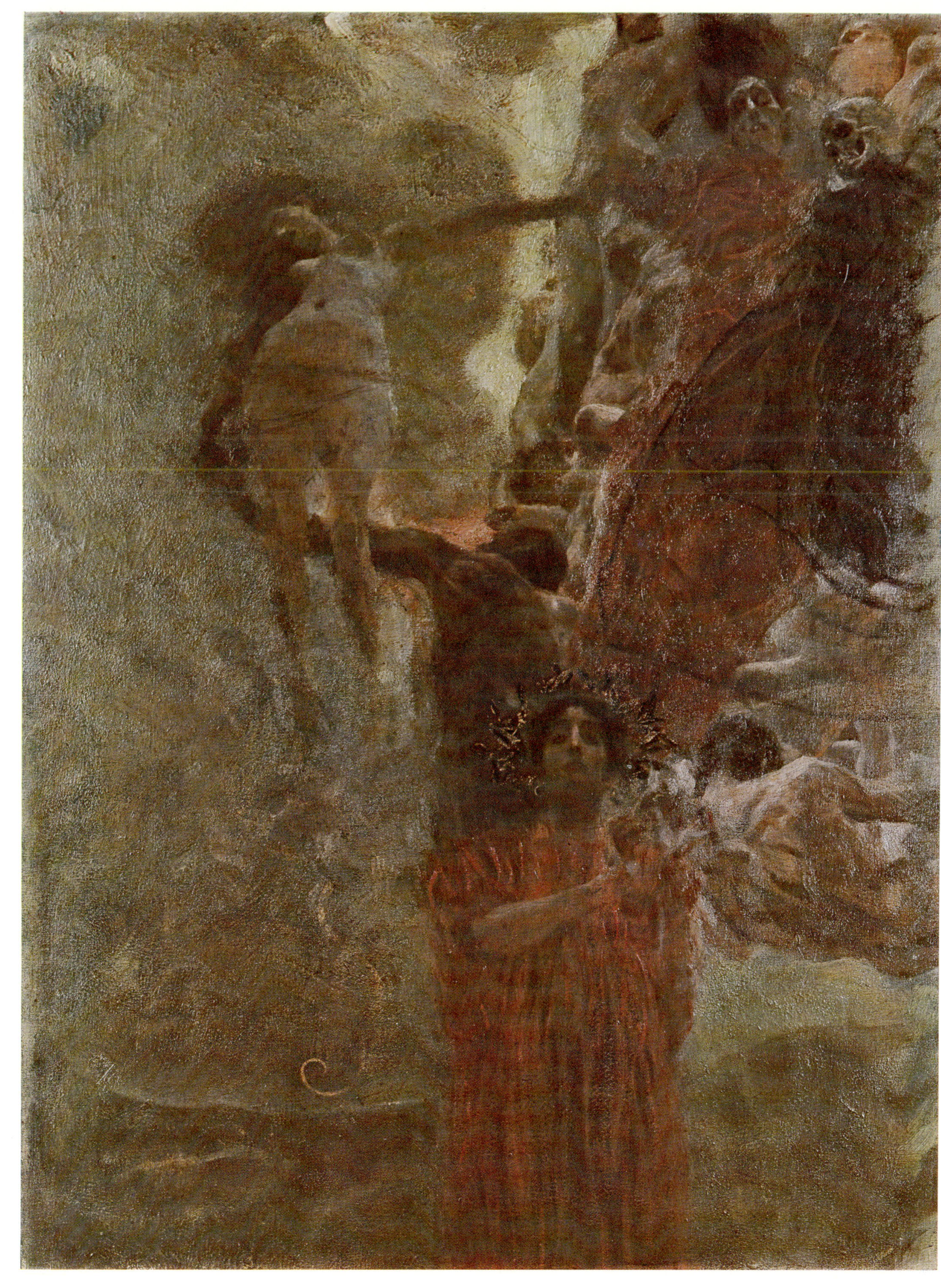

13 MEDICINE, composition study, 1897 — 98 (D. 88)

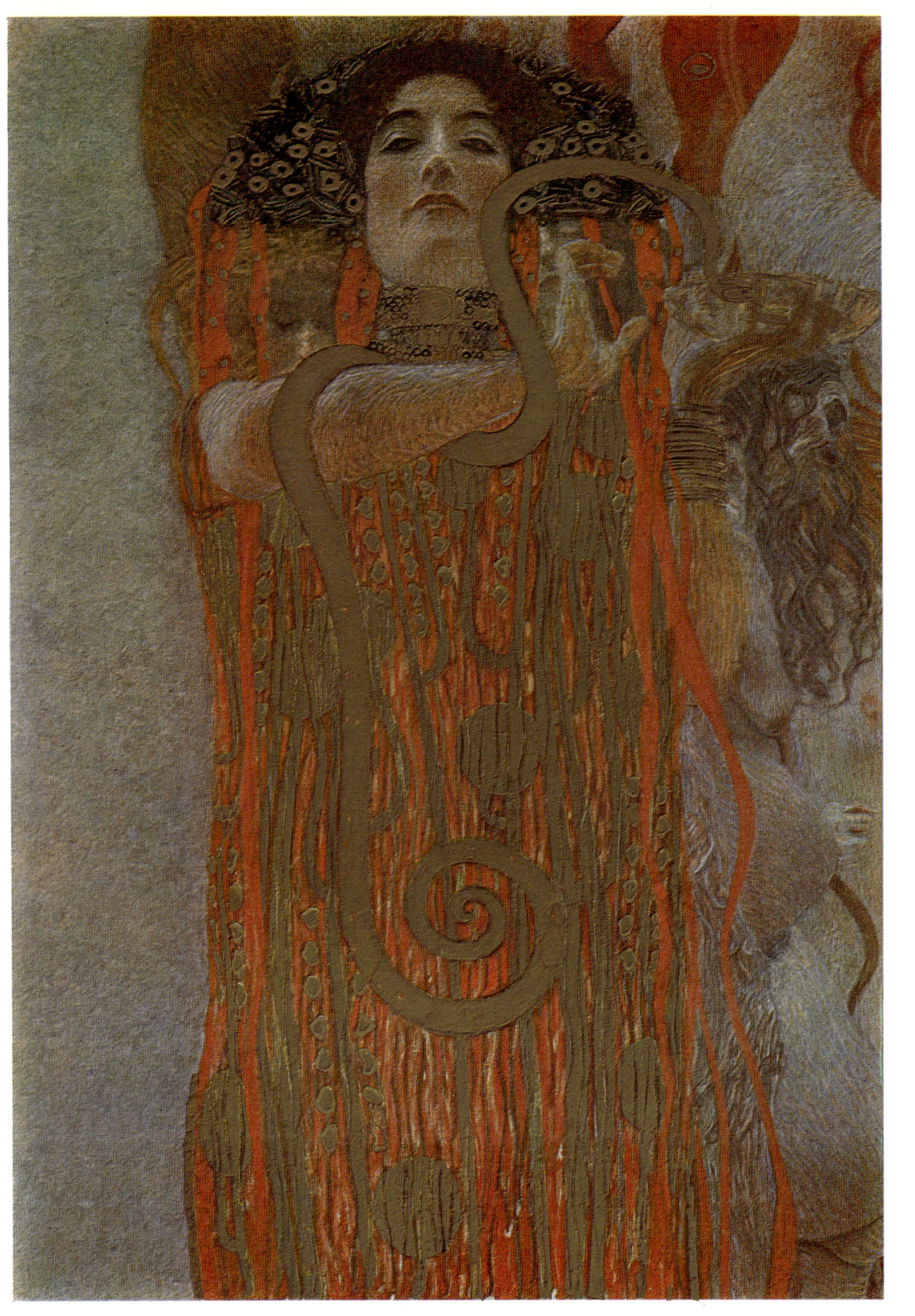

14 HYGIEIA, detail from medicine, 1900 – 07 (D. 112)

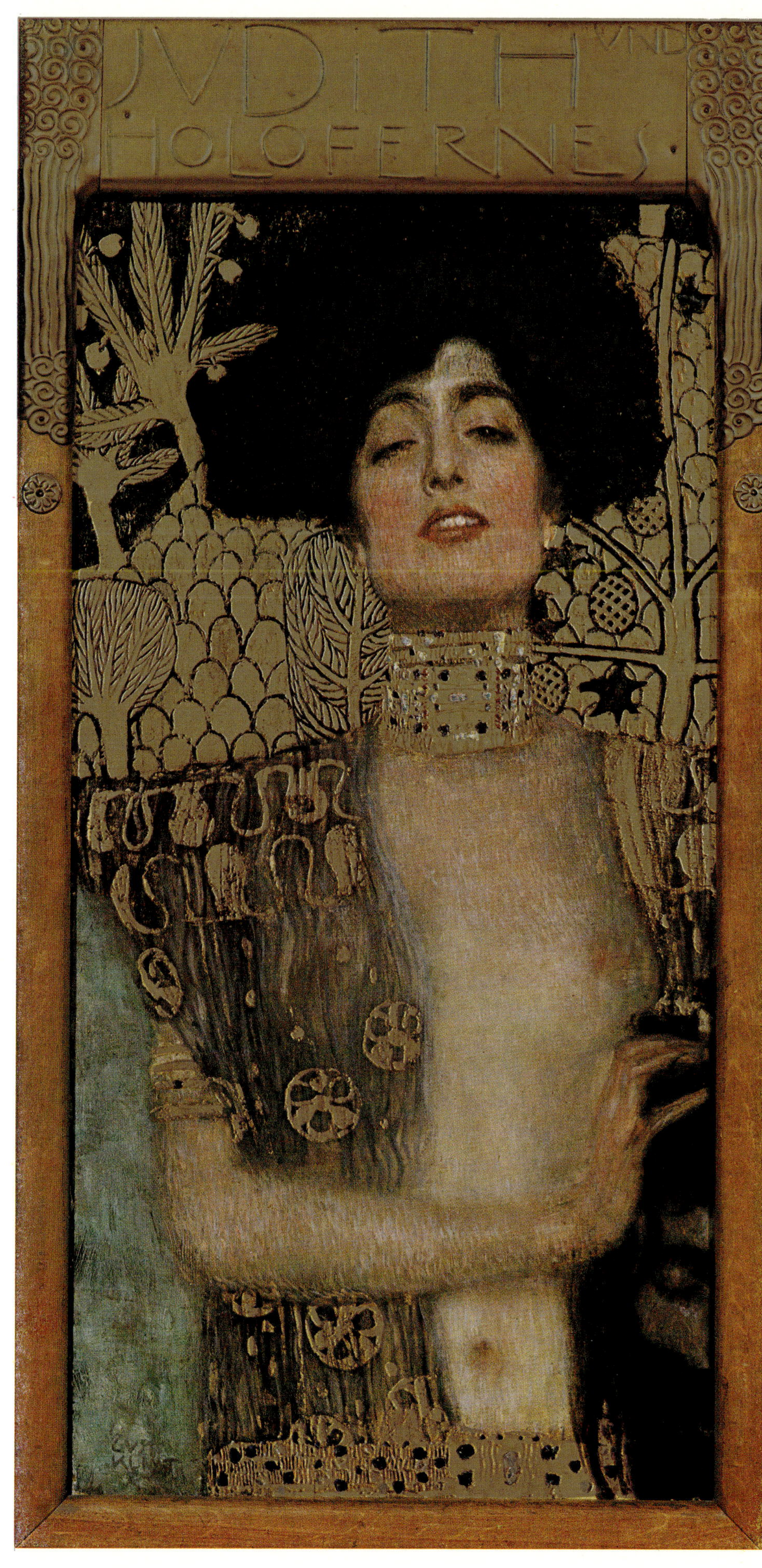

15 JUDITH I, 1901 (D. 113)

16 FARMHOUSE WITH BIRCH TREES, 1900 (D. 110)

following pages:

17 THE SWAMP, 1900 (D. 109)

18 PINE FOREST I, 1901 (D. 120)

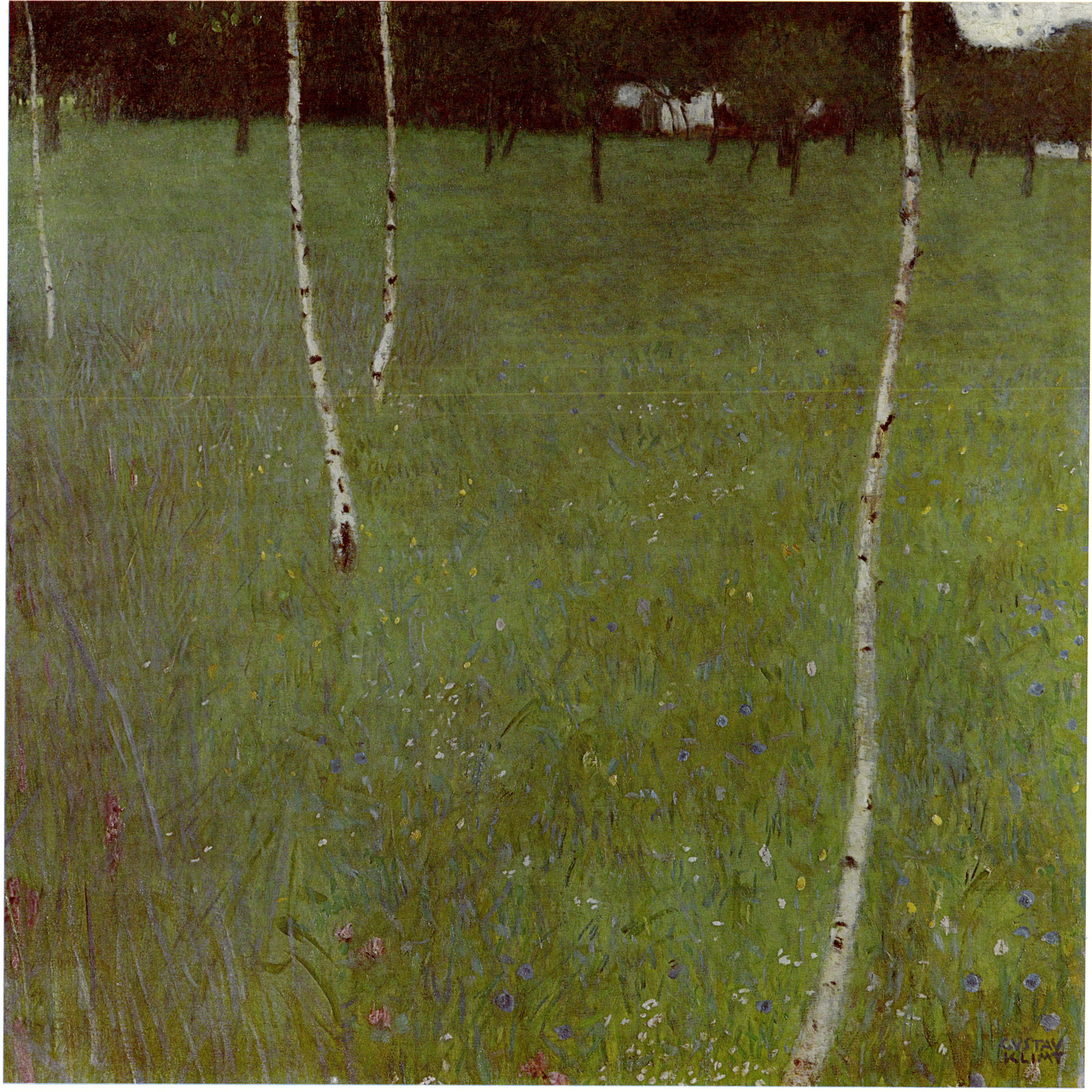
GUSTAV
KLIMT

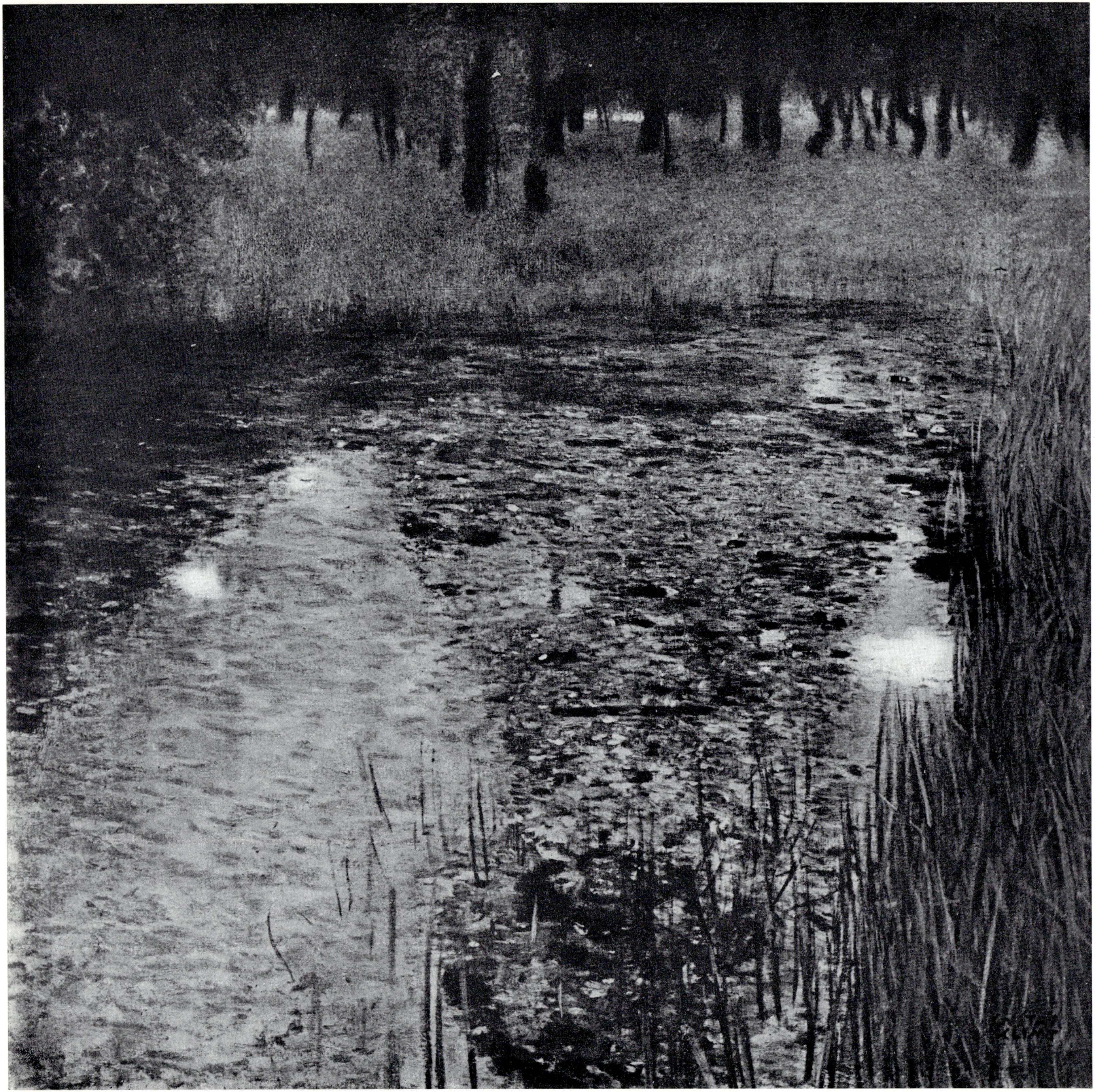

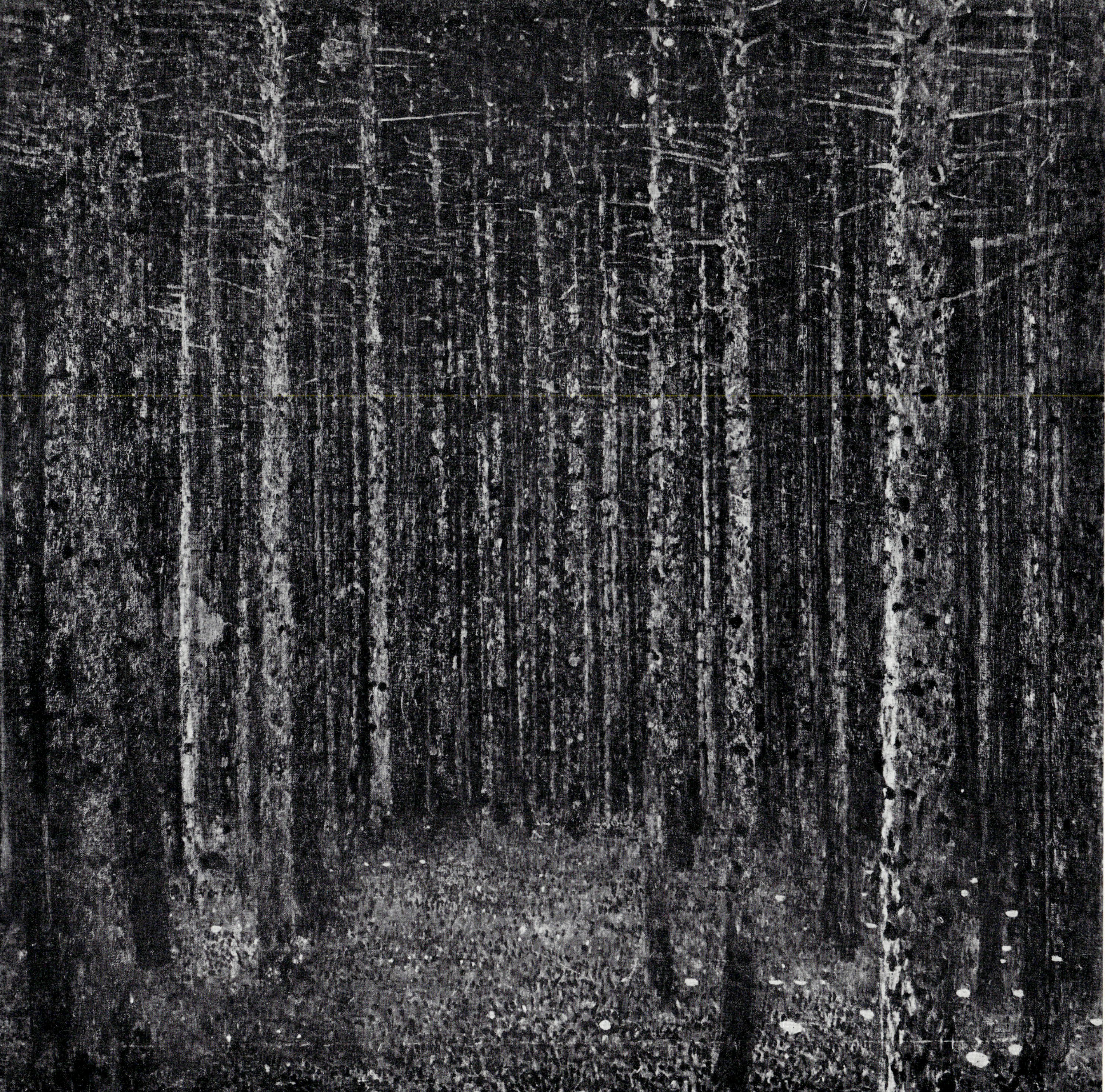

19 BEECH FOREST I, c. 1902 (D. 122)

following pages:

20 ATTERSEE I, c. 1900 (D. 116)

21 TALL POPLARS I, 1900 (D. 111)

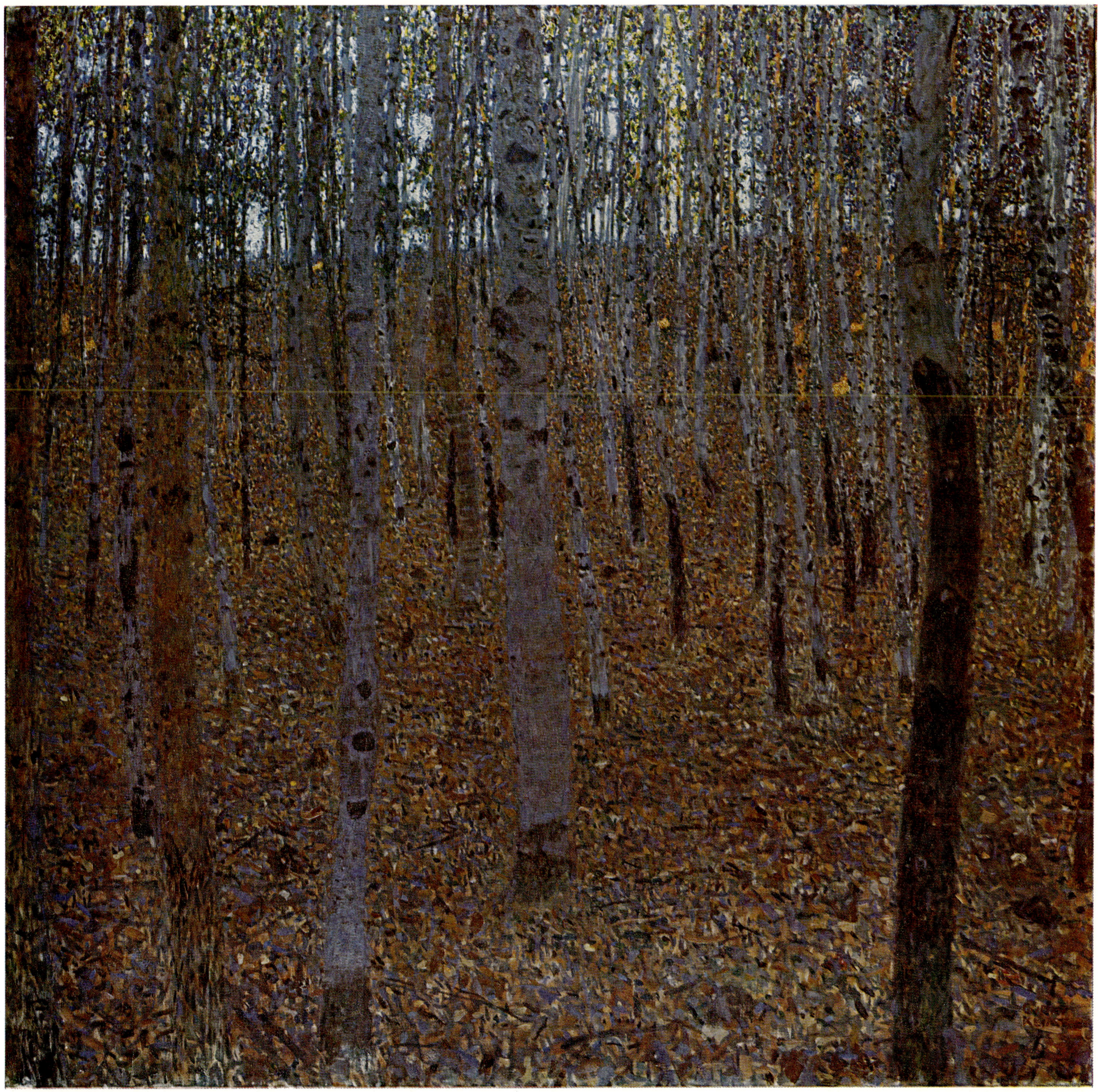

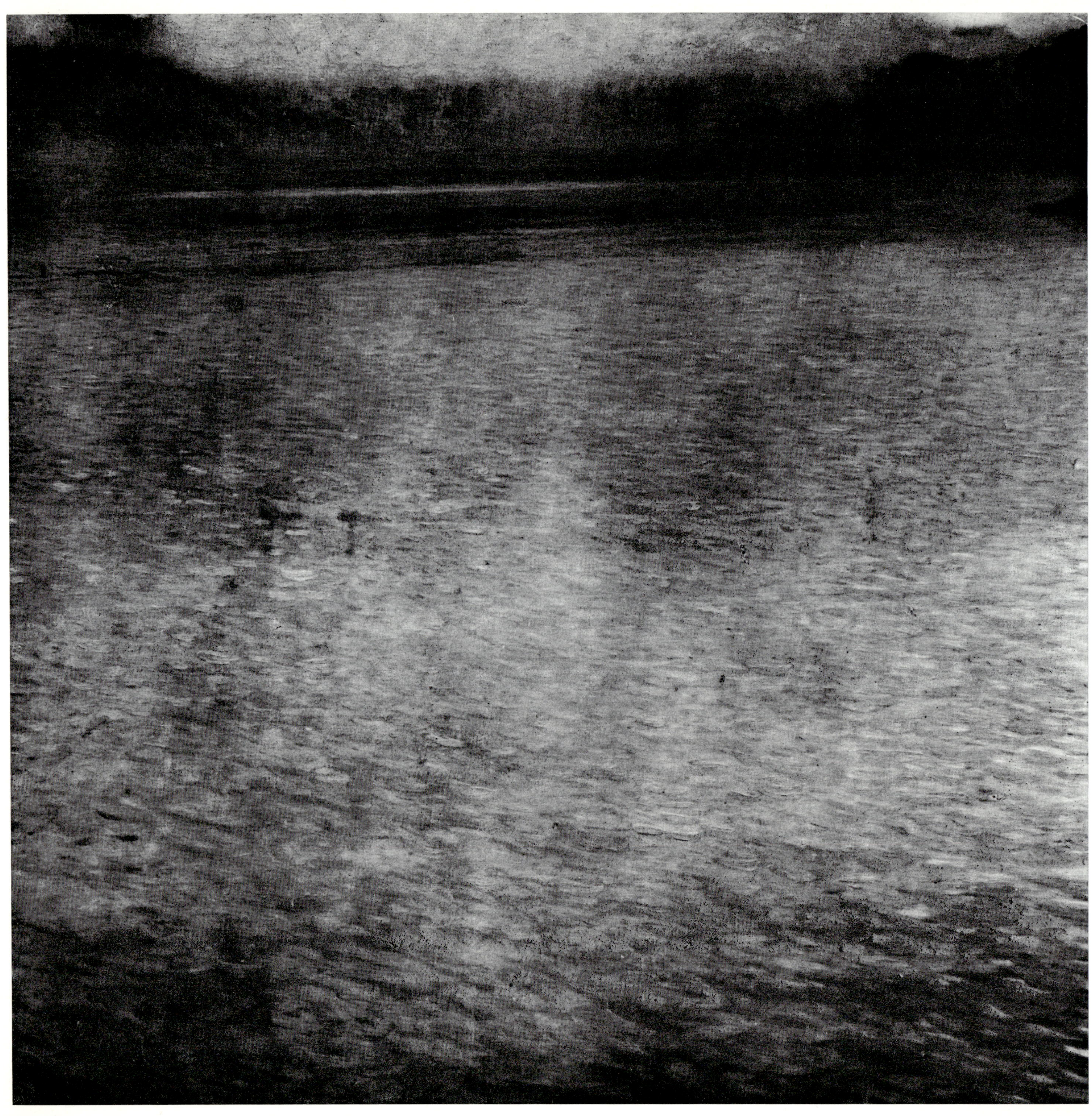

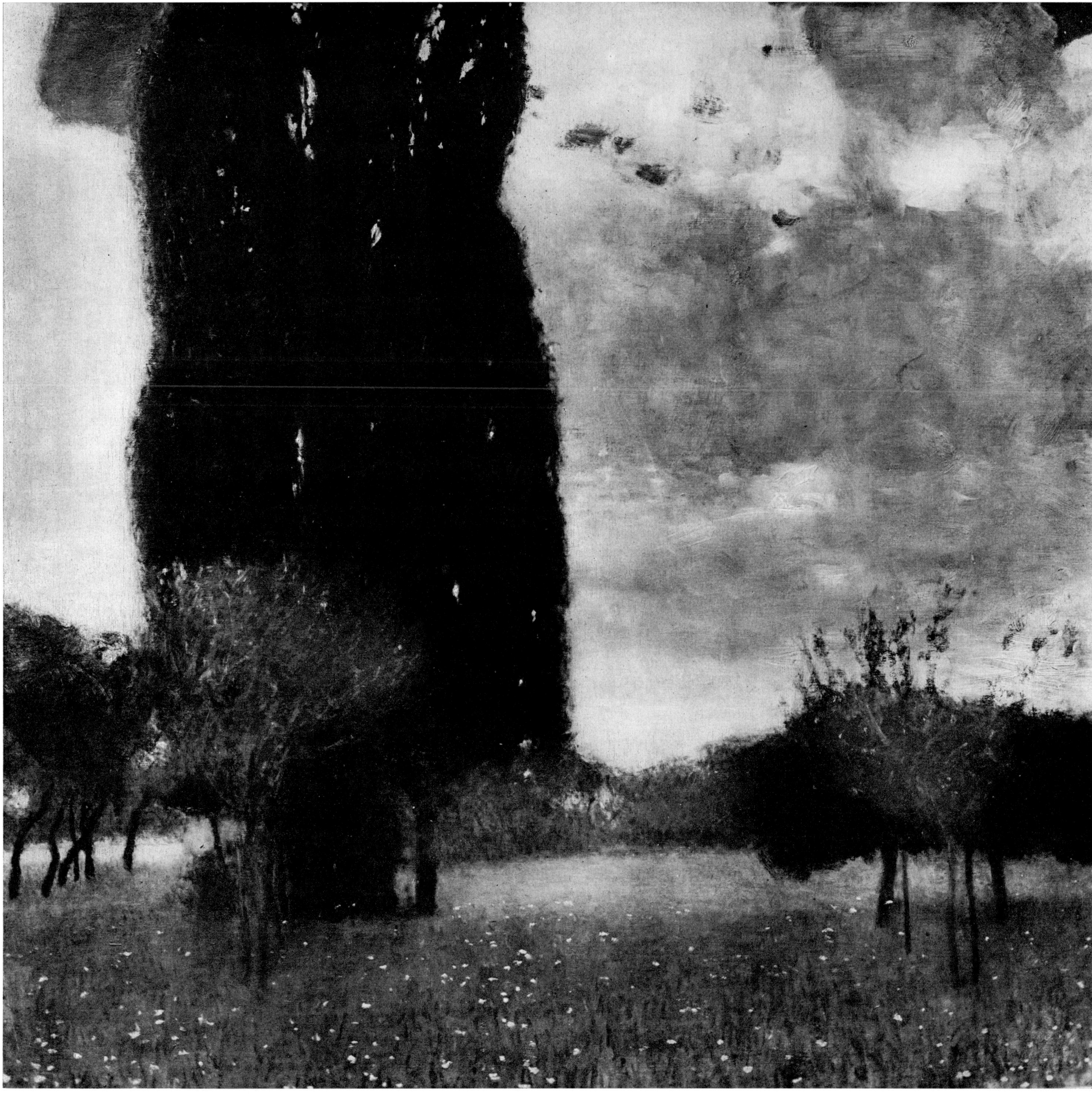

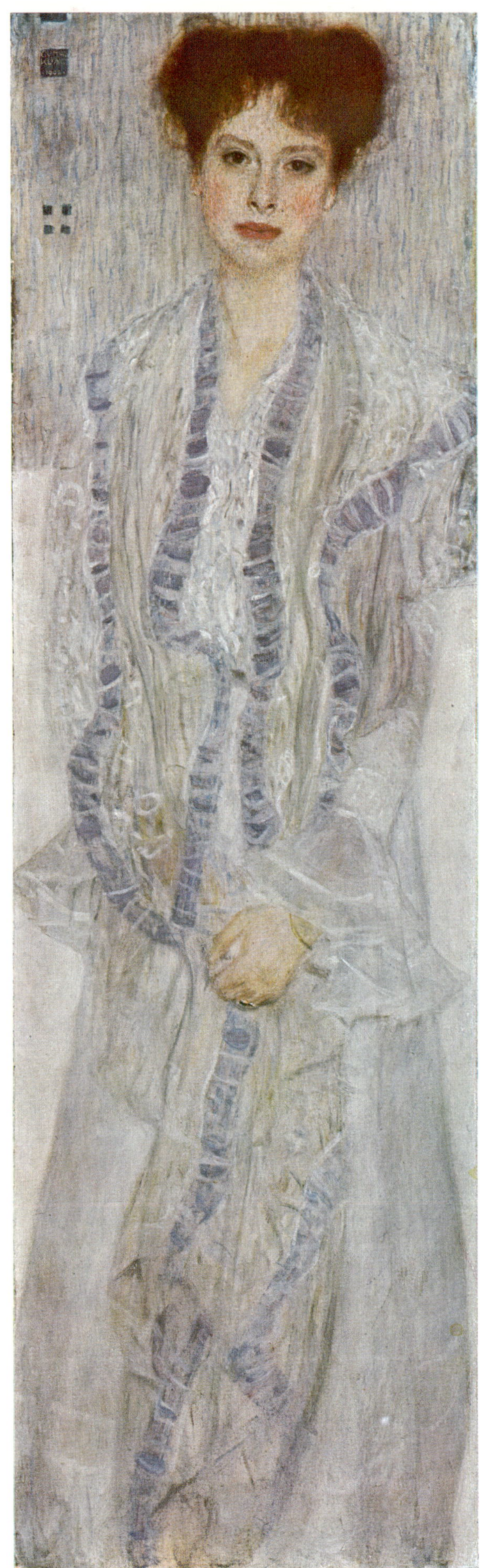

22 PORTRAIT OF GERTHA FELSÖVANYI, 1902 (D. 125)

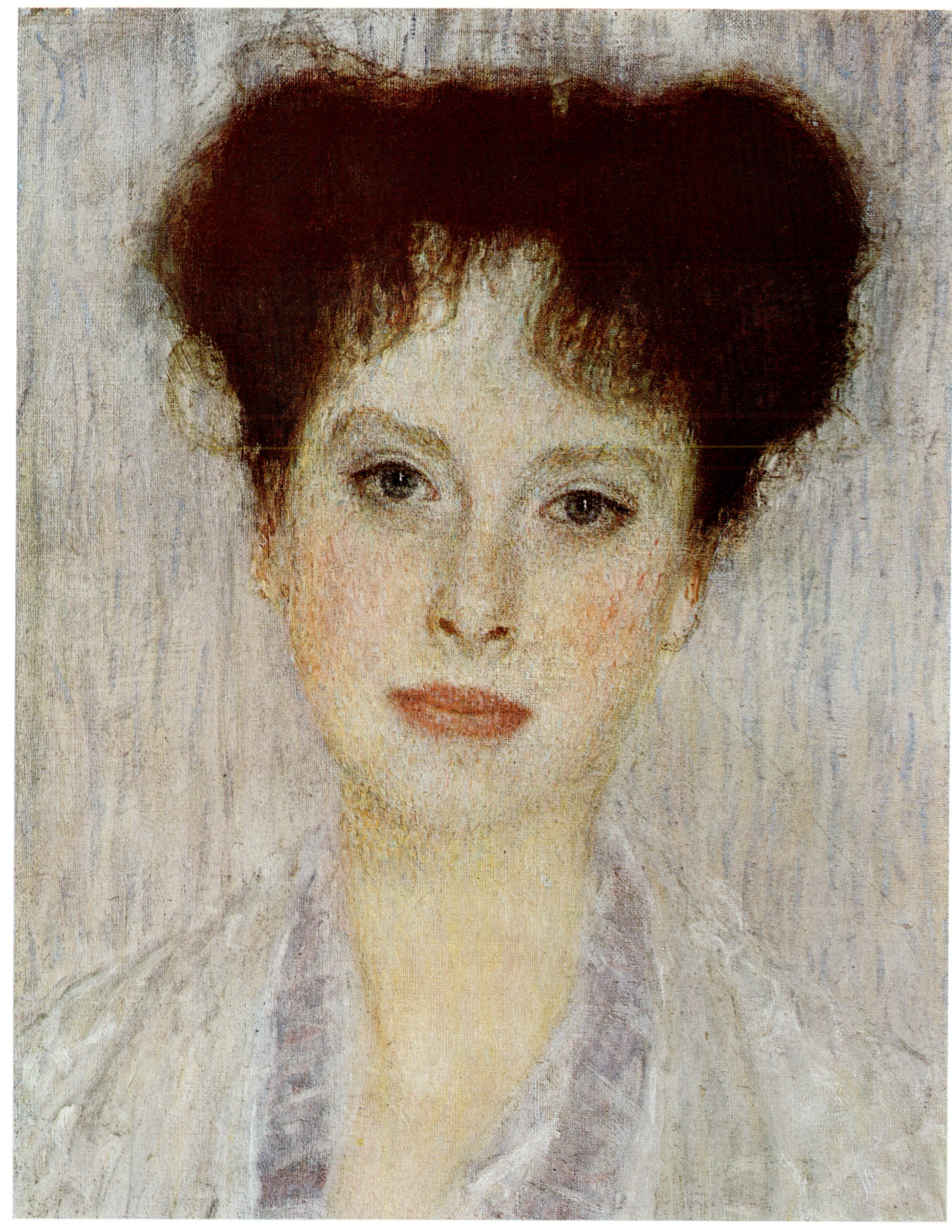

23 DETAIL

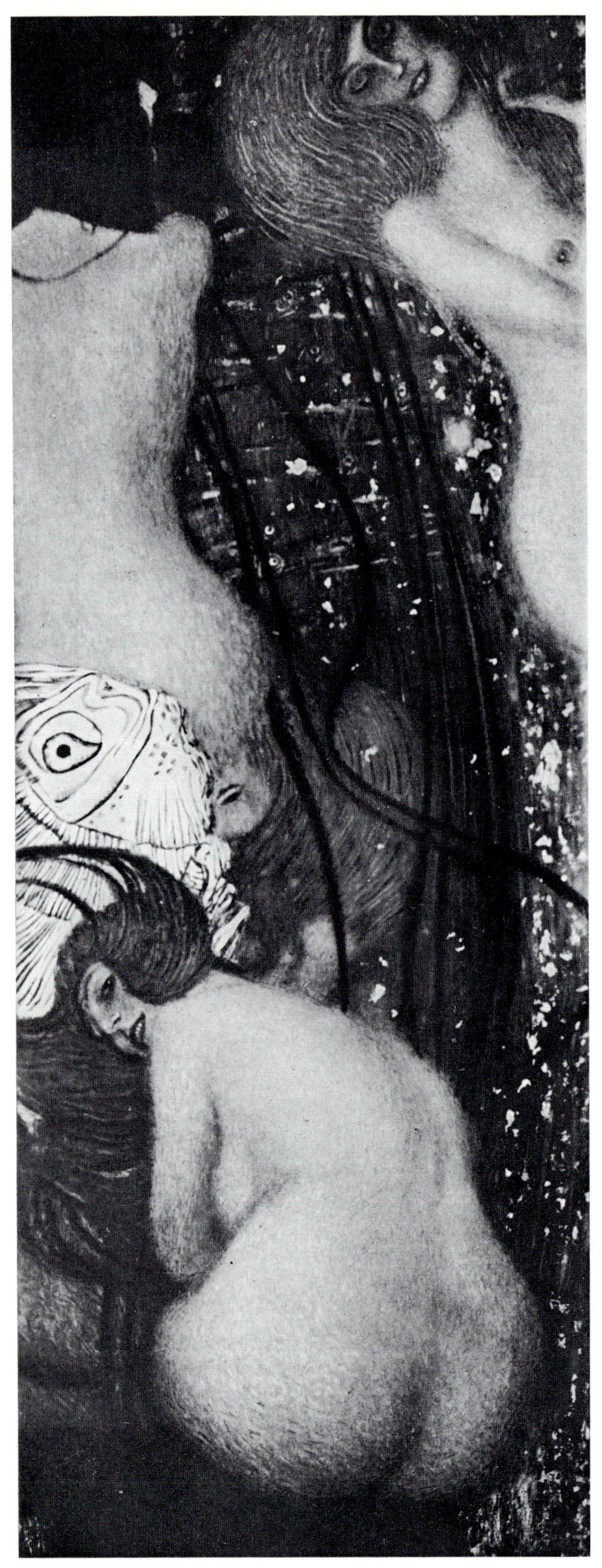

24 GOLDFISH, 1901 – 02 (D. 124)

25 PROCESSION OF THE DEAD, 1903 (D. 131)

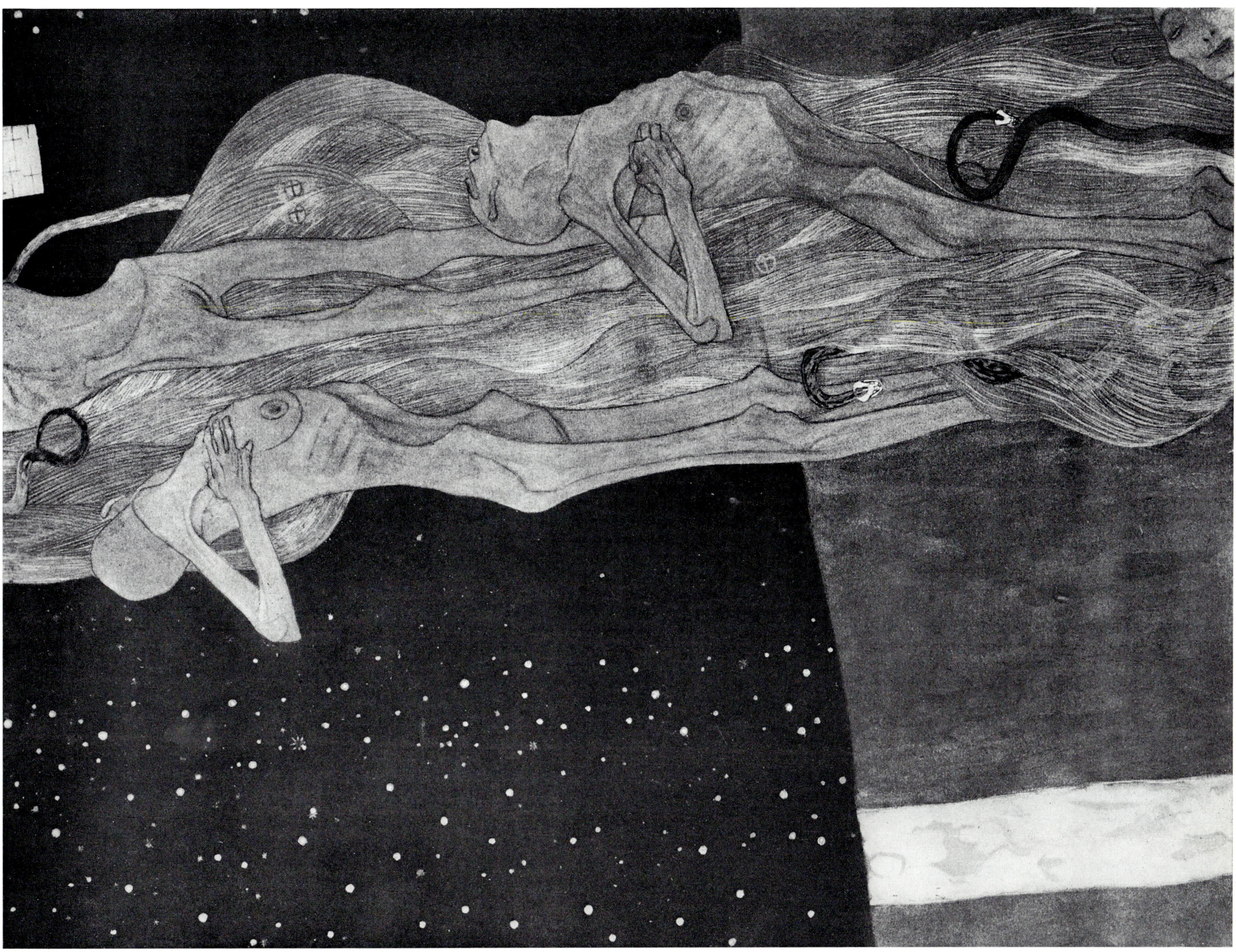

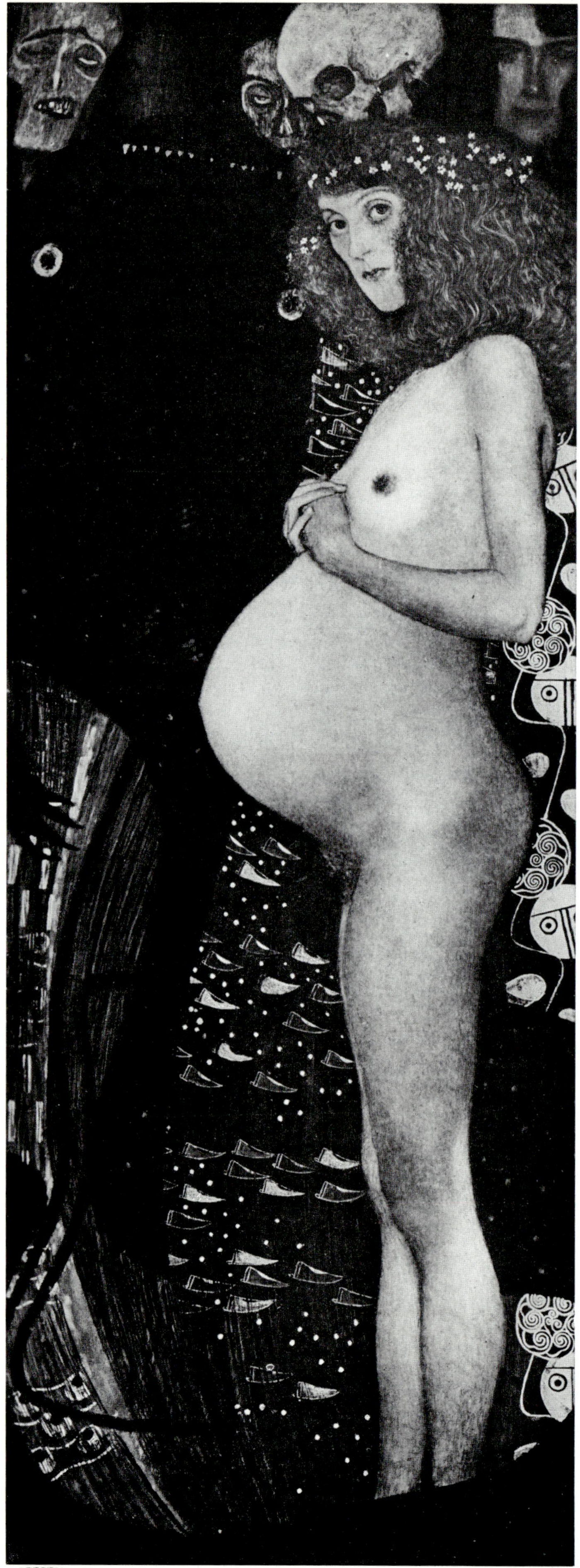

26 HOPE I, 1903 (D. 129)

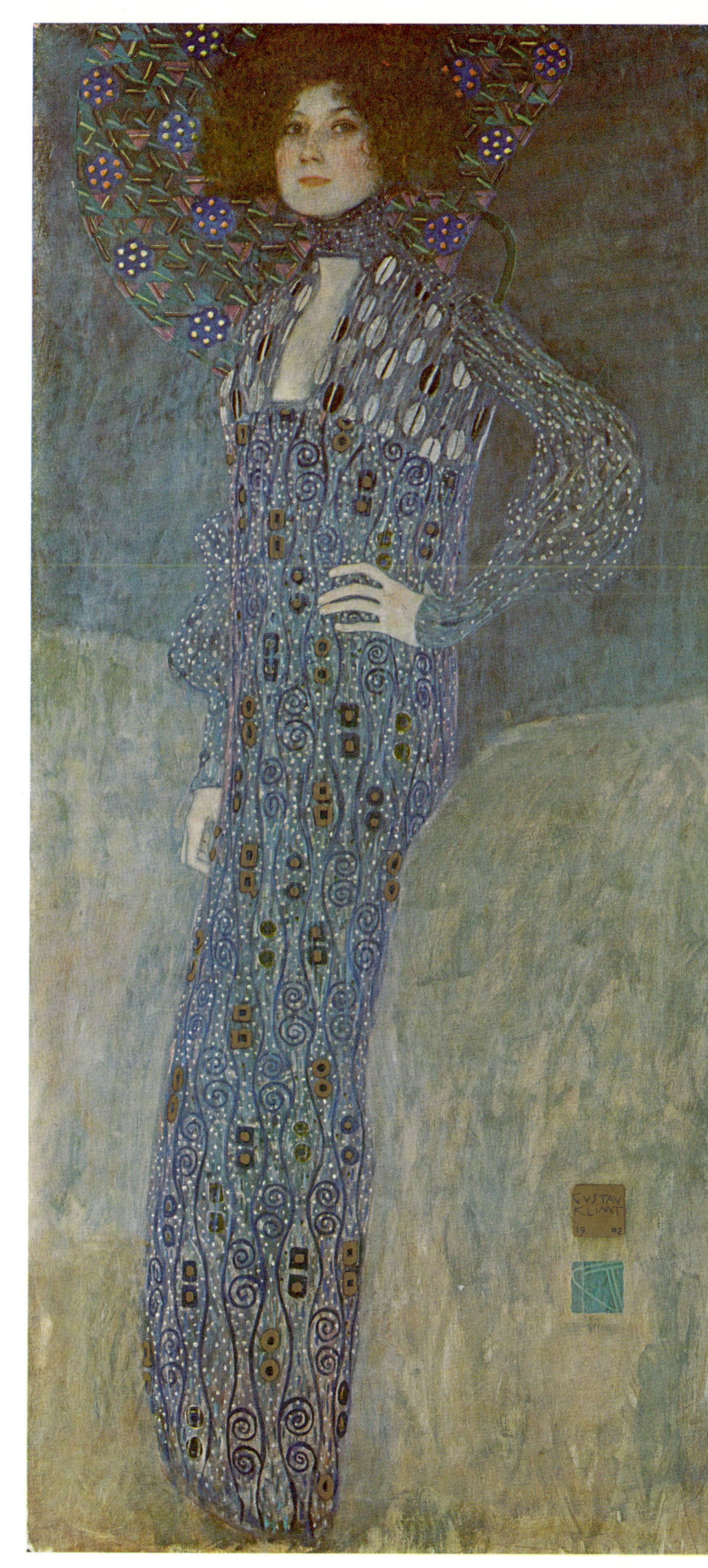

27 PORTRAIT OF EMILIE FLÖGE, 1902 (D. 126)

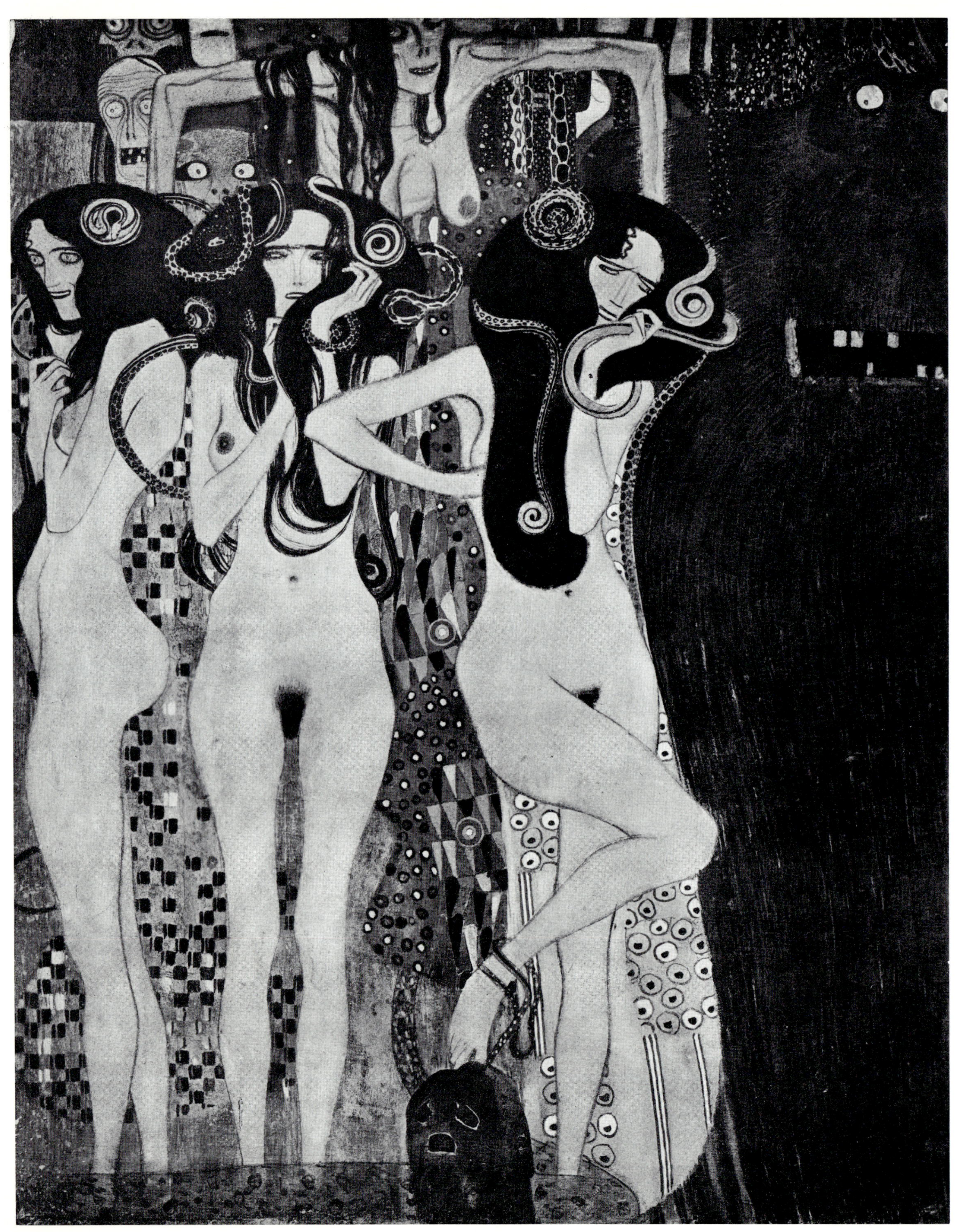

28/29
DETAILS FROM THE BEETHOVEN FRIEZE, 1902 (D. 127)

left: wall 2, THE HOSTILE POWERS
right: wall 3, JOY

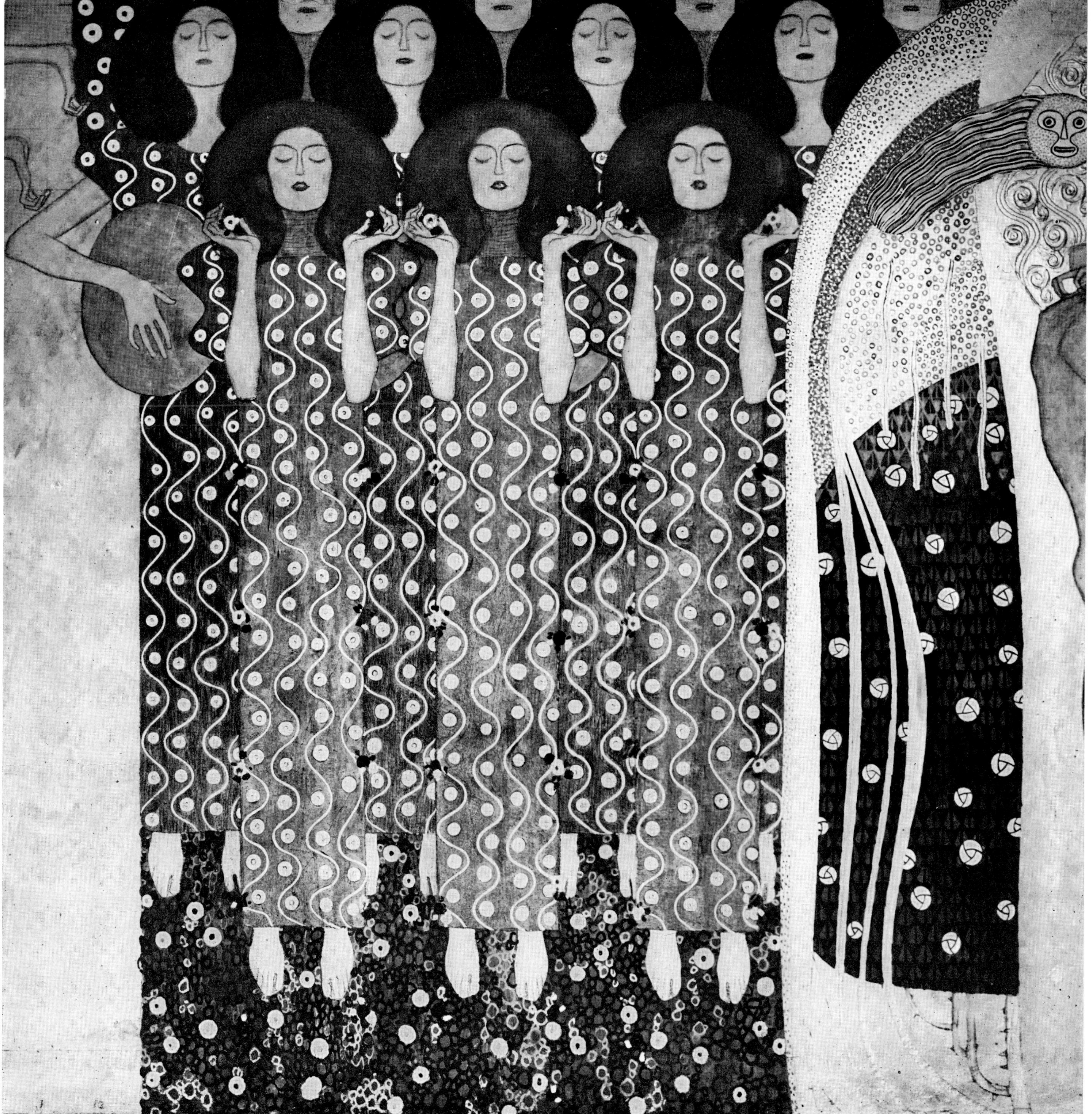

30 THREE AGES OF WOMAN, 1905 (D. 141)

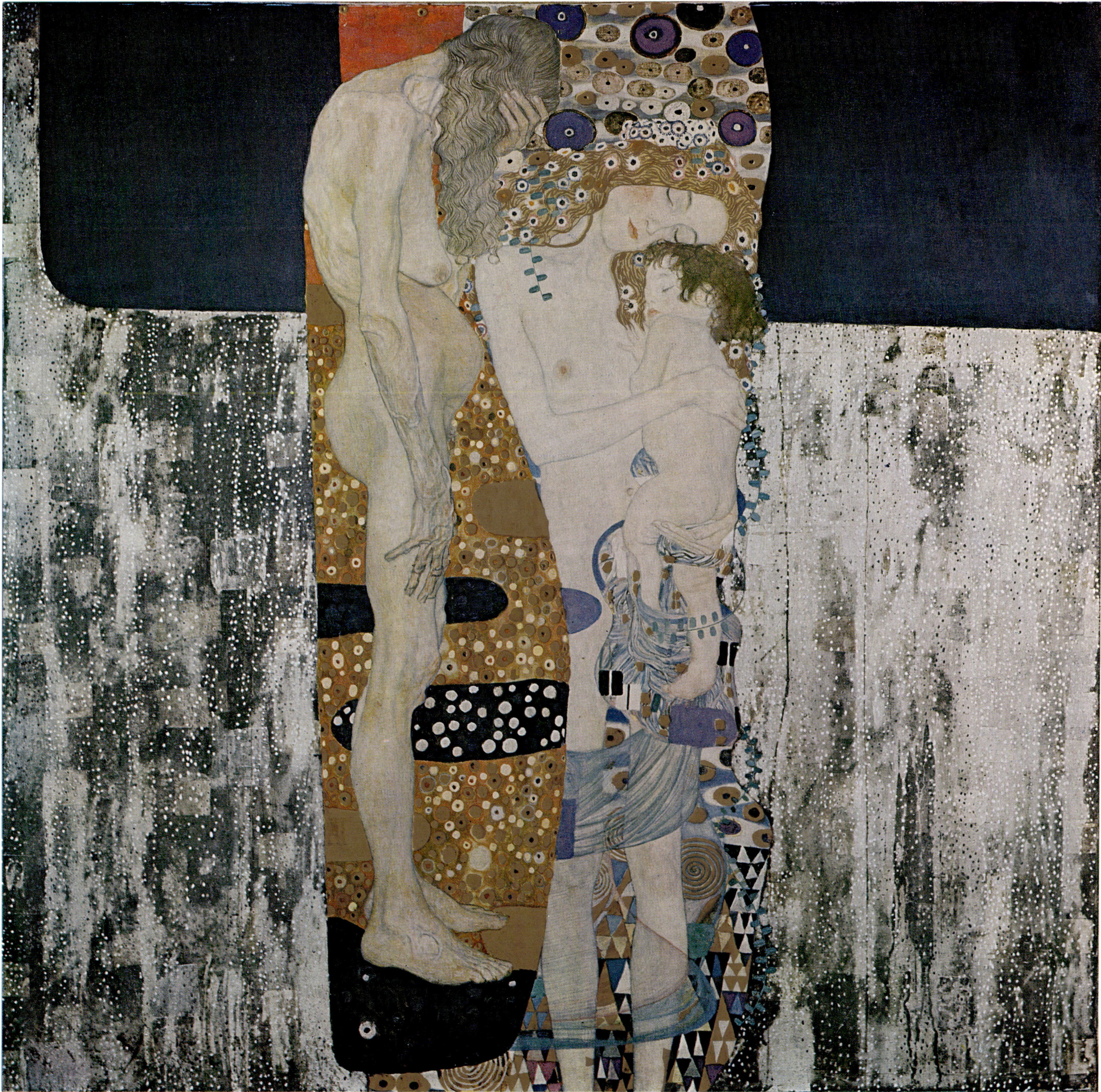

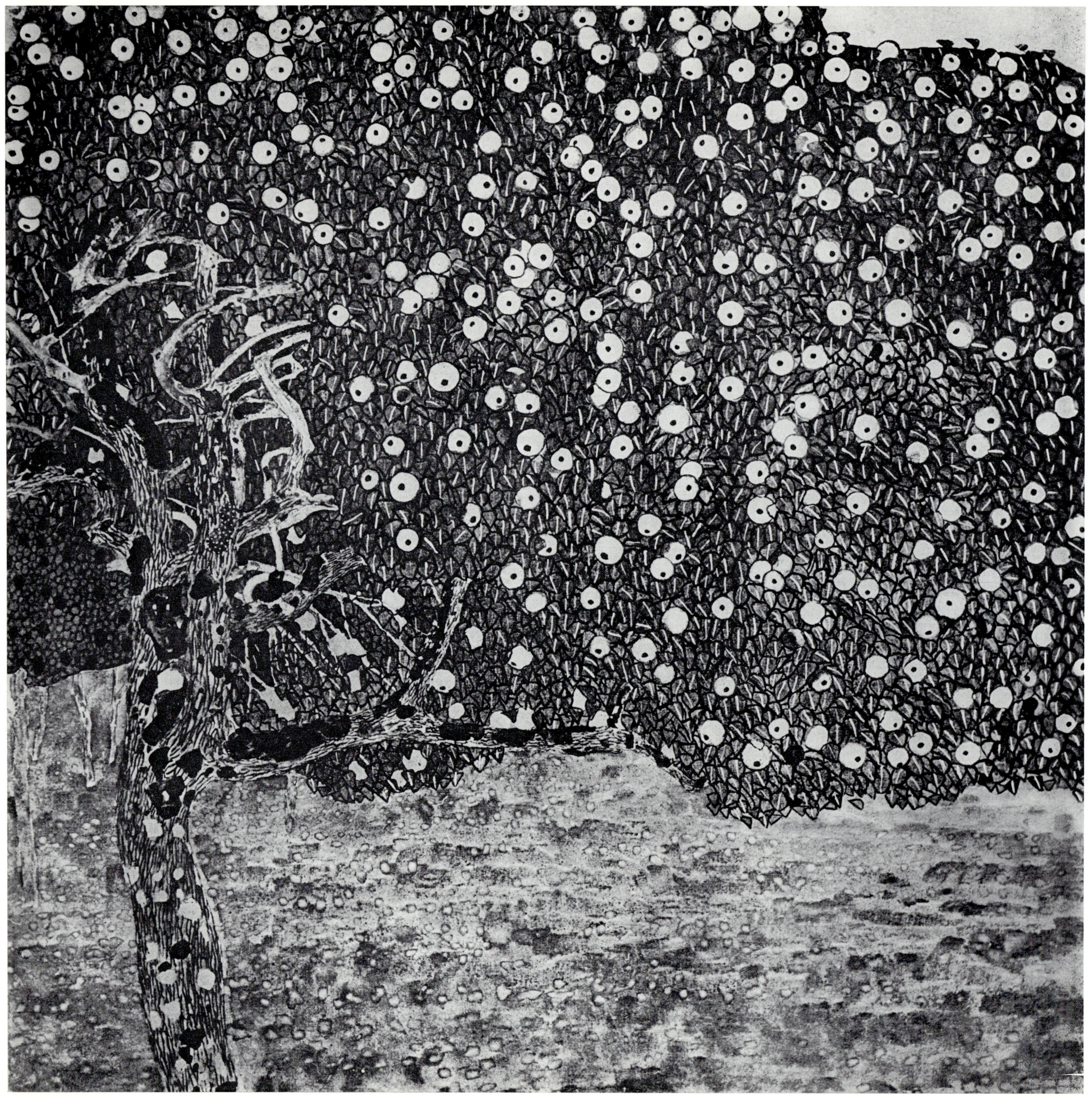

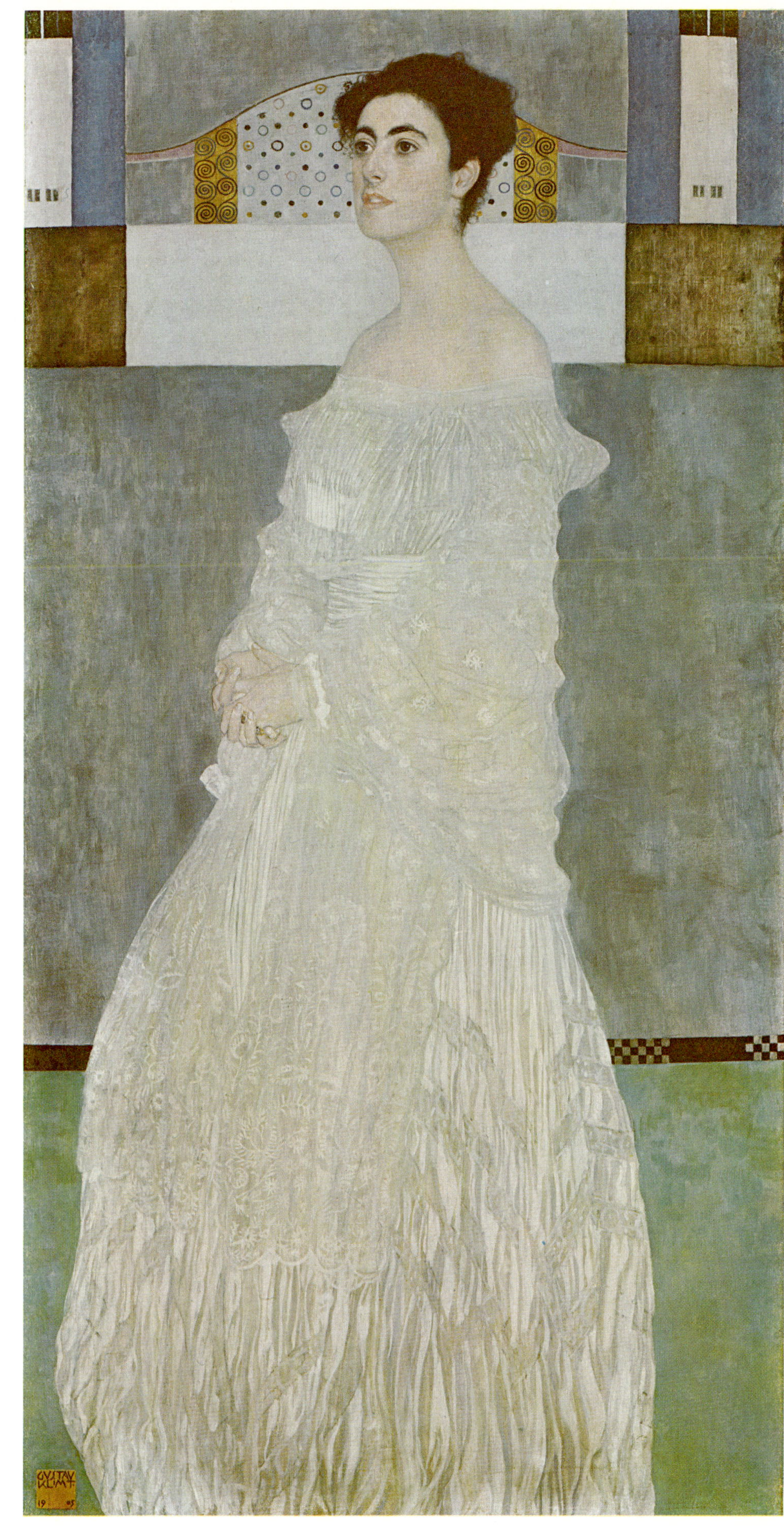

◀ 31 GOLDEN APPLE-TREE, 1903 (D. 133)

32 PORTRAIT OF MARGARET STONBOROUGH-WITTGENSTEIN, 1905 (D. 142)

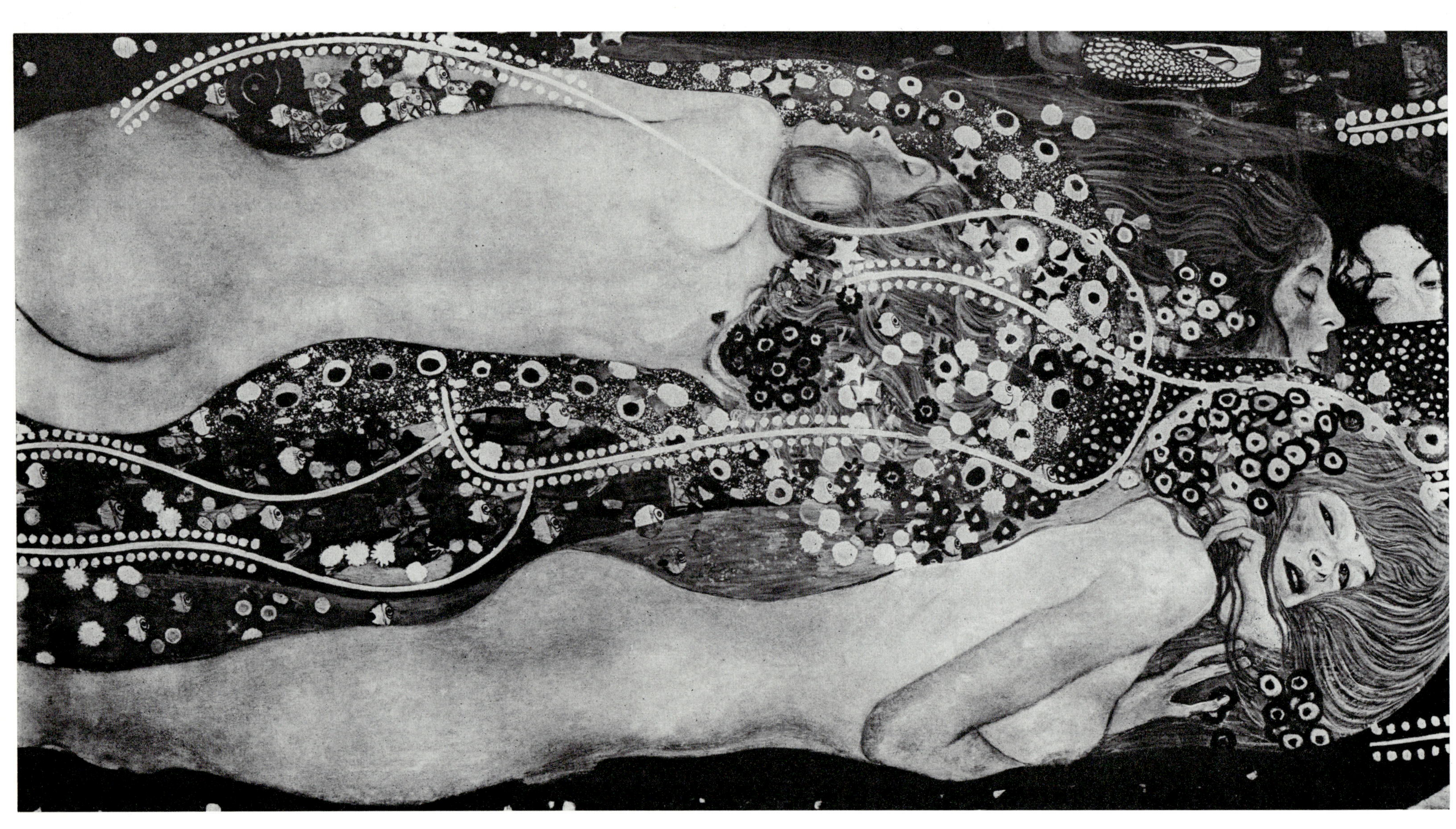

33 WATER SERPENTS II, 1904 — 07 (D. 140)

34 WATER SERPENTS I, c. 1904 — 07 (D. 139)

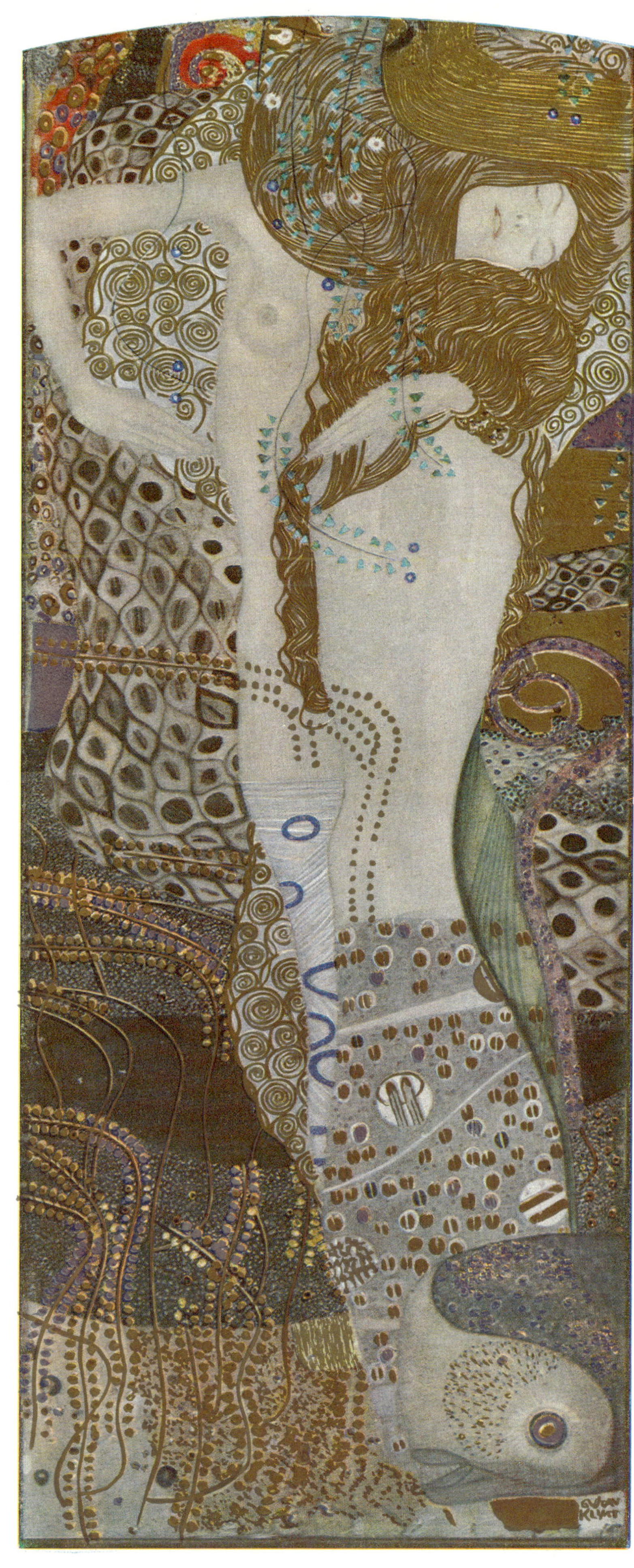

35 PORTRAIT OF FRITZA RIEDLER, 1906 (D. 143)

following pages:

36 THE SUNFLOWER, c. 1906 — 07 (D. 146)

37 FARM GARDEN WITH SUNFLOWERS, c. 1905 — 06 (D. 145)

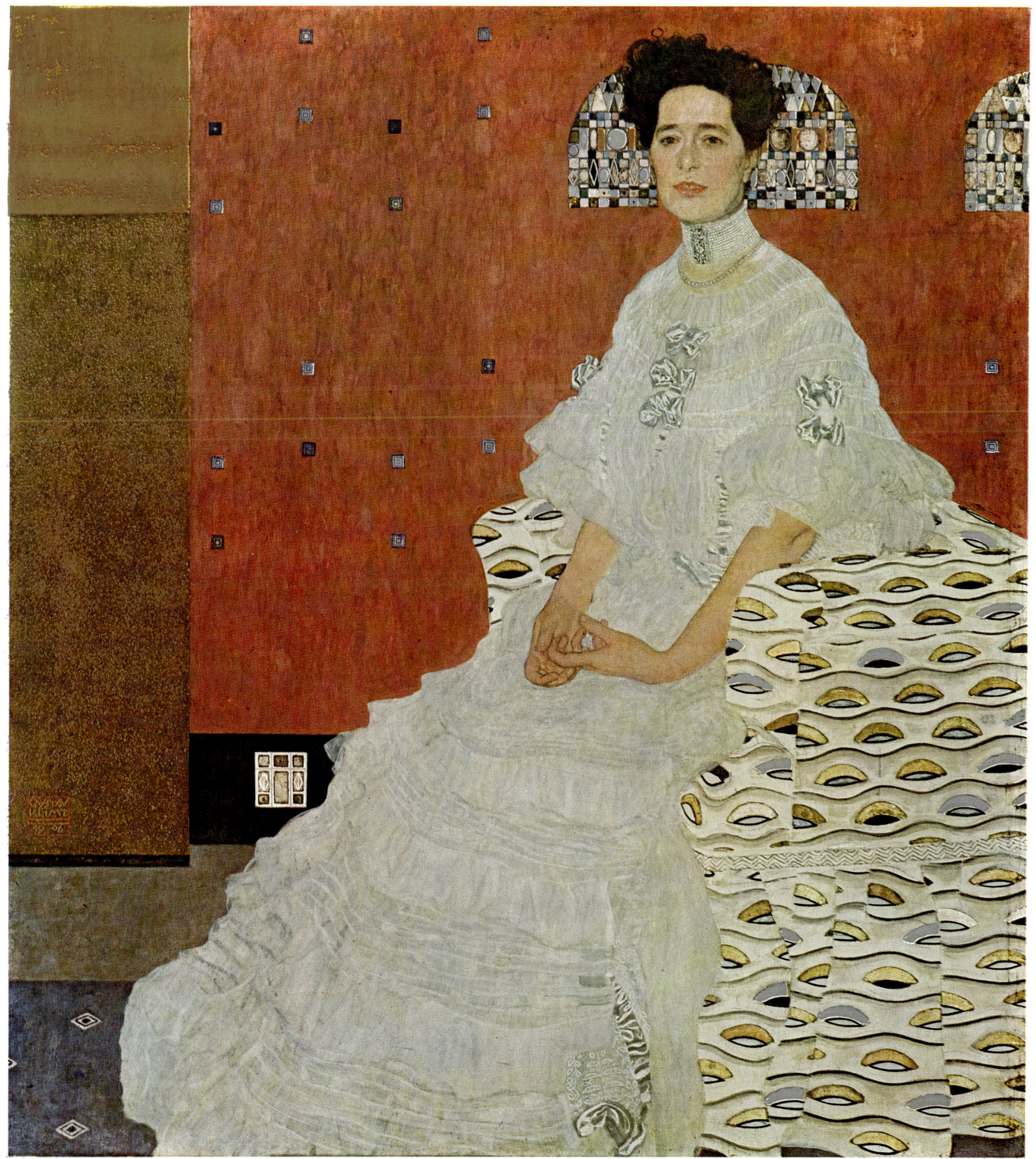
GUSTAV
KLIMT
19 06

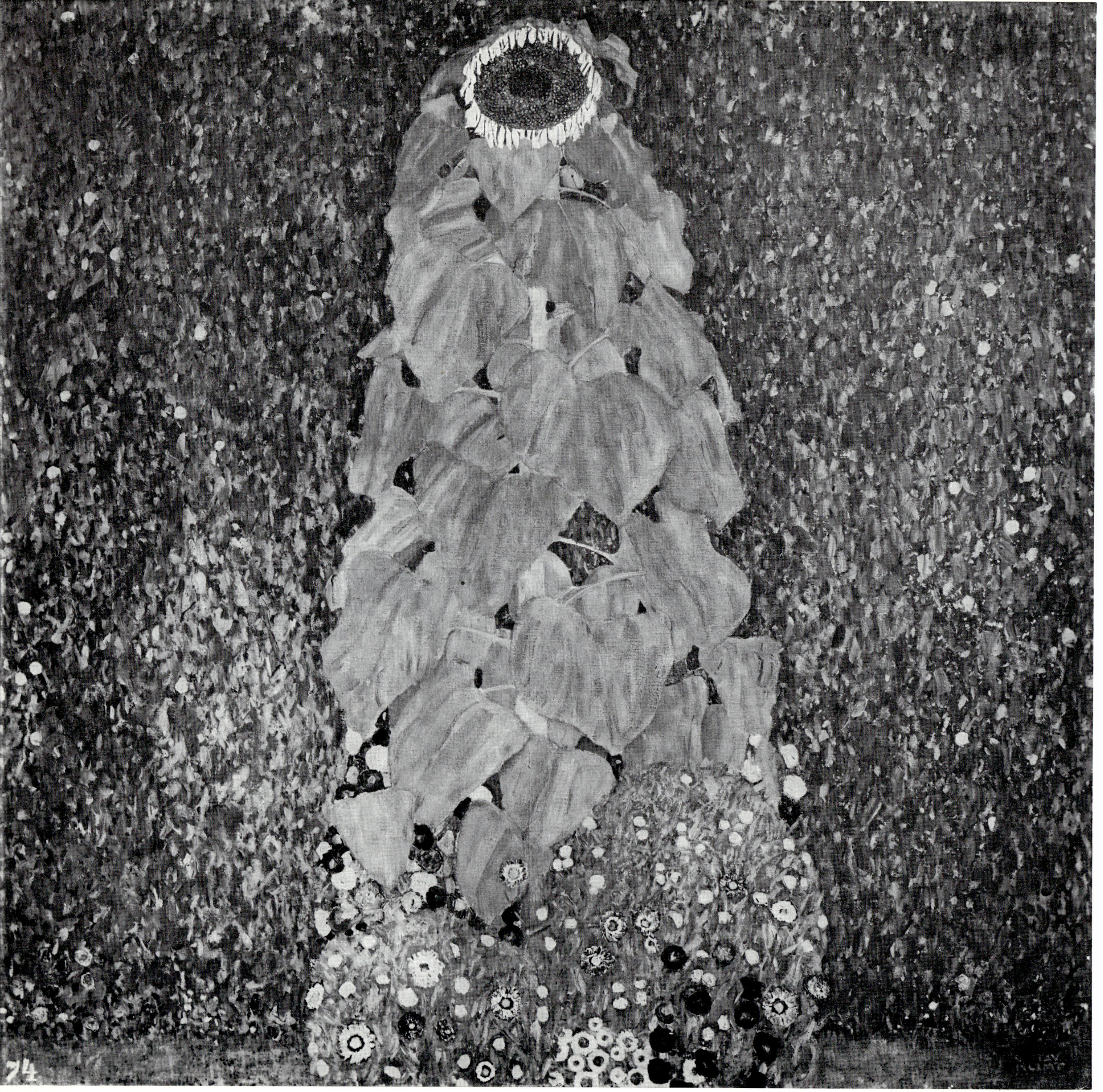
74

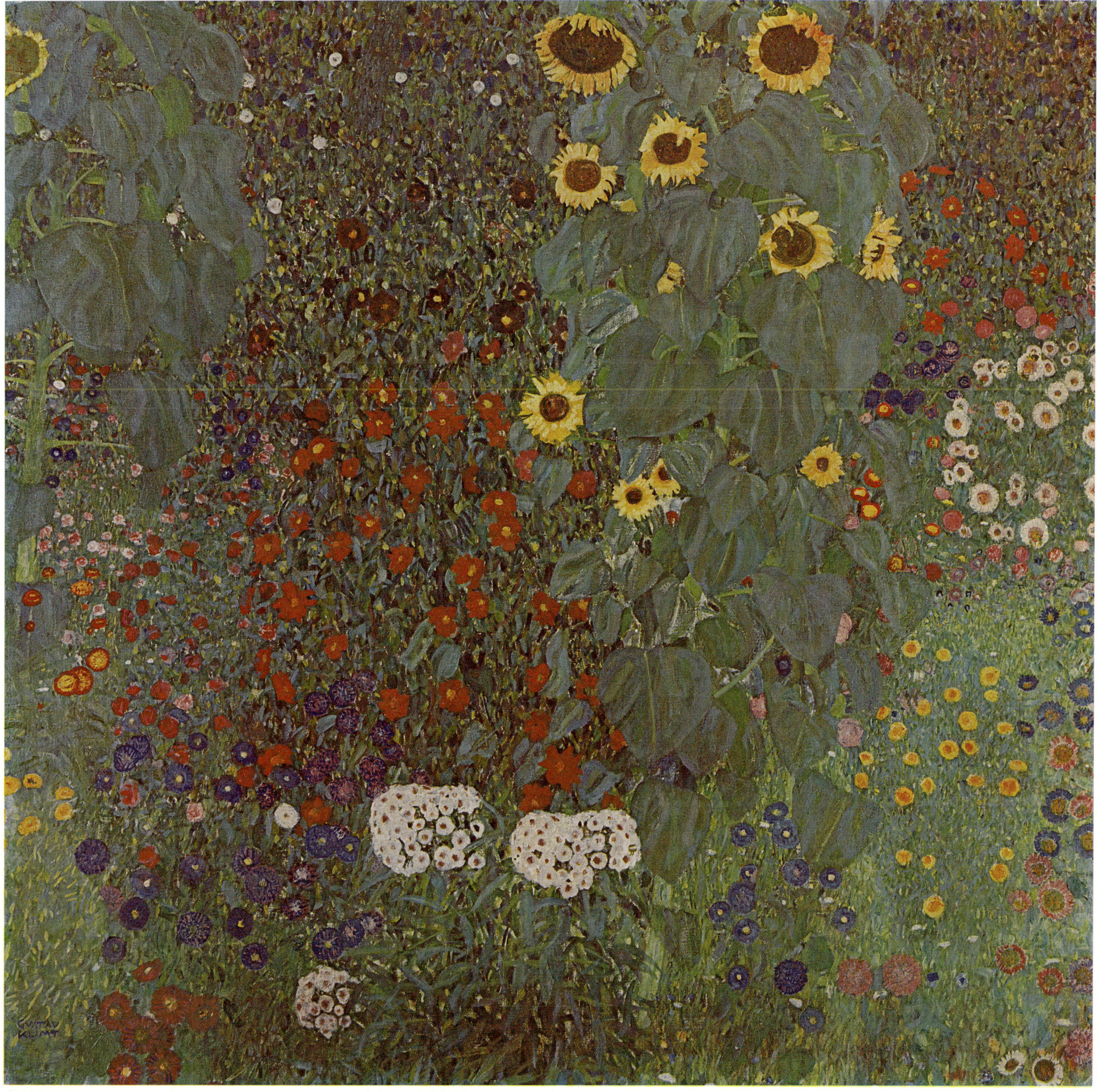
GVSTAV
KLIMT

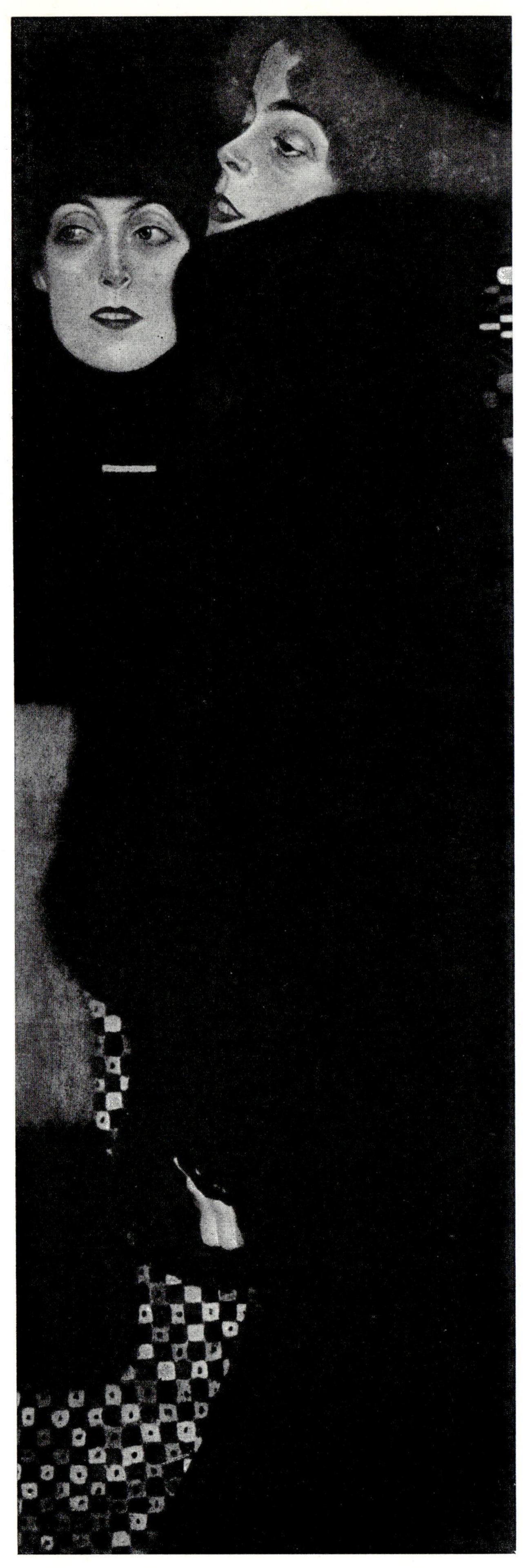

38 THE SISTERS, 1907 — 08 (D. 157)

39 DANAE, c. 1907 — 08 (D. 151)

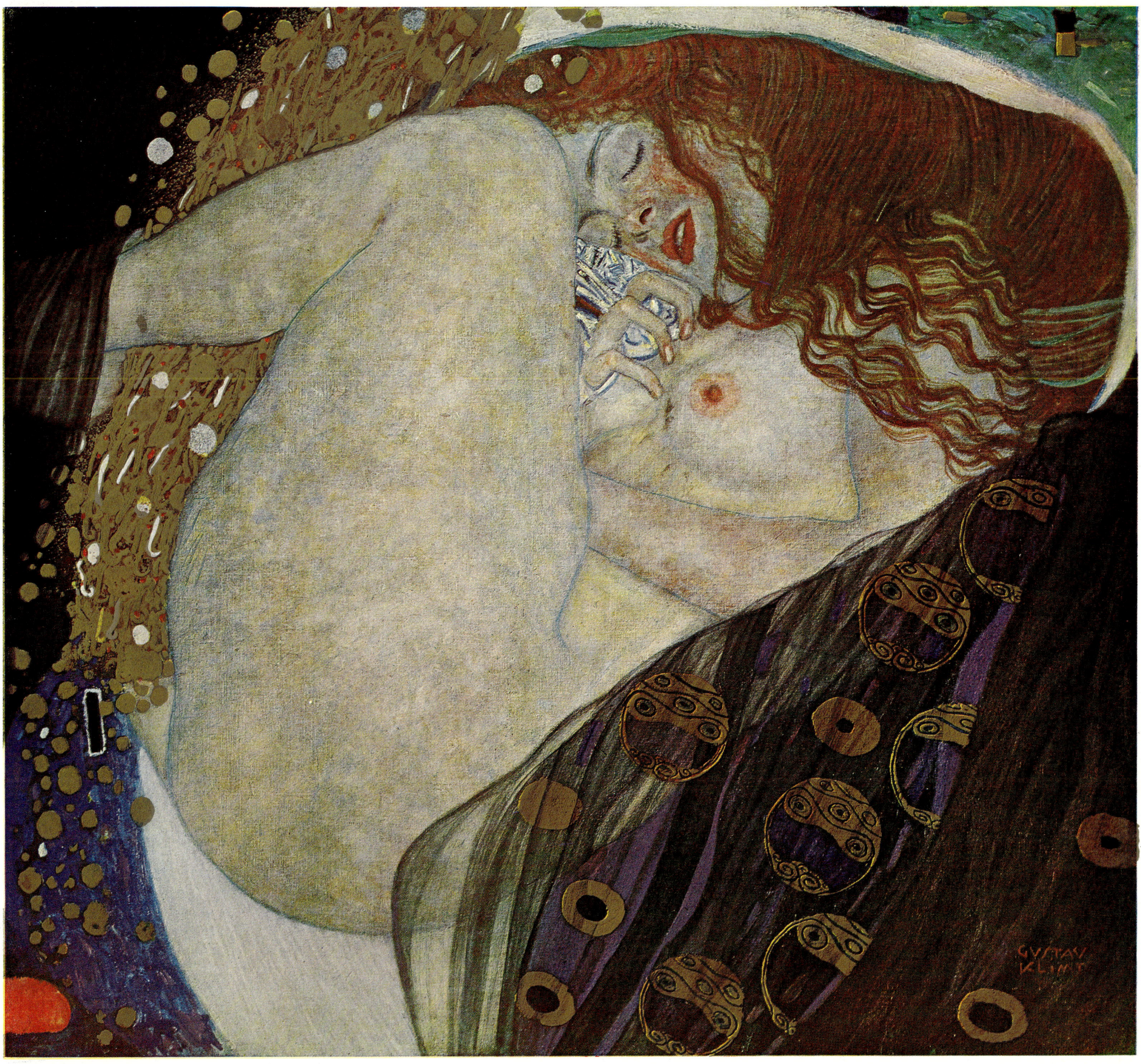
GUSTAV
KLIMT

40 POPPY FIELD, 1907 (D. 149)

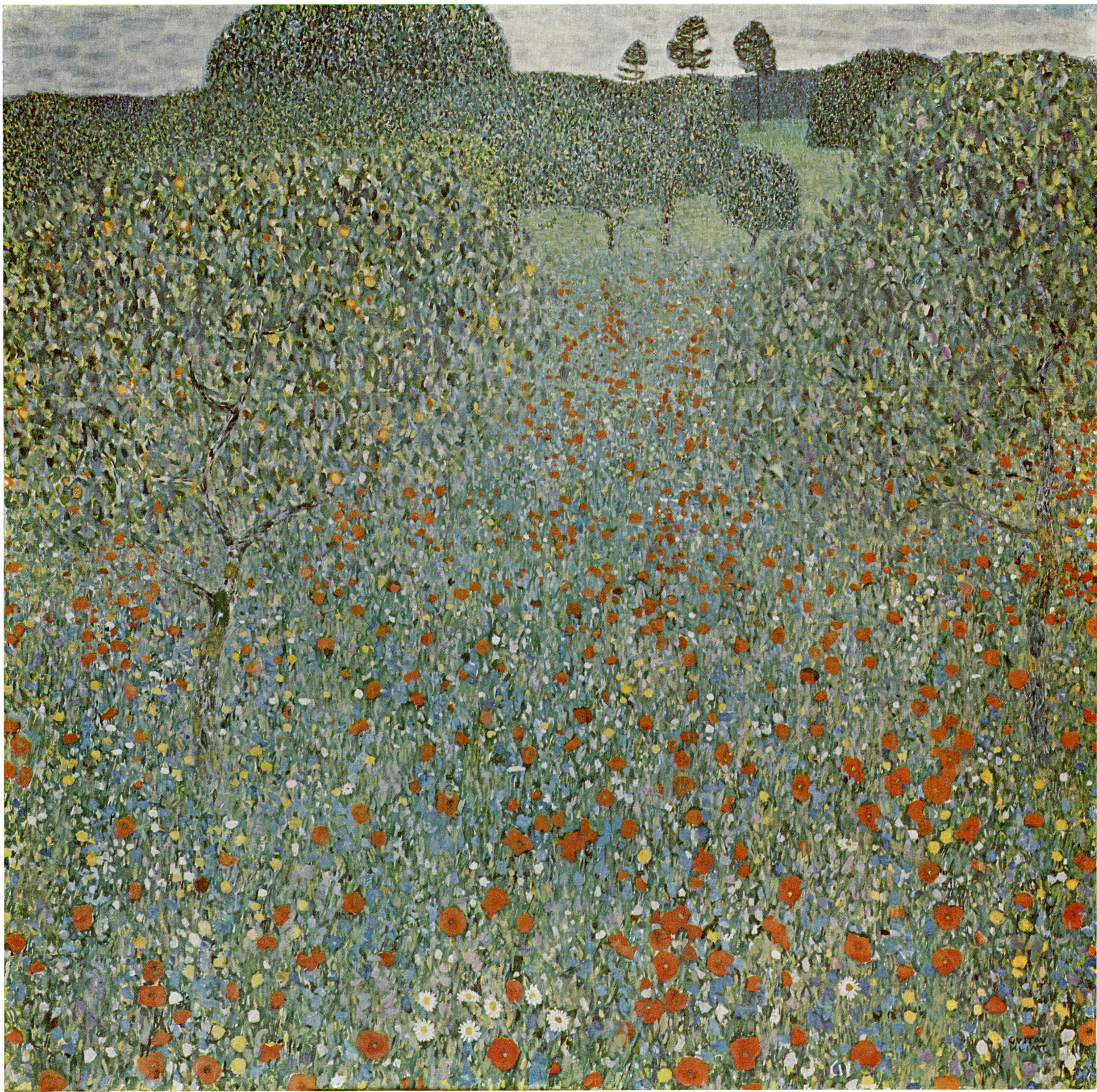

41 FARM GARDEN, c. 1905 — 06 (D. 144)

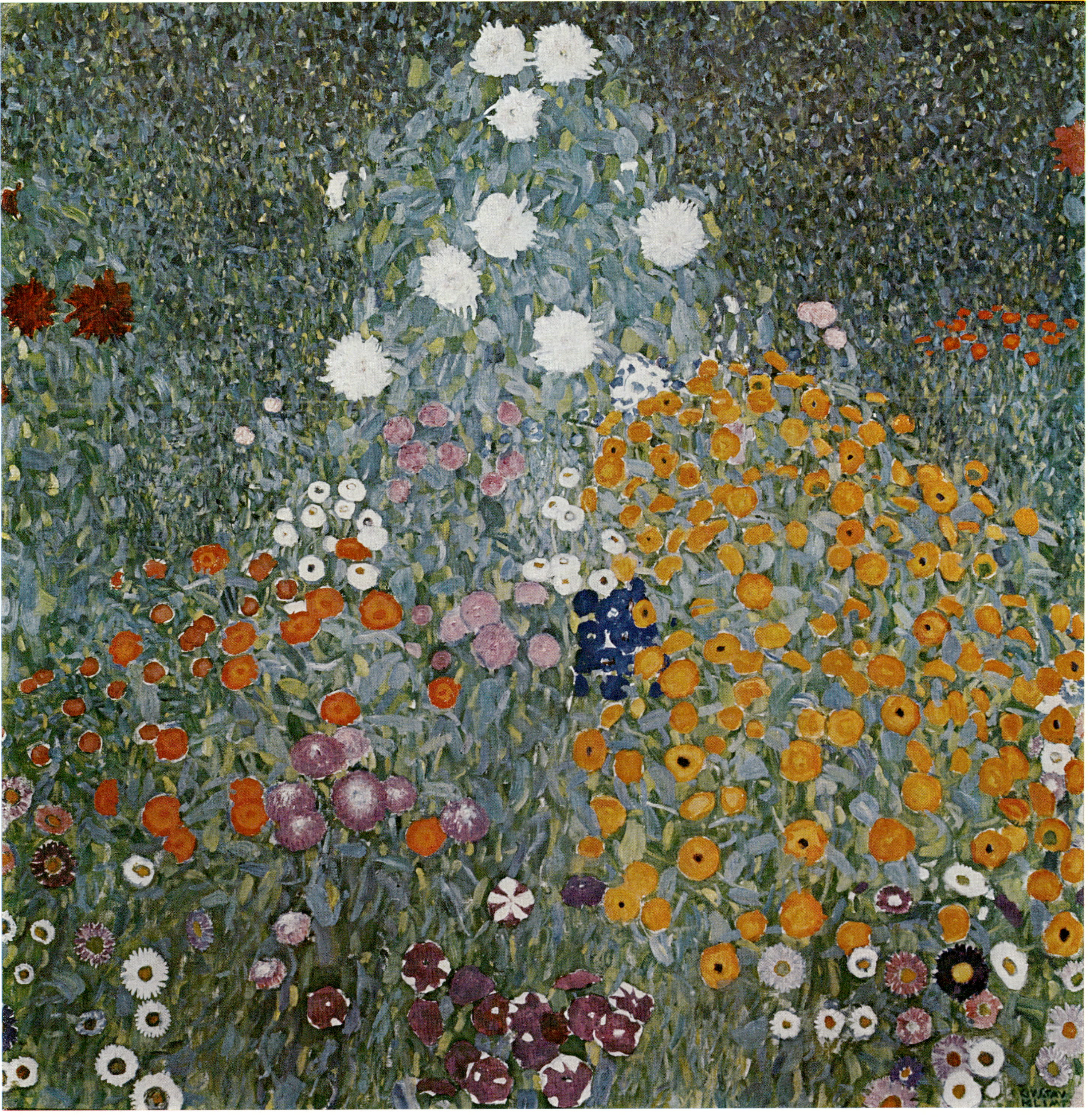

42 PORTRAIT OF ADELE BLOCH-BAUER I, 1907 (D. 150)

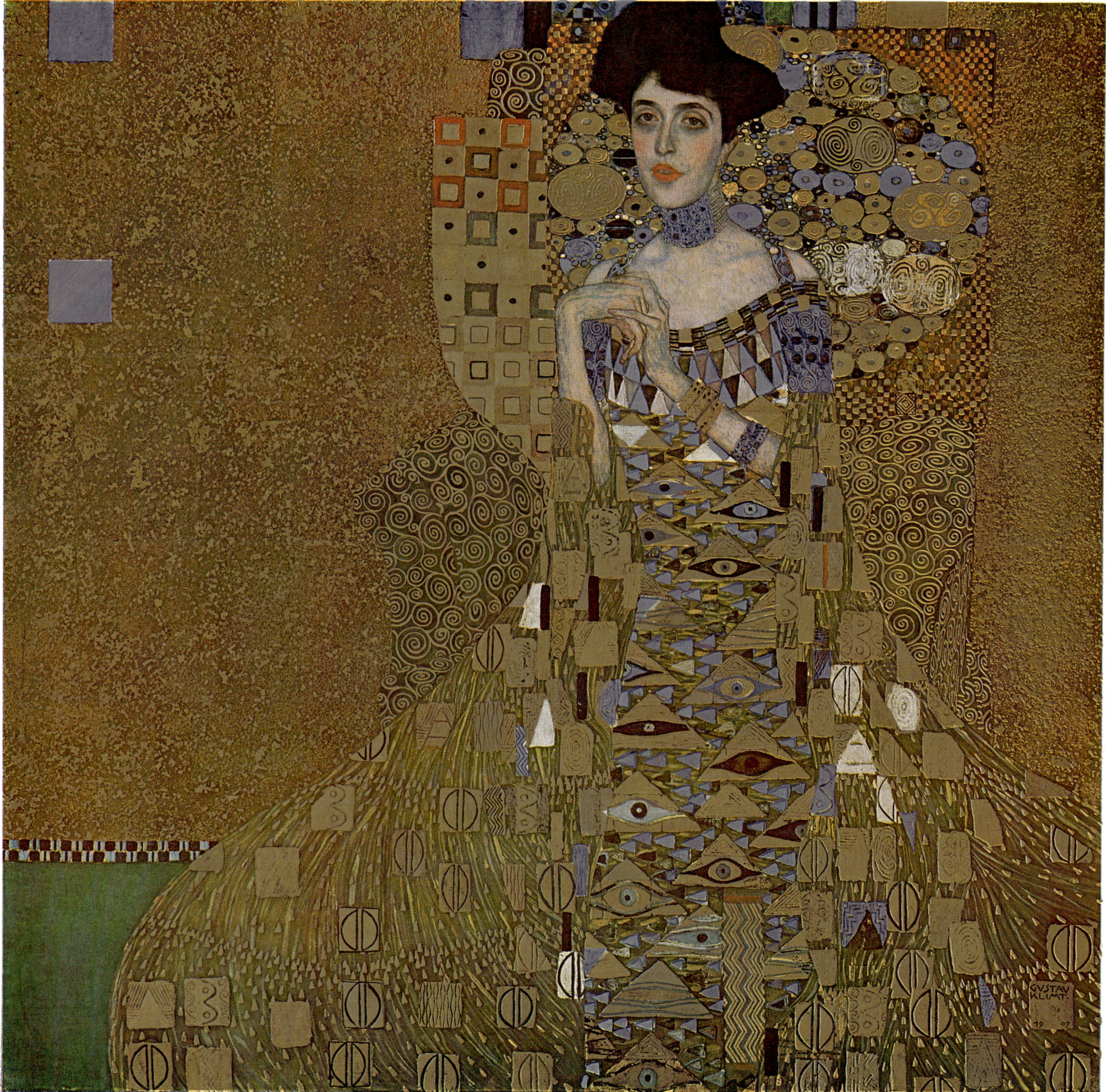
GVSTAV
KLIMT.
19 07

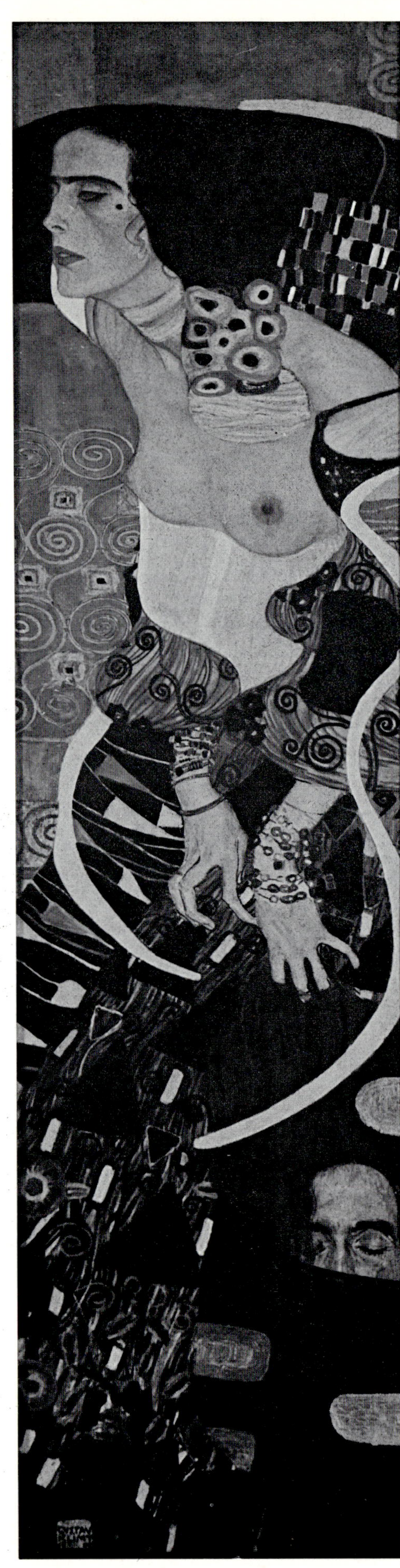

43 JUDITH II (Salome), 1909 (D. 160)

44 LADY WITH HAT AND FEATHER BOA,
1909 (D. 161) ▸

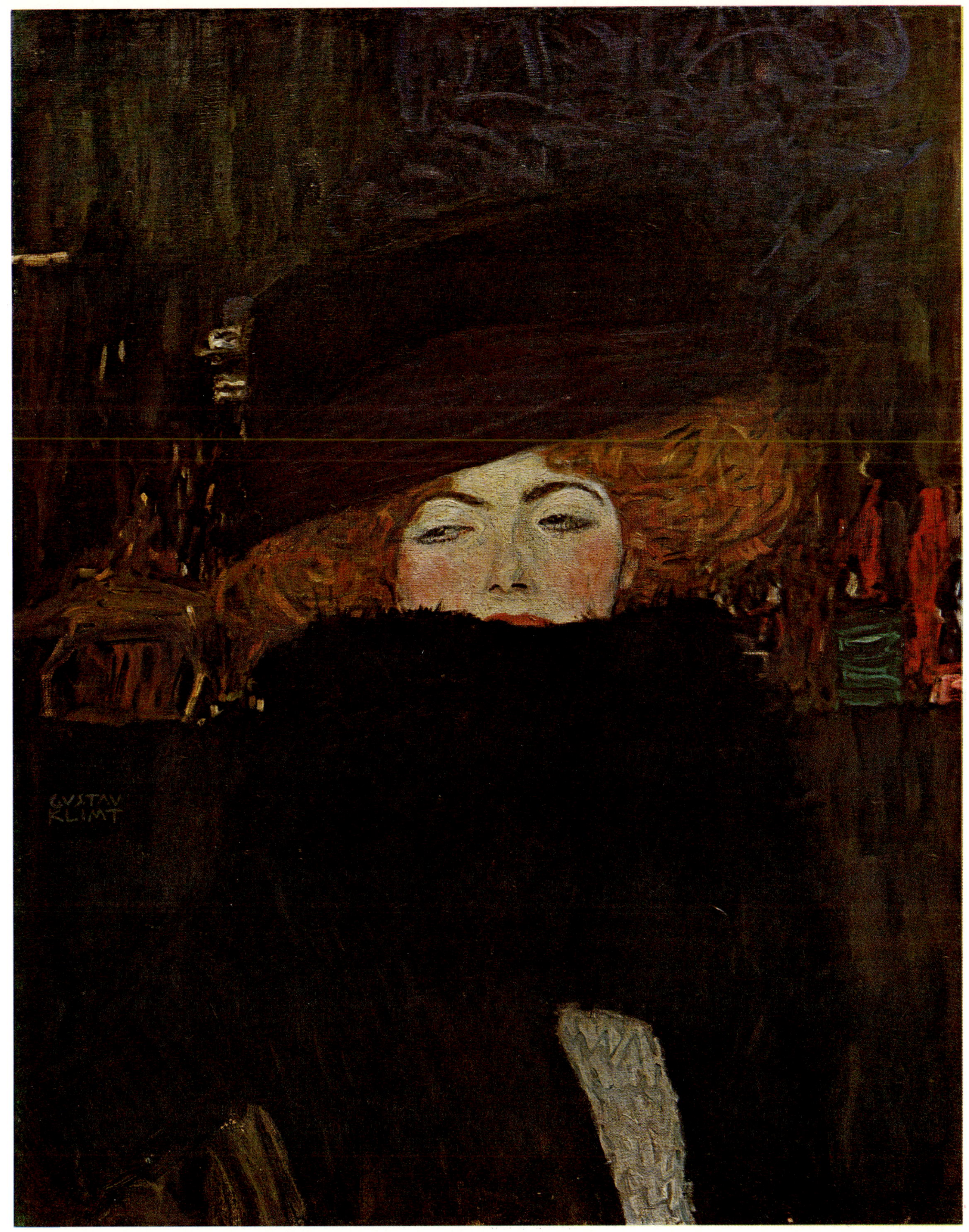
GVSTAV
KLIMT

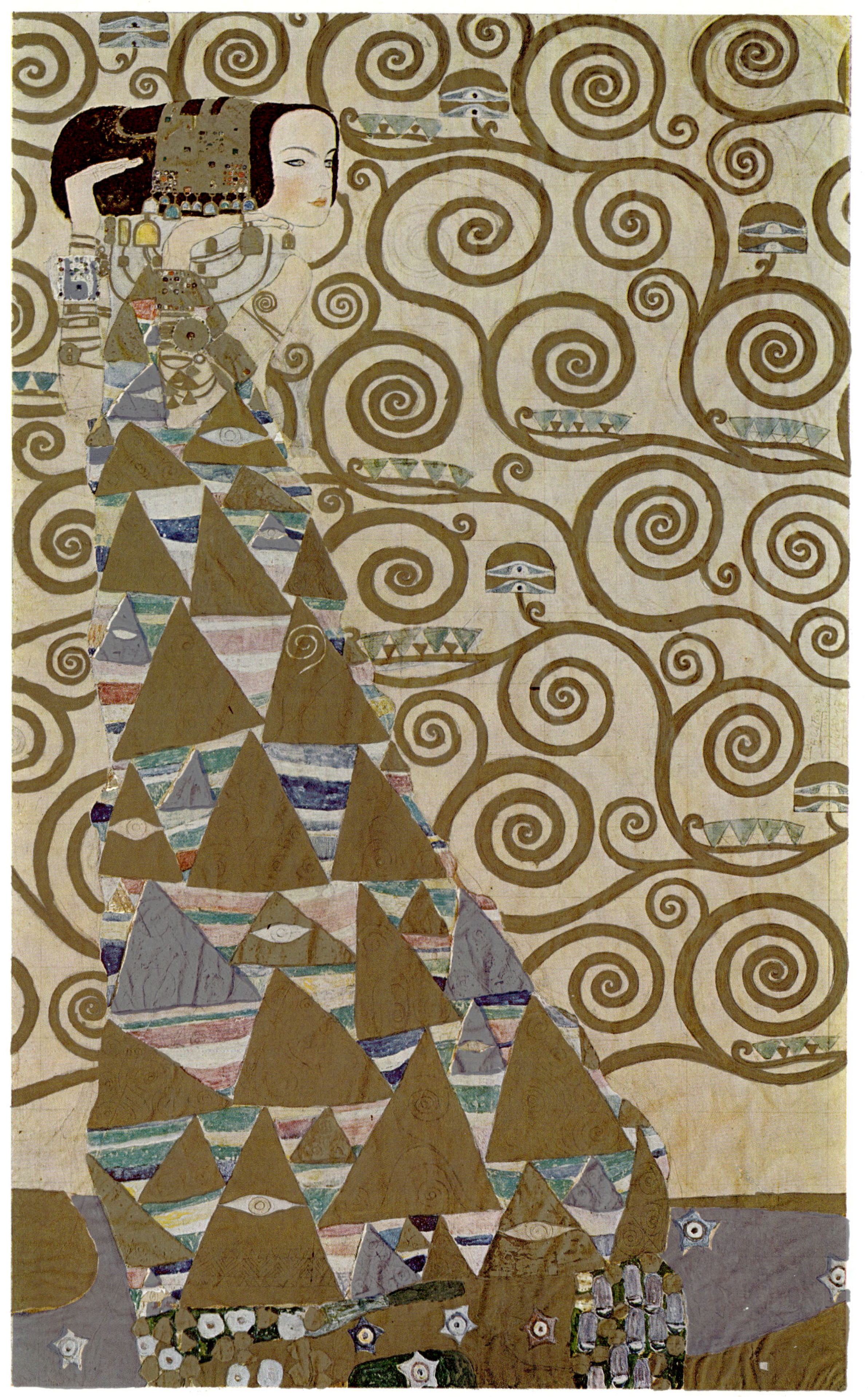

45 EXPECTATION, Cartoon for the Stoclet frieze, c. 1905 — 09 (D. 152 B)

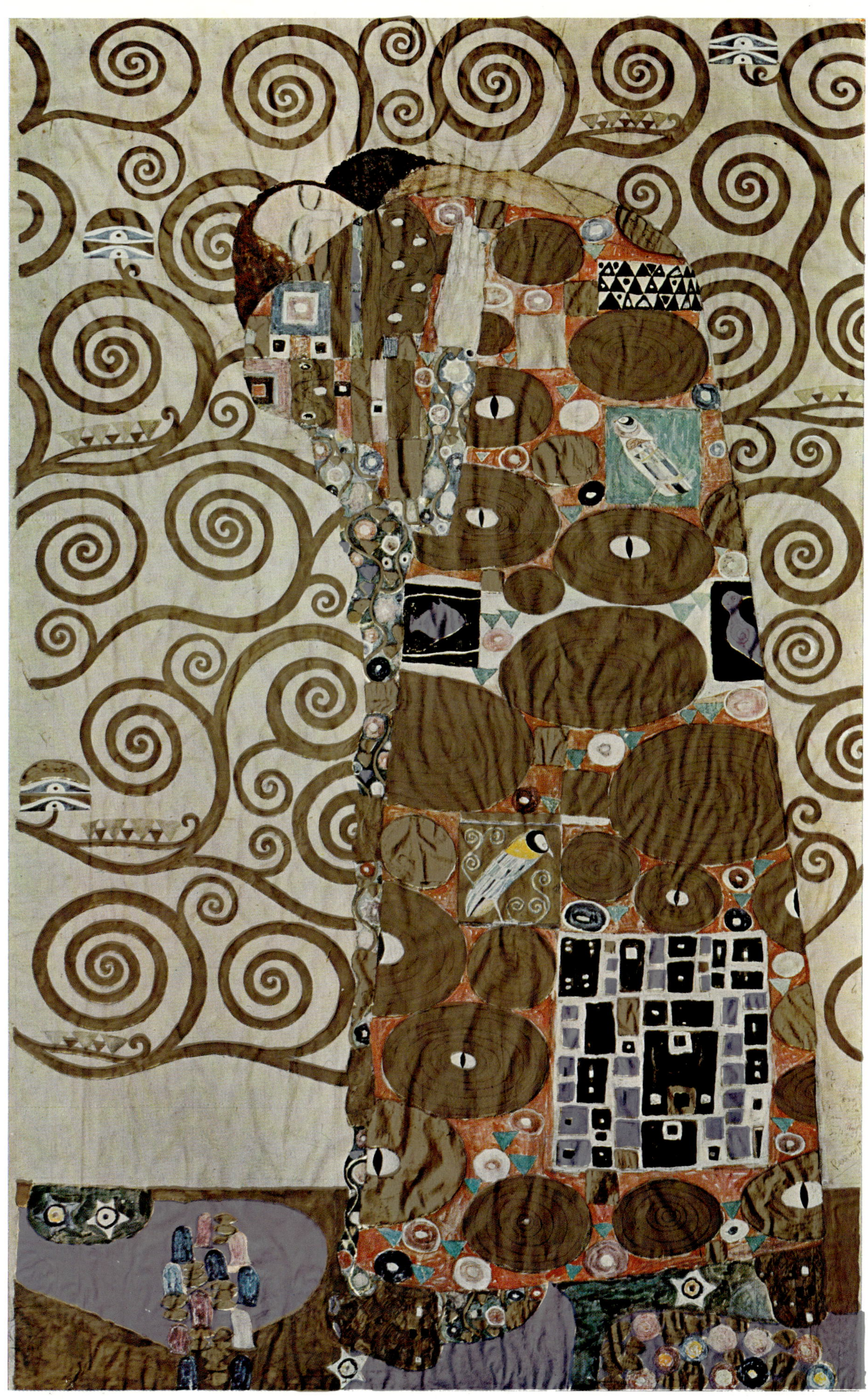

46 FULFILMENT, Cartoon for the Stoclet frieze, c. 1905 — 09 (D. 152 I)

47 THE KISS, 1907 — 08 (D. 154)

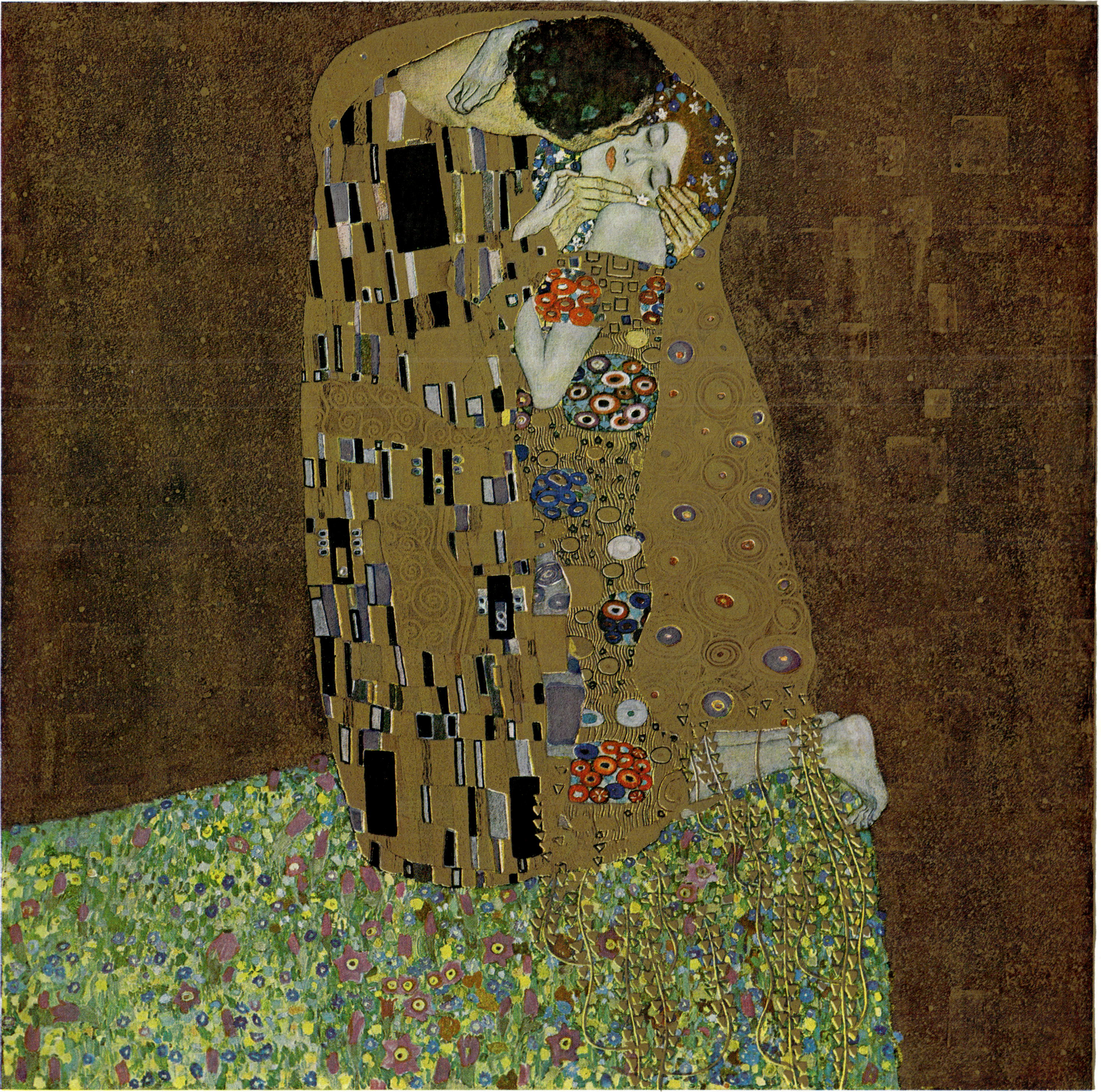

48 MOTHER WITH CHILDREN (Family), 1909 — 10 (D. 163)

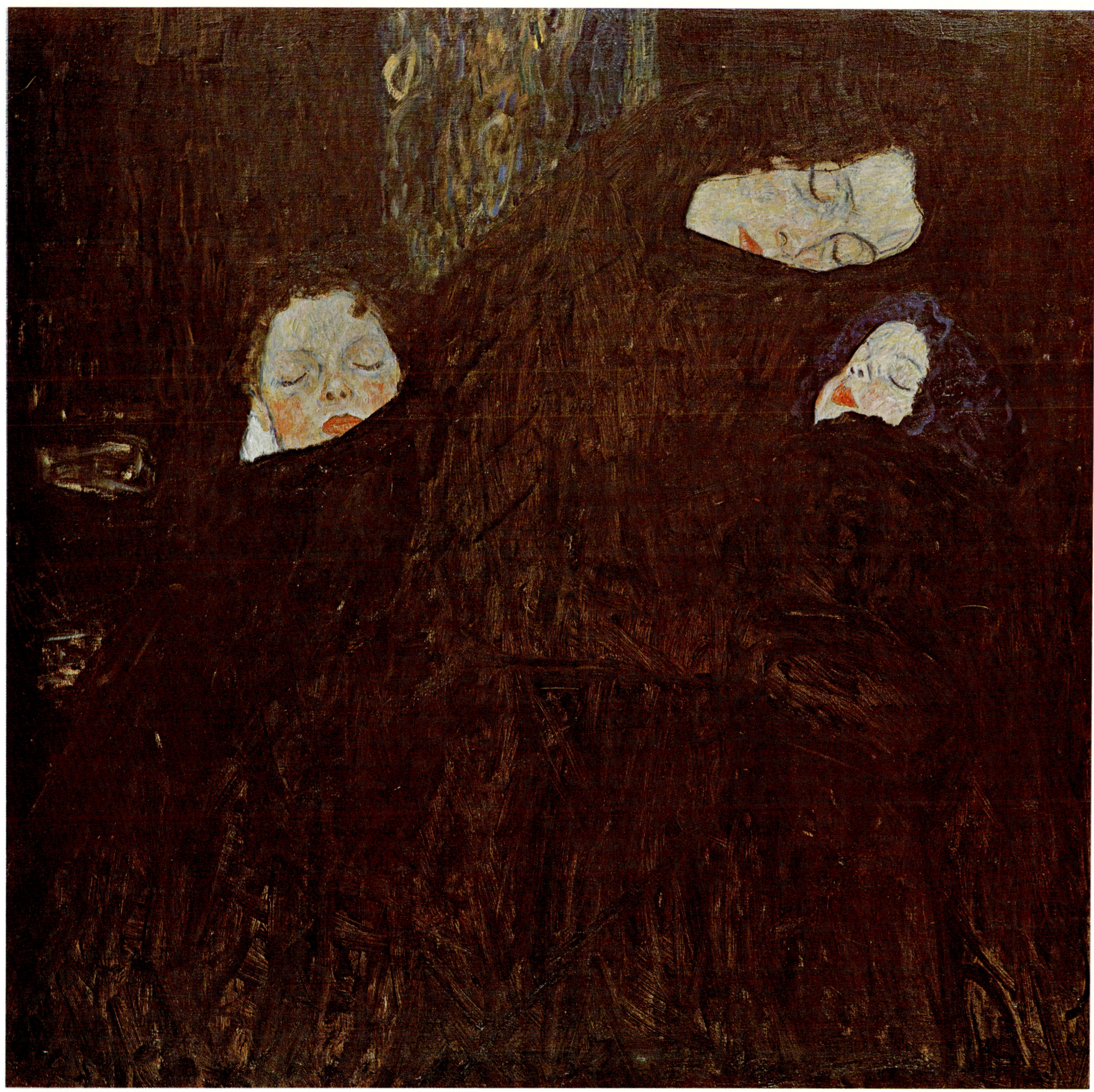

49 PARK, before 1910 (D. 165)

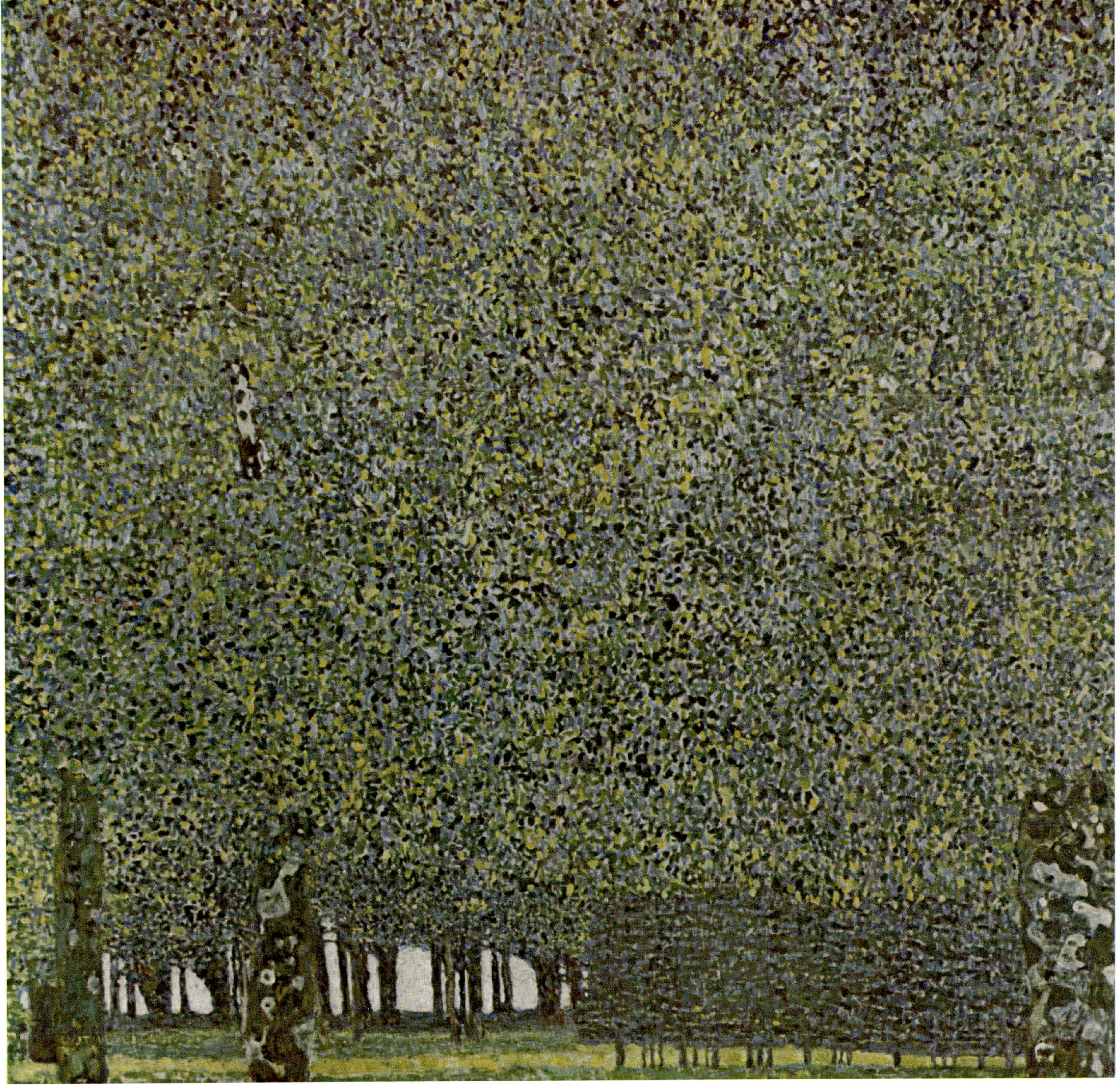

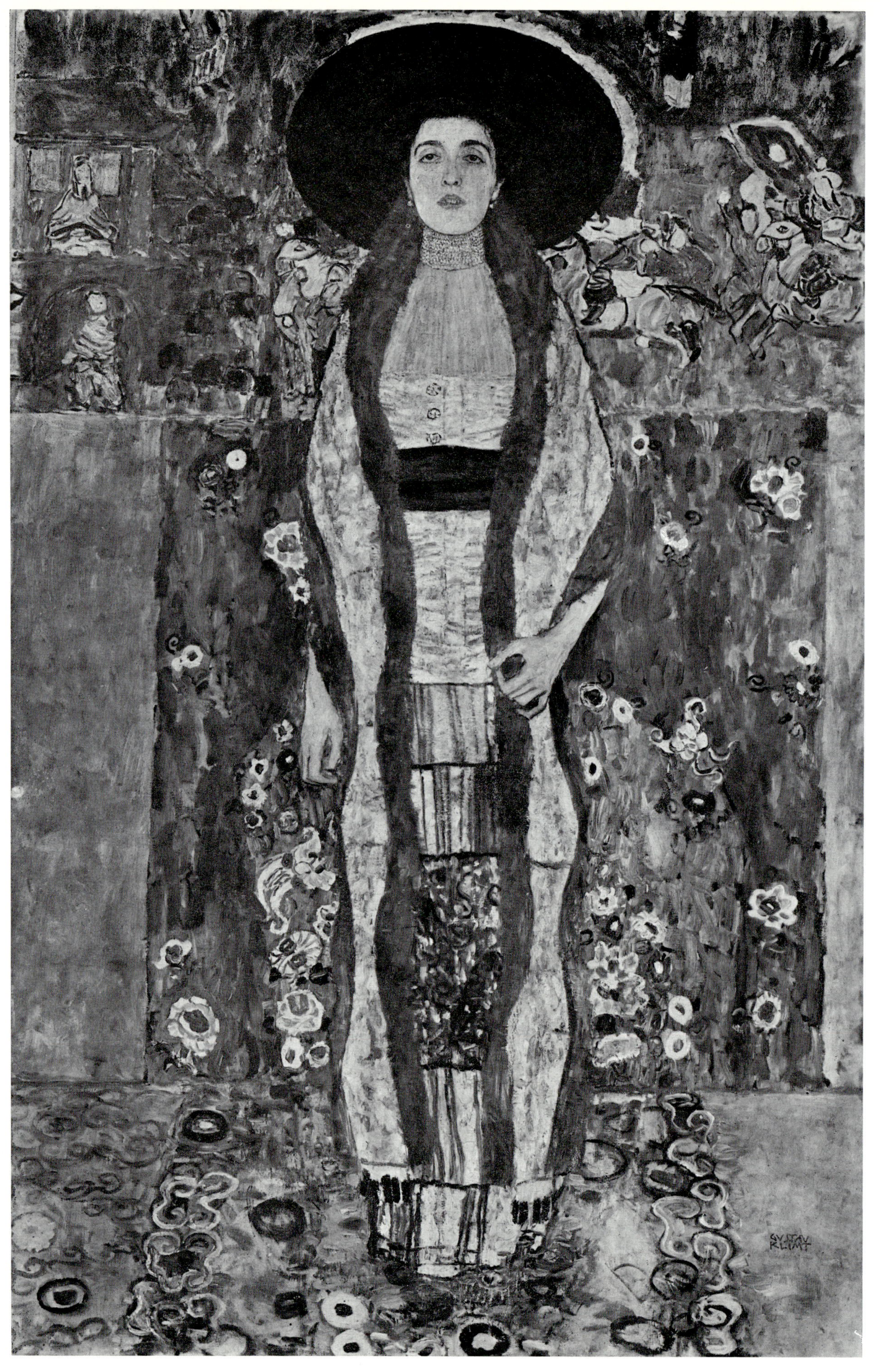

50 PORTRAIT OF ADELE BLOCH-BAUER II, 1912 (D. 177)

51 THE BLACK FEATHER HAT, 1910 (D. 168) ▸

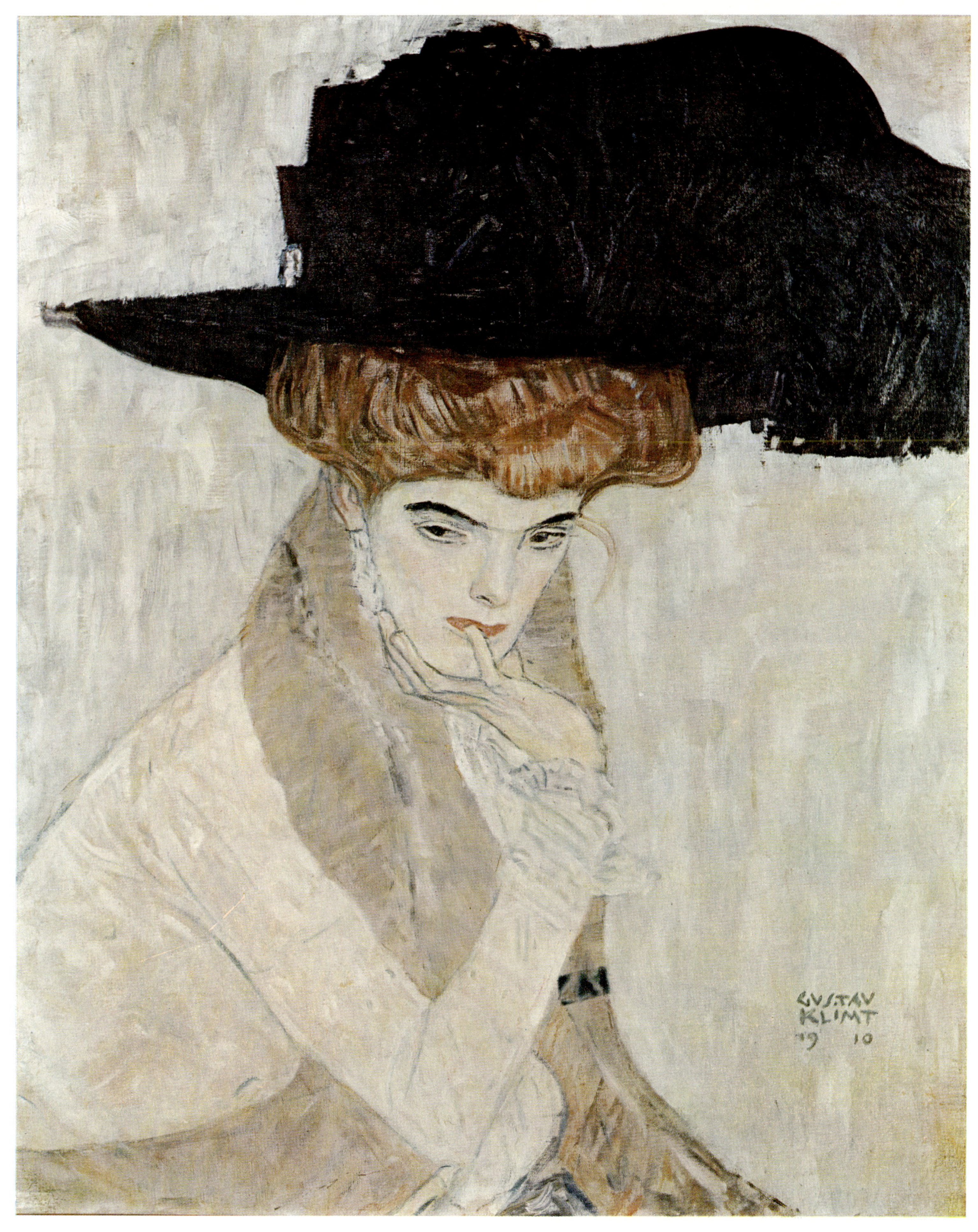
GVSTAV
KLIMT
19 10

52 SCHLOSS KAMMER ON THE ATTERSEE III, 1910 (D. 171)

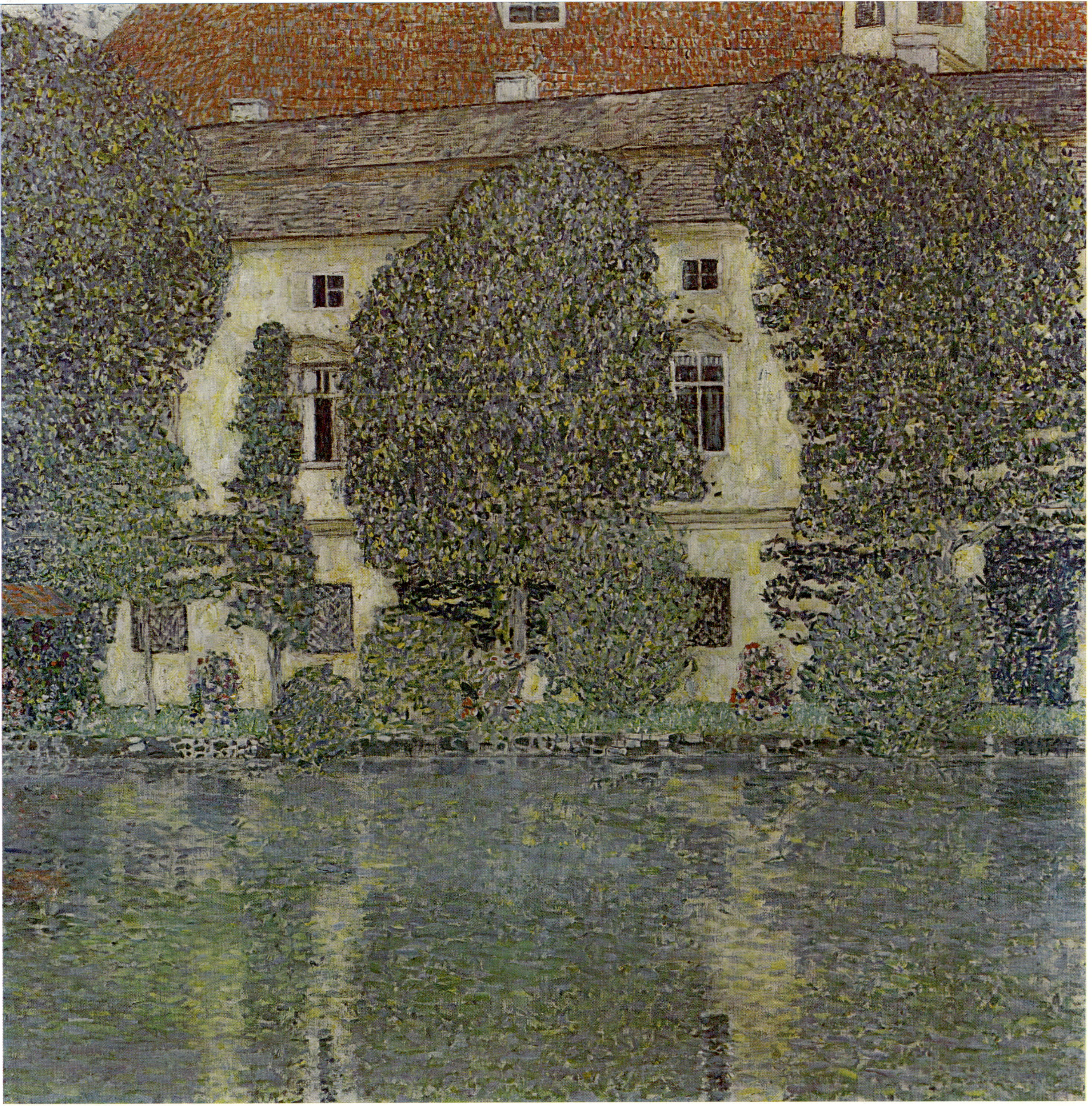

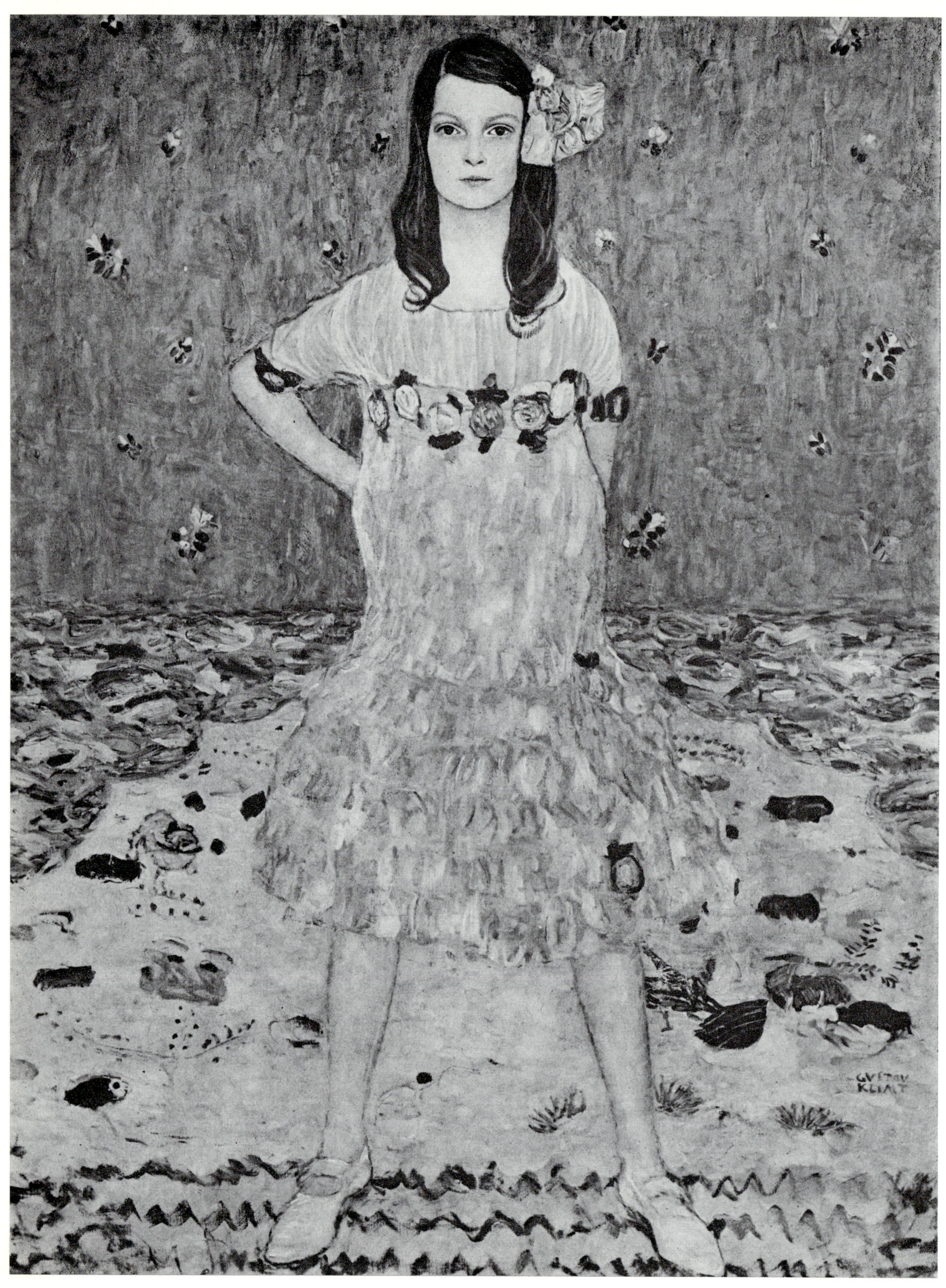

53 PORTRAIT OF MÄDA PRIMAVESI, c. 1912 (D. 179)

54 THE MAIDEN, 1913 (D. 184) ▸

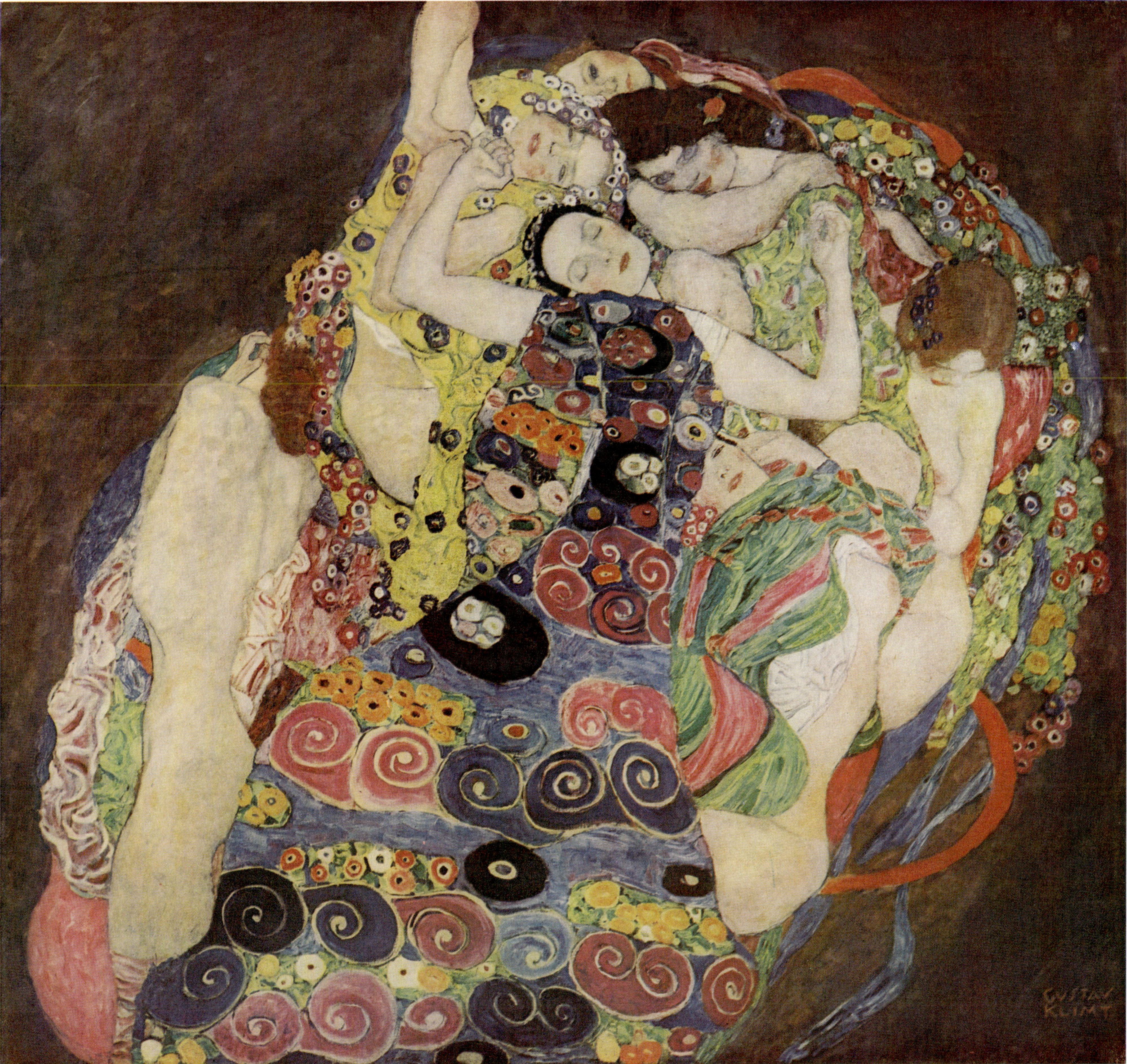
GUSTAV
KLIMT

55 APPLE-TREE I, c. 1912 (D. 180)

following pages:

56 AVENUE IN SCHLOSS KAMMER PARK, 1912 (D. 181)

57 FORESTER'S HOUSE IN WEISSENBACH ON THE ATTERSEE, 1912 (D. 182)

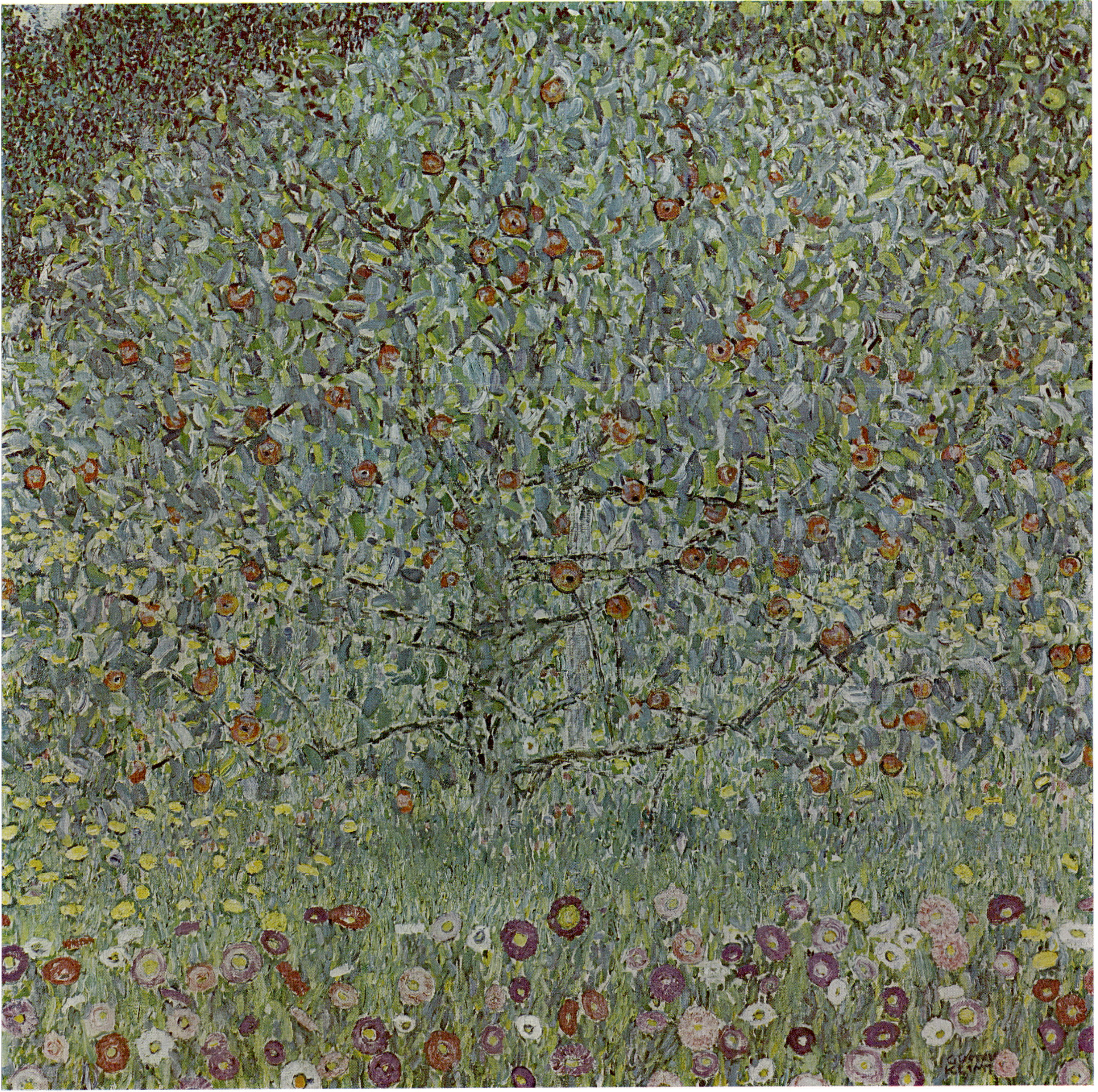

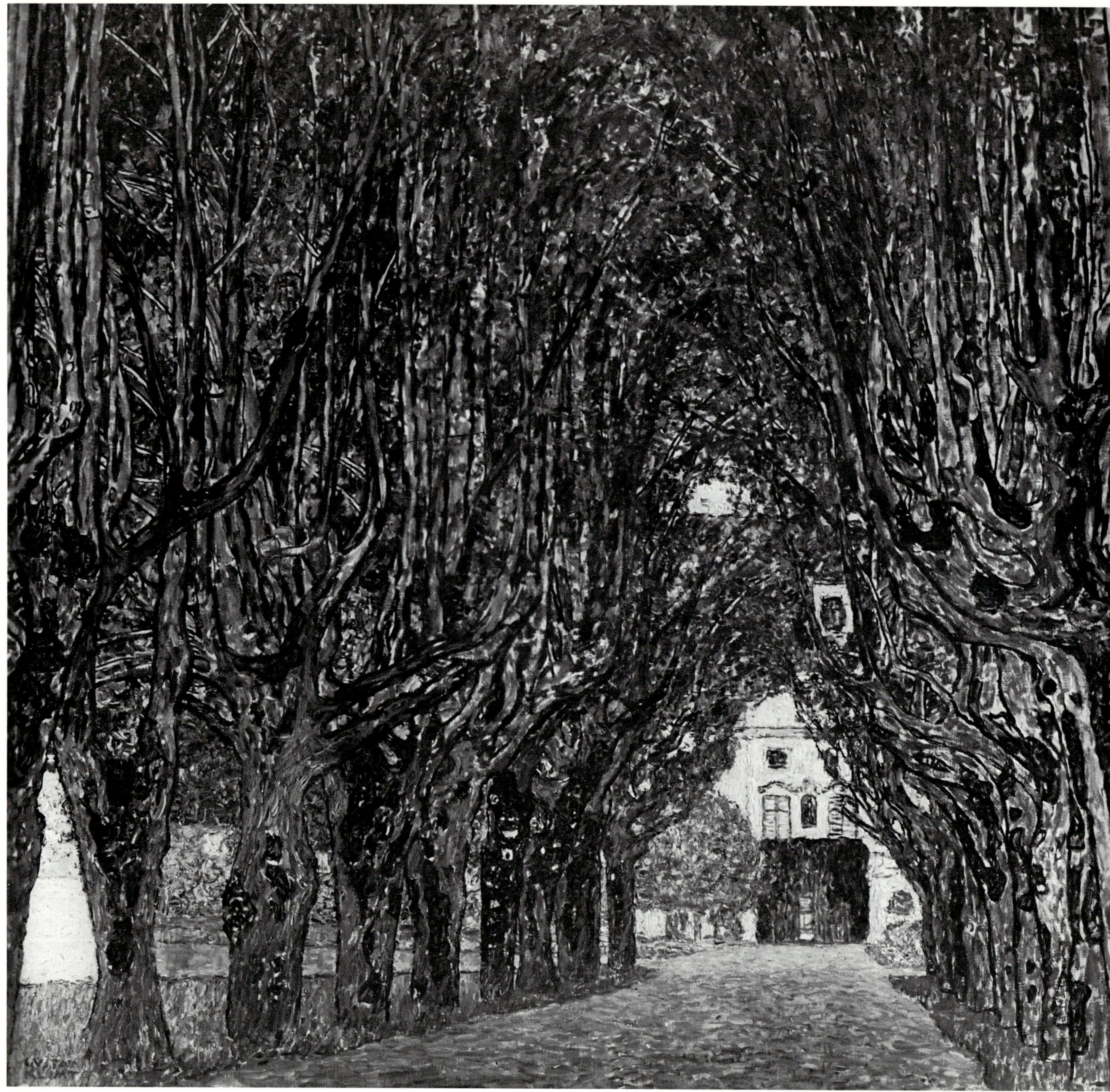

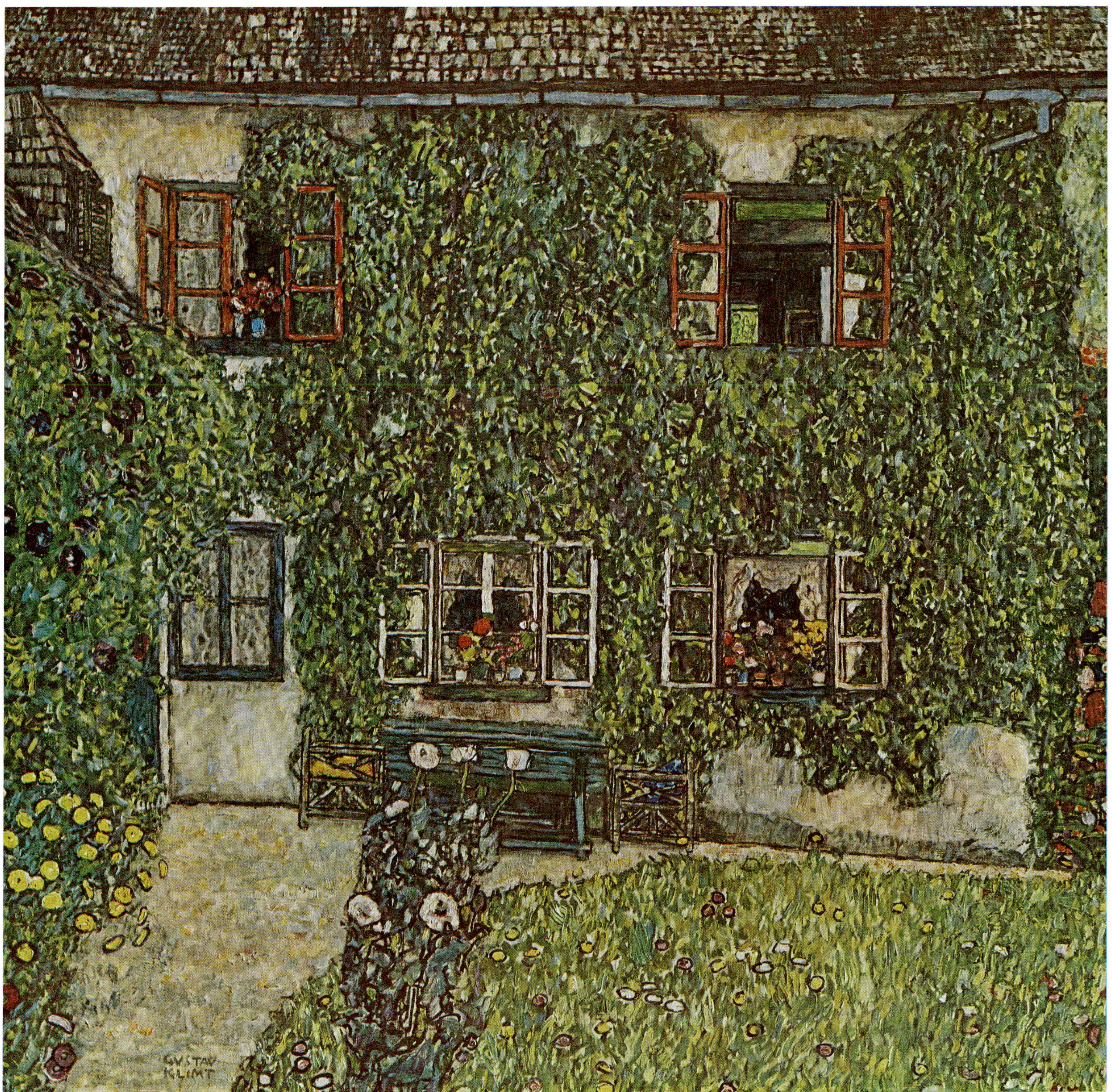
GVSTAV
KLIMT

58 DEATH AND LIFE, before 1911,
revised 1915 (D. 183)

following pages:

59 CHURCH IN CASSONE, 1913 (D. 185)

60 MALCESINE ON LAKE GARDA,
1913 (D. 186)

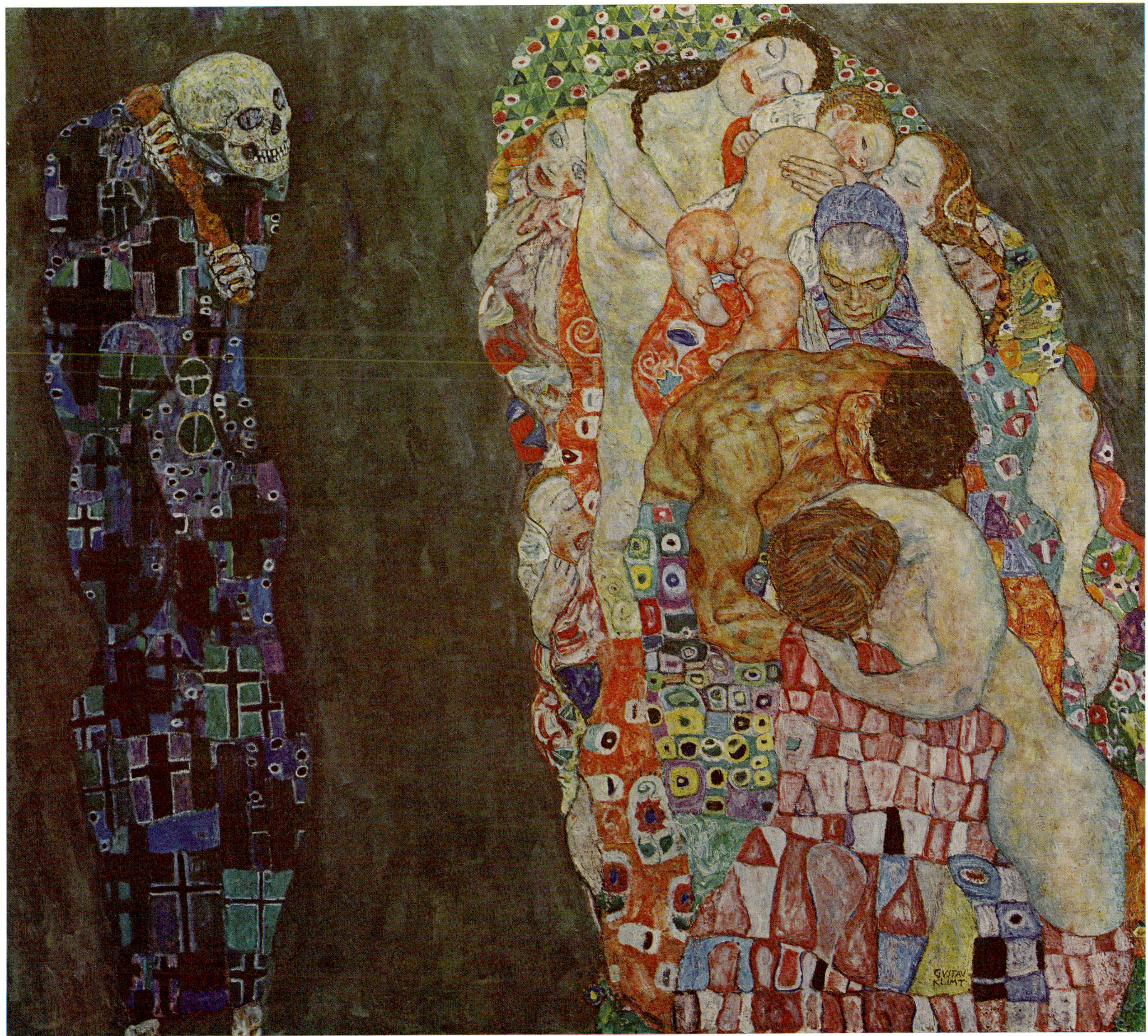
GVSTAV
KLIMT

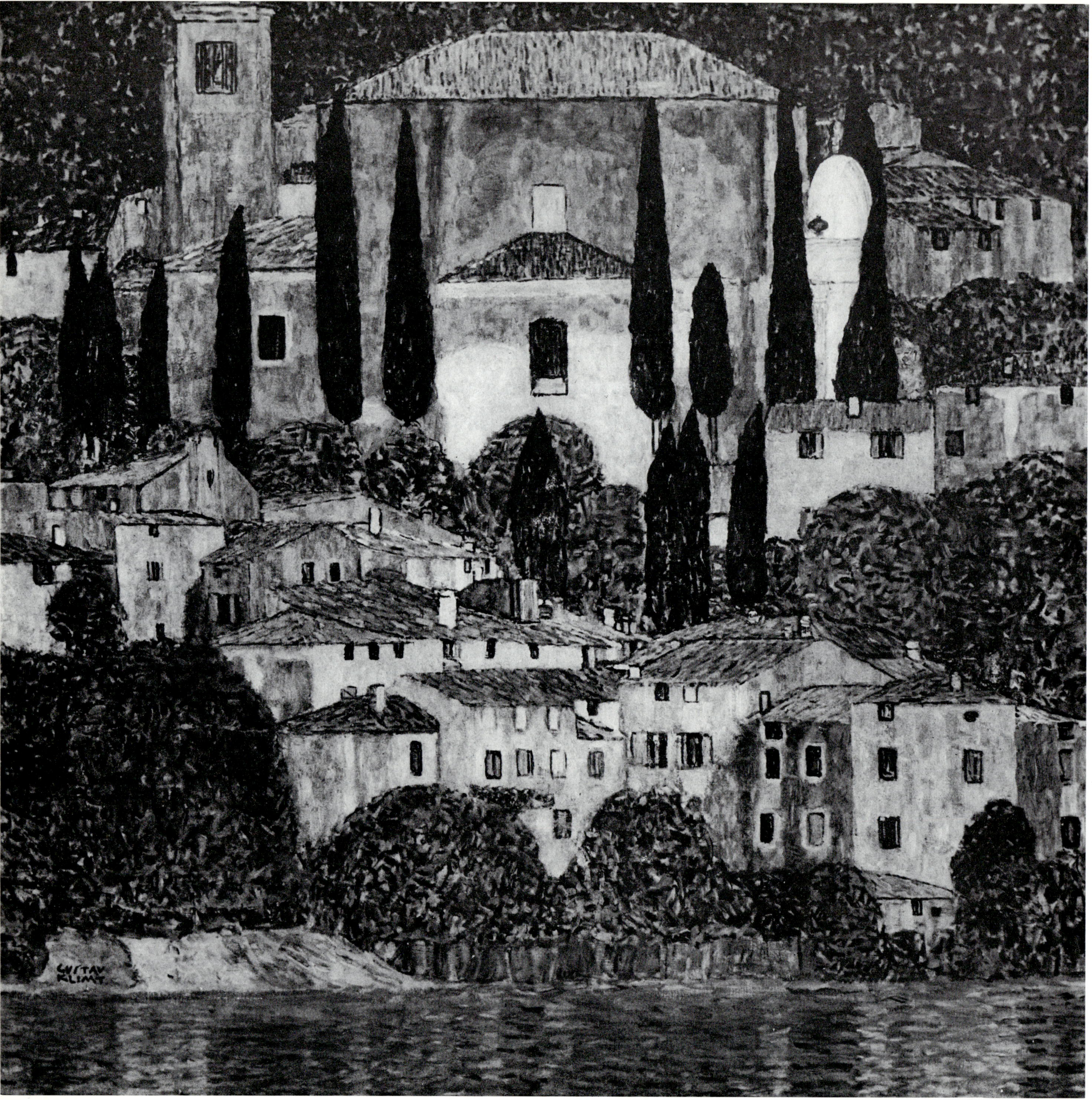
GVSTAV
KLIMT

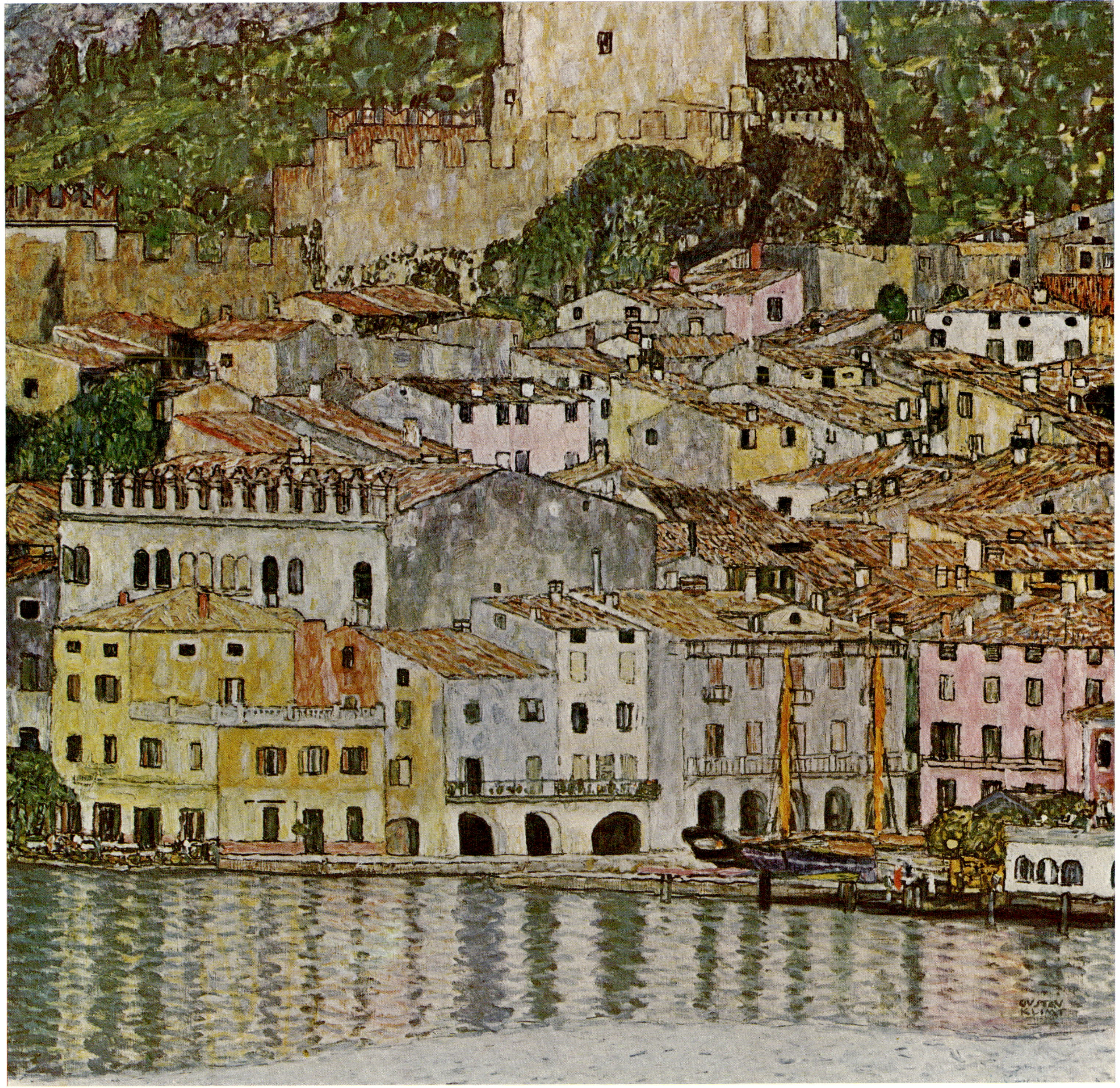
GUSTAV
KLIMT

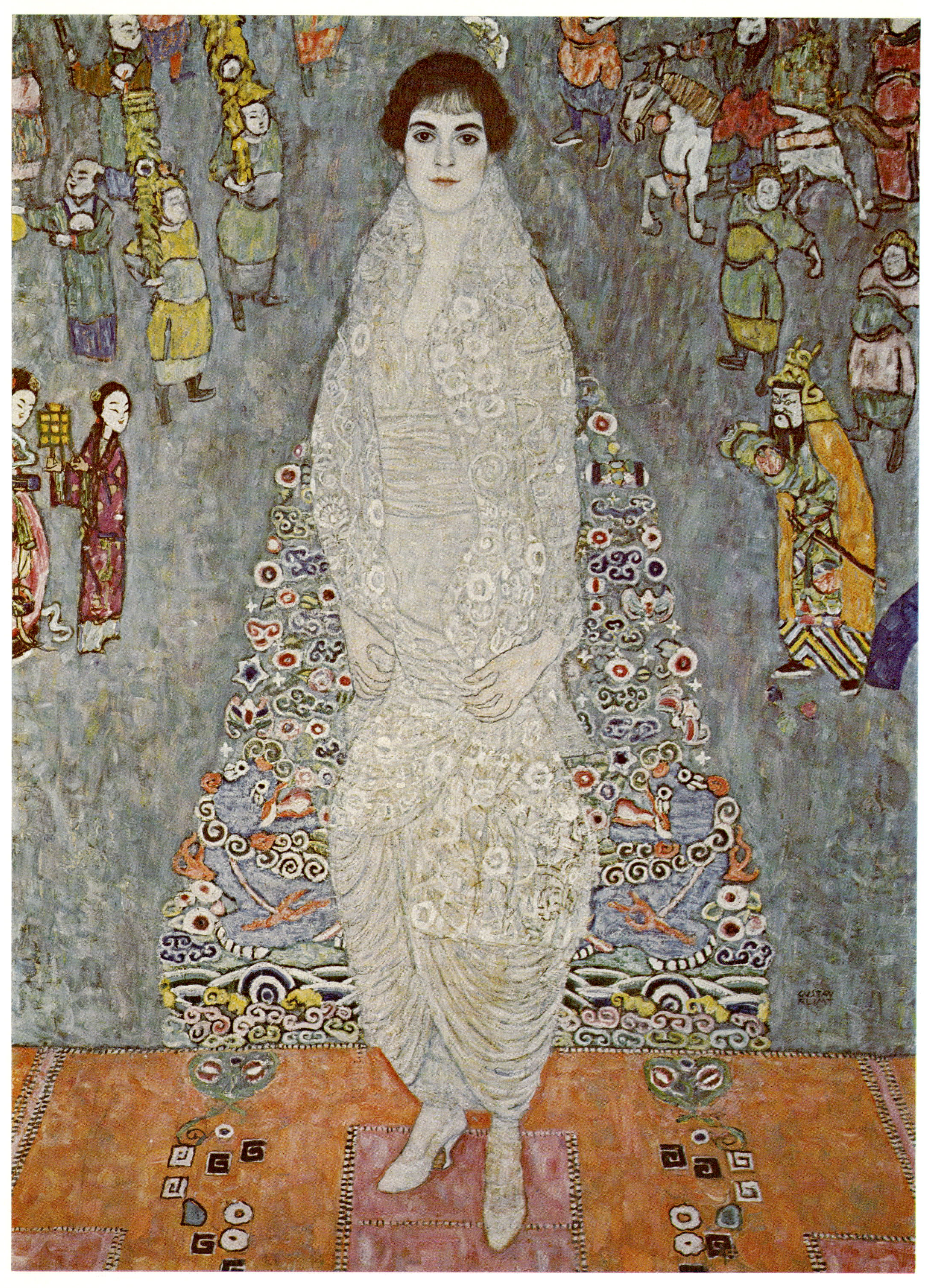

61 PORTRAIT OF THE BARONESS ELISABETH BACHOFEN-ECHT, c. 1914 (D. 188)

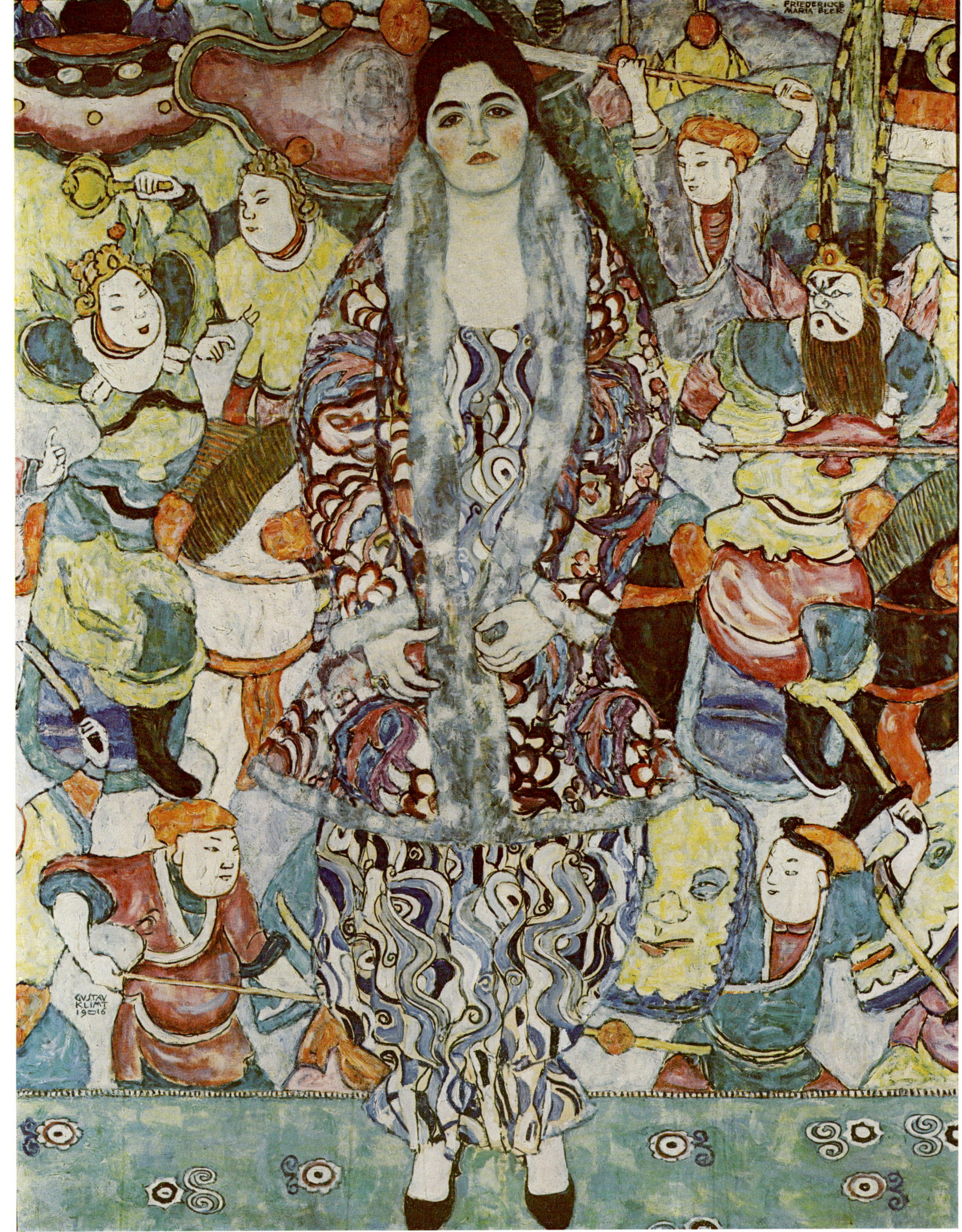

62 PORTRAIT OF FRIEDERIKE MARIA BEER, 1916 (D. 196)

following pages:
63 APPLE-TREE II, c. 1916 (D. 195)
64 THE LITZLBERGERKELLER ON THE ATTERSEE, 1915 – 16 (D. 193)

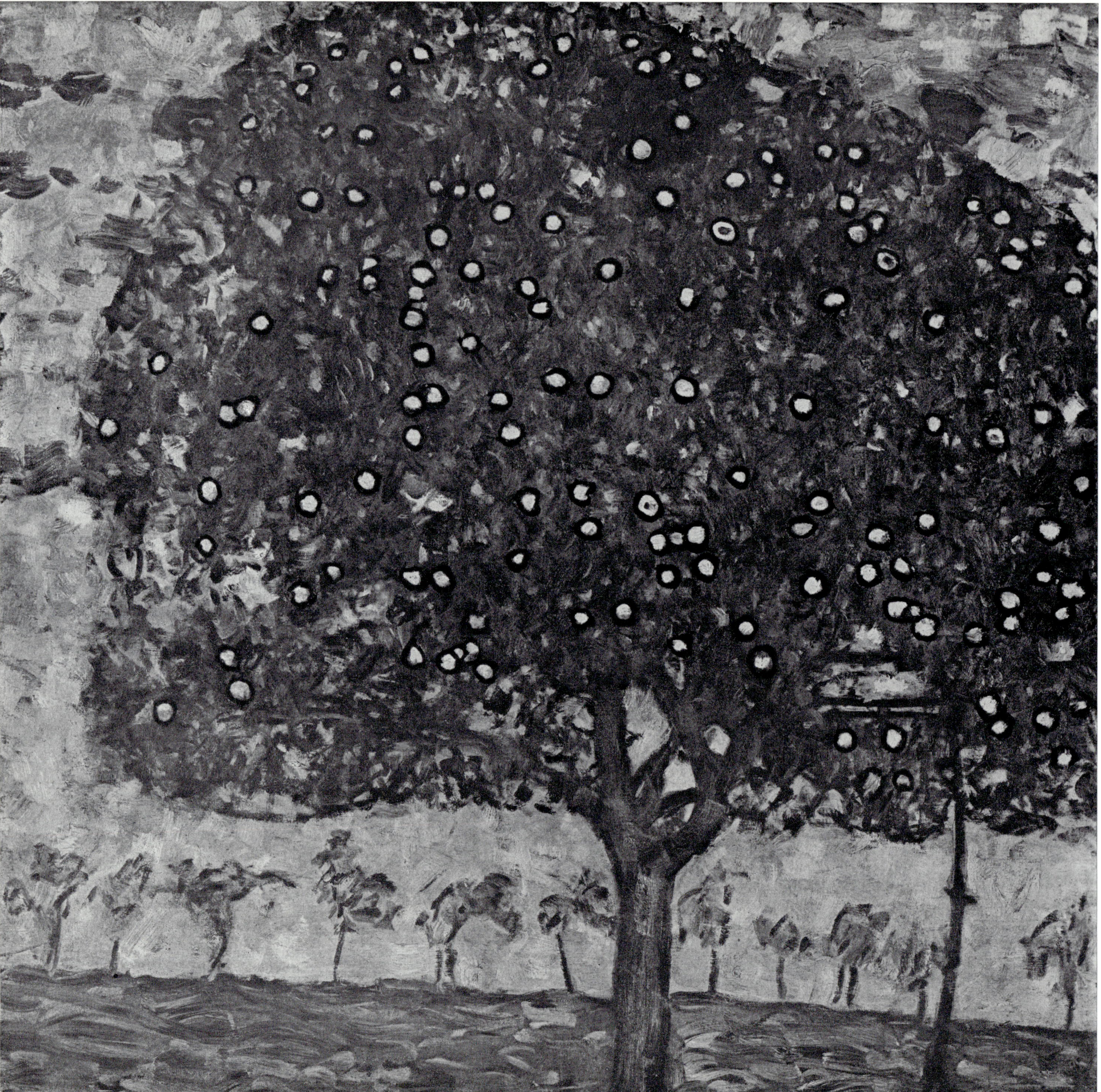

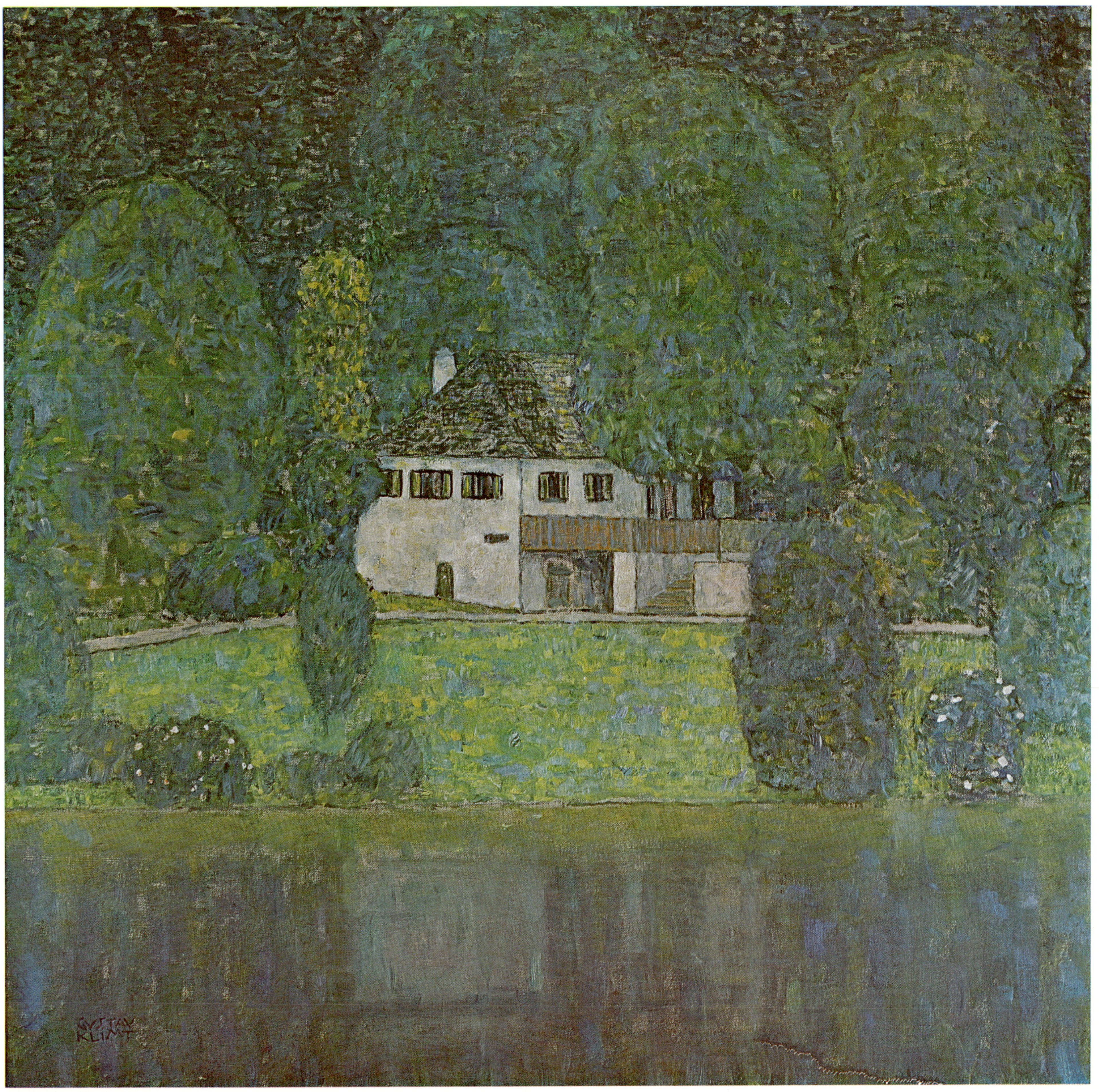
GVSTAV
KLIMT

65 SCHÖNBRUNN PARK, 1916 (D. 194)

following pages:

66 VILLA ON THE ATTERSEE, c. 1914 (D. 189)

67 CHURCH AT UNTERACH ON THE ATTERSEE, 1916 (D. 198)

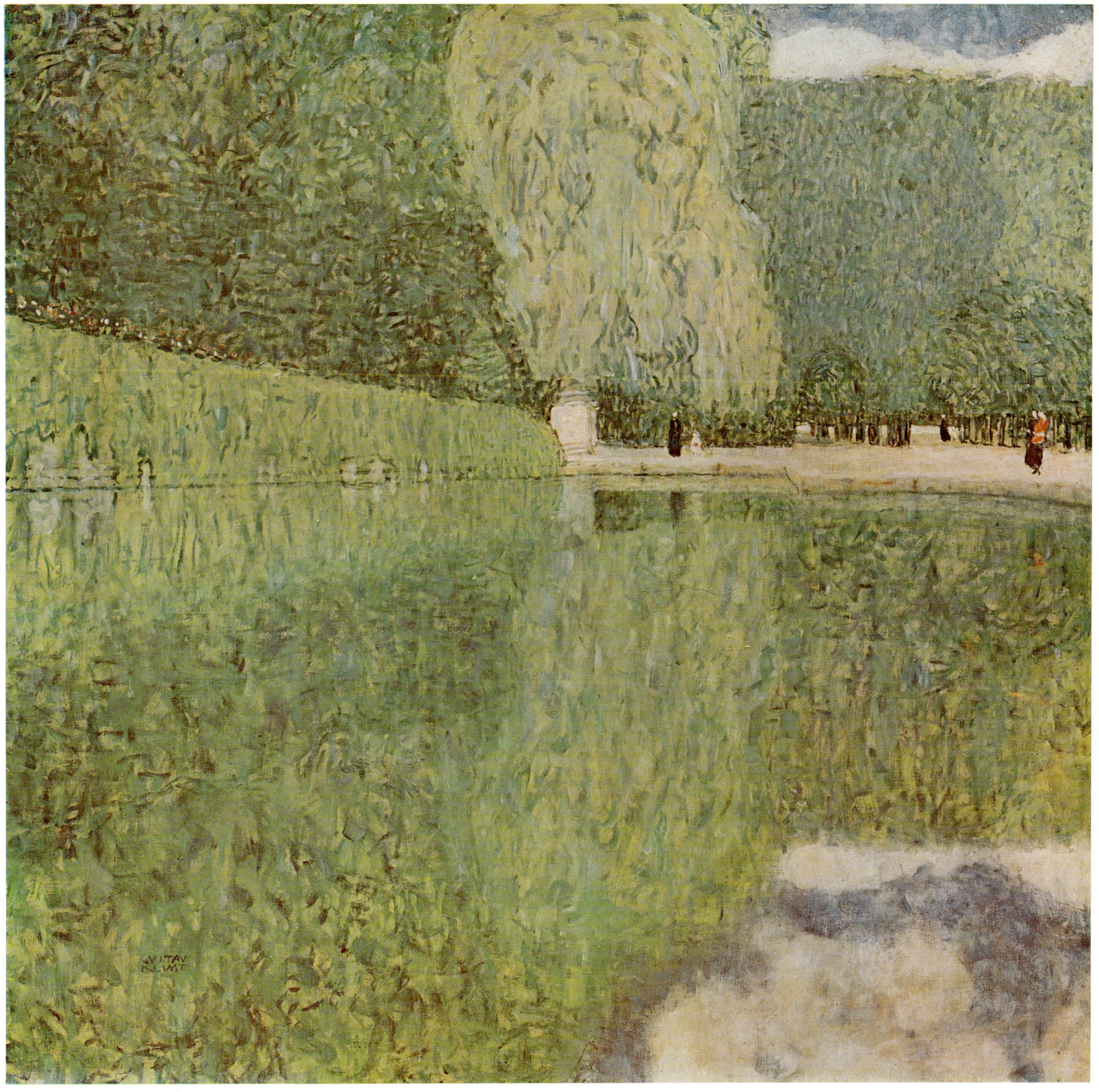

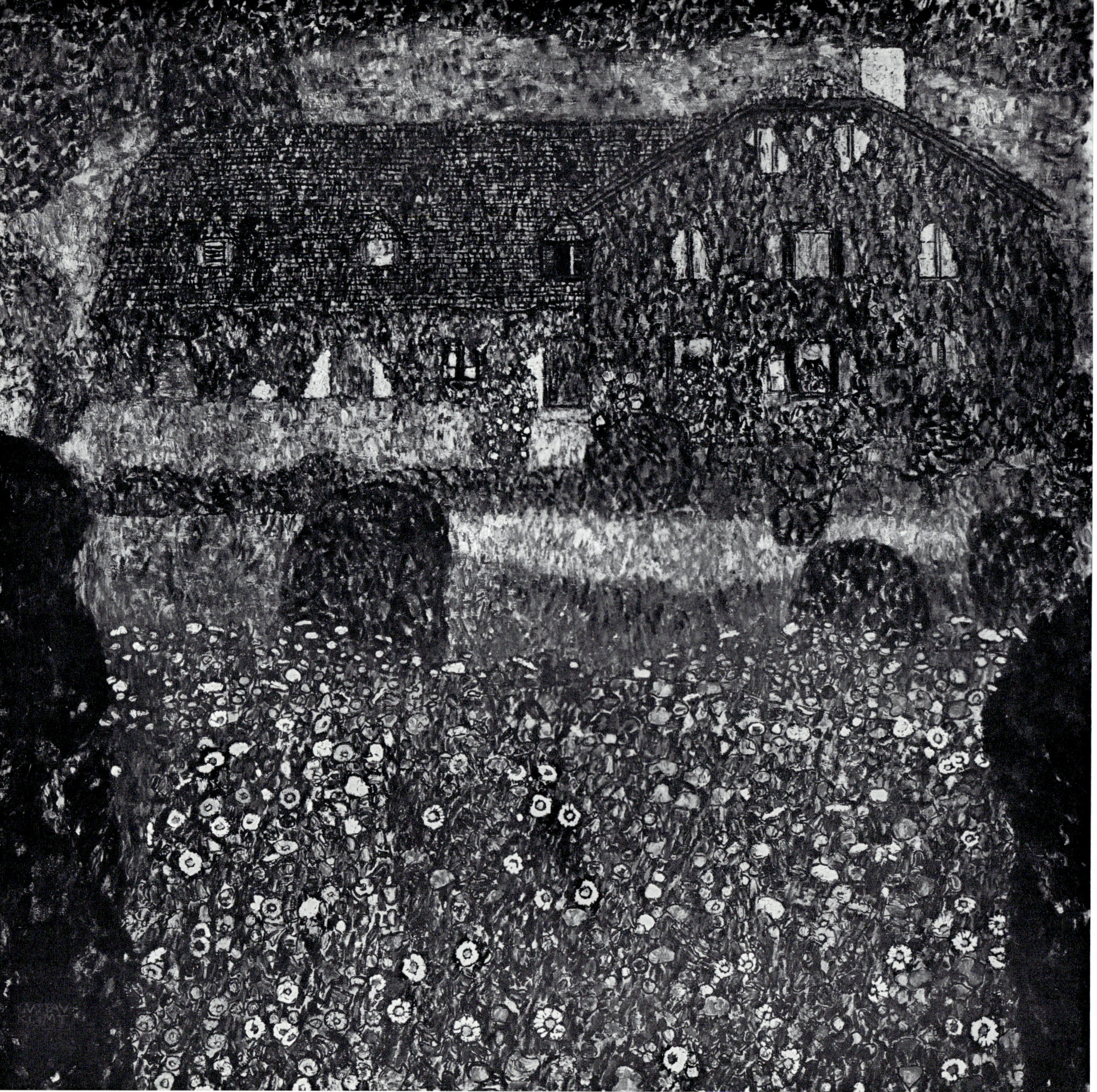

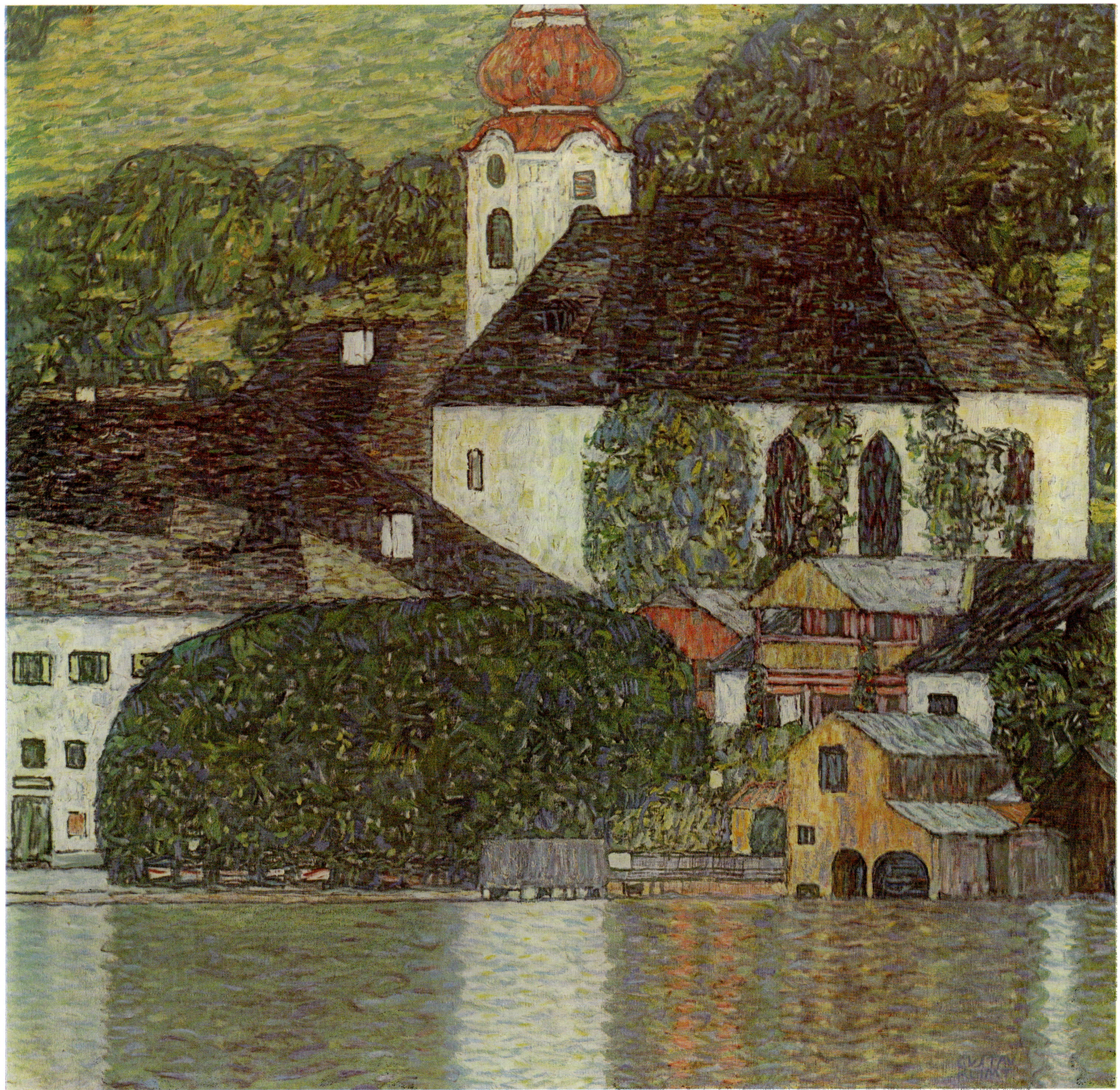

68 THE WOMEN FRIENDS, 1916 – 17 (D. 201)

following pages:

69 LEDA, 1917 (D. 202)

70 WALLY, 1916 (D. 200)

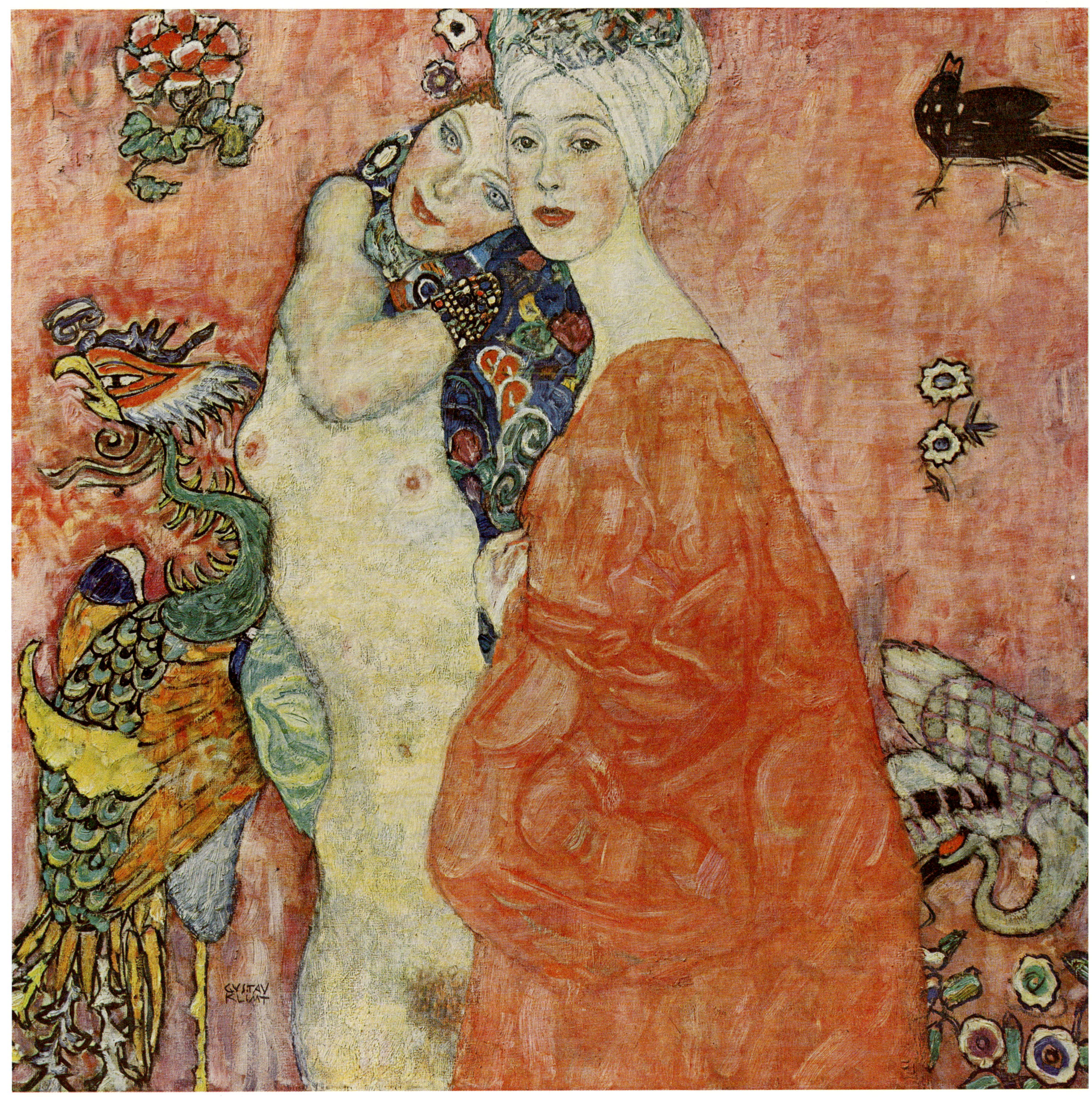
GVSTAV
KLIMT

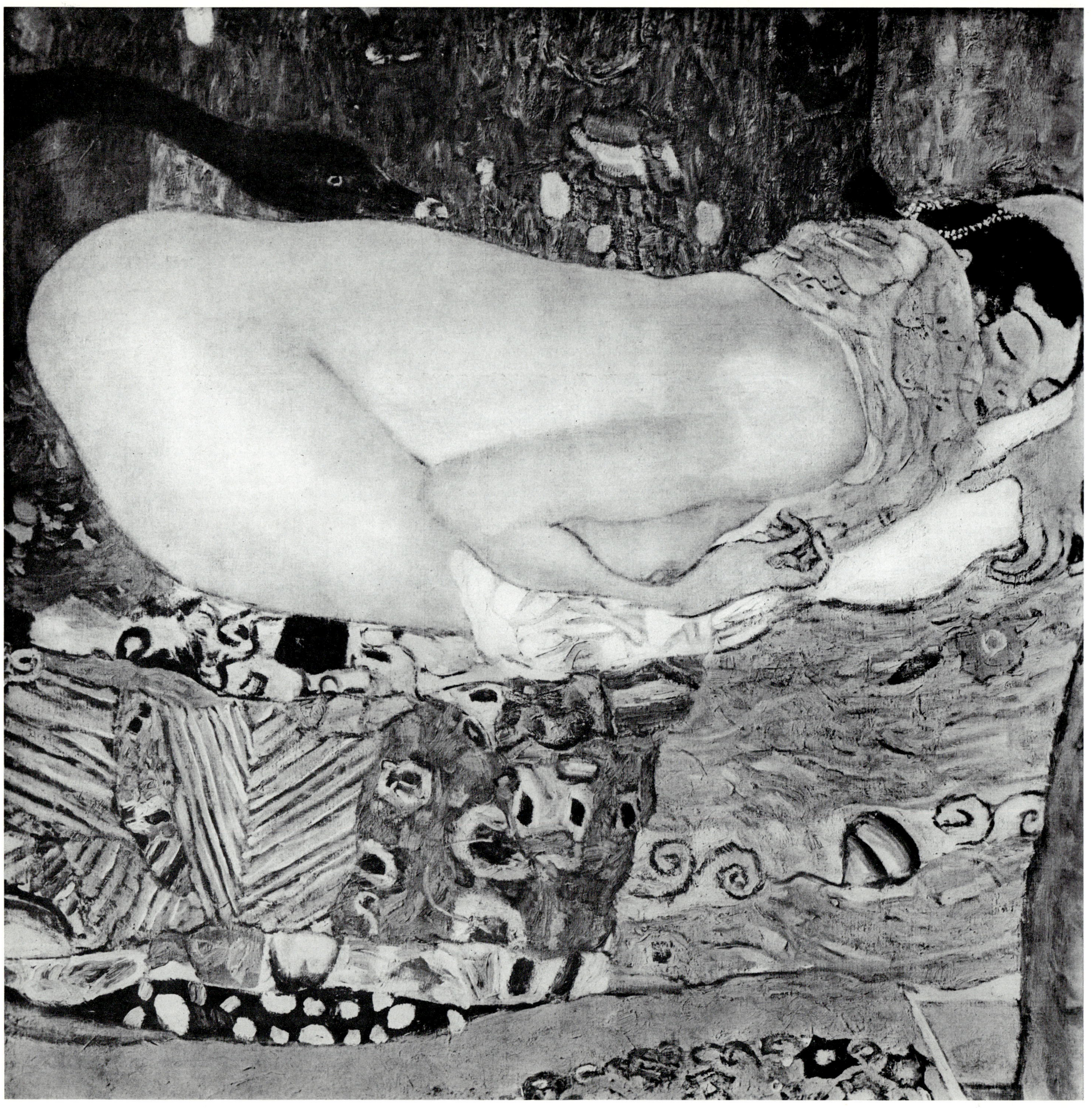

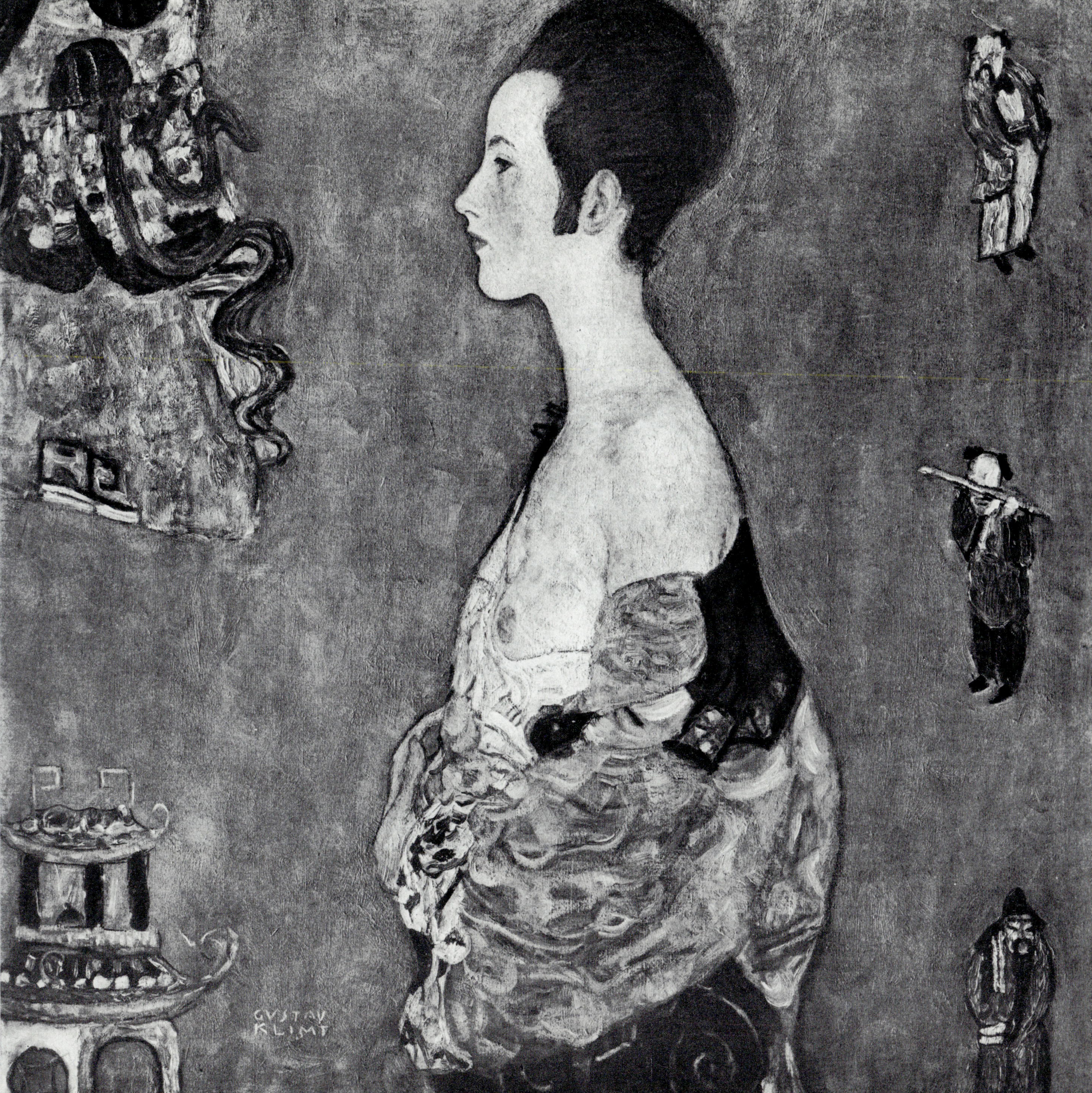
GVSTAV
KLIMT

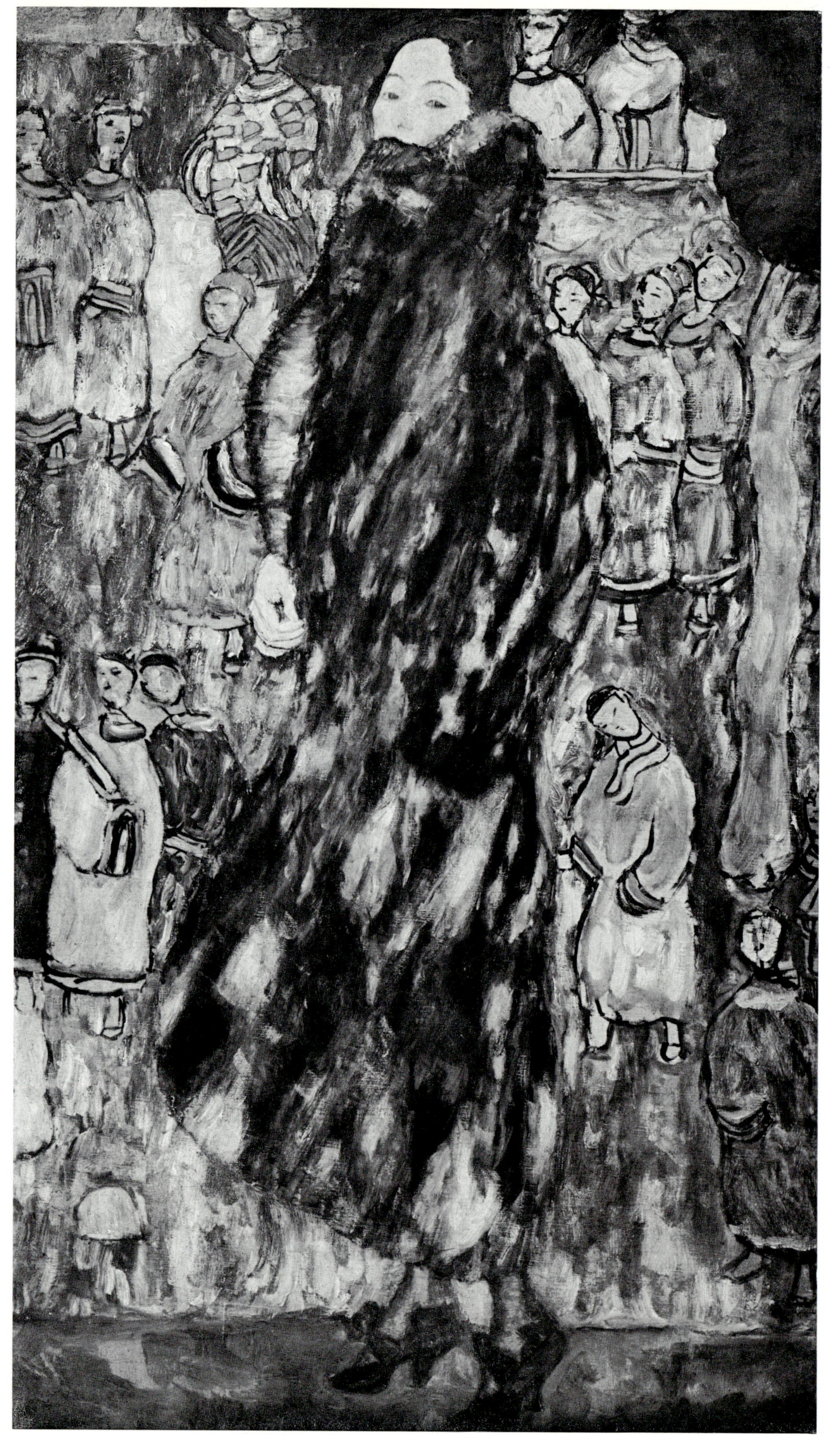

71 THE POLECAT FUR, 1916 — 18, unfinished (D. 206)

72 LADY WITH FAN, 1917 — 18 (D. 203) ▸

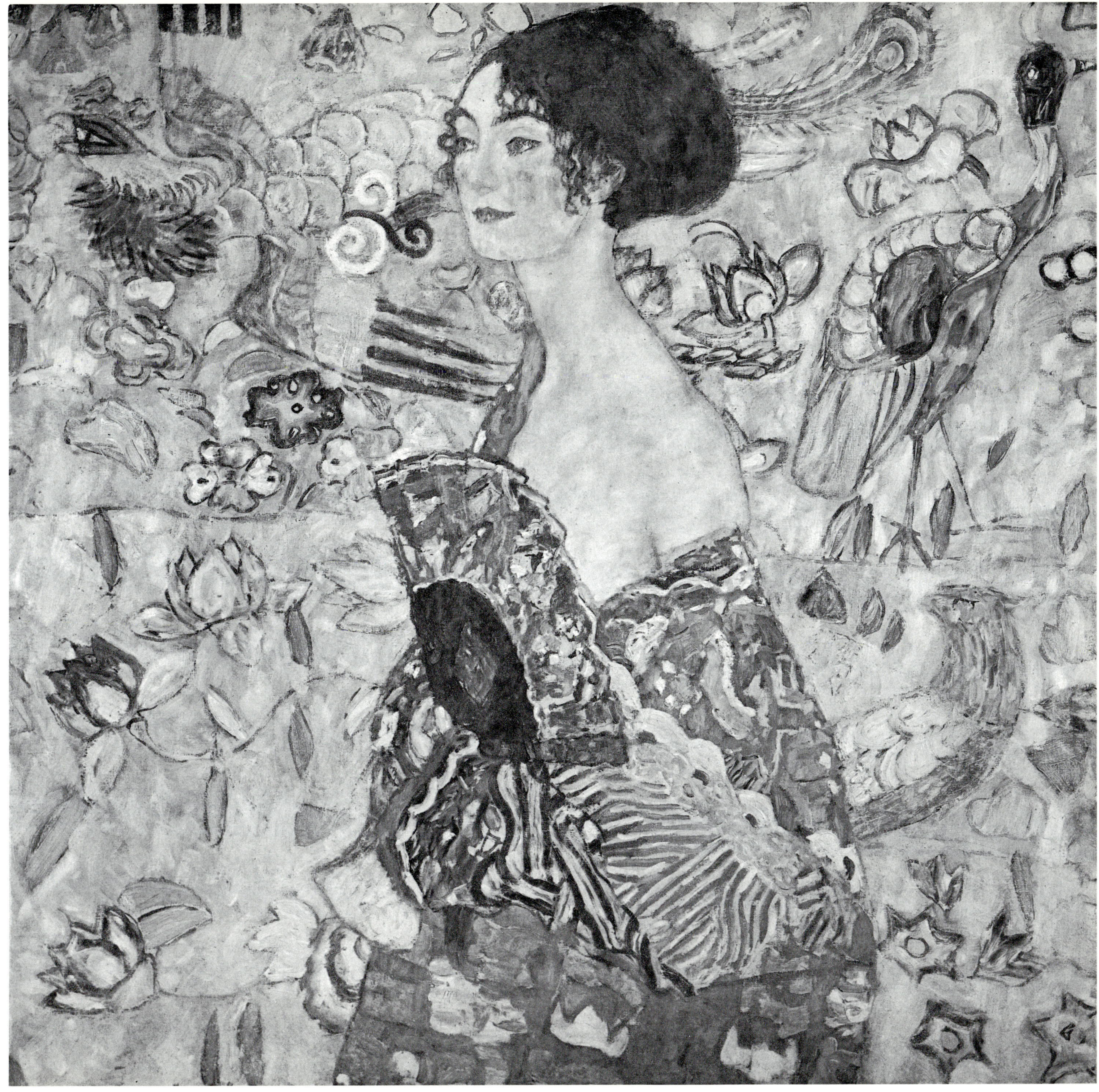

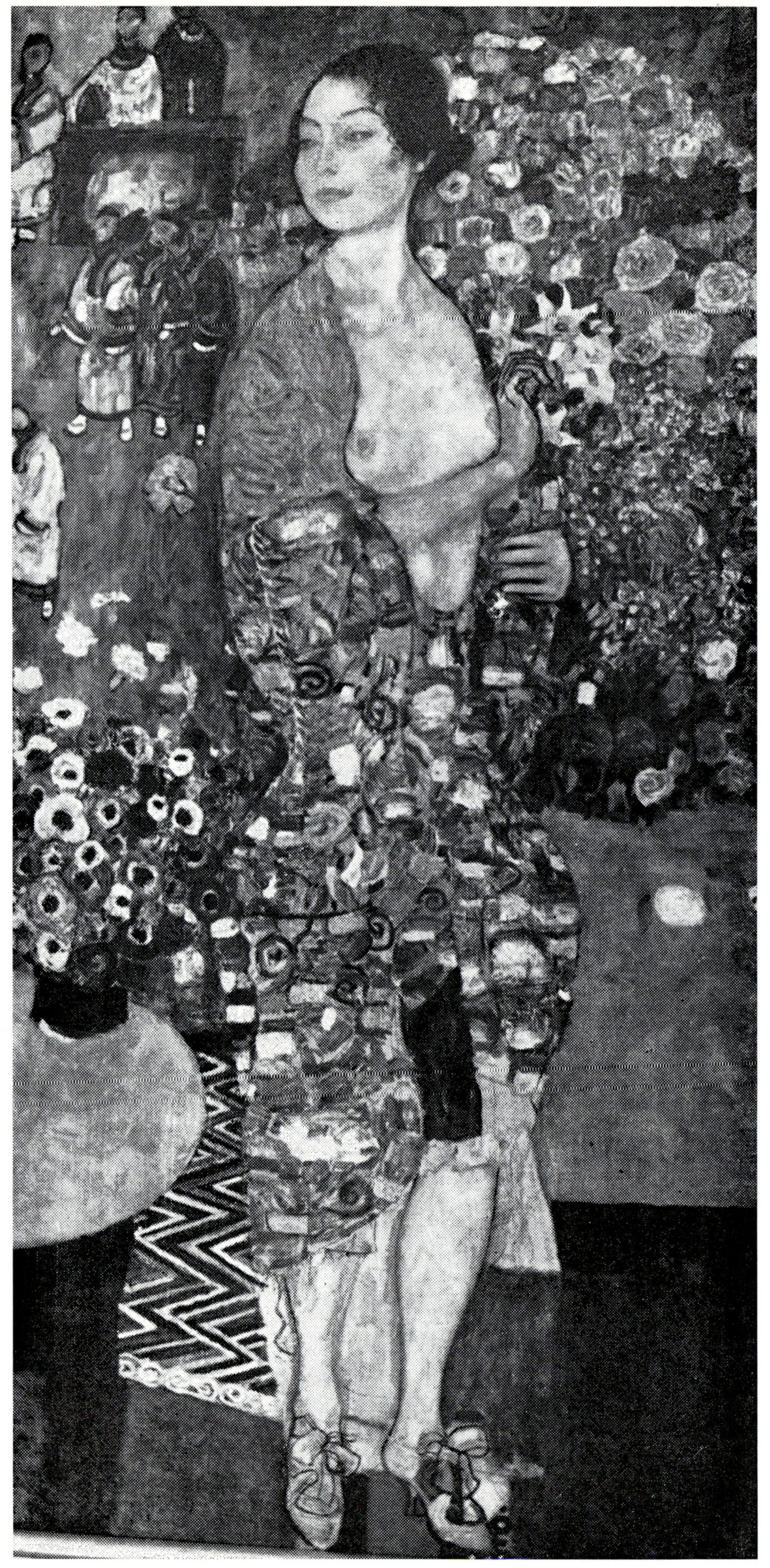

73 THE DANCER, c. 1916 — 18 (D. 208)

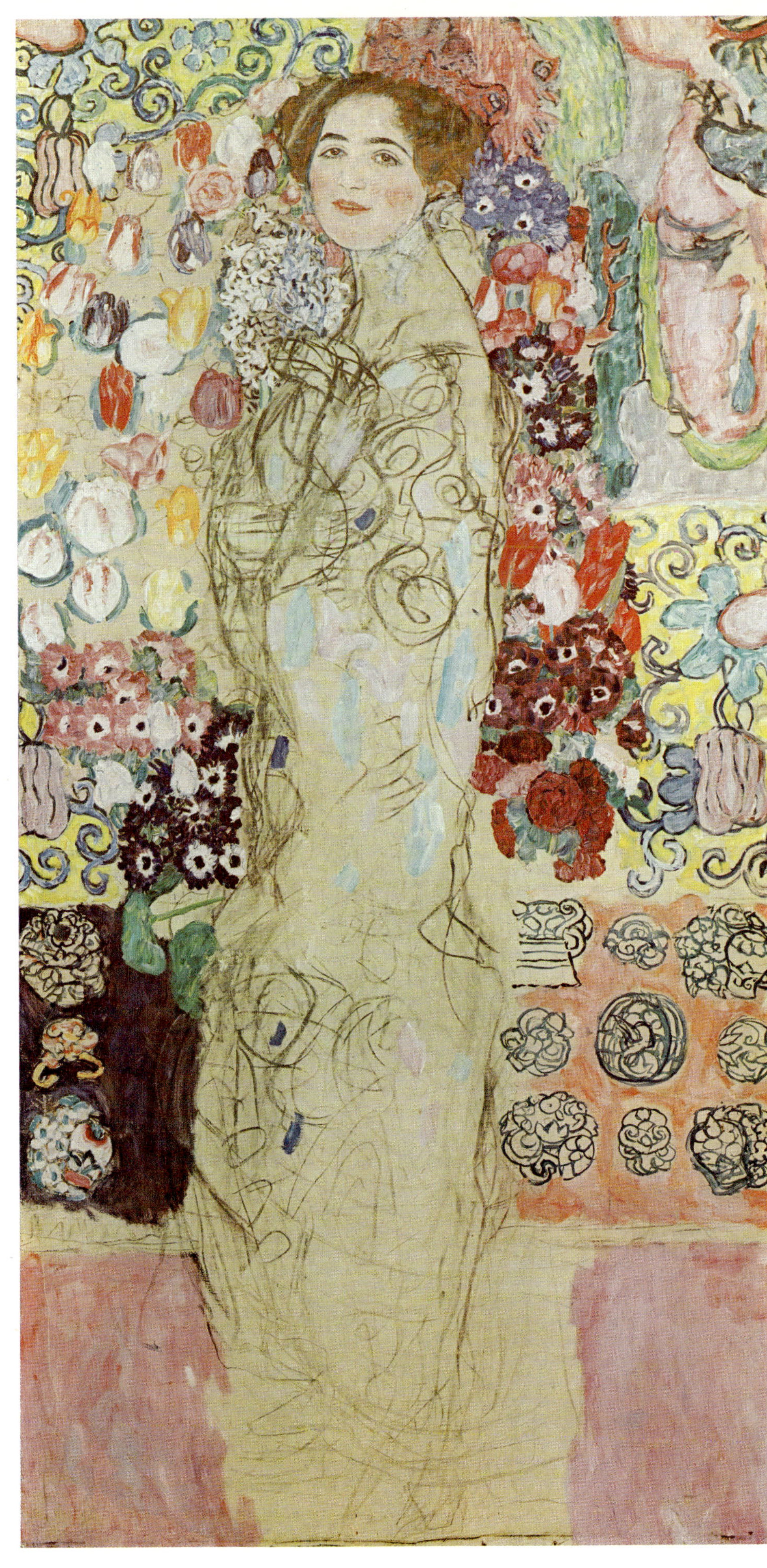

74 PORTRAIT OF A LADY, 1917 — 18, unfinished (D. 209)

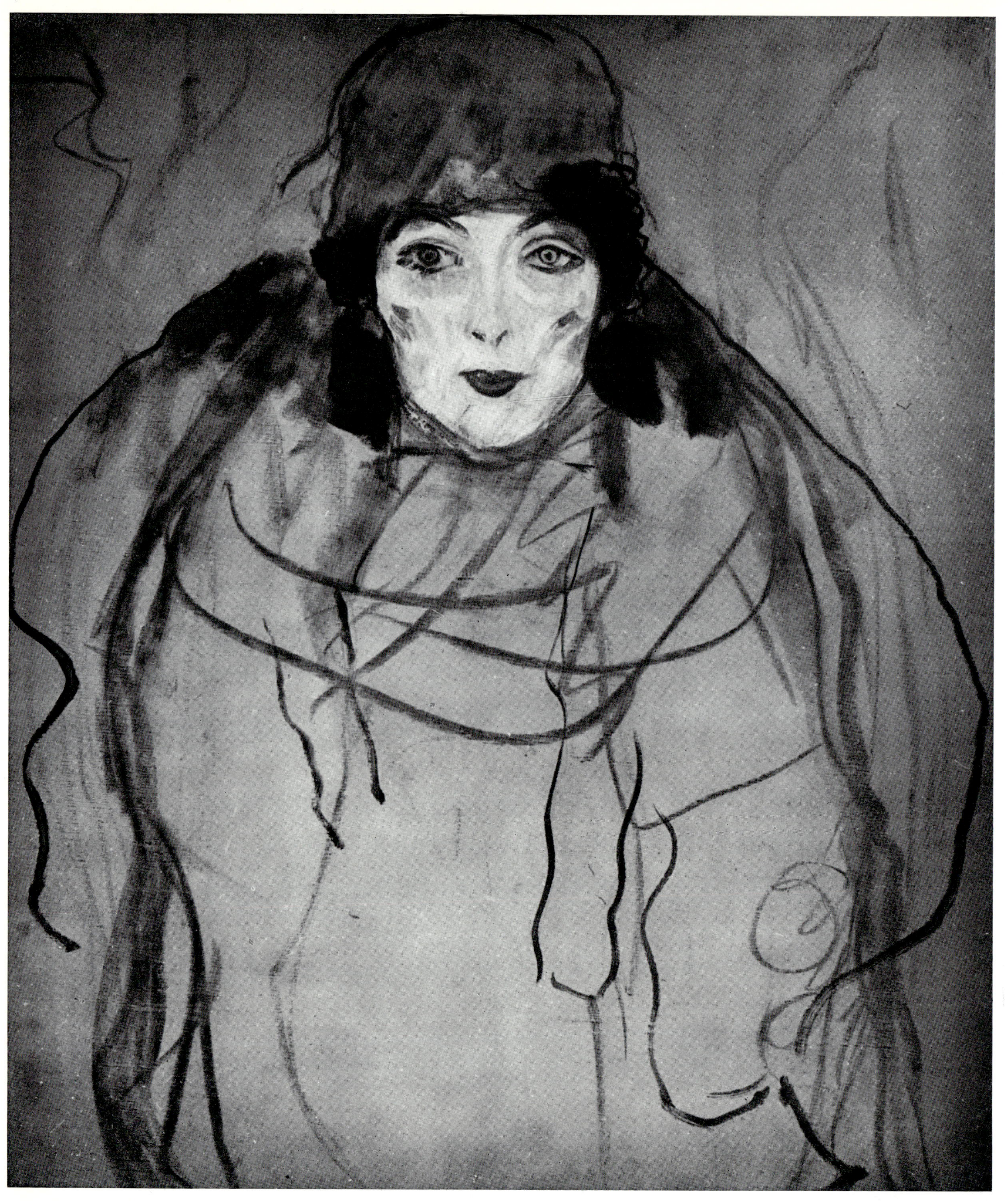

75 FULL-FACE PORTRAIT OF A LADY, 1917 – 18, unfinished (D. 212)

76 PORTRAIT OF FRAU AMALIE ZUCKERKANDL, 1917 – 18, unfinished (D. 213) ▸

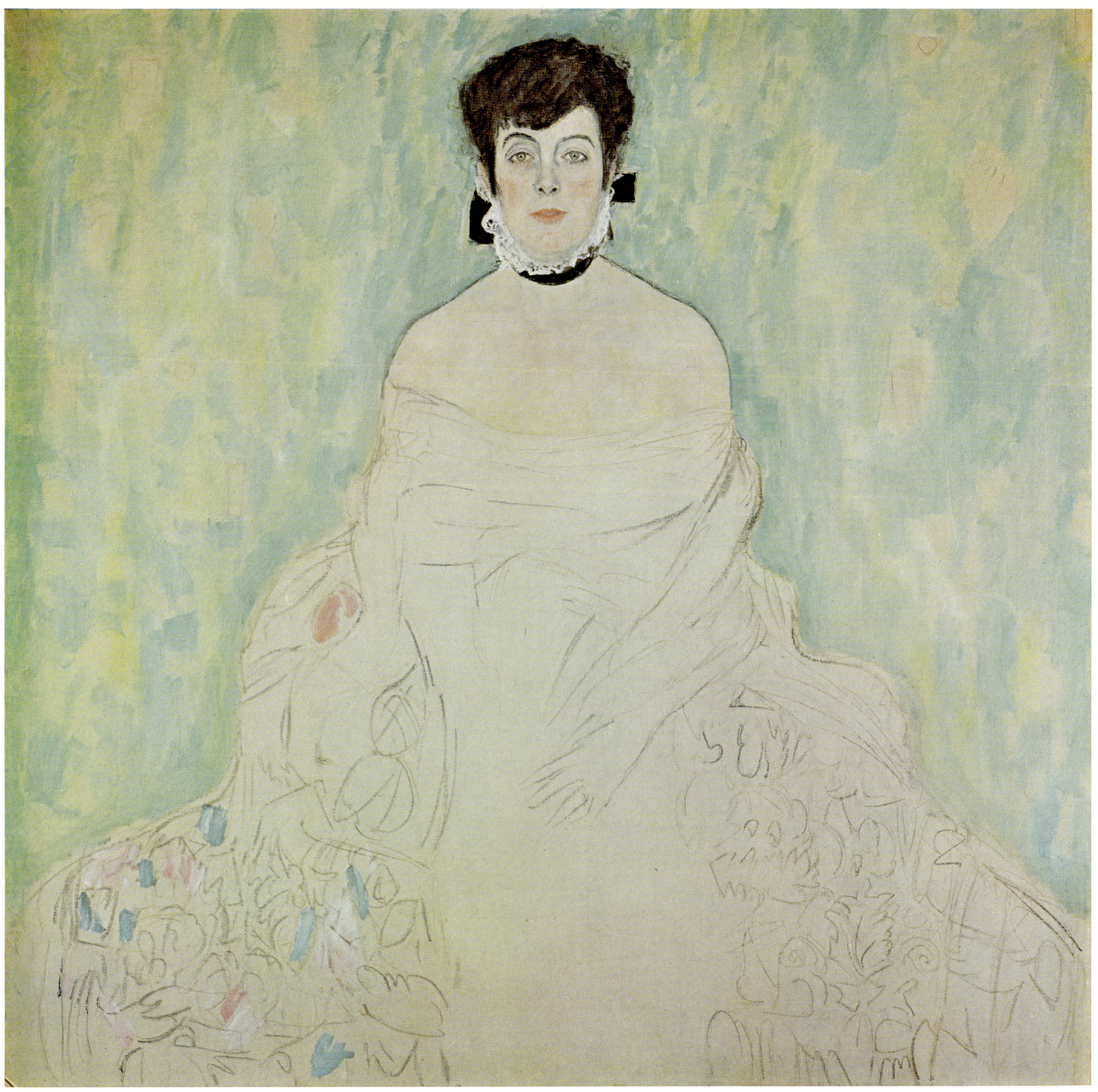

77 VINEYARD PRESSING-HOUSE ON THE ATTERSEE, 1917 (D. 217)

following pages:

78 GARDEN LANDSCAPE WITH HILLTOP, 1917 (D. 216)

79 GARDEN PATH WITH CHICKENS, 1917 (D. 215)

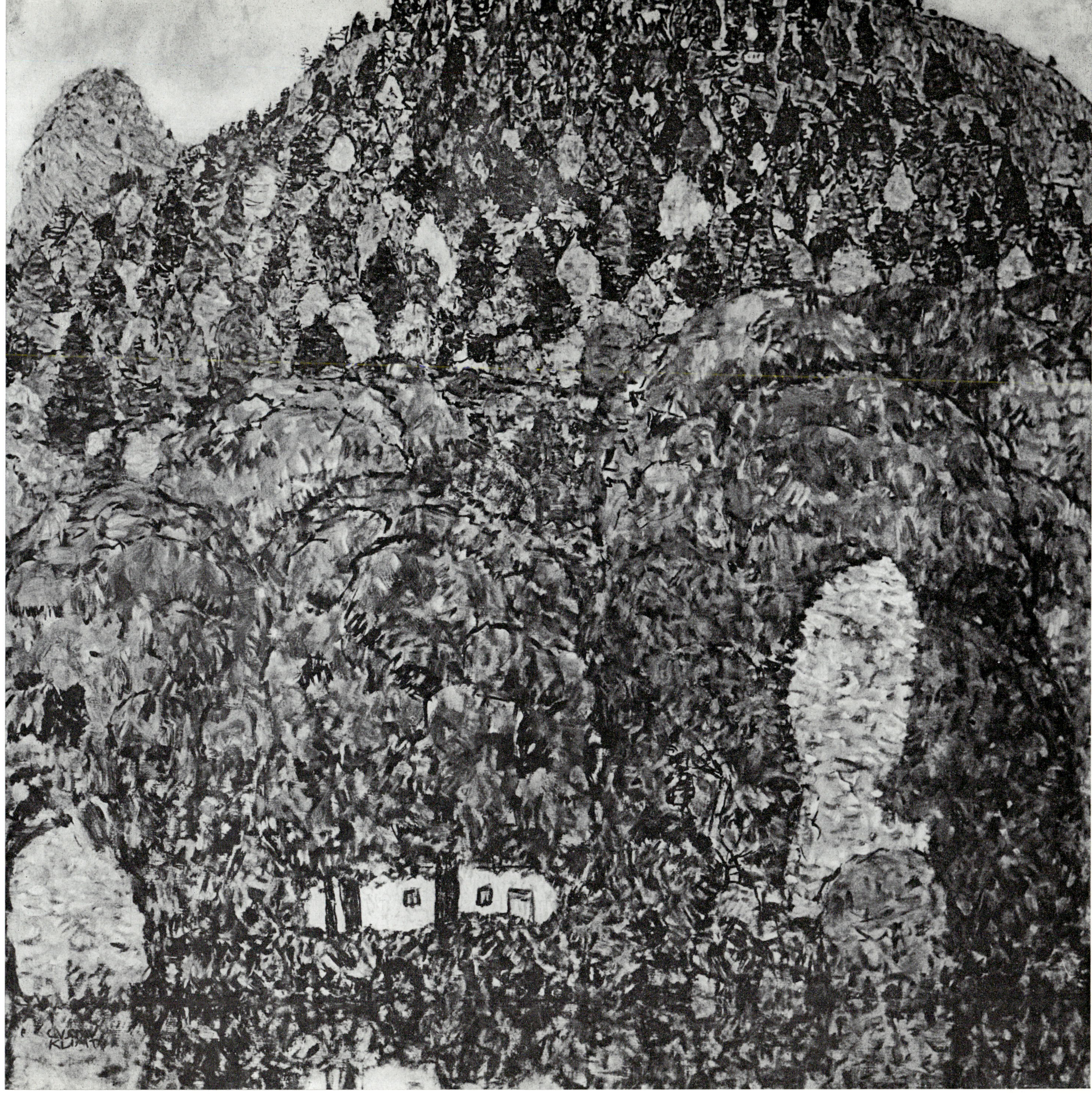

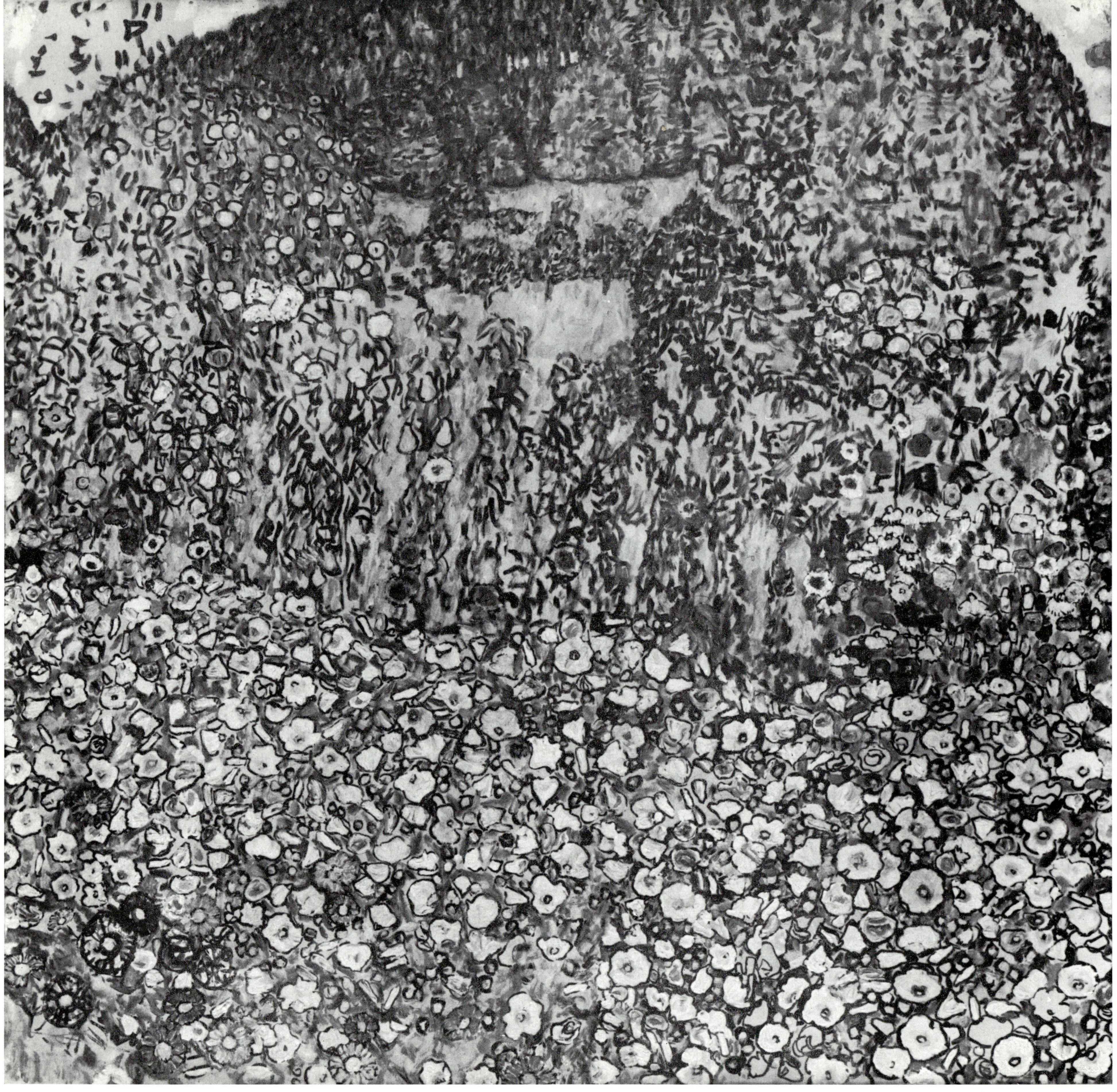

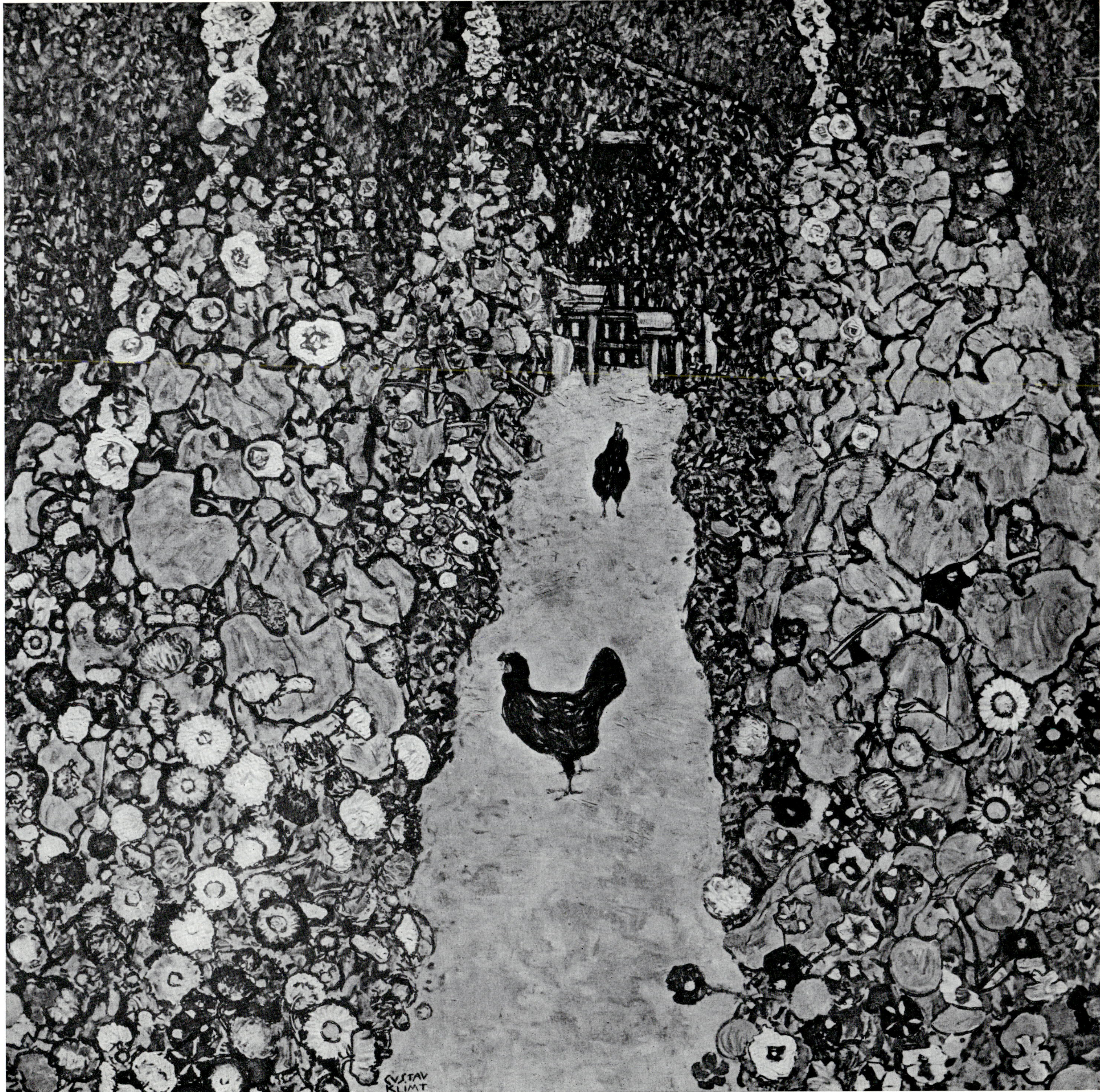
GVSTAV
KLIMT

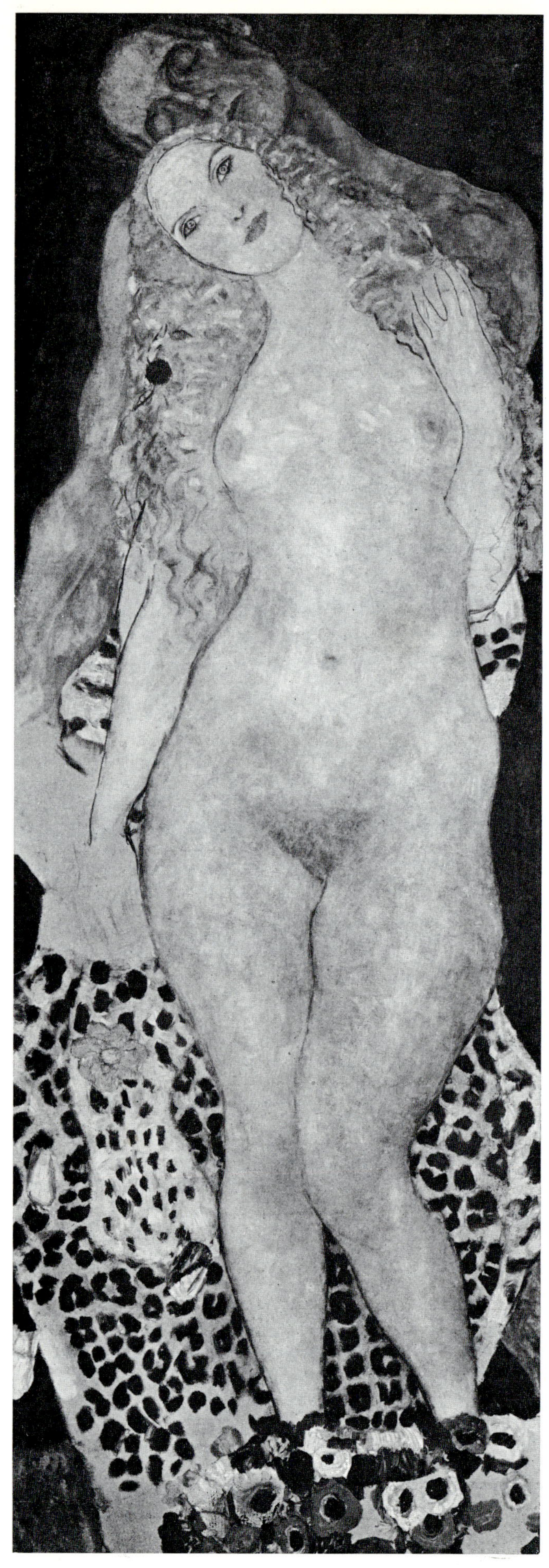

80 ADAM AND EVE, 1917 — 18, unfinished (D. 220)

81 BABY, 1917 — 18, unfinished, ▸ (D. 221)

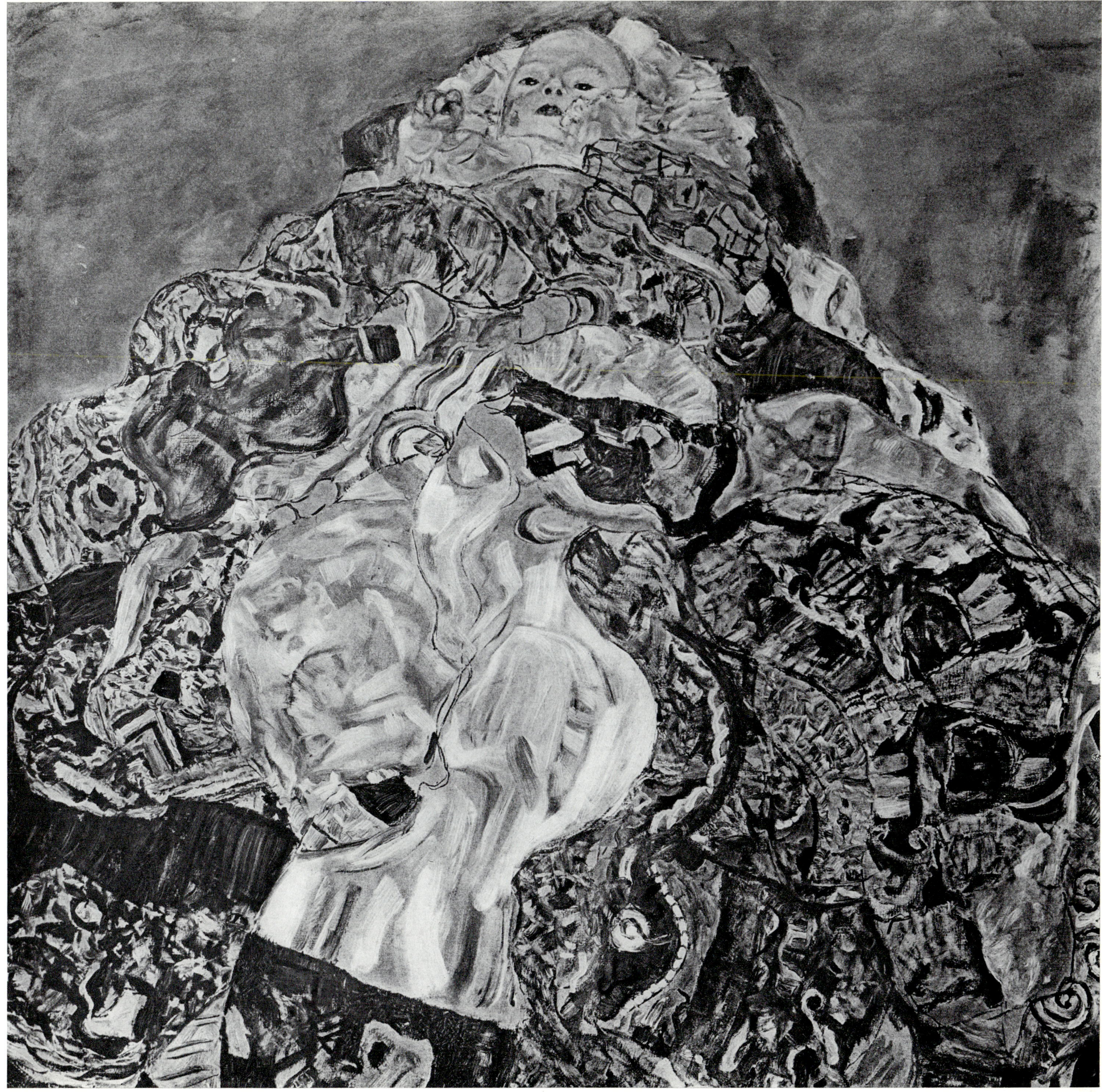

82 THE BRIDE, 1917 — 18, unfinished (D. 222)

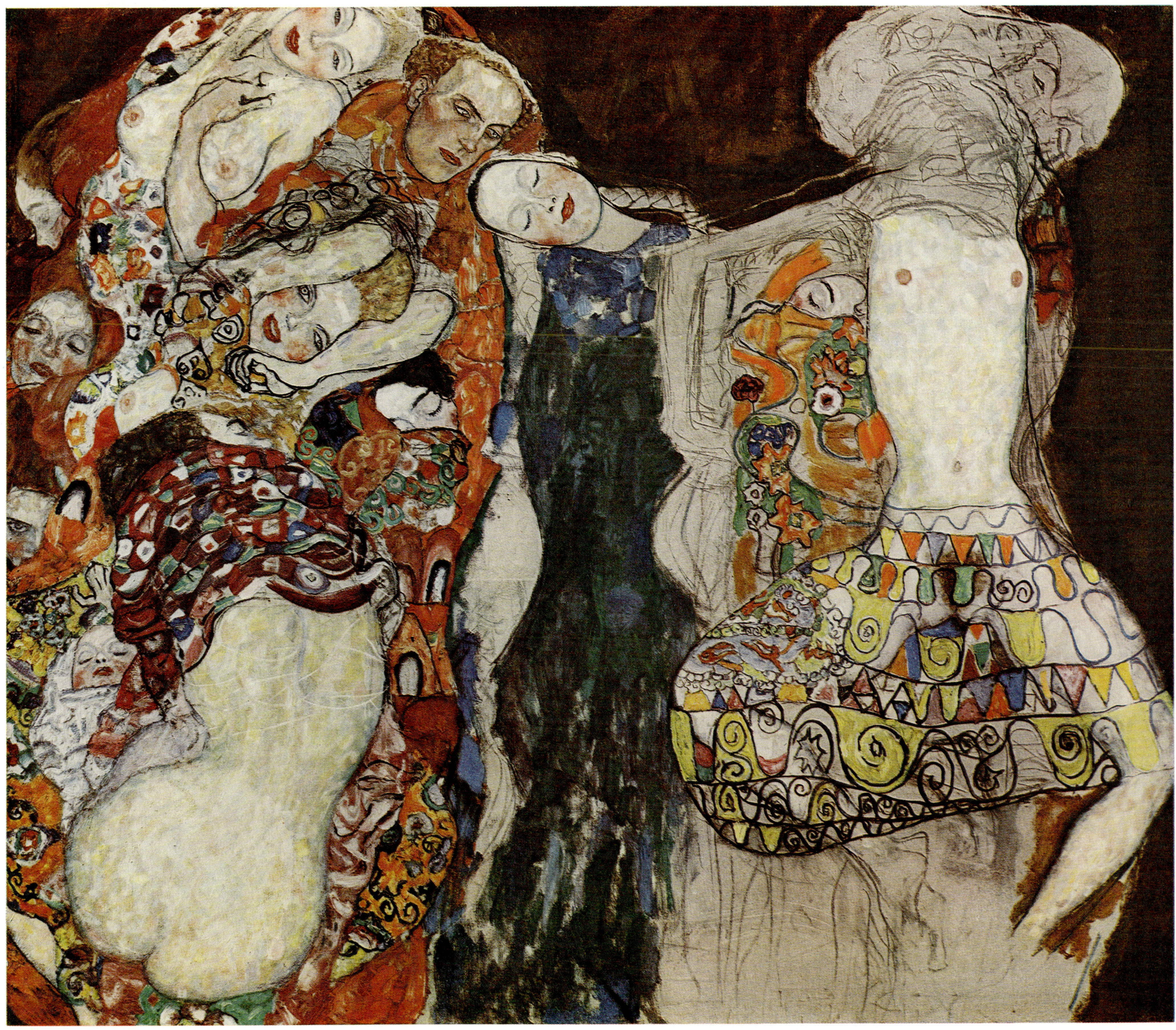

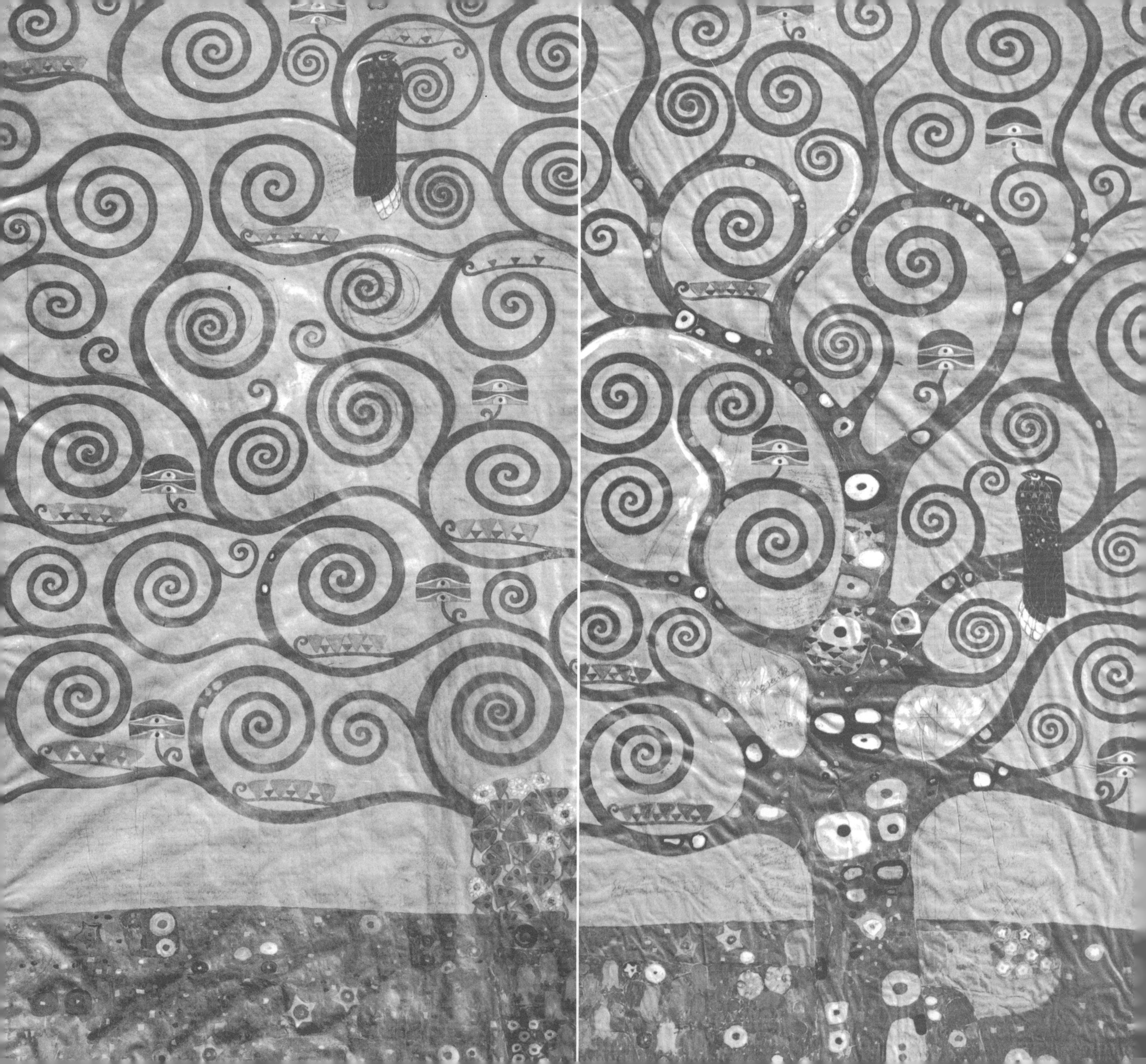